D1548549

Selected Plays of
Louis MacNeice

SELECTED PLAYS OF LOUIS MACNEICE

Edited by

Alan Heuser and Peter McDonald

CLARENDON PRESS · OXFORD

1993

Oxford University Press, Walton Street, Oxford OX2 6DP
Oxford New York Toronto
Delhi Bombay Calcutta Madras Karachi
Kuala Lumpur Singapore Hong Kong Tokyo
Nairobi Dar es Salaam Cape Town
Melbourne Auckland Madrid
and associated companies in
Berlin Ibadan

Oxford is a trade mark of Oxford University Press

Published in the United States
by Oxford University Press Inc., New York

British Library Cataloguing in Publication Data
Data available

Library of Congress Cataloging in Publication Data
MacNeice, Louis, 1907–1963.
[Plays. Selections]
Selected plays of Louis MacNeice / edited by Alan Heuser and
Peter McDonald
Includes bibliographical references.
(acid-free paper)
I. Heuser, Alan. II. McDonald, Peter. III. Title.
PR6025.A316A6 1993
822'.912—dc20 93-19748
ISBN 0-19-811245-9

Typeset by Rowland Phototypesetting Ltd.
Bury St Edmunds, Suffolk
Printed in Great Britain
on acid-free paper by
Bookcraft Ltd
Midsomer Norton, Bath

To Jon Stallworthy

Acknowledgements

It gives us, the editors, great pleasure to thank all those who have contributed to the making of this book of Louis MacNeice's plays. For permission to publish the eight plays herein, grateful acknowledgement is made to MacNeice's literary executor, Professor Jon Stallworthy, the MacNeice Estate, the British Broadcasting Corporation, Faber and Faber Limited, and MacNeice's literary agents, David Higham Associates Limited.

The chief repositories of MacNeice's playscripts (mainly typescripts, some holograph manuscripts and notes, also microfilms) are: the BBC Play Library in Broadcasting House, London, together with the BBC Written Archives Centre, Caversham Park, Reading; the Berg Collection in the New York Public Library; and the Humanities Research Center at the University of Texas at Austin; all of these have graciously responded with assistance, duly acknowledged here. We thank particularly the archivists, librarians, and other staff at these repositories for careful photographic reproduction of the texts, especially Carole Burchett, John Jordan, Julian Rickards, and Neil Somerville of the BBC WAC, Caversham Park; Berdeen E. Pigorsh, Reprographic Services, The New York Public Library; and Cynthia Farar of the HRC, The University of Texas, Austin.

For facilitating the listening to tapes of MacNeice's radio productions, acknowledgement must be made to The National Sound Archive, London, and its head, Toby Oakes. For further assistance, Alan Heuser wishes gratefully to thank John Tydeman, Head, Drama, BBC Radio, and two of his staff, Sarah Kilgarriff and Jonathan Cook.

The late R. D. (Reggie) Smith's list of MacNeice's 'Radio Scripts 1941–1963' in *Time Was Away*, edited by Terence Brown and Alec Reid (1974), and Christopher M. Armitage and Neil Clark's MacNeice *Bibliography* (1973), are to be acknowledged as pioneering works in the field. Barbara Coulton's book, *Louis MacNeice in the BBC* (1980), and Christopher Holme's chapter on 'The radio drama of Louis MacNeice' in *British Radio Drama*, edited by John Drakakis (1981), still provide helpful guides to the plays.

By Alan Heuser: I wish heartily to thank the Social Sciences and Humanities Research Council of Canada and its English Literature Committee (1991) for a generous Standard Research Grant. I am also grateful to

McGill University for a sabbatic leave in 1991–2, the reference and inter-library loan librarians of McLennan Library for assistance, as well as Professor Michael Maxwell, the then Dean of Arts, and my chairman, Professor John Ripley of the Department of English at McGill, for encouraging this project. My deepest debt is owed to my wife Margaret for patience, encouragement, and support.

A.H.   P.McD.
McGill University   University of Bristol

May 1992

Contents

Introduction

Louis MacNeice's involvement with the BBC, which lasted from 1941 until his death in 1963, gave rise to the great bulk of his dramatic writing: over the twenty-two years, he wrote more than 120 scripts, for most of which he was also the producer. The line between a radio 'feature' and a drama is an extremely difficult one to draw, but some seventeen original plays and a dozen or so adaptations of literary material can be laid to MacNeice's account during his time at the BBC, as well as much semi-dramatized *reportage* on an extremely diverse range of subjects written and produced for the Features Department. Even this does not quite account for all of MacNeice's dramatic output: there were plays for Rupert Doone's Group Theatre (and others) in the 1930s, the stage play *One for the Grave* in 1958, and a play for television in 1960. Taken together, this amounts to a body of work more than substantial enough to permit consideration of MacNeice as a playwright as well as a poet. However, critics of MacNeice's poetry have always expressed some unease on this point, responding perhaps to a genuine ambivalence registered by MacNeice himself: the poet's work is marked inevitably by the routine out of which — and within which — so much of it was written, and admiration for its various qualities cannot but be tempered by speculation on the cost, for MacNeice's poetry, of such professional successes. In providing texts for some of the best of the plays, it is hoped that critical discussion of this kind can now move on to firmer ground, and that MacNeice's poetic profits, as well as supposed losses, might begin to figure in the argument.

If MacNeice's career at the BBC began as a compromise (on his return to Britain from the USA, the poet was declared physically unfit for service in the Royal Navy), the business he was called upon to perform there was in its turn marked by the need for compromise, albeit of a kind which the Features Department carried off with aplomb in the War years and afterwards. There was often, in the wartime work, the imperative of providing propaganda, a pressure which MacNeice and his colleagues contrived to meet and resist at the same time. Another problem, linked to this, was presented by the demands of writing for a mass audience in search of 'entertainment'. MacNeice's Introduction to the published text of *Christopher Columbus* (1944) gives some idea of what was involved:

All the arts, to varying degrees, involve some kind of a compromise. This being so, how far need the radio dramatist go to meet the public without losing sight of himself and his own standards of value? He obviously cannot aspire to the freedom of lyric poetry written for the page; he must work to the limitations, already described, imposed both by medium and audience.

MacNeice's solutions to such problems responded to the various creative restraints with optimism and resource, and he held firmly to the belief that radio was a medium particularly suited to the talents of poets.

The buoyant confidence evident in MacNeice's earlier thoughts about radio — and evident indeed in the pace, scope, and assurance of a work like *Christopher Columbus* itself — was in part a confidence born of the discovery of a new genre: radio drama seemed, to MacNeice and many others, essentially a new dramatic form, the creative demands of which imposed novel and liberating disciplines upon the imaginative writer. Radio drama was not simply to be poetry by other means, but a fresh (and, importantly, a collaborative) form within which the poetic intelligence might be braced by encountering the demands of a mass audience. Radio drama was seen as generating its own aesthetics, founded on the controlling of different elements of a production, its various voices, effects, and (as is often the case with MacNeice's work) its music, as well as its exploitation of freedom from the visual logic and constraint of the stage. MacNeice's great triumph of the 1940s, *The Dark Tower*, full of deftly shifting scenes and placeless voices, and with a musical score by Benjamin Britten, exploits such freedom brilliantly, while other early works like *Christopher Columbus* and *He Had A Date* also break new ground in the techniques and possibilities of radio drama.

Although MacNeice's time at the BBC began with a subtly uncompromised understanding of various kinds of artistic compromise, it continued into a period when such dealings became more perplexing, and clear-cut issues grew more blurred. The advent of the Third Programme in 1946 was undoubtedly a watershed: while the new channel offered a remarkable degree of creative freedom to writers like MacNeice, it also brought their radio work into the realm of 'minority-interest'. The rise of television, in turn, made radio itself less central as a form of mass communication. By 1963, introducing the last of his radio plays that he was to collect for publication, MacNeice was voicing an attitude very different to that of the war years:

Obsolescent or not, sound radio, in Britain at least, is not the *mass* medium it used to be, television having stolen most of its public though it cannot take over most of its territory. Sound radio can do things no other medium can and, if 'sound' dies, those things will not be done.

Even though MacNeice's claims may well be correct ones (and he speaks here with the considerable authority given by his own important achievements in the medium), his suspicion that radio drama is 'a peculiar genus which may soon become a historical curiosity' reveals a changed world, in which the once-compromising pressure represented by the 'audience' seems itself to have become anachronistic.

It is against such a background that the development of MacNeice as a playwright must be considered. It is obvious that the best of his dramatic work remains as more than a 'historical curiosity', but it is also true that the bulk of this writing is of its time, and that some aspects of its idiom have ceased to be current, so that a degree of historical understanding has become necessary for its appreciation. The need for this kind of understanding is apparent, as are perhaps some of the benefits it might bring, in the two plays included in the present edition though never prepared for publication by MacNeice himself: *He Had A Date* and *Prisoner's Progress*. Both these plays explore areas of closely personal significance to their author — the life and the premature death of a friend, and the meanings and possibilities of 'escape' — in somewhat stylized dramatic idioms which aim at immediate accessibility. To say that these texts are 'of their time' is not to criticize them, but to offer a way of interpreting their dramatic manners which may help in the recognition of their deliberate placing in different historical moments of the life of a generation.

The deep concerns of MacNeice's plays, and the shapes which these concerns take, are parts of a larger creative development to be seen in his poetry; unlike the poetry, however, the plays' mode of expression is an extremely public one, which must set out to 'entertain' before all else. Introducing the text of *The Dark Tower*, MacNeice noted that a character in a radio play 'may say things that actually he never would or could say — the author may be making him utter what is only known to his unconscious'. Whether the unconscious in question is that of character or author is left unclear, but this element of partially occluded meaning in the fabric of plays ('once, to use a horrible piece of jargon, the subjective is objectified') is especially what MacNeice sees drama as being capable of getting away with: 'you can get away with anything *so long as you entertain*.' In fact, the themes at the heart of MacNeice's plays tend to conform to two basic patterns: the Morality and the Quest. Beneath the apparent variety of MacNeice's dramatic subjects, the same patterns and thematic motifs recur, often as elements of what the author thought of as a parable content, a subterranean stream of meaning that runs beneath the surface level of professional 'entertainment'.

In 1963, MacNeice defined parable as 'a kind of double-level writing, or, if you prefer it, sleight-of-hand', and the definition seems to be indebted at some level to earlier insistences on what the poet 'can get away with' in the radio medium. The aesthetics of MacNeice's work for radio depend importantly on the ability to pass off one thing for another by 'sleight-of-hand', uniting the conjuring-tricks of the radio studio with the parabolic doubleness of the skilled literary craftsman. MacNeice got away with a good deal here, and his occasional unsuccesses in writing for radio are more than compensated for by the quality of his successful plays; but it is remarkable that the 'double-level' process should seem itself to furnish a convincing metaphor for the thematic preoccupations of so many of these works. Time and again, MacNeice's plays feature characters (or often simply voices) of a constantly-shifting nature, whose identities change as often (and of course, this being radio drama, as invisibly) as their settings. The phantasmagoric world of *The Mad Islands* permits characters to change and change again, withholding their 'true' identities throughout; Roland, in *The Dark Tower*, must pass through landscapes where nothing is stable, and where everything is always on the verge of becoming something else. Even the perplexing presence crucial to the play, that of the Dark Tower itself, is in the end a something out of nothing. Christopher Columbus discovers something where previously nothing had seemed to be; the prisoners in *Prisoner's Progress*, in stumbling upon a neolithic passage-grave, uncover a reality underlying that of their captivity; finally Hank, in *Persons From Porlock*, discovers a subterranean world in which the failures and frustrations of his life above ground might be transformed into artistic coherence. In *They Met On Good Friday* the battle of Clontarf is both a historically placed event and an emblematic expression of enduring Irish dilemmas, while the television studio of *One for the Grave* provides a visual equivalent for the double-level puns which its hero, a bewildered Everyman, must embody. In all these cases, double-level writing becomes something more than a literary device, and seems to express the very condition which the plays themselves contemplate: in getting away with so much, MacNeice engages obliquely with the areas his writing is attempting to get away *from*, with whatever degree of success. Here, critical judgement has often treated the plays more harshly than the best of them deserve, failing to pursue their complex resonances and ambiguities within MacNeice's work as a whole.

MacNeice's significance as a poet is perhaps the major reason for directing attention to his dramatic work, but it is certainly not the only one, and the plays' inherent merits, as well as their place in the history of dramatic writing for radio, argue strongly against neglect. The plays collected here by no means exhaust all that is accomplished, imaginative, and striking in the large *corpus* of MacNeice's dramatic work; taken together, however, they do suggest the nature and extent of his achievement. At all events, there are ample grounds to be thankful that in his long career in the BBC Louis MacNeice got away with so much, with such purpose and style.

A Note on the Text: In this volume each MacNeice play is introduced by an editorial headnote (stating production, thematic, and textual particulars), the author's introduction or introductory note, and a list of characters or voices. The editors have made every attempt to locate and transcribe accurately the most authoritative text of each play. Alan Heuser edited all the plays except *He Had a Date* and *Prisoner's Progress*, which were transcribed and edited by Peter McDonald. Heuser wrote all the headnotes and McDonald the Introduction. After the eight plays two appendices are printed: these are general statements on radio drama, written by MacNeice in the 1940s to introduce his *Christopher Columbus* and *The Dark Tower*, which have more than historical interest. Authorial and editorial notes appear in a single sequence at the end of the book.

CHRISTOPHER COLUMBUS

a radio play

MacNeice's *Christopher Columbus*, an ambitious BBC feature produced by Dallas Bower, was written on the occasion of America's entry into the war and broadcast 12 October 1942 (Home Service) on the 450th anniversary of Columbus' arrival in the New World. This long verse play was based on Samuel Eliot Morison's new book *Admiral of the Ocean Sea* (1942) and conceived as 'a one man, one idea programme' of an uncompromising egoist 'motivated by a mystical *idée fixe*', an epic quest 'with a romantic yet ruthless hero'[1] set to an outstanding score by William Walton. Laurence Olivier played Columbus, and other parts of the large cast were taken by Marius Goring and Robert Speaight, Hedli Anderson, Margaret Rawlings, and Gladys Young. The play has been published twice by Faber (March 1944 with a long introduction of 'Some Comments on Radio Drama' published at the end of this volume as Appendix 1 – and September 1963 in a school edition with a partly new, shortened introduction and the same notes, both of which are printed here).[2] For the quincentenary of 1492–1992 the BBC presented an entirely new production on Radio Three, 26 January 1992. The text of the play used here is that of MacNeice's 1963 edition – with a few missing punctuation marks supplied from the playscript held by the Humanities Research Center, University of Texas at Austin.

AUTHOR'S INTRODUCTION (1963)

My radio play *Christopher Columbus* was first broadcast in 1942 and first published in 1944. Many years later, rereading both the play itself and my own Introduction to it, I feel I am returning to an innocent but quaint and archaic period. The nickname 'steam radio' is properly nostalgic: rarely has such an up-to-date medium matured, and indeed aged, so rapidly (even the silent film had hardly a shorter run before the talkies came to supersede it). So people, including myself, no longer write pieces like *Christopher Columbus* (for one thing the production is far too expensive). And nowadays looking at my Introduction to it, written in 1943, I find that I protested too much: I was still trying to sell radio drama to a public which I hoped, not too confidently, might include a few 'intellectuals'. A few years later this would hardly have been necessary. A few years later again, once the juggernaut of television had got into top gear, it would have been not only unnecessary but irrelevant. The public for a sound radio play like *Columbus* is perhaps five per cent of what it was during the war but, because it would now be pigeon-holed in the Third Programme (which then, of course, did not exist), it would contain a large number of highbrows, not only relatively but absolutely.

There is no need here to labour the very rapid changes of the last two decades except for one very brief word about television. In an introduction to a later radio play of mine, *The Dark Tower* (published 1947), I wrote: 'It would be a great pity if television were ever completely to supersede sound broadcasting as the talkies superseded the silent films.' I still agree with this but I am afraid, when two sentences later I wrote that 'sound alone is for most people more potent, more pregnant, more subtle than pictures alone', history has proved me wrong: it may be more pregnant and more subtle but it is certainly not more potent. Television is addiction-forming to a far greater degree than sound ever was. And most people, after all, are lazy. Listening to radio is far harder work than just watching a baby screen: without any visual aids you have not only to follow carefully but also to use your imagination. So instead of making propaganda for sound as *against* television (which would now be like trying to drag people away from the greyhound tracks to the theatre), let us simply consider what *are* the peculiar virtues of the sound radio play.

It is to be doubted if it can compete with television in the naturalistic presentation of everyday life. But then that is what television can do best; in most other spheres it has still to prove itself and there are certainly very great difficulties facing any television writer or director who wants to get away from naturalism or to do things *larger* than life. Sound radio is free from these difficulties: as in most artistic media, its very limitations can be turned into assets. The complete *lack* of the visual element allows the radio playwright to jump about not only in time and place but on different planes of reality. Thus it is admirably suited to fantasy: even Cocteau's grotesqueries in the cinema tend to creak or to appear 'contrived' but in radio a witch or a talking animal can comparatively easily escape the suggestion of pantomime. It is also suited to the dramatized chronicle, which is larger than or simpler than life, a species of *pageant* less cumbrous and less cardboard than the traditional visual kind.[3] This is where *Christopher Columbus* comes in.

This radio play was written to order to celebrate the 450th anniversary of the discovery of America. For this reason I ended the story with Columbus's triumphant return to Spain, ignoring his later (most tragic) career, which would have required a very different treatment. My main concern was theme, not character, and this is one reason why I wrote it in verse (admittedly a pretty elastic sort of verse). In most of my later radio plays (for the same reason I suppose as the more *poetic* of contemporary writers for the *theatre*) I avoided verse and preferred a kind of sleight-of-hand colloquial dialogue. But in such plays my objectives were quite different. For further comments on what is now something of a 'period piece' (though I note with pleasure that schools and amateur societies are rather fond of performing it, in some token sort of way, on the stage) I will quote what I wrote in 1943.

Christopher Columbus is an untypical radio play (by which I mean play written specially for radio) both because it is so long and because it involved so much music, and particularly vocal music. I have decided not to indicate all the places in the text where music was used but, as an example of its importance, I can point out that the whole of Columbus's triumphant procession from Seville to Barcelona had processional music in the background; this meant that the running commentaries in verse during these sequences were delivered, over the music, with much the same tempo and punch that characterize a real running commentary delivered over the noise of a crowd on a sportsground. William Walton's music, I should add, served its purpose admirably; i.e. it was structural.

The vocal interludes require an additional comment from a literary angle. The work as a whole being a stylized treatment of a simple heroic theme, these interludes served some of the same purposes as the choruses in a Greek tragedy. It will be noticed that the two verse-speakers and the two semi-choruses are neither characters nor, in the ordinary sense, narrators[4] but are the mouthpieces of two opposed principles, doubt and faith — a projection as it were of Columbus's inner dialectic; being thus projected outside the protagonist, they allowed me to keep him as simple and wedge-like as I wanted.

Since *Christopher Columbus* is so long, the sequences too are unusually long and the build unusually leisurely. It therefore looks more 'literary' than most radio scripts while it lacks those surprises and twists which, in a script of normal length, are often required to make a point in a flash — a dynamic *multum in parvo*. I rather regret the absence of such tricks but the tempo of the work did not require them and they might have conflicted with the one-way dignity of the theme. The temptation to stunt in this way might also have involved the wider temptation to debunk the Columbus legend. Columbus, a man who like Hitler relied on his intuitions and was rather an offensive character, should after all be a Godsend to those who enjoy debunking. My concern, however, was first with the Discovery and then with the Discoverer with a capital D. The small d, the small columbus, could be shelved.

This brings me to the question of history, Columbus became a legend first in his own mind, and to all romantics since. Radio drama, like all other forms of drama, being primarily directed to the emotions, my first object was to retain the *emotional* truth preserved in the legend rather than to let it dissolve in a maelstrom of historical details. On the other hand, in treating such a very *historical* event as the discovery of America, I did not consider myself entitled to alter the main outlines of the discovery and what led up to it or to misrepresent — except by simplification — the character of the discoverer *qua* discoverer. One thing that seems to be agreed about Columbus is that, whether or not he was a first-class navigator, he was a man of one idea with an almost mystical faith in his mission. This is how I have tried to portray him.

It should be remembered that many of the 'facts' about Columbus are still open to controversy. The Notes at the end of this book will make some historical points which may not be clear in history or in the script. It will be seen that, for dramatic reasons, I have done some minor transpositions and made some minor exaggerations. In the same way I have throughout used the name Christopher Columbus; he was of course Christóbal Colón.

CHARACTERS

THE VOICE OF DOUBT   BEATRIZ
THE VOICE OF FAITH   A WAITING WOMAN
JOSÉ   OBSERVER
ARTUR   VASCO
ALFREDO   LUIS
BARTOLOMÉ   A TOWN CRIER
CARLOS   MARTÍN PINZÓN
FRANCISCO   A STOREKEEPER
BROTHER PEDRO   A SERVANT
PRIOR   A SAILOR'S VOICE 1
COLUMBUS   A SAILOR'S VOICE 2
ANTONIO   MATE
THE HERALD   A WOMAN
TALAVERA   SPOKESMAN OF CREW
MEDINA CELI   GUTIÉRREZ
MEDINA SIDONIA   SÁNCHEZ
MENDOZA   VICENTE PINZÓN
1ST LACKEY   ESCOVEDO
2ND LACKEY   SEGOVIA
MARQUESA   HIDALGO
QUEEN ISABELLA   A PEASANT
DIEGO DE DEZA   A CLERIC
MANUEL   AN ONLOOKER
TAPSTRESS   SPOKESMAN OF THE PROCESSION
JUAN

CHRISTOPHER COLUMBUS

ACT ONE

DOUBT No, it cannot be done, it cannot be done.
  Here on the shore of the final sea
  Our windows open on unreality,
  The bitter rubric of the sinking sun —
  Ne plus ultra. This is the Western edge
  Of the established world, the ocean wall
  Beyond which none may pass. To pass
  Would lead to nothing at all.
DOUBT CHORUS West of Europe all is dark
  Water and uncertainty;
  Never seaman dare embark
  On that desert of the sea;
  On those waves of nullity
  Never venturer may sail —
  All who try shall fail, shall fail.
FAITH Yes, but it *can* be done, it *can* be done.
  Wise men have proved the world is round:
  Follow the sun to the west and you are bound
  To come on unknown lands which know the sun.
  Westward! Westward! Legendary isles
  Call our ships to sea and who knows where
  We shall come to port! We know,
  We know there is something *there*.
FAITH CHORUS West of Europe lies a world
  Never heard of, never seen,
  But the sails that still are furled
  Soon shall reach a new demesne.
  All the things that might have been —
  When we cross the Western Sea,
  All those things, shall be, shall be.

*(A room in Lisbon, 1484. Three middle-aged Portuguese are having
a friendly back-bite)*

JOSÉ Who is this man Columbus?

ARTUR Christopher Columbus!

ALFREDO A madman!

ARTUR Not a madman, my friend. An impostor.

JOSÉ What's he doing in Portugal?
  Where does he come from anyway?

ALFREDO He comes from God knows where.

ARTUR A very shady customer.

ALFREDO Think of him going to the King![5]

ARTUR Well, the King wouldn't take any nonsense.

ALFREDO Nonsense isn't the word for it.
  That man's schemes are lunacy.

JOSÉ Either of you ever seen him?

ALFREDO I've seen him. He's dangerous.

ARTUR I've seen him. He's deep.
  Here in Lisbon I saw him one time in a bookshop
  Taking down notes when he thought no one was looking.
  His hair's going grey, he's got a hooky nose —

ALFREDO And a mad look in his eye.
  Time I saw him he couldn't stop talking —
  Went on and on and on about his land in the West.
  Land in the West! You'd have thought
  You were listening to a drunken sailor;
  That's the kind of talk you hear in the taverns on the quay.

  (*A guitar creeps in and takes you to a tavern on the quay. Three rough
  sailors are swapping stories*)

BARTOLOMÉ I tell you I seen it. With my own eyes I seen it.

FRANCISCO Go on, Pedro. Have another drink.

BARTOLOMÉ It was when we was becalmed in Madeira.
  On certain days in Madeira
  You can see high land to the West.

FRANCISCO Aye, when you've been drinking.

CARLOS Easy there. I've seen things too. On the island of Graciosa —

FRANCISCO Lay off it, the pair of you.

CARLOS There was two corpses washed up on to the beach —
  Must have drifted in from the West.
  Wide cheekbones they had and a yellow skin —

BARTOLOMÉ And you know what *I* seen?
  We was sailing off the Azores and we picked up a piece of wood —

Carved wood it was, with queer figures on it,
Not like aught any of *us* had met with.
FRANCISCO To hell with all these stories. I suppose
You'll be telling me next you believe in Atlantis
And all them other places — Zipangu and Antilia!
CARLOS I believe in 'em surely. Why, man, don't you find 'em
Marked on our sheepskin charts?
BARTOLOMÉ That's right. Antilia and Zipangu . . .
Aye, and Vineland and Hy Brasil . . .
And the Isle of the Seven Cities.
CARLOS And the Fortunate Islands where no one grows old.
BARTOLOMÉ And the islands of dog-headed men.
And men with only one eye . . .
(*The guitar stops and the voices die away*)
CARLOS Hy Brasil . . .
FRANCISCO The Fortunate Islands . . .
BARTOLOMÉ Zipangu . . .
CARLOS Antilia . . .
FRANCISCO Atlantis . . .
(*The indignant Portuguese continue their indignation*)
ALFREDO The kind of talk you hear from drunken sailors!
What right have these damned foreigners
To think they can come to Lisbon and sell us something for nothing,
Sell us a midsummer dream of Land in the West
Or a western route to Asia?
I wish the fellows would get out of Portugal.
ARTUR They say that he's got out already.
To escape arrest, so they say.
JOSÉ That's good news. Where'll he go to?
ARTUR Spain presumably. Same old story.
Work away like a mole till he gets a royal audience —
In Spain that will take some time —
Then he will go to the King or the Queen or both
And tell them he knows for certain —
Mark what I say: for certain —
That, if they give him a ship, he will sail her West,
Discover islands and mainlands in the Ocean Sea —
ALFREDO Well, the Spanish Court won't believe *that*.
JOSÉ Haven't the money if they did.
Far too busy fighting the Moors at Granada.
ALFREDO If Columbus goes to Spain they'll probably put him in gaol.

ARTUR God knows where they will put him. The man has no place in
a modern community.
He has no place and he has no future.

JOSÉ No future. He has no future at all.

ALFREDO NO FUTURE AT ALL...

(*There is a pause and you hear the chanting of monks. This is the end
of Compline in the monastery of La Rabida. This is Spain in 1484*)

PEDRO Father Prior! Father Prior!

PRIOR What is it, Brother Pedro?

PEDRO There is a man at the gate. Am I to let him come in?

PRIOR You know our rules, Brother Pedro:
Admit all strangers who ask for shelter.

PEDRO Yes, but this man is different.
One ought to be careful these days.
Before I joined the Order of St Francis
I was, as you know, a soldier;
I know a dangerous man when I see one.

PRIOR So do I, Brother Pedro;
You forget I have lived many years in the Court.
What kind of a man is this dangerous stranger?

PEDRO He is in rags and covered with dust.
He looks like a beggar — except for his manner.
He looks very tired — except for his eyes.

PRIOR Go and admit him at once.

PEDRO But Father Prior, he may be a thief or a murderer;
Here at La Rabida
They sneak over here — over the frontier — from Portugal.

PRIOR I do not care if he *is* a thief or a murderer.
Our Holy Founder would not have cared either.
Go and admit him at once.

PEDRO Yes, Father Prior.

PRIOR And bring him in here.
I like to meet dangerous men.

(*While Pedro goes to the gate, the monks chant the* Salve *in the background*)

PEDRO This way please, Señor.
This is the Prior of our monastery, the Reverend Juan Pérez.

PRIOR Welcome, my son. Welcome to La Rabida.
> (*Pause*)

May I ask you your name?

COLUMBUS I am a man from Nowhere. They call me Christopher
Columbus.

My trade is the sea; I am a stranger in Spain —

A voice crying in the wilderness.

I knock at the doors of Kings to offer them an empire;

But — since they refuse it — I beg my bread.
> (*Pedro laughs*)

PRIOR Brother Pedro!

Kindly go to the refectory.

Fetch some food and some wine for Señor Columbus.

PEDRO Yes, Father Prior.
> (*Pedro goes out*)

PRIOR Now, my son, if you will sit here . . .

You are tired? You have come a long way?

COLUMBUS I have come a long way . . . It is only the beginning.

PRIOR You say your trade is the sea? Where did you learn it?

COLUMBUS At the age of ten in Genoa.

I come of a family of wool-weavers and tapsters

But God gave me a feeling for ships.

PRIOR So you are a native of Genoa?

COLUMBUS I am a native of the Kingdom of God.

PRIOR Here in La Rabida we know about ships;

We are only a couple of miles from the port of Palos —

COLUMBUS Palos? That looks west.

PRIOR Yes, they sail from there down the coast of Africa.
> (*Pedro returns*)

PEDRO Father Prior, here is the food and wine.

COLUMBUS I am not hungry, Father Prior.

PRIOR But surely — When did you last eat?

COLUMBUS This morning, I think. Or maybe yesterday.

But I have no hunger for bread or meat.

Only a hunger to talk.

PRIOR That can be easily satisfied.

Brother Pedro, go to Brother Antonio.[6]

Tell him we have a guest who shares his interests,

Ask him to join us.

PEDRO Yes, Father Prior.
> (*Pedro goes out*)

PRIOR Antonio de Marchena — You will like him,
  He knows about astrology and cosmography.
  And, Brother Pedro, tell him to bring his charts —
  His charts and the Mappa Mundi.
PEDRO Yes, Father Prior.
COLUMBUS Charts? The charts are all wrong.
  Except maybe Toscanelli's —
PRIOR Who did you say?
COLUMBUS No matter. It was a map
  I saw in Lisbon but I knew it before;
  I knew it all in my blood.
      (*Pedro returns with Antonio*)
PEDRO Here is Brother Antonio.
PRIOR Come in, Brother Antonio.
  This is our guest, Señor Christopher Columbus.
ANTONIO I am happy to meet you, Señor.
COLUMBUS You are a cosmographer?
ANTONIO It is my amusement.
COLUMBUS You know that the world is round?[7]
ANTONIO There are learned men — eccentrics — who don't admit
    it.
COLUMBUS But *you* admit it?
ANTONIO Certainly.
COLUMBUS Good. Then listen to me.
PEDRO (*aside*) The man will be talking all night.
PRIOR Brother Pedro,
  It is time you returned to your duties.
PEDRO Yes, Father Prior.
      (*Pedro goes out for good*)
COLUMBUS Right. The world is round. That is Point One.
  Point Two, Brother Antonio, is this:
  You know that in order to reach Asia
  People till now have gone to the East?
PRIOR How else would they go, my son?
COLUMBUS They would turn their backs on Europe and sail to the
    west.
  And, if the world is round, that would bring them to Asia.
ANTONIO That may be so. No one would dare to try it,
  And sail beneath the earth —
COLUMBUS *I* would dare.
ANTONIO Has it occurred to you, Señor,

That, if you *did* sail out to the west,

There might be other lands between here and Asia?

COLUMBUS Yes, there is Zipangu.

PRIOR Zipangu! A story of Marco Polo's.

ANTONIO I myself, Father Prior, believe Marco Polo.

I know he did not visit Zipangu himself

But his evidence for it is good.

He says there are many islands in the sea to the east of Asia.

Seven thousand islands.

COLUMBUS Seven thousand, four hundred and forty.

PRIOR Seven thousand islands that have never heard of Christ.

COLUMBUS They will hear of Him soon.

PRIOR Why do you think so?

COLUMBUS My name is Christopher — that is the Bearer of Christ.

My name is Columbus — that is the Dove.

You remember the dove of Noah?

It flew across the waters bearing a branch of olive.

PRIOR So you want to carry Christ to the Unknown World?

COLUMBUS That is my mission.

PRIOR You cannot do that alone.

You will need material things, you will need official support.

And I fear you will meet with a refusal.

COLUMBUS I have met with refusals already.

I have been refused by Kings.

PRIOR What Kings, my son?

COLUMBUS Portugal. Portugal refused me.

PRIOR So now you are trying Spain?

COLUMBUS

Spain . . . England . . . France. . . . Anyone who will have me.

ANTONIO Spain, I fear, will be the same as Portugal.

They will refuse you too.

PRIOR That is not certain, Brother Antonio.

Our Queen Isabella has faith.

ANTONIO Yes, she has faith, but her treasury is empty.

Besides, our King, Ferdinand . . .

He likes to be sure of his returns.

PRIOR Speak softly, Brother Antonio. . . .

Yes, Señor, it is true. The State Treasuries are empty.

The war with the Moors is still going on —

God knows when it will end.

Aragon and Castile are drained of money and blood;

Our first business is to take Granada,
To purge our land of the Sign of the Crescent.
And we cannot run after the moon while the earth is in chaos.
You are impatient, my son, to find new worlds,
But before we do that, we must put the old in order.

COLUMBUS My new world, Father Prior, might help the old.

PRIOR My son, you are younger than I am.
You must forgive me if in my old age
My vision is narrower than yours.
All I can see is Europe and that is enough —
Quarrels within the state and quarrels without
And, above all, the threat of the false gods.
It is only thirty years since Constantinople,
The second pillar of Christendom, fell to the Infidel.
You would not remember that personally.

COLUMBUS I remember all things personally.
All that has happened to man since the fall of Adam.

PRIOR And you know why Adam fell?
Because he had eaten the fruit of the Tree of Knowledge —
The forbidden tree that gives men fancies,
That makes them cry for the moon.
You yourself, my son —
The taste of that fruit is strong in your mouth.

ANTONIO Father Prior!

PRIOR
What is it, Brother Antonio? I thought you were falling asleep.

ANTONIO I've never been less asleep in my life.
It is this map. There!
        (*Antonio tears up his chart*)

PRIOR What are you doing? Why have you torn it up?

ANTONIO Because it is wrong. It is a lie.

PRIOR It's your own map. Didn't you make it yourself?

ANTONIO I made it myself and it's wrong.
This man has proved it is wrong.
Señor Columbus, I thank you.
My map ended on the shore of Europe
But you have shown me the truth.
The shore of Europe was the end of the world
But from this day on the world is endless.
I shall make a new map tomorrow.

PRIOR Señor Columbus,

You seem to have made an impression on Brother Antonio;
That is something unusual.
Brother Antonio,
Do you really believe that Señor Columbus —
Or anyone else for that matter —
Could sail out west from Europe and come to land?
ANTONIO I would not have believed it before tonight. . . .
But now I do, Father Prior, now I do.
PRIOR In that case we must see what can be done.
Señor Columbus,
You do not know it but I have the ear of the Queen,
For many years I was her Father Confessor —
COLUMBUS Then you will send me to the Queen?
PRIOR Not so fast, my son. Their Catholic Majesties
Are not so easy to approach.
The Queen's Confessor now is Hernando de Talavera.
I will give you an introduction to Talavera.
ANTONIO And there he had better be careful.
PRIOR That is true. I must warn you.
Talavera is a holy man but he is not like myself
Or Brother Antonio here.
You, my son, have a strange manner of speaking,
So be careful when you meet Talavera;
Pride is something he hates.
You must approach him with proper humility,
Explain your scheme to him in moderate language —
COLUMBUS I will tell Talavera the truth.
That is all he can ask for.
ANTONIO Perhaps it is more than he asks for.
PRIOR Yes, my son. Talavera,
He has no interest in knowledge for itself,
He has no interest in worldly glory.
He is a servant of God.
He may very possibly think your scheme is mad
And, what is worse, he may think it sacrilegious.
COLUMBUS That is all right. I will quote him the Bible.
Where can I find him?
PRIOR He is at the moment in Cordoba.
I will send you there in a few days' time.
It is a short journey.
ANTONIO I would call it a long one.

DOUBT Finding his way by starts and gleams,
   Plotting imponderable schemes,
   A haggard pilgrim drunk with dreams
   He plods the dusty land of Spain
   To call upon the indifferent Court,
   On priests and nobles for support,
   But he will call in vain, in vain.
DOUBT CHORUS Endeavour as it can
   The over-eager soul
   Shall never reach its goal —
   The truth denied to man.
FAITH The man the populace despise —
   There is a flame that never dies
   Upon the altars of his eyes;
   He will not break, he will not bend,
   His hands are tied by Church and State,
   He runs the gauntlet of the great
   But he shall conquer in the end.
FAITH CHORUS His inner eye is true,
   He knows that he is free
   To see what none can see,
   What none can do, to do.

COLUMBUS Now the game is beginning; now I am on the move.
   Whether they want to or not, they will have to listen.
   I am Christopher, the Bearer of Christ,
   I am the Dove that travels the world,
   And the words that I speak are the words that I hear
   And the words that I hear are the words of God.
   I am the last Apostle. Let them give me a ship
   And I will carry Christ to the world that no one knows,
   I will remake the maps and I will remake
   The destinies of the human race. Give me a ship
   And I will pass the gates of the West and build
   A bridge across the Future. Look out there —
   All you see is a waste of waters, the heaving
   Bosom of the indifferent childless sea,
   The drunken marble of the toppling wave,
   The edge of the horizon or the explosive
   Filigree of spindrift — That is all you see

But I see so much more.
In my hand I hold the key of the West,
I have come to Spain with that key in my hand,
I shall open my hand to the powers of Spain
And say: 'Do you see this?
This is the key to glory, the key to a new world.
Will you allow me to use it?'
That is what I shall say to the powers of Spain
And, whether they want or not, they will have to listen.

(*Fanfare*)
HERALD Fray Hernando de Talavera, Monte Jerónimo,
Confessor to Her Catholic Majesty; Bishop of Avila!
The Lord Bishop is granting an audience
To an unknown person, one Christopher Columbus.
(*Pause*)
TALAVERA Señor Columbus
I cannot really think that you are serious;
You come to me here out of nowhere,
A foreigner with no credentials,
And you ask me to procure you an audience
With her Catholic Majesty herself.
Her Majesty, Queen Isabella of Spain,
Is busy with the war with the Moors;
She has other things to think of
Than a wild goose chase after something that does not exist.
You have not, Señor, given me a single ground
To think your proposals feasible. I admit
You have quoted the Holy Scriptures to me; perhaps
I ought to remind you of the saying
That the devil can quote scripture to his purpose.
Your language, Señor, has been immoderate. However,
I cannot recommend you to the Queen, but seeing
That you are adrift in Spain, I will give you
A letter to one of the grandees of Andalusia,
The Duke of Medina-Sidonia....
(*Fanfare*)
HERALD The Most Excellent Señor Don Enrique de Guzmán,
Duke of Medina-Sidonia,
Count of Niebla and Señor of Sanlúcar de Barrameda.

MEDINA-SIDONIA Señor Columbus,
  I have listened to your project with the utmost attention;
  It has, I may say, the charm of novelty
  At the same time it takes me back to my youth;
  I remember when I had dreams like that myself . . .
  However, Señor, I am a busy man,
  Running my own estates takes me all my time —
  If you want someone who likes adventure
  And might have more time to discuss this matter,
  I will give you a letter to my peer, the Duke of Medina Celi,
  Whose exploits you will have heard of against the Moors.
      (*Fanfare*)
HERALD The most Excellent Señor Don Luís de la Cerda,
  Duke of Medina Celi,
  (Count of Puerto de Santa Maria),
  Señor of Cogolludo, of Gibraleón,
  Of Bembibre, Castrobalcón and of la Peña de Valdeña.
MEDINA CELI Señor Columbus
  I am a man of action. What you have told me
  Sounds like a fairy story but it stirs my blood.
  If it were not for this war with the Moors
  I would be half inclined . . . But, apart from that,
  Even a Spanish grandee could not espouse your cause
  Without the royal authority.
  I know that you want to go direct to the Queen
  But that is quite impossible. For myself,
  I shall be pleased to offer you hospitality.
  Stay in my household as long as you wish. If you will only be patient,
  I will, in due time, when circumstances permit,
  Give you a letter to the man who, after Their Majesties themselves,
  Is the greatest power in Aragon or Castile —
  I mean Mendoza himself,
  The Grand Cardinal of Spain.
      (*Fanfare*)
HERALD His Eminency the Cardinal,
  Don Pedro Gonzalez de Mendoza,
  Archbishop of Seville!
MENDOZA Now, Señor Columbus,
  You have come to me from the Duke of Medina Celi,
  In whose household you have stayed two years;
  You were sent to him by the Duke of Medina Sidonia

To whom you were sent by Hernando de Talavera
To whom you were sent by the Prior of La Rabida.
Where is all this leading you?

COLUMBUS I hope, my Lord, to the Queen.

MENDOZA You have a sanguine temperament.
I have here a letter about you from the Queen's Confessor,
The most reverend Hernando de Talavera.
You have not seen him, I take it, for two years.

COLUMBUS He writes to support my cause?

MENDOZA He writes to tell me you are mad.
   (*Pause*)
Talavera is the Queen's Confessor,
She pays great attention to all that he says.
It is a pity you have set him against you.

COLUMBUS Very well. If Spain will not have me,
I will go to France or England.

MENDOZA A moment, Señor. Talavera is powerful.
So am I, Señor Columbus.
I will arrange you an audience with the Queen.

   (*The Court of Castile. Two lackeys*)

1ST LACKEY Who is that fellow sitting in the ante-room?

2ND LACKEY Sitting? He's been walking up and down,
Up and down the carpet like a caged tiger.
He's waiting to see the Queen.

1ST LACKEY See the Queen! Who is he?
He looks no better than us.

2ND LACKEY He's one of those mad foreigners,
You ought to have heard how he spoke to me —
Looked right through me as if I was a sieve.
I only hope Her Majesty keeps him waiting.

1ST LACKEY He'll be kept waiting all right.
She's busy with the Marquesa.

2ND LACKEY Marquesa de Moya?

1ST LACKEY Who else? She's the only woman she trusts.

   (*The Queen's Room*)

MARQUESA Your Majesty?

ISABELLA What is it now, my friend?

MARQUESA May I not stay for this interview?

ISABELLA I have told you once. You may not.

MARQUESA But this man Columbus —
  My husband has been talking to Diego de Deza
  And Deza had been talking to the Cardinal of Spain —

ISABELLA You all of you talk too much.

MARQUESA But this man Columbus seems a phenomenon.

ISABELLA My Father Confessor tells me he's a menace.

MARQUESA Diego de Deza, so my husband says,
  Thinks that his scheme is possible.
  If that is so and if you would further it,
  Think what you would be doing for Spain.

ISABELLA I hope God will forgive me if I say
  I have done certain things for Spain already;
  Put down faction and cleaned out heresy,
  Reunited the country,
  Restored our old universities,
  Revived the arts and humanities.
  If I can only also defeat the Moors
  I shall not feel ashamed.

MARQUESA No, Your Majesty, but —

ISABELLA But what?

MARQUESA But look at Portugal.
  Look how the Portuguese explored the coasts of Africa
  And took it all for themselves.
  Why shouldn't *we* do something like that?

ISABELLA Africa, my dear friend, happened to exist.
  If you sail along a coast you can be sure
  That you will discover something.
  What Señor Columbus asks is a very different matter.

MARQUESA But it is much more exciting.

ISABELLA We do not make our decisions on grounds of excitement.
  My friend, I shall see this man now.
  I must ask you to go next door;
  Go and practise your instrument.

  (*The Marquesa goes next door and practises her instrument*)
MARQUESA (*sings*)[8]
  'Down in the Kingdom of Granada
  Our soldiers are fighting the Moors,

Our soldiers are all at the wars
Under the Sierra Nevada.'
What can they be talking about so long?
'The snow remains on the peaks
The night is ebony and silver,
And death is a dark river,
Down in the Kingdom of Granada'
I wonder what this man Columbus is like?
They are having a marathon interview
The evening sun is crawling over the floor . . .
'The scimitars of the Moors
Flash on the towers of the Alhambra;
The cross of Our Lord Christ
Is broken on the Alcazaba.
Orange groves and olive,
Orange blossom and mimosa,
Grow in the shadow of Death
Under the Sierra Nevada.'
What can he be like? Perhaps if I just creep over . . .
Perhaps if I listen at the door . . .
Very dishonourable of me . . .
    (*Faint murmuring of Isabella's voice; then of Columbus*)
That is Columbus now . . .
Perhaps if I open it, just the tiniest chink . . .
I *must* just see what he's like . . .
COLUMBUS (*from the next room*)
Your Majesty,
I must beg leave to correct you.
MARQUESA God preserve us!
COLUMBUS You used the word possibility.
What I am proposing is a certainty.
MARQUESA God in his mercy protect us!
So that is Christopher Columbus!
The man who corrects Isabella.
MARQUESA (*sings*)
'Down in the Kingdom of Granada
The cavaliers and the Hidalgos
Are driving the cattle of the Moors,
Are driving the cavalgada;
The rocks are stained with blood,
Our bones are cold and silver,

For Death is a dark river,
Under the Sierra Nevada.'

(*The Marquesa's singing recedes as we move next door*)
ISABELLA Señor Columbus,
We Isabella, Queen of Castile and Aragon,
Have listened to all you say,
And we would suggest to you, Señor,
A greater discretion of speech.
It is not the custom in Spain to contradict the Throne;
But, for this one time, we will pass that over.
Now, Señor, we will speak to you openly.
Our Father Confessor told us you were mad
But your words have stirred our fancy.
You ask us to give you a ship
And to authorize you to sail to the end of the world;
You ask us to send you out into an ocean of guess-work.
COLUMBUS Give me a ship and you need not guess any more.
Only give me a ship.
ISABELLA Matters like this, Señor, are not decided in a word.
We shall have to consult our partner on the Throne
Who is at this moment attacking Granada.
Apart from that we shall have to consult the authorities.
COLUMBUS Who are *they*, Your Majesty?
ISABELLA Señor, we ask you again to remember to whom you are
    speaking;
We are not accustomed to be interrupted and questioned.
By the authorities we mean an assemblage of learned men,
With knowledge of the world and of books,
With knowledge of the soul and of God.
What you propose may be factually impossible,
It may also be morally wrong.
These two points must be decided.
I will refer them to a Royal Commission
Consisting of wise men and fathers of the Church;
They shall decide whether you are right,
They shall decide whether there is land in the West.
COLUMBUS But how can they know?
How can they know I am wrong until I have proved myself right?
How can they know what there is in the West

While the West is still uncharted?
Here am I. Give me a ship.
Let me go to the West and then let them prove me wrong.
ISABELLA We did not say they will prove you wrong —
We hope ourselves they will not —
But we will not undertake this thing without their authority.
COLUMBUS Authority! Authority! Authority!
What authority had Moses to go out into the desert?
ISABELLA He had the authority of God.
COLUMBUS Yes, Your Majesty, but I dare swear
He did not have to wait for the learned men
To niggle over their books and mumble into their beards
Before he set out on the path that he knew was his.
ISABELLA Señor, you forget yourself.
We, Isabella, Queen of Castile and Aragon,
Have told you what we will do.
We will call a Royal Commission.[9]
That is all, Señor.
Now you will leave our presence.
    (*In the other room the Marquesa is still singing*)
MARQUESA (*sings*)
    'The fountains of the Alhambra
    Are playing upon the marble;
    The hungry eagle hovers
    On the hill of the Alcazaba.'
ISABELLA (*entering*) Marquesa!
MARQUESA Your Majesty.
ISABELLA You may stop making music now.
Your Señor Columbus has gone.
MARQUESA Oh he was wonderful.
ISABELLA How do you know he was wonderful?
The ladies of my Court do not listen at doors.
MARQUESA I am sorry, Your Majesty.
I only listened for a minute.
Are you going to give him your support?
ISABELLA I am appointing a Royal Commission.
I shall make Talavera its president.
MARQUESA Talavera! But he hates him.
ISABELLA Talavera is impartial.
The Commission will meet in Salamanca
In the Monastery of St Stephen.

(There is a pause and you hear The Commissioners singing the Veni Creator; this is drowned in the murmuring of a crowd)

TALAVERA Silence in the Court of the Commission!

(The murmuring dies down)

Fathers of the Church, Doctors of the Law and Masters of Letters,
As President of this Commission
Appointed by Her Catholic Majesty Queen Isabella
To investigate the case of Christopher Columbus,
I here and now after three days' session on this subject,
Consider that the time has come to make our decision.
If anyone here present wants any further discussion —

1ST VOICE No, we don't.

2ND VOICE We've heard enough already.

3RD VOICE Enough and more than enough.

TALAVERA Order in the Court!

Does anyone here present want any further discussion?

DIEGO DE DEZA I do, my Lord President.

(Murmuring)

TALAVERA It seems our learned Brother Diego de Deza
Wants some more discussion.

1ST VOICE No! No! No! No more discussion!

TALAVERA What are your grounds, Señor, for holding up our verdict?

DIEGO DE DEZA My grounds, my Lord President, are these.
We have now been in session three days
Debating the proposals of Christopher Columbus.
Three days, one would have thought were enough —

2ND VOICE They *are* enough!

3RD VOICE Enough and more than enough!

DIEGO DE DEZA They would have been had you had open minds
And kept to the point in debate —
But you have done no such thing.

CHORUS Shame! Shame!

1ST VOICE Sit down, Señor, sit down.

DIEGO DE DEZA I regret very much, my Lord President,
In such a distinguished gathering
To have to lodge a complaint of emotional prejudice —

1ST VOICE Sit down, can't you?

DIEGO DE DEZA The applicant to our Commission,
Señor Christopher Columbus —

(Murmuring)

Has come before us with a perfectly serious proposal —

2ND VOICE Perfectly serious!
   (*Laughter*)
DIEGO DE DEZA This proposal merits our gravest consideration
  And that for a number of reasons —
3RD VOICE Tell us *one*!
DIEGO DE DEZA One reason, my brother, is this:
  That, if what Señor Columbus says be true —
VOICES True! It's *not* true! How could it be true?
TALAVERA Order in the Court!
  Let our Fellow Commissioner proceed.
DIEGO DE DEZA
  If what he says be true then we should give him our aid
  Because, if his project succeeds —
2ND VOICE Away with all these ifs.
  If he fails he will make us a laughing stock.
DIEGO DE DEZA Why take failure for granted?
  And why be afraid of laughter?
  The thing after all is possible.
  We admit that the world is a sphere —
3RD VOICE No, we don't. We don't admit any such thing.
DIEGO DE DEZA I appeal to you, my Lord President.
  I thought it had been agreed that the world is a sphere.
TALAVERA No, Señor, the question whether the world is a sphere
  Is still, it would seem, open to dispute.
  In the present discussion, however, this question is irrelevant.
DIEGO DE DEZA
  I beg your pardon, my Lord, but it is not in the least irrelevant.
  If the world is a sphere —
TALAVERA Brother Diego de Deza,
  We cannot hold up these proceedings for one dissentient.
  I therefore propose without any further ado,
  Seeing that no one has anything further to say —
COLUMBUS *I* have something to say.
TALAVERA You have said your piece, Señor Columbus.
  Further remarks from you would be out of order.
    (*Pause*)
  Gentlemen of the Commission,
  The question before you is twofold.
  Señor Columbus has come before this Court
  To expound a certain theory
  And make a certain proposal;

We have to decide whether his theory is true
And, if it is true, whether his proposal is practical.
Previous to your decision
I propose to summarise the evidence —
1ST VOICE Is that necessary, my Lord President?
TALAVERA It may not be necessary, Señor.
It is the custom.
    (*Pause*)
Señor Christopher Columbus,
Will you oblige me by standing on the rostrum?
4TH VOICE (*aside*) The man's all a-quiver.
5TH VOICE (*aside*) He knows what's coming.
TALAVERA Thank you, Señor.
Christopher Columbus, citizen of Genoa —
COLUMBUS I am *not* a citizen of Genoa.
TALAVERA You are not a citizen of Spain
You are not a citizen of Portugal;
A man must have some country —
COLUMBUS My country, my Lord, is the Future.
    (*Pause: laughter and catcalls*)
3RD VOICE Then what are you doing here?
    (*More laughter*)
TALAVERA Order in the Court!
I would remind the Commissioners of their dignity.
    (*Pause*)
Christopher Columbus, you have told us your theory;
And you have explained to us your project.
In my opinion — but I do not know
Whether the Commission will agree with me —
5TH VOICE (*aside*) He doesn't know!
4TH VOICE (*aside*) Oh no!
TALAVERA In my opinion your theory is downright false —
CHORUS Hear! Hear! ... Hear! Hear! ...
TALAVERA Your theory is contrary to common sense —
CHORUS Hear! Hear!
TALAVERA Your theory is contrary to Reason —
CHORUS Hear! Hear! ... Hear! Hear!
TALAVERA Your theory is contrary to Holy Writ
And the accepted doctrines of the Church.
CHORUS Hear! Hear! ... *Hear! Hear!* ... HEAR! HEAR!
    (*Pause*)

TALAVERA Many Commissioners have made that point;
  They have quoted the Scriptures to disprove you,
  They have quoted the Christian Fathers,
  They have quoted St Lactantius and St Augustine,
  They have quoted the Law and the Prophets.
COLUMBUS Prophets!
  What do they know about prophets?
  What do you, my Lord President, know about prophets?
TALAVERA Silence, Señor!
COLUMBUS Have I not quoted you back the prophet Isaiah?
  Have I not quoted you back the prophet Esdras?
  Have I not told you the words that I hear myself in the night —
  The still small voice of Almighty God Himself?
      (*Uproar; cries of 'Shame!', 'Blasphemy!'*)
TALAVERA Señor Columbus! I call you to order!
  What you have just said is not only contempt of court,
  What you have said is blasphemy.
2ND VOICE That's right. Blasphemy.
1ST VOICE Give him to the Inquisition.
CHORUS Down with Columbus! Down with Columbus! Down with
    Columbus!
TALAVERA Order in the Court!
  Christopher Columbus,
  What you have just said precludes further debate.
  You have stood here before this Royal Commission
  Consisting of learned men and dignitaries of the Church,
  You have stood here and thrown God in our teeth.
  This being so, Señor,
  My patience is now at an end —
COLUMBUS And so is mine, my Lord.
  You and your Royal Commission —
  For three days you have baulked the issue,
  Three days of prevarication and obscuration,
  Three days of the closed mind and the lying tongue —
CHORUS Shame! Shame! Shame!
COLUMBUS (*against uproar*)
  I have heard the opinions of your learned body;
  They are like so many dead leaves
  Blown hither and thither in an endless maze
  Of ancient ignorance and prejudice —
  A labyrinth of lies.

(*Uproar*)

TALAVERA Order in the Court!
My fellow Commissioners,
I am not surprised this time at your loss of control.
This man has convicted himself out of his own mouth
As either a wilful heretic or a madman.
There is no need for me to conclude my summary.
This man has asked us for our official approval.
There is only one answer to give.

CHORUS (*mounting*)
No! No! No!
No! No! No!

(*The repeated negatives mount into a musical chorus*)

DOUBT CHORUS No ... No ... No ...
Never again!
His hope was thrown away
And all his work in vain.

DOUBT Broken the golden bowl
And gone the morning dream,
No one can now redeem
The desolated soul.
Alone he toils along
A never-ending street
Where all his hopes are wrong
And all his life defeat.

DOUBT CHORUS Defeat! Defeat! Defeat!
Defeat! Defeat!
He knows his hopes are wrong
And all his life defeat.

(*There is a pause as several years elapse. A guitar emerging from tipsy chatter takes us to a humble tavern*)

MANUEL Wine there! Wine!

TAPSTRESS Not so fast, fellow. How many hands have I got?
You've both had a skinful already. Why can't you behave?
Why can't you be decent and quiet like the gentleman over in the
corner?

MANUEL Because we bain't gentlemen.

JUAN What's that fellow in the corner anyway?

I seen him before some place.

MANUEL He looks a bit crazy to me.

TAPSTRESS He's a man that's come down in the world.

He was news one time.

Used to be received by the nobility.

JUAN Fancy that now. Look at his ragged cloak.

MANUEL Let's go and give him a drink.

TAPSTRESS Don't you go near him. He's touchy.

JUAN You can't frighten *us*. What's his name?

TAPSTRESS Señor Columbus.

JUAN Hey you, Señor! Señor Columbus!

We want you to drink with us.

TAPSTRESS Leave him alone.

1ST PEASANT (*loudly*) Maybe he's deaf.

Drink, Señor, drink!

We want you to drink with us.

COLUMBUS You want me to drink with you?

JUAN That's right.

MANUEL Your health, Señor Columbus.

COLUMBUS Thank you. Thank you very much.

JUAN What are you thinking about, Señor?

Remembering something?

COLUMBUS No, my friend, I'm forgetting something.

(*Laughter*)

JUAN That's a good one. Forgetting something!

Have another drink if you want to forget,

Have another drink and forget the whole world.

COLUMBUS And forget the whole world?

It will do if I forget just half of it.

MANUEL Half of it?

JUAN He must mean women.

COLUMBUS No, my friend, I don't mean women.

There is one woman I love but she is easy to forget.

JUAN They all are. They all are.

COLUMBUS

When you have seen someone then you can forget them.

But what you have never seen — that's what sticks in your mind.

MANUEL I don't tumble to that.

JUAN Don't understand what you mean.

COLUMBUS Look at it like this.

You know what it is to be homesick?

MANUEL I have never been away from my home.

COLUMBUS That makes no difference.

Maybe you've been homesick for the home you never had.

MANUEL That makes no sense neither.

COLUMBUS Oh yes, it does. Go and look at the sunset
When the sky is a lather of crimson and coral
And the bulging sun, over-ripe with knowledge,
Glides back into the womb of the sea.
Don't you feel as you watch him sink —
Don't you feel an envy of the sun?
It is so easy for him to travel out to the West
And see what none of us have seen.
(Pause)

JUAN You want to be like the sun?
If that's so, you've got no right to be here.
What are you doing sitting here in the corner?
The sun don't sit in no corners.
Always moving the sun is. Always moving.

COLUMBUS You are quite right, my friend.
(Pause)
Yes, you're right.
It's time for me to move on.

MANUEL Hey! What's the hurry?

JUAN I didn't mean it serious.
Sit down, Señor. Have another drink.

COLUMBUS No; you've taught me my lesson. Now I must leave you.

JUAN It's too late to travel this time of night.

COLUMBUS It's never too late to travel.

JUAN But where in God's name are you going?

COLUMBUS I'm going out of this country
I'm shaking the dust of Spain from my feet.
I'm going where men will know who I am.
(Pause)
But first I must call at Cordoba.

JUAN Cordoba? I know a woman in Cordoba.

COLUMBUS So do I. That's why I'm going there.
Beatriz Enríquez.[10] I have to say goodbye to her.

JUAN So she's expecting you?

COLUMBUS No, she's not. Why should she be?
I haven't seen her for years.
She does not expect me back.

(In Cordoba someone is singing)

BEATRIZ *(sings)* When will he return?
Only to depart.
Harrowed by the omen
Of his restless heart;
Bondsman of the Voice,
Rival of the Sun,
Viceroy of the sunset
Till his task be done.

Though he is my love
He is not for me;
What he loves is over
Loveless miles of sea
Haunted by the West,
Eating out his heart —
When will he return?
Only to depart.

(As she stops singing her woman cries from the doorway)

WAITING WOMAN Doña Beatriz! Doña Beatriz!

BEATRIZ What is it, Maria?
Have you seen a ghost?.

WAITING WOMAN He has come back, Doña Beatriz.
He is here.

BEATRIZ Who has come back?
(Pause)
You do not mean . . .

WAITING WOMAN Yes, Doña Beatriz. Señor Columbus.
He arrived in Cordoba this morning.

BEATRIZ Where is he now?

WAITING WOMAN Here, Doña Beatriz, here. Go to the window.
He is down in the patio sitting on the edge of the fountain.
Go to the window and see him.
Or shall I tell him to come up?

BEATRIZ Tell him nothing . . . Leave me alone.
Get back to your room and stay there.

WAITING WOMAN Yes, Doña Beatriz.
(The waiting woman goes out. Beatriz goes to the window and looks down into the patio)

BEATRIZ Now . . . Softly . . . Softly . . .
No, there is no one in the patio,

I cannot see for the sun
And the leaves and the shadows of leaves, the net of shadow and
    dazzle.
Would that be him sitting on the edge of the fountain?
Or is that a shadow too?
If I shade my eyes with my hand . . .
    (*Pause*)
Yes, it is, it is . . . How grey his hair is.
It is so like him to come and sit in the patio
When he knows I must be here.
Softly, Beatriz, do not cry out;
He must not see you; no,
You must take your cloak and slip away.
What right has he after these years
To come back into my life like a burning ghost
And sit on the edge of my fountain troubling the water with a stick,
Teasing the carp? What right
Has this man who is always passing through,
Passing by and beyond, to turn again
And knock at a door that is overgrown with ivy?
No, I will take my cloak, I will close my lips,
Once and for all I will —
    (*As she is turning from the window Columbus catches sight of her*)
COLUMBUS (*from below*) Beatriz!
    (*Pause*)
Beatriz! Is that you?
BEATRIZ Why have you come back?
COLUMBUS To say goodbye.
BEATRIZ You said goodbye to me before,
  When you left me to go to Salamanca,
  When you left me to go before the Royal Commission —
COLUMBUS Don't mention that;
  All that is Ancient History.
  May I come up?
BEATRIZ No, you had better not. What is the use?
  When you come on a visit
  The light is always behind you,
  The shadow of your departure crosses the door before you;
  I am too tired, Christopher . . .
  Where are you going this time?
COLUMBUS I am on my way out of Spain.

I am looking for a country where men have faith
And where their rulers have vision.
BEATRIZ No one has more vision — or faith — than Isabella.
COLUMBUS Don't talk to me about your Queen Isabella.
   All you Spaniards have betrayed me.
   Your Queen is afraid of her Confessor, Talavera,
   Your King thinks only of himself,
   Your Court is a circus of knaves and fools,
   Of short-sighted bigots and long-fingered thieves.
       (*Pause*)
   May I come up now?
BEATRIZ I told you it is no use.
   So you are leaving Spain? By land or sea?
COLUMBUS By sea, from Palos.
   I shall call on the way at La Rabida
   To say goodbye to Prior Juan Pérez.
   Now, Beatriz, since you will not let me come up
   I will take this rose from your patio
   And I will be on my way.
BEATRIZ But, Christopher, wait . . . Wait!
   You have no right to take a rose from my patio.
   You have no right to come here at all, but now you have come,
   You cannot leave me like that . . .
   Yes, you had better come up.

       (*After another pause you hear the monks again, chanting the Kyrie
       Eleison. Columbus is back at La Rabida*)
PRIOR So, my son, you are leaving Spain?
COLUMBUS I am leaving Spain for good.
PRIOR That is a great mistake. Haven't you heard the news?
COLUMBUS What news, Father Prior?
PRIOR Granada is about to capitulate.
   The war with the Moors is finished.
COLUMBUS Praised be God for that!
   All the same I am leaving this country.
PRIOR In spite of the Fall of Granada?
COLUMBUS How can that affect me?
PRIOR Don't be so foolish, my son.
   I know your sojourn in Spain
   Has been long and hard and disappointing . . .

But now Spain will be different.
The victory over the Moors is a great one,
A new life will come into this people,
There is no telling what they may undertake
That before they would not have dreamt of.
No, my son, do not be stubborn.
Granada is about to surrender:
Take a horse — the best horse that you can —
And ride to Granada at once,
Wait for the Queen when she enters Granada,
Press your suit while the moment is ripe,
Ride to Granada at once, ride to Granada . . .

(*After a pause a triumphant chorus is heard. You are now in the streets of Granada*)

CHORUS (*singing*) Granada has fallen! Granada has fallen!
The triumph of Spain has atoned for her loss.
Granada has fallen; the sign of the Crescent
Has bowed in the end to the sign of the Cross.
Granada has fallen. Our Queen Isabella
Has entered Granada with pennons and drums.
The Old Age was iron; the New Age is golden;
The Gold Age is coming — oh see where it comes!
Granada has fallen. The long days of torment
And bloodshed are over; the battle is done
And we are the victors. Granada has fallen
And Spain's resurrection today has begun.
OBSERVER Today . . . Today . . . Today!
The most wonderful day in our history.
From where I stand on the top of this turret
The whole of this city of Granada is a sea of sound and colour —
Brass and brocade, jewels and banners,
The plumes of the knights like spray
When the sun is dancing on the sea.
The Royal Procession is winding through the resounding streets,
Ferdinand in silver and gold, Isabella in diamonds,
The sunlight catches in her auburn hair
And her horse's trappings reach to the ground.
Yes, I can see it all but I cannot take it in;
This is the end of our Ten Years' War,

This is the end of the Moorish occupation,
The end of a number of things,
The beginning of many more . . .
The whole town is drunk with drums and trumpets,
The eyes of all the world are fixed upon Granada —
Yes, I can see it all . . . I can see it all . . .

COLUMBUS And I too — I can see it all:
The cavalcade of those who have won Granada,
Of those who have failed Columbus.
Here I stand, unmarked, among the goggling crowd,
In the shimmer of silks and the clamour of bronze,
And I alone have no feeling of triumph.
Or rather I have — but it is not enough;
I must go to the Queen and tell her it is not enough.
I can imagine a greater day than this,
A greater conquest; I see
The banners of Castile and of Christ
Carried in triumph, entering
Nobler gates than the gates of Granada —
I mean the Gates of the West.
I must go to the Queen at once and point across the sea
To those invisible gates and open my hand thus
And say 'Your Majesty, here is the key;
Only give me a ship.'

(*After a pause Columbus repeats himself. But now Isabella is really
there to hear him*)

COLUMBUS Give me a ship, Your Majesty, give me a ship.
Need we delay any longer?
ISABELLA We shall not delay any longer;
Your project, Señor Columbus,
Your proposed voyage of discovery —
Now that our hands are no longer tied by the Moors —
Excites our warmest interest.
What we propose is this:
We shall appoint another Royal Commission —
What is wrong, Señor?
COLUMBUS If you appoint another Royal Commission,
I might as well jump off the top of the Alhambra.
ISABELLA Control your impatience, Señor.

This is a great — a momentous — undertaking.
It has to be begun under the proper auspices.

COLUMBUS And who, may I ask Your Majesty,
I ask it with all humility,
Who is to be the president of this Commission?

ISABELLA The Commission will be on the same basis as before.
Its President will be the same as before.

COLUMBUS You mean Talavera? In that case —

ISABELLA A moment, Señor. It is several years now
Since you appeared before him. At that time
Your conduct before the Court was such
As to excite his displeasure —

COLUMBUS As to excite his hatred.

ISABELLA Our Father Confessor does not hate;
He is a saintly character. However,
It is true that he can be provoked; therefore, Señor Columbus,
We would remind you to exercise discretion.
You are going before this Commission
With our own recommendation;
All you need do is to be discreet.
There are certain formalities to be settled,
And your own status made clear;
So, whatever you do, make a show of humility,
Do not offend Talavera again,
Moderate your demands.

(*A fanfare introduces the Second Commission*)

TALAVERA Señor Columbus,
As president of this Commission called by royal demand
To authorize your voyage into the Western Ocean,
It is my duty to tell you that our body
If it is to sanction your undertaking,
Can only give its sanction on certain terms.

COLUMBUS Thank you, my Lord President. I have terms of my own.
(*Murmuring*)

TALAVERA Indeed, Señor? What are they?

COLUMBUS My Lord President, Members of the Commission,
If I undertake this voyage of discovery,
I demand in return —

TALAVERA You *demand*, Señor?

(*Louder murmuring*)

COLUMBUS I demand in return the following things as my right:
First, the position of Viceroy and Governor-General
Over all islands and continents that I discover —

1ST VOICE Viceroy and Governor-General!
(*Laughter and murmurs*)

COLUMBUS And further, I demand to be appointed
Admiral of the Western Ocean; and further —
I demand a tenth part of all the treasure —
Pearls, diamonds, silver, spices, gold —
That shall be found in the lands that I discover.

3RD VOICE Counting his chickens!

2ND VOICE He's mad!

COLUMBUS And further, I demand exclusive
Ownership of one eighth part
Of all the lands discovered, and one eighth part
Of all the revenues therefrom; and further —

TALAVERA That is enough, Señor.

COLUMBUS Further, I tell you;
I demand that all these rights and dignities and titles
Shall be, by Royal charter, made hereditary,
Confirmed to my descendants, from first-born to first-born.
(*Pause*)

TALAVERA Is that all, Señor Columbus?

COLUMBUS That is all, my Lord President.
(*Hostile laughter*)

TALAVERA Very good, Señor.
I think the Commission will agree with me
That these demands are absurd.
Unless you withdraw them one and all,
We cannot sanction your enterprise.

COLUMBUS I will not withdraw anything.
Unless I am made Viceroy and Governor-General
Of the lands that I have discovered,
Unless I am made Grand Admiral of the Ocean,
Unless you grant me every title I ask,
I will not sail at all.

1ST VOICE You won't sail at all!
(*Laughter*)

TALAVERA I give you your last chance.
Will you withdraw these demands?

COLUMBUS No, I will not.

TALAVERA In that case, as President of this Commission,
I refuse you all further support.

CHORUS Hear! Hear! . . . Hear! Hear! . . . Hear! Hear!

2ND VOICE That'll be the end of *you*, Señor Columbus.

COLUMBUS You are wrong, Señor.
Your Royal Commission for the second time has rejected me.
I shall not trouble you again.

3RD VOICE Thank God for that!

COLUMBUS No, my very dear friends,
I shall go over your heads.
You are not the only people who count in Spain.
There *are* some people who believe in me,
I dare say you may have heard of them.
There is Don Andrés de Cabrera, Marquis of Moya,
There is Don Luís de Santangel, Chancellor of the Treasury,[11]
There is his Eminency the Cardinal —
Don Pedro Gonzalez de Mendoza.
There is also Isabella of Castile.

(A fanfare takes you back to the Court)

ISABELLA Marquesa, what is the news from your husband?

MARQUESA He has been talking to Luís de Santangel.
Santangel will loan you the money —
If you wish to accept it.

ISABELLA Of course I wish to accept it.

MARQUESA His Majesty will not like it.

ISABELLA Listen, my dear friend.
I am Queen of Castile in my own right;
If I decide to borrow money from my Treasurer
In order to further any particular project —

MARQUESA So you do want to help Columbus?

ISABELLA You knew that surely?
That man's ideas have kept me awake in the night.
It is time for him to put them into action.

MARQUESA But what about Talavera?
He thinks the whole scheme is unholy.

ISABELLA Even Talavera may be wrong.
Mendoza thinks the opposite.
His Majesty, I know, agrees with Talavera,

Or rather he doesn't think that the scheme is unholy —
He merely thinks it a waste of time and money.
MARQUESA But Santangel on the other hand —
He has a head for business —
He thinks that Columbus may bring you in millions.
ISABELLA Quite so. Opinion is divided.
What do we do when opinion is divided in our Court?
We do, my dear Marquesa, what we want to.
    (*Pause*)
And Ferdinand will have to agree to it.

    (*Ferdinand agreed to it. A Fanfare introduces the Herald*)
HERALD On this day the thirteenth of April
In the year of Our Lord Fourteen Hundred and Ninety-two
In the name of the Holy Trinity and Eternal Unity,
We Don Ferdinand and Doña Isabella,
By the grace of God, King and Queen of Castile,
Leon, Aragon, Sicily, Granada, Toledo, Valencia,
Galacia, Majorca, Seville, Sardinia, Corsica,
Murcia, Jaén, Algarve, Algesiras, Gibraltar and the Canary Islands,
Count and Countess of Barcelona,
Lords of Biscay and Molina,
Dukes of Athens and Neopatria,
Counts of Roussillon and Cerdan,
Marquises of Orestan and Goziano,
Have seen a patent of grace signed with our names and sealed with
    our seal,
Drawn up as follows . . .
COLUMBUS They have given me all that I asked —
Let Talavera laugh it off if he can.
Admiral of the untravelled ocean!
Viceroy of the Unknown World!
They have promised me three ships. I shall sail from Palos.

END OF ACT I

ACT TWO

(You hear the music and chatter of a port. This is Palos. Two old longshoremen are gossiping on the quay)

VASCO What be goin' on in port?

LUÍS Hast not heard? 'Tis they three ships.
Fittin' of 'em up for Columbus.

VASCO Ha! Ha! Ha!
Martín Pinzón, I hear, be a-goin' too.

LUÍS Martín Pinzón? 'Tis true.
I'd have thought he'd have more sense.
He's a rare good seaman, Martín Pinzón.

VASCO What can he want, takin' up with Columbus?

LUÍS God knows what he can want. He has his work cut out,
Tryin' for to sign on crews.
Nobody wants to sail with 'un.
You can't blame 'em neither.
No one in his senses would go on this here trip;
When they get out West there they'll topple off of the world,
Go right over the edge.

VASCO So no one will sign on?

LUÍS Hardly a dozen so far.
And they three ships be small 'uns.
The Santa Maria — and she be biggest of three —
She be two hundred tons or two hundred and thirty.
Nay, man, they'll never raise their crews.
Not unless they opens the jails.

VASCO Wouldn't do that, would they?

LUÍS No knowing what they would do.
Whole business be crazy.

TOWN CRIER Oyez! Oyez! Oyez!
Hearken to the Royal Proclamation:
We Don Ferdinand and Doña Isabella,
By the grace of God, King and Queen of Castile,
To all magistrates, in our cities and towns,
To all officers of the law and governors of the prisons:
Be it known to you that we

Have ordered Christopher Columbus
To proceed to sea for the despatch of certain
Business in our service. And in so much as
He has met with difficulty for this purpose
In the raising the proper crews,
We hereby proclaim an amnesty
To all such persons at present in prison
Fòr the breaking the laws of this realm
As will consent to report at our port of Palos
To man the three ships of the said Christopher Columbus.

(*Now you hear the tramp of the jail-birds*[12])

PINZÓN[13] Keep in line there. Keep in the line.
   Who comes next?
BARTOLOMÉ I do, master.
PINZÓN Where are you from?
BARTOLOMÉ Prison in Seville.
PINZÓN What were you in for?
BARTOLOMÉ Robbery with violence.
PINZÓN Very good. Sign on at the quay.
   Who comes next?
CARLOS I do.
PINZÓN Where are you from?
CARLOS Prison in Ronda.
PINZÓN What were you in for?
CARLOS Coining false money.
PINZÓN Sign on at the quay. Next!
   Where are you from?
FRANCISCO Prison in Cabra.
PINZÓN What were you in for?
FRANCISCO Murder.
PINZÓN Right. Sign on at the quay.
   It looks as if we shall have a crew after all.

STOREKEEPER (*check these over*)
   A third of hard tack, a third of salted flour ...
   Wine, bacon, vinegar, oil,
   Cheese, peas, beeves, beans,
   Stockfish, lentils, honey, raisins,

Hoops, pitch, nails, nets,
Hardware, tallow, oakum . . .

(*As the storekeeper's inventory fades away you hear a woman singing in empty space*)
There be three ships
  Down on the quay
Waiting to sail
  The Western Sea;
Three lonely ships
  Will leave this shore
And we shall see them
  Nevermore.

Three ships upon
  A hopeless quest
To break the spell
  That binds the West,
Three lonely ships
  Will leave this shore
And we shall see them
  Nevermore.

(*The voice of Pinzón brings back the world of business*)
PINZÓN Señor Columbus.
COLUMBUS What is it, Señor Pinzón?
PINZÓN All three ships are ready and seaworthy.
  Laden and manned and ready to sail.
COLUMBUS In that case, Señor Pinzón . . .
  In that case we sail tomorrow.
PINZÓN Very good, Señor. Tomorrow.
SERVANT (*entering*) Señor Columbus! Señor Columbus!
COLUMBUS Why do you come in my presence without knocking?
SERVANT I am sorry, Señor. There is a lady outside.
COLUMBUS Ask her to come in.
PINZÓN I will leave you then.
COLUMBUS I will see you tomorrow, Señor Pinzón.
  Remember to check that matter of the biscuits.
PINZÓN One pound of biscuits per man per day,
  Two litres of wine per man per day,

Two thirds of a pound — But it's not so easy;
How can we possibly know how many days —
COLUMBUS That, Señor, is irrelevant.
PINZÓN Very good, Señor. Hasta la vista.
COLUMBUS Hasta la vista.
    (*The servant re-enters*)
SERVANT Doña Beatriz Enríquez.
COLUMBUS Leave me.
    (*Pause*)
Beatriz . . .
BEATRIZ I heard you were due to sail.
I came on horseback from Cordoba.
COLUMBUS That was a mistake, Beatriz.
BEATRIZ I wouldn't have come but I had something to tell you.
COLUMBUS You cannot have anything new to tell me.
BEATRIZ Yes, I have. Something entirely new.
Or perhaps I should say it is something very old —
Old for the race of women but new for me.
COLUMBUS If you want me back, Beatriz —
BEATRIZ I do not want you back, Señor.
I know you are going away for ever —
But then you've always been away.
When you and I were together in a locked room
You still were further away than the furthest planet.
COLUMBUS If you know that, why've you come here now?
BEATRIZ Because I have something to tell you.
COLUMBUS Then for God's sake tell me. I have no time to spare.
BEATRIZ No . . . I cannot tell you. You have no imagination.
COLUMBUS *I* have no imagination!
BEATRIZ When are you sailing?
COLUMBUS Tomorrow. Early in the morning.
BEATRIZ Then perhaps tonight . . .
COLUMBUS Tonight I shall go to the monastery of La Rabida
And spend the night on my knees.
BEATRIZ You have good reason.
    (*Pause*)
Goodbye.
COLUMBUS Beatriz . . .
BEATRIZ If you are praying the whole night
You might say a prayer for me.
Goodbye, Christopher, goodbye . . .

(*Beatriz vanishes and morning succeeds her. A crowd has come to the quay to see Columbus off. The gulls are crying and the two old longshoremen are waiting for something sensational*)

VASCO A fine morning, Luís.

LUÍS Aye, 'tis a fine morning.

   You be up early.

VASCO I want to be in at the death.

LUÍS So do whole town seemingly.

   Never seen such a crowd here.

VASCO Where be old madman himself?

   'Captain Christopher Columbus'?

LUÍS On his way down from La Rabida.

   They say as he spent the night a-praying.

VASCO Reckon he had good need to.

   And all them other poor devils.

LUÍS *They* spent night in pot-houses.

VASCO 'Let us eat and drink for tomorrow us die.'

   Lord have mercy on all of 'em.

      (*Now we hear the drumming*)

LUÍS That'll be 'un now. Look 'ee yonder.

   Yon be banner of Castile — the gold castle on the red ground.

VASCO Aye, and yon be friars of St Francis —

   See their brown hoods in crowd.

   Who be they two fellows in front?

   One of 'em walking with great big strides

   And the tall one a-going along as if he was floating.

LUÍS The tall one look like old Juan Pérez —

   He be prior of La Rabida.

   One that's striding must be Columbus himself.

VASCO Be that Columbus himself?

   Ha! Ha! Ha! What's all the hurry?

      (*The crowd swells up and the drums come nearer*)

VASCO What be old Prior up to?

   He bain't sailing, surely?

LUÍS (*shouting*) What did 'ee say? Can't hear.

VASCO (*shouting*) Prior? *He* bain't sailing?

LUÍS Prior of La Rabida? Nay.

   He be come to bless the ships.

      (*There is dead silence for the Blessing*)

PRIOR O God, Lord of the Heaven and Earth and of the wide sea, we humbly pray Thee out of Thy infinite mercy to bless and hallow these three ships, sailing today from this port of Palos to a bourne which no man knows.

Per Dominum.

CHORUS Per Dominum.

(*The crowd begins to chant the Litany of the Saints. Columbus is heard crying with full voice over it*)

COLUMBUS In the name of the Holy Trinity —

Weigh the anchor.

VOICE Aye, aye, Captain. Anchor up.

MATE Hands to the capstan. Break her out.

(*The Litany continues but is drowned in a Capstan Shanty*[14])

SOLO We're bound upon a wild goose quest —

CHORUS pero yo ya no soy yo —

SOLO To find an empire in the West —

CHORUS ni mi casa es ya mi casa.

SOLO Goodbye to Spain and the Spanish shore —

CHORUS pero yo ya no soy yo —

SOLO For *we* won't see our wives no more —

CHORUS ni mi casa es ya mi casa.

SOLO The life on shore was not so bad —

CHORUS pero yo ya no soy yo —

SOLO And now we're here we know we're mad —

CHORUS ni mi casa es ya mi casa.

SOLO So goodbye father and mother mine —

CHORUS pero yo ya no soy yo —

SOLO You can drink my health in muscadine —

CHORUS ni mi casa es ya mi casa.

(*As the sailors' voices fade away your attention comes back to the crowd on the shore who are still chanting the Litany. The two longshoremen are looking out to sea*)

VASCO So that be end of that!

LUÍS Not a bad start, howsomever.

They sail better'n I thought.

Pity the *Niña* got lateen sails.

VASCO *Pinta* can go a lick though.

LUÍS Aye, got a lovely run off a fair wind.

Pretty sight they make surely;

Wind filling out the sails with a red cross on each of 'em

And the sun shining on the gold trucks and the taffrail —
(*A woman is heard sobbing*)
What be wrong with *you*?

WOMAN They've taken away my man.
He's on the *Santa Maria*.
I'll never see him again.

VASCO Reckon you won't.

LUÍS Don't say that, you fool . . .
Stiff ships, bain't they. Look at their wake.

WOMAN I'll never see him again.
I'll never see him again.

VASCO Well, you're not the only one.

BEATRIZ No, she's not the only one.

VASCO Beg your pardon, lady. I didn't see you.
Lady like you oughtn't to be in this crowd.

BEATRIZ A lady like me oughtn't to be alive.

LUÍS (*humming*) La-la-la-la-la . . .
All this unhappiness!
The white horses be happy enough;
Look at 'em leaping at the stem.

BEATRIZ White horses? The horses of the sea.
The horses of the sea are taking him away.

LUÍS You don't look well, Señora. You ought to go home.

BEATRIZ There is no point in my going home.

LUÍS Any connection of yours sail on them ships?

BEATRIZ Any connection of mine?

VASCO He means husband or father or summat.

BEATRIZ No, my friends. Nothing like that.
It is only someone I used to know —
He's out there now on the poop of the *Santa Maria*
But he is not any connection of mine.

VASCO Then you're lucky. This poor creature here —
Look how she's a-crying of her eyes out.

BEATRIZ Poor thing. I almost wish
I could cry my eyes out too —
But that would be out of proportion.
I can hardly see him now, standing there in the stern;
He thinks he knows where he's going,
He will never know what he's leaving behind.

VASCO And what may he be leaving behind?

BEATRIZ Only a woman he does not love . . .

Only that and a child he will never know.
On those ships they are singing.
Singing away in time to their work,
Singing away without ceasing
As if this voyage would go on for ever —
And so it will, so it will;
None of those ships will ever come back.
And the man standing there on the poop —
The father of my child to be —
He too will never come back.
Not in a month of parboiled days,
Not in a year of palsied months,
Not in an age of haunted years —
He won't come back, he won't come back.
    (*Pause*)
(*fading*) And all they can do is sing!

    (*That is what they are doing. A Hauling Shanty creeps up into the
    foreground*)
SOLO We're gone away for ever, for ever on the ocean,
CHORUS Gone away for ever, for ever and a day,
SOLO Gone away for ever, for ever on the ocean,
CHORUS Gone away for ever, for ever and a day.

SOLO In sunlight and starlight, in springtime and autumn,
CHORUS Gone away for ever, for ever and a day,
SOLO In snowfall and nightfall, in darkness and downfall,
CHORUS Gone away for ever, for ever and a day.

SOLO Out upon the ocean we're flotsam and jetsam,
CHORUS Gone away for ever, for ever and a day,
SOLO We're ragtag and bobtail, we're lost and we're lonely,
CHORUS Gone away for ever, for ever and a day.

    (*From the sailors' voices you move to the captain's cabin*)
COLUMBUS (*writing in journal*) 'Friday, August the third, Fourteen-
Ninety-Two: Set sail from the bar of Saltes in Palos at eight o'clock
and proceeded with a strong breeze till sunset, fifteen leagues South
afterwards South-West and South by West which is the direction of
the Canaries.'

'September the sixth: Cleared from the Canaries and sailed due West.'

'September the ninth: Sailed this day nineteen leagues, and determined to count less than the true number, that the crew might not be discouraged if the voyage should prove long . . .

The sailors steered badly, causing the vessels to fall to leeward toward the North East, for which the admiral reprimanded them repeatedly.'

(*From the captain's cabin you move back to the sailors*)

BARTOLOMÉ Told us off he did. How can *us* help it?

FRANCISCO That's right. What do he think we are?

BARTOLOMÉ Damned galley slaves — that's what he thinks we are.

FRANCISCO Sooner be back in prison.

CARLOS You know what *I* think? I think he's mad.

FRANCISCO Reckon you're right. I'll tell 'ee what I saw only last night it was. I were on watch in the bits and there he were a-standing up on the forward castle, standing up there like a statue up on a church — and talking to himself he was, face didn't seem to move but he were a-talking to himself — talking right out loud to the sea and the moon.

(*Night-music now throws a light on Columbus talking to himself*)

COLUMBUS 'Where shall wisdom be found and where is the abode of understanding?

God makes the weight for his winds and he weigheth the waters by measure.'

They knew that I was to come.

Isaiah and Esdras and Job and John the Divine —

They knew that I was to come.

And the Roman poet, Seneca, knew it too — [15]

. . . venient annis

Saecula seris quibus oceanus

Vincula rerum laxet . . .

'The time will come in a late

Century when the sea

Will loose the knots of fate

And the earth will be opened up

And the rolled map unfurled

And a new sailor sail

To uncover a new world.'

'The time will come . . .' The time has come already.
There are strange things happening.

(*The night-music fades away and we are back with the sailors*)

FRANCISCO See that? Do 'ee see it? Do 'ee see it or don't 'ee?

BARTOLOMÉ I see it all right. It's just I don't believe it.

FRANCISCO Hey, Carlos, come and look at this.

CARLOS Look at what? What's wrong with you?

FRANCISCO The needle, Carlos, the compass needle,
The needle, the fly, the lily.
Come and look at this here lunatic needle.

CARLOS The needle, Francisco? What's wrong with her?

BARTOLOMÉ Witchcraft. That's what's wrong with her.

CARLOS Well. Let's have a look.

FRANCISCO A moment, Carlos. Tell me —
You know this magnetic needle —
What way be she meant to point?

CARLOS Why, we all know that. She points due North,
She points to the Stella Maris.

FRANCISCO Very well, Carlos. Come ye here and see.
(*Pause*)

CARLOS Nombre de Dios!

FRANCISCO Well, Carlos? What way be she pointing now?

CARLOS But this is mad. She's swung to the West,
She's pointing well North-West,
Pointing North-West a fourth of the wind.

FRANCISCO A fourth of the wind, eh? Well, Carlos?
What do 'ee think of that?

BARTOLOMÉ It's summat no one's ever heard of.
Us was wrong to come on this voyage.

FRANCISCO Wrong! Us was signing our death-warrant.
Better have taken our twenty years in jail.
The laws of Man be one thing,
The laws of Nature be another —
Way out here in this here empty sea
The laws of Nature don't work no more;
Nature — as us knew her — Nature don't exist.

BARTOLOMÉ 'Tis the Devil that rules out here.

CARLOS The Devil? I don't know about that —
But we've got a devil of our own right here on board

And it's him that gives us our orders.

FRANCISCO He won't be giving us orders not much longer —
Not if this here sort of thing go on.

BARTOLOMÉ A sailor's life be a hard life but this beats all.

FRANCISCO Nothing from day to day nor week to week
But steel band of horizon
Like a steel collar on your throat;
It make me feel I'm choking.

CARLOS What does he care if you choke?
A man like that who never sleeps a wink,
A man like that who talks to himself —

FRANCISCO And 'tain't as if he only talked to himself.
I've watched him there in the night. He talk a spell
And then he stop and listen.
What do 'ee think he listen to?

CARLOS Don't ask *me*. I never learned black magic.

FRANCISCO No, but I tell 'ee; I've seen it —
There he stand listening and listening.
What do 'ee think he listen to?

(*What do you think?*)

FAITH You shall achieve what you have designed —
ECHO you have designed.

DOUBT The steed you are riding is doomed to a fall —
ECHO doomed to a fall.

FAITH Beyond the horizon is something to find —
ECHO something to find.

DOUBT Beyond the horizon is nothing at all —
nothing at all.

FAITH Your name is Christopher, Bearer of Christ —
ECHO Bearer of Christ.

DOUBT You are the Dove that cannot get free —
ECHO cannot get free.

FAITH What you shall find is a world unpriced —
ECHO a world unpriced.

DOUBT What you are seeking is lost in the sea —
lost in the sea.

FAITH Forward and follow the star in your mind —
ECHO star in your mind.

DOUBT Better turn back or worse will befall —
ECHO worse will befall.
FAITH Beyond the horizon is something to find —
ECHO something to find.
DOUBT Beyond the horizon is nothing at all —
  nothing at all.
COLUMBUS Nothing at all? That is not true,
  For the last few days there have been signs.
  Floating grasses, a live crab —
  Never found beyond eighty leagues of land;
  A whale — whales are always near the land;
  A floating branch with berries — that means land too,
  And those white birds flying south-west —
  Where could they be going if not to land?
  Land ... land ... land ...
FAITH Land is ahead, so be not depressed —
ECHO be not depressed.
DOUBT All is mirage. Disappointment is all —
ECHO disappointment is all.
FAITH Keep on your course. There is land in the West —
  land in the West.
DOUBT Better turn back or worse will befall —
  worse will befall.
COLUMBUS Better turn back? Turn back!
  Who dares tell me that?
  Man — or more than man — who dares use those words?
SPOKESMAN OF CREW Turn back, Captain, turn back.
COLUMBUS What's that? Who said that?
SPOKESMAN OF CREW 'Turn back, Captain.' I said that.
  I am the spokesman of your crew.
  We have gone as long as we can.
  We cannot go on any more.
COLUMBUS Indeed, Señor?
  You say you speak for the crew.
  I do not believe you.
SPOKESMAN OF CREW
  You don't believe me? Look out on the deck.
COLUMBUS You're a mutineer. I'll put you in irons.
SPOKESMAN OF CREW You can't put us all in irons.
  Look out on the deck, I tell you.
    (*Murmurs from the crew*)

COLUMBUS What are the fools doing? Why are they not at their posts?
  Hallo there! Why are you not at your posts?
VOICE (*distant*) Because we want an answer.
COLUMBUS Answer to what, you fools?
VOICE (*distant*) Will you turn back — or won't you?
CREW (*chanting*) We want to go back.
  We want to go back.
  We want to go back.
SPOKESMAN OF CREW You see, Captain?
COLUMBUS I see.
  I will have a few words with this scum.
CREW (*nearer and crescendo*) We want to go back.
  We want to go back.
  We want to go back.
COLUMBUS Silence there!
  So you want to go back?
  You disappoint me, gentlemen.
  Don't you know our voyage is nearly done?
  We are within a few days' sail of land.
VOICE Who says so?
COLUMBUS I say so, my friend. I have seen the signs.
VOICE Signs!
    (*Murmurs from the crew*)
COLUMBUS All last night I heard — and so did you —
  All last night we heard birds passing
  Flying West South West.
  That means land.
1ST VOICE I don't believe it.
2ND VOICE Why should it mean land?
COLUMBUS You fool! What else could it mean?
2ND VOICE I'll tell you what it could mean.
  Back in the seas of Europe birds are a sign of land
  But away out here on the rimless rim of the world
  Things are different, signs are no longer signs,
  And birds are no longer birds. How do we know
  These birds that pass in the night are not a trick
  Of the Devil to lead us on
  To one mirage of land after another
  Until our food is gone and our ship falls to pieces
  And we ourselves are madmen, drowned in a mad sea?
1ST VOICE He's right, Captain, he's right.

We've gone as far as we can. It's time to turn back.

CREW We want to go back.

We want to go back.

WE WANT TO GO BACK.

COLUMBUS Silence, you knock-kneed trash. You're wasting your time.
I am Christopher Columbus. I do *not* turn back.

2ND VOICE Oh yes you will, if we say so.

1ST VOICE If you won't yield to reason, you'll yield to force.

SPOKESMAN OF CREW He's right, Captain. You can't keep on
If all your crew are against you.

COLUMBUS I know that. Keep quiet.
Listen to me, Señores,
Today is October the eighth; it is my reckoning
We shall strike land within three days. Give me five —
If by then the land has failed us,
Then we shall reconsider what we must do.
Only wait five days. I know it in my heart
That land is over there. Señor Pinzón,
Captain of the *Pinta*, thinks so too —
And he, as you know, is a master seaman,
Well, Señores, if he and I are right,
All your troubles are over. What remains is glory —
Glory, my friends, and gold. We have good reason
To think that over there there is gold in plenty,
Just beyond the horizon. The land out there —
The land to which those white birds keep flying —
Is a land where gold flows in the streams, where gold
Drips from the trees, where gold
Litters the shores and lies pell-mell in the fields.
Gold, señores, gold . . .
Gold, gold, gold, gold.

CREW (*whispering*) Gold . . . gold . . . gold . . .
Gold . . . gold . . . gold . . .

COLUMBUS Give me five days more.

CREW (*louder*) Gold, gold, gold, gold,
Gold, gold, gold, gold . . .

COLUMBUS Give me five days more.

CREW (*loud and crescendo*)
Gold, gold, gold, gold gold,
Gold, gold, gold, gold, GOLD.

VOICE Captain!

COLUMBUS Yes?

VOICE We will go on.

CREW (*to themselves*) Gold ... gold ... gold ... gold ...

(*When their murmuring has faded away Columbus is heard making another entry in his diary*)

COLUMBUS 'October the eleventh: This day the *Pinta* picked up a reed and a stick, and another stick carved, as it seemed, with iron tools ... and some grass which grows on land ... and a tablet of wood. The crew on seeing these signs breathed and felt great joy!'

BARTOLOMÉ Hear what the *Pinta* found today?

FRANCISCO Course I heard. Things be lookin' up.

BARTOLOMÉ Captain's ordered a special watch. First as sights land, he'll get a rare reward.

FRANCISCO What be time now?

BARTOLOMÉ Near two hours till midnight. Dark night bain't it?

FRANCISCO Ssh! Here comes Captain.

(*Pause*)

COLUMBUS All correct here?

BARTOLOMÉ All correct, Captain.

COLUMBUS Either of you seen anything?

BARTOLOMÉ \
FRANCISCO / No, Captain, nothing.

COLUMBUS Keep your eyes skinned.

What's that yonder?

BARTOLOMÉ What, Captain?

FRANCISCO I can't see nothing.

COLUMBUS That little light.[16]

FRANCISCO Light?

BARTOLOMÉ Light?

COLUMBUS You're blind, you fools, you're blind.

Where's Pedro Gutiérrez? *He's* got eyes.

FRANCISCO I'll fetch him for 'ee, Captain.

COLUMBUS Light, of course it's a light ... But it comes and goes,

Like a taper of wax rising and falling —

BARTOLOMÉ Maybe it's just a star.

COLUMBUS Star, you fool?

Who ever saw a star moving from side to side

Dipping and jerking? This —

If it's not an illusion — this is a sign of life,
This is a sign of land —

FRANCISCO Here 'ee be, Captain.
Here's Gutiérrez, and Rodrigo Sánchez too —
Another fellow with gimlet eyes.

COLUMBUS Come here, Gutiérrez. And you too, Sánchez.
Look over there where I point.
What do you see, Gutiérrez?

GUTIÉRREZ Where, Captain? I see nothing.

COLUMBUS Look where I'm pointing, damn you. Don't you see a light?
No it's gone out now. Wait.
Keep your eyes over there.

GUTIÉRREZ Right, Captain. I'm waiting.

COLUMBUS Now! Do you see it?

GUTIÉRREZ No.

COLUMBUS It's gone out again. Keep looking.
Now!

GUTIÉRREZ Where? Where? . . . Mother of God!
Yes, I see it.
Yes, it *is* a light. A light.

COLUMBUS And you, Sánchez, do you see it?

SÁNCHEZ Can't say as I do.

COLUMBUS Don't you see any light?

SÁNCHEZ Nay, Captain. Can't see nothing.

COLUMBUS But you must. You must see it, you must.

SÁNCHEZ Nay, Captain, I don't.

COLUMBUS But you see it, don't you, Gutiérrez?

GUTIÉRREZ I see it surely. By God I see it.

COLUMBUS Then it is land at last.

FRANCISCO That's what *he* says.

BARTOLOMÉ Reckon he's right. It's land.

FRANCISCO Sánchez don't see it.

BARTOLOMÉ No, but Gutiérrez do.

FRANCISCO Well, we shall know at dawn.

COLUMBUS Stand by for the dawn!

CHORUS Look . . . Look . . . Look!
What do we see in the dawn?
What do we see in the dawn?

DOUBT You see a mirage like many before;

A misty shape that is merely mist.
CHORUS No ... No ... No!
  It is something else we see.
  What can it be we see?
FAITH You see what you have sailed to find.
  You see what none has found before.
CHORUS Land ... Land ... Land!
  Taking shape in the rising sun,
  A green land with a golden beach,
  A land of colour, a land of life,
  A land, a land, a land!

      (*The* Te Deum *swells up from the decks of the ships and mingles with
      the chanting of the Indians on the shore*)
BARTOLOMÉ Look 'ee yonder. Look on the shore.
  What be they on shore?
  What in God's name be *they*?
FRANCISCO Yon be living men.
  Ask Gutiérrez here,
  Hey, Gutiérrez, you have eyes like a needle.
  Yon things moving on the island —
  Tell us if they be men.
GUTIÉRREZ Of course they're men. Wait and I'll describe them.
  They're moving down to the bay from the green hill —
  A whole crowd of naked men and women
  Bronze in colour, lithe as gazelles,
  They've feathers on their heads, they're jumping
  From rock to rock like goats;
  Here they come now, down to the frills of the surf,
  They're gathering there in their ranks, they're lifting their arms to
    the sky,
  And bowing themselves to the sand; I cannot hear a sound
  But it looks as if they're singing or praying,
  I think they're singing or praying ...

INDIAN CHORUS Guanahani! Guanahani!
LEADER Who come now to Guanahani?
CHORUS Over sea. Over sea.
LEADER The gods are come from over sea.

CHORUS The gods are come to Guanahani.

INDIAN CHORUS Guanahani! Guanahani!

LEADER From the birthplace of the sun,

CHORUS With the sun to Guanahani,

LEADER Come the children of the sun,

CHORUS White gods to Guanahani.

INDIAN CHORUS To the shore of Guanahani

LEADER Here they come, here they come,

CHORUS Here they come to Guanahani,

LEADER The white gods are come, are come,

CHORUS To the shore of Guanahani.

    (*The Spaniards are now wading ashore through the surf*)

INDIAN CHORUS Guanahani! Guanahani!

LEADER Stepping through the silver foam

CHORUS On the sands of Guanahani

LEADER Come the shining sons of Heaven

CHORUS To our land of Guanahani.

INDIAN CHORUS Guanahani! Guanahani!

LEADER Let us pray. Let us pray.

CHORUS Pray! Pray! Pray! Pray!

LEADER To these gods who step ashore,

CHORUS Step ashore on Guanahani.

    (*The Spaniards are now drawn up on the beach*)

COLUMBUS Are you here, Martín Pinzón, Captain of the *Pinta*?

MARTÍN PINZÓN Aye, my Lord Admiral.

COLUMBUS And you, Vicente Pinzón, Captain of the *Nina*?

VICENTE PINZÓN Aye, my Lord Admiral.

COLUMBUS And you, Rodrigo de Segovia, Inspector of the Fleet?

SEGOVIA Aye, my Lord Admiral.

COLUMBUS Good. Stand by and take note.

    (*Fanfare*)

  In the name of the Holy Trinity

  I here upon this hitherto heathen land —

  In the year of Our Lord Fourteen Hundred and Ninety-two

  And the twelfth day of October —

  Erect the cross of Christ.

CHORUS Per Dominum!

COLUMBUS And in the name of their Catholic Majesties

  I raise the banner of Castile.

  And I thus take over this island in the name of their Catholic majesties.

Señor de Escovedo, enter the same in your record.

ESCOVEDO I will, my Lord Admiral.

COLUMBUS And I hereby name this island . . .
San Salvador.[17]

CHORUS Per Dominum! Per Dominum! Per Dominum!

COLUMBUS And I now instruct you all:
You see this island — it is like the garden of Eden,
And you see its naked inhabitants
Who are like Adam and Eve, knowing not good or evil.
Here they lie on their faces before us,
Grovelling to us as gods.
It is for us to teach them good,
It is for us to save them from evil.
Therefore, Señores, in this new world
Conduct yourselves as worthy sons of Spain
And true servants of Christ.

CHORUS We will, Señor, we will!

INDIAN CHORUS (*mid-distance*) Guanahani! Guanahani!

LEADER These are gods. These are gods.

CHORUS These are gods in Guanahani.

LEADER They have come but they will go,

CHORUS Go again from Guanahani.

COLUMBUS Señor de Escovedo.

ESCOVEDO Here my Lord Admiral.

COLUMBUS You are to keep a full record of all my proceedings here;
Leave no chink for the fingers of malice.
I intend to explore this island and all the lands adjacent,
Discovering all they contain of interest or treasure
And making a report of the same for Her Majesty Queen Isabella.

ESCOVEDO Yes, my Lord Admiral.

COLUMBUS This part of the world, as you can see, is rich —
Blessed with the bounty of God in plants and precious stones,
Cinnamon, musk and aloes and who knows what?
I also expect gold —
You have seen the gold rings they wear in their noses —
But more important than that,
More important than this or the next door island
Is the continent lying beyond us,
The realm of the Great Khan.
We are now on the fringe of Asia.

ESCOVEDO You think so, my Lord Admiral?

COLUMBUS I know so. Why! If we are not near Asia,
Where in the round world are we?

ESCOVEDO I couldn't tell you. I have never been here.
It only occurred to me that between Europe and Asia
There might be something else.

COLUMBUS And so there is, Señor. There is this island
And many another like it.
These are the islands which Marco Polo spoke of;
One of them is Zipangu.

ESCOVEDO I was not thinking of islands —
Or not, at least, of Marco Polo's islands.
I was thinking that maybe — maybe, my Lord Admiral —
We may have struck a new mainland.

COLUMBUS Señor de Escovedo, you are my notary.
You are not a cosmographer.
I tell you, Señor, what we have done
Is to find the western passage to Asia;
This island on which we stand is off the shore of Asia.

ESCOVEDO You know best, my Lord Admiral.

COLUMBUS That being so, since we know where we stand,
My plan of action is this:
I shall remain here but a couple of months,
Exploring, collecting, recording.
Then I shall sail for home with the news —
'News', Señor! The word is too weak;
What I shall tell them in Spain is more than news, it's a gospel —
The epilogue to the previous history of Man,
The prelude to his future.

ESCOVEDO Yes, my lord Admiral.
So we shall sail for home?

COLUMBUS We shall, Señor. In two or three months from now.

(*The Indian song comes up again and covers Columbus's departure for Europe*)

INDIAN CHORUS Guanahani! Guanahani!

LEADER The white gods have left the shore.

CHORUS Left the shore of Guanahani,

LEADER Gone again into the sunrise,

CHORUS Gone again from Guanahani.

(*The Indian voices fade into nothing; this nothing resolves to the shore of Europe*)

HIDALGO What are you doing there, fellow?

PEASANT Eh?

HIDALGO What are you doing perched up there on that rock
Straining your eyes on the sea?
I've been watching you, my man;
You've been stuck up there an hour.

PEASANT I've been stuck up here for weeks.

HIDALGO What for, my man, what for?

PEASANT I'm keeping a look-out.

HIDALGO A look-out?

PEASANT Aye, I come from Cordoba.

HIDALGO Cordoba? What's that got to do with it?

PEASANT 'Twas a lady in Cordoba sent me here.
She told me for to keep look-out.

HIDALGO Stop talking like an idiot.
What did this lady in Cordoba send you here to look out for?

PEASANT Why, for Señor Columbus.

HIDALGO Señor...? Nombre de Dios!
You mean Columbus that sailed to the West last year?

PEASANT Aye, that be the one.

HIDALGO And you mean to say you're sitting here
Day after day, week after week,
Waiting for *him*! You're mad,
As mad as Columbus himself.

PEASANT Doña Beatriz — she had a dream.

HIDALGO A dream! She must have had several.
Your Señor Columbus will never come back to Spain.
We all knew that when he sailed.

PEASANT No matter. I keep my look-out.
The lady in Cordoba pays me.

HIDALGO I hope she pays you well.
Columbus, you see, will never come back to Europe.
Columbus will never come back — not in a thousand years.

(*Music answers back the hidalgo and prepares you for the Return*)

VASCO Heard the news?

LUÍS What news, Vasco?

VASCO Columbus be back.

LUÍS *Who* be back?

VASCO Columbus. Christopher Columbus. He just put into port.

PRIOR Heard the news, Brother Antonio?

ANTONIO What news, Father Prior?

PRIOR Our friend Columbus is back. He has found his land in the West.

ANTONIO I always knew he would. Thank God!

PRIOR Thank God!

CLERIC Have you heard the news, Your Grace?

TALAVERA What news, Señor?

CLERIC Christopher Columbus has arrived in Palos.

TALAVERA I do not believe it, Señor.

CLERIC And what is more, he has found his land in the West.

TALAVERA I tell you, I do not believe it.

WAITING WOMAN Doña Beatriz! Doña Beatriz!

BEATRIZ Yes, what is it?

WAITING WOMAN Have you heard the news?

BEATRIZ Yes, Maria, I have.

 (*Pause*)

I heard it before anyone.

WAITING WOMAN And what are you going to do?

BEATRIZ Do, Maria? Nothing.

 (*Pause*)

If he comes through Cordoba perhaps I will watch from the window.

ISABELLA Heard the news, Marquesa?

MARQUESA What news, Your Majesty?

ISABELLA Columbus has come back.

MARQUESA Columbus has come back!

ISABELLA Yes, my friend, and he's found it.

MARQUESA Found ... *it*?

ISABELLA Found what we hoped he would. God is great.

MARQUESA And where is Columbus now?

ISABELLA In Seville. Waiting instructions.
MARQUESA Then he will come to the Court?
   He will come here to Barcelona?
ISABELLA Yes, he will come to Barcelona.

        (*Processional music anticipates the procession*)
ONLOOKER Here they come now, here they come now,
   The long procession leaving the gates of Seville,
   En route for Barcelona.
   Have a good look, ladies and gentlemen, never again
   Will this city of Seville see such a wild to-do.
   Look at the shining soldiers bearing coffers of gold,
   Look at the tattered banners bleached with the brine,
   Look at the red savages crowned with feathers —
   Gold rings in their noses and popinjays on their shoulders —
   Look at the golden masks, the pearls and mother of pearl,
   And look at who comes here — the Discoverer himself,
   The man who is now the talk of Europe, the Very Magnificent Lord
   Admiral of the Ocean Sea, Viceroy of the Western World,
   With his pale face and burning eyes, sitting his horse
   Like a Roman Emperor . . . or
   It might be fitter to say like the fifth
   Horseman of the Apocalypse.
        (*The procession draws level. Columbus's followers are chanting in the
        manner of a Round*)
   Back from the West

   Beyond the world
   Back from the West

   We have returned
   Beyond the world
   Back from the West

   And here we are
   We have returned
   Beyond the world
   Back from the West

   And here we are
   We have returned
   Beyond the world
   And here we are

We have returned
And here we are!

ALL TOGETHER
Back from the West
Beyond the world
We have returned
And here we are.

SPOKESMAN OF PROCESSION
From Seville over the Sierras, bound for the Royal Court,
By a dusty road to the banks of the Guadalquivir,
To a Moorish city of winding streets and gardens
Set among groves of olive and orange,
Here we come in our Admiral's train
Bearing the wealth of the West and the news of the Indies
Here we come to Cordoba, here
Through Cordoba we come riding.

(*As the cheers of the onlookers recede you notice Doña Beatriz in a balcony*)

WAITING WOMAN
Doña Beatriz! Doña Beatriz! Did you see him?
BEATRIZ Yes, but he didn't see *me*.
He rode by in the way that he would —
Looking neither to right nor to left.
WAITING WOMAN This is a day for him!
A day of triumph.
BEATRIZ A day — I would say — of miracle.
But he will die unhappy.

(*The music surges back, Beatriz is left behind and we ride on with Columbus*)

SPOKESMAN OF PROCESSION
From Cordoba we go on, from Cordoba to Montoro,
From Montoro to Jaén huddled on wooded hills,
From Jaén to Orihuela on the banks of the Segura
And thence to Alicante with its palm-trees by the sea;
And everywhere the crowds come out to meet us and they throw
Flowers upon our heads and we ride on
With our Indians and our popinjays and gold;

We ride on, ride on.

CHORUS Back from the West
  Beyond the world
  We have returned
  And here we are.

SPOKESMAN OF PROCESSION
  And now we come to the great white port of Valencia
  With its multitude of roofs and its towering campanile
  And the people of Valencia bring us flowers and bring us fruit,
  Blow us kisses as we were lovers and look up to us as gods —
  And we smile the smile of gods and we ride on.
  And we come to Catalunya, to Roman Tarragona,
  With its dark cobbled alleys clambering up the hill
  And the smell of fish and wine
  And the broken Roman arches that betoken
  So much glory of the past
  Which is nothing to the glory that is ours
  That surrounds us as we ride to the King and Queen of Spain
  Holding court in Barcelona . . .

HERALD Holding court in Barcelona!

  (*The processional music ends and silence introduces the Court at
  Barcelona*)

ISABELLA Señor Don Christopher Columbus!
  We Isabella, Queen of Castile and Aragon,
  Do here before the assembled peers of our land
  Welcome you back to Spain and give you our royal thanks
  For that against the odds you have done what you have done
  To the greater glory of God and the honour of Spain.
  Of your achievements we have already heard
  And here we see their tangible evidence —
  The gold, the pearls, and these strange men;
  But we ask you now, Señor, out of your own mouth
  Here to address the Crown and the Peers of Spain —
  Aye, and the whole of the serried Christian world —
  And tell us your own story and what it means.

COLUMBUS Your Catholic Majesties . . . it is hard for me
  On such a day and before such an audience,
  Feeling myself on a pinnacle high among clouds of dream,
  To find the words — it is hard to find the words

For a theme that no man yet has phrased or painted —
The passage where no passage lay,
The world where no world was before.
But this is what I have done:
I took three ships and sailed them into the teeth of the West,
Into what seemed the certainty of death
And against the veto of Nature.
Weeks went by and no land came, I might have
Well turned back but I did not, I went on
And in the ripeness of God's will I found
The second Earthly Paradise and there
I raised the cross of Christ and the banner of Castile.
Your Majesties, look out yonder,
Look out yonder along the line of my arm
Across Tibidabo and the hills of Spain:
Four thousand miles out there to the West
Lie uncharted lands — they are yours to chart,
Uncounted treasure — yours for the taking,
Aye and countless hordes of heathen men
Who are from now your subjects,
Unenlightened souls who wait the light.
Aye, your Majesties, this new world
That I have opened up through the will of God —
Only God can tell what is its total worth,
And God alone knows what it will become
Or what may be the blessings that late or soon
May flow from thence to Europe —
Aye, and to all mankind from this new world.
This is my story and this is what it means:
Here and now at your court in Barcelona
In the year of Our Lord Fourteen-Hundred-And-Ninety-
     Three,
Before the Throne of Spain and the eyes and ears of Europe
And before the crowded jury of posterity —
I have brought you a new world.[18]
     (*The crowd then sing in triumph*)
LEADER Glory, glory to God.
  Joy in the land of Spain.
  They sailed away to the West,
  Now they are here again.

CHORUS Glory, glory to God.
Joy in the land of Spain.

LEADER They sailed away to the West,
Now they are here again.
They tracked the sun to his lair,
They found the Golden Main.

CHORUS They sailed away to the West,
Now they are here again.

COLUMBUS (*calling from distance*)
I have brought you a new world.

LEADER The world that we have found
Shall never be lost again.
The voyage that we made —
We made it not in vain.

CHORUS The world that we have found
Shall never be lost again.

AUTHOR'S ADDENDA (1963)

The Transitions between the many scenes in this play were effected in various ways, often with the help of music. Where the original script contained technical directions for these, I have substituted something more readable.

Cuts: This printed version includes some passages (e.g. the list of titles on page 39) which were cut in the radio transmission and probably ought to be cut in any repeat performance. I have printed them here for the fun of it.

Religion: Not being a Roman Catholic, I have not dared to dwell more than a little on that aspect of this story which for a writer like Paul Claudel is the primary one and which most probably must be treated as primary by anyone who hopes to create out of this subject a major work of art.

HE HAD A DATE
OR, WHAT BEARING?

a radio play

He Had a Date is a radio play in two versions (28 June 1944, Home Service; 14 February 1949, Third Programme), the second of which is published here, as it incorporates MacNeice's more mature thoughts — from a typescript used for the 1949 production (now held at the Humanities Research Center, University of Texas, Austin), with manuscript annotations and alterations, mainly expansions, by MacNeice. This play commemorates his school friend Graham Shepard (commemorated more explicitly in his poem 'The Casualty', *c.*1943, in *Collected Poems*, 245–8) who had been drowned at sea while serving with Atlantic convoys in the Royal Navy in 1942. The play is conceived as a biography of an average man of his time in the form of a flashback of his life. It opens with the protagonist Tom Varney on duty, on watch; then follows, as he is meditating, 'a private newsreel of his life' set against a background of public events. The command 'What bearing?' is applied to his own changeable life, characterizing 'the uncertainty of purpose and belief' of the times.[1] Then Varney's ship is hit by an enemy torpedo, and, as he is drowning, voices from his past sound in his head. The play is an experiment in radio biography.

Tom Varney was intended to be typical of his period (1907–42) and to reflect in passing the effect of public events on his generation. An uneasy intellectual from the upper classes, he is shown reacting against his own background and upbringing. His parents, kindly but unimaginative Tories, give him a public school and Oxford education, a moulding process in which he avoids being moulded. He is not a 'heroic' hero; he has vitality but even in his last phase, when he to some extent 'finds himself' on the lower deck, it has not been properly canalized; he remains confused and inconsistent.

Some listeners, when the programme was first broadcast during the war, found his inconsistency and his 'psychological complexity' incredible; I can only say that among my own contemporaries I have known many people with a similar background whose actions revealed an equal or a greater inconsistency and complexity.

This portrait of Tom is meant to be true to life; he is not idealized (that is, simplified) and while typical of his kind he is also, I trust, an individual. Apart from some stylized soliloquies at the beginning and end of the programme where he is allowed to summarize his own situation — first, when in the cradle, and, last, when drowning — he is presented naturalistically and is never given more heightened or more lucid speech than such a character would really use. So both his own reactions to things and the things to which he is reacting are revealed in an offhand manner. He is never fully explicit either about his family and his love affairs or about the issues involved in the General Strike of 1926, the Spanish Civil War, or the World War, and what other people say to him or about him is as important as what he says himself. For, true to his time and class, he will not often give himself away.

In form the programme was something of an experiment — the application to a fictitious character of a radio method generally reserved for factual histories; though the story is invention, the form is that of a feature programme. We begin with Tom on the bridge of his ship when it is about to be torpedoed and then have one long flashback lasting from the cradle to the bridge again. The missing years are spotlighted and separated by the popular songs of the day from 'I do like to be beside the seaside' to 'You are my sunshine'; apart from their use in planting the passage of time these serve as a sort of ironic chorus —

Tom is both serious and intellectual but this is the world he lives in. The final sequence relies on an old but still, I think, legitimate device which Mr Tyrone Guthrie used most effectively in the early days of radio drama; voices from Tom's past come in on his drowning consciousness, these fragments succeeding each other against a background of music (an arrangement for strings by Alan Rawsthorne of the nursery cradle song 'Rockabye Baby').

The revival of *He Had a Date* was proposed partly because someone who died in 1942, even if he was fictitious, can now be seen more in perspective, partly because the programme had never yet been heard as it was written. Its first production on 28 June 1944, suffered from being cut to ribbons owing to a grave miscalculation on my part of the length of the script. The new version not only restores the passages cut but has here and there been rewritten to eliminate earlier crudities. The popular tunes which originally were meant to be whistled in the studio are now more effectively rendered by George Mitchell's Choir. Lastly, the 1944 production took place in a quite unsuitable studio; this time we have the chance to vary our acoustics decently, as is desirable in a programme with so many scenes ranging from a cricket match at Lord's to a barricaded building in Madrid.

CHARACTERS

OFFICER OF THE WATCH

TOM

MOTHER

FATHER

MRS ARROW

UNCLE DES

ANNIE

BLACK

FLAHERTY

HARRINGER

TERRY

STRIKER

TUTOR

JANE

CITY POLICEMAN

DETECTIVE

COUNTY POLICEMAN

ELSIE

CHIEF REPORTER

EDITOR

MARY

DUNCAN

NEWSBOY

AMERICAN

WAITER

LOUD VOICE

CROWD

1ST FOREIGN VOICE

2ND FOREIGN VOICE

COMPANY COMMANDER

VOLUNTEER

OBSERVER

1ST SPECTATOR

2ND SPECTATOR

VOICES

WARDEN

FOREMAN

DIVVY OFFICER

1ST SAILOR

2ND SAILOR

HE HAD A DATE
OR, WHAT BEARING?

ANNOUNCER *He Had a Date* was conceived as a private news-reel of episodes from one man's life. The hero — who is not in the ordinary sense a hero (some might dismiss him as a fool, a failure, or even a cad) — is a fictitious character but typical of his period. He belongs to a generation which was not sure of its bearings and to a class of which *he* was not sure himself. And already — like the Nineteen-Twenties and the Nineteen-Thirties, like the Bright Young People and the General Strike, like the Spanish Civil War and the Battle of Britain, like the popular songs of the day before yesterday — we can see him receding into Ancient History.

He was born in 1907 and died in 1942. He had — you see — a Date.

(*Pause; fade up Tom whistling Himno de Riego*)

OFFICER OF THE WATCH What the Devil! Who's that whistling? (*Whistling stops abruptly*) Port lookout!

TOM Sir?

OFFICER OF THE WATCH Was that you whistling?

TOM Er ... Yes, sir.

OFFICER OF THE WATCH What's your name?

TOM Varney, sir.

OFFICER OF THE WATCH How long have you been in this ship?

TOM A year and four months, sir.

OFFICER OF THE WATCH Well, Varney, don't you know the rule about whistling?

TOM Aye, aye, sir. I'm sorry, sir.

OFFICER OF THE WATCH Lucky for you the Captain's not on the bridge. All right; don't do it again.

TOM No, sir.

(*Pause; to self*) What a fool ... what a fool I am ... everyone knows whistling's taboo in the Navy ... brings bad luck or something ... habit of mine, though —

Eh, what's that now? (*To Officer*) Floating object in the water to port, sir.

OFFICER OF THE WATCH What bearing?

TOM Er ... Red Four O, sir.

OFFICER OF THE WATCH I see it. Just a bit of gash. But, while we're on the subject, Port Lookout, wake your ideas up when you report these things. Give the correct bearing without me having to ask you.

TOM Aye, aye, sir.

(*Pause*) Spherical object red Nine O, sir.

OFFICER OF THE WATCH Red Nine O? ... Yes, I see it. Only a barrel.

(*Pause*)

TOM (*to self*) He always sees it — makes me feel kind of superfluous ... funny to think, if our leave hadn't been cut short, I had a date today. I had a date to — God, what's that?

(*To Officer*) Track in the water on port bow, sir, approaching.

OFFICER OF THE WATCH What bearing?

TOM (*to self*) What bearing? Track in the water approaching. Tin fish — Jack-in-the-Box — matter of seconds — bearing? Bearing, bearing, Able Seaman Varney? Suggestive phrase — 'what bearing'? Might apply to anything. Life, death, your life, mine. Mary and me, Jane and me, Spain and me, Mum and me. Poor Mum! Her only child. What did she hope with me in the cradle? What thoughts? What bearing?

(*Fade up Mother singing softly 'Rockabye Baby', then, after one verse, humming and breaking off in the middle*)

MOTHER Ah, he's asleep at last.

TOM Yes, I'm asleep at last. Drowned in muslin flounces, I am only six months old, I cannot crawl, I cannot speak, when I am hungry I feel myself all mouth. But once that mouth has been filled, then I have eyes and fingers. My fingers crook round coral or ivory, my eyes are drawn to the tasselled oil-lamp, to the bubbling fire in the grate, to my mother's brooch, to a bright button. Mouth, eyes, fingers — but somewhere beneath is a mind. A mind like a Japanese flower that is still quite small and crumpled. But some fine day its petals will open in water. In the meantime I must sleep.

FATHER (*approaching*) Constance! Heard the latest? They say the suffragettes have —

MOTHER Ned! Tommy's asleep.

FATHER Sorry, dear; I —

MOTHER Come and have a look at him.

FATHER Hm? Hands above his head. Sign of good health, that.

MOTHER There speaks my old GP. He always sleeps like that. (*Pause*) I wonder what he'll be ... when he grows up.

FATHER Early to think of that. If we give him a good start — Thank God I've got those savings — well, he might be anything. But what *I* look forward to's five or six years from now. Nice age that, take him to the seaside, give him a spade and a bucket —

MOTHER *And* a sailor cap, Ned.

FATHER If you like, why not? He might be a sailor some day.

(*Fade up Choir: 'I do like to be Beside the Seaside', peak, and lose behind*)

MRS ARROW Oh, Mrs Varney! Is that your little boy?

MOTHER Yes, that's Tommy. He's turning seven.

MRS ARROW Really? How big for his age, my dear. Mine are too, you know. You've seen them, haven't you? George, Edith, Francis —

MOTHER Excuse me, Mrs Arrow. (*Calling*) Tommy! ... Tommy! ... Don't go out on that rock.

MRS ARROW George, Edith, Francis, and Dorothy. They're all big for their age. We were going to take them abroad this year but ... my husband thought this was more sensible.

MOTHER Yes, yes, *my* husband — he's a doctor, you know — he says the English seaside is quite the most healthy place you can —

MRS ARROW *No*, my dear, what *my* husband meant was —

MOTHER (*calling*) Tommy! Not on that rock! Forgive me, Mrs Arrow, you were saying?

MRS ARROW What *my* husband meant was Kaiser Wilhelm.

MOTHER Oh, really? Kaiser Wil —

MRS ARROW Not that I believe in it completely myself but —

MOTHER (*calling*) Tommy! I've told you already. You're *not* to go out on that rock!

TOM (*intimate*) I *will* go out on this rock; I will, I will, I will. Mummy is just wicked. If I can get hold of that seaweed to hang on the wall by my bed, I'll know when it's going to rain. And I *will* enjoy myself, I *will* forget these nightmares. The big black Jack-in-the-Box that jumps out of the night. And sometimes it talks like Dad and sometimes it talks like Mum but most times it talks ... like ... like something you never heard. And it wants to eat me up, that big Jack-in-the-Box; it wants to eat me up ...

MRS ARROW Oh but, Mrs Varney, one *must* take account of the Kaiser.

My husband was talking to a man in the Foreign Office and he told
my husband — in confidence, you know —

(*Fade up Choir — 'Tipperary' — peak, and lose behind*)
MOTHER Tommy! Tommy! Guess who's here. Your uncle —
UNCLE DES Your Uncle Des! (*Laughs*) My word, Tommy, you've
grown.
MOTHER Say something, Tommy. *You're* not shy of Uncle Des.
TOM (*intimate*) Oh yes, I am. That's why I won't say a word. Uncle
Des used to be just an uncle but now he makes me shy. With his
bright buttons and his Sam Browne belt. How can I open my mouth?
He's going off to be a hero.

(*Fade up disc of 'It's a Long, Long Trail', mix with train, then to
background; knock on door and door opens*)
ANNIE It's a telegram, Ma'am. From the Office of War, Ma'am.
MOTHER Oh ... Thank you, Annie. (*Pause*) Oh!
TOM There you are. He *was* a hero.

TOM And I'm going off to school. (*He croons:*)
   'It's a long, long trail w-winding
   To my jol-lee prep school . . .'
   (*Fade out; then door-knock as before*)
MOTHER Oh *why* does that postman always knock so loudly?
   (*Door opens*)
ANNIE A letter from Tommy, Ma'am.
MOTHER Thank you, Annie. Ned dear, a letter from Tommy.
FATHER Tommy? Nice work. Read it out to me.
MOTHER (*reading*) 'Dear Mum: This is a nice school but I do not like
corned beef. There is a boy called Evans who does conjuring tricks' —
conjuring spelt congering — 'There is a master who is funny too. He
is different to the other masters and he cannot write on the black-
board. His name is Flaherty, he loses his temper a lot. We call him
Flaggers. One of the boys called Black says Flaggers' breath is bad
because' . . . 'because he drinks whisky'.
FATHER Upon my soul!
MOTHER (*reading*) 'We all stamp our feet when he breaks the chalk
but Black says some day he will run a muck'–'run amuck. Black says' —

FATHER I don't believe a word of it. That class of school! What else does Black say?

MOTHER Black says: 'Some day Flaggers will lose his temper so bad that Mr Anson will have to send him away'.

BLACK You'll see, Varney, you bally little muff. Some day Flaggers will lose his temper so bad that Mr Anson will have to send him away . . .

FLAHERTY Now, boys, this is an isosceles triangle. I will call this angle X, this angle Y, and this angle — Ah, blast the chalk! Take that, ye beggar, take that! (*Stamping of feet*) What are ye stamping your feet for? Quiet there! Quiet! (*Feet out*) I suppose ye think I'm funny because I swear at the chalk. I suppose your parents have told you how it's ill-bred to swear. Well maybe I *am* ill-bred. But I'll tell you something, boys. I've served me time in the trenches — (*Rude whistle*) Who was that? Was it you, Evans? Don't try it again now or — or I'll clout the head off ye. (*Stamping and hold behind*) Stop that, will ye! Quiet! (*More stamping*) So this is mutiny, is it? (*Catcall*) All right then, have it your own way. But let me tell ye this. I went out to the Front to fight for the likes of you. Well . . . I'm sorry I did! I got myself shell-shocked too. Maybe ye don't believe me — (*More stamping*) Go on, stamp yer feet. Class dismissed! I'm quittin'. (*Fade out stamping*)

FATHER (*reading*) 'Dear Dad: Thank you for the butterfly net. Flaggers has gone away. He ran a muck and swore and shouted — ' Well, good Lord, I — 'Evans has learnt a new congering trick. We are having a half-holiday on Thursday — '

MOTHER How callous children are.

FATHER Just as well, my dear. If Tommy'd really understood, this business of this fellow Flaherty — well, it might have really upset him. But boys being what they are . . .

MOTHER I suppose so, Ned. But I wish it hadn't happened.

TOM I wish . . . I wish . . . I wish it hadn't happened. Flaggers has gone away. He was unhappy; I just thought he was funny. Something to do with the war. Uncle Des was a hero but Flaggers . . . It's like what I used to feel about that Jack-in-the-Box. Black says Anson 'fired' him. It makes me feel . . . queer. But I won't let on to anyone. I'll go to the changing-room now — see if Blackfield has finished blowing that egg. But I wish I could grow up quickly.

(Fade up Choir: 'Margie' — and behind)

MOTHER Dear me, how quickly the years pass.

FATHER 'm. Tempo of everything seems to be quickening up. You and I'll have to look alive, dear; this is what they call the Jazz Age.

(Peak Choir, accelerando, and out)

MOTHER Look alive, Ned, did you say? Then where's that horrible inventory? This is my chief puzzle, Ned; 'three pairs of boots or shoes, black.'

FATHER Why?

MOTHER Well, which ought they to be? Tommy's always had boots but maybe a public school's different.

FATHER Keep him on boots, Constance. Boys of thirteen should never wear shoes. I've seen enough weak ankles professionally —

MOTHER All right, Ned dear, boots. I'll go out and buy them today.

FATHER Yes, yes, yes, the world's moving faster and faster. But am I wrong or is it also getting out of tune?

(Fade up school bell, speed up and out)

TOM Sunday ... Sunday letter ... 'September 25th 1921 ... Dear Mum and Dad. It seems a long time since I came here on Friday. I like it very much but it is awfully big. My dormitory has twenty boys, they are all quite nice — ' All quite nice? Well, it's no good explaining. That beastly swine Harringer — No, I can't tell them that.

HARRINGER Varney? That your name? Varney! I see you wear boots, Varney. That's not done, you know. Only cads wear boots. People like grocers' sons. But perhaps your people are like that. New boots too, aren't they, Varney? I suppose your people thought they were doing you proud, did they? Well, tell them it's not done. Hey, fellows, come here! See this new boy Varney? See what he's wearing? Boots! Isn't it priceless? Boots! *(Into a high cackle and fade)*

TOM No, I can't tell them that. Hurt their feelings — but why must they be so stupid? You wait till I'm a blood. I'll have pointed shoes and coloured socks with arrows and all the boys will look up to me. I'll show the swine, I'll show them! I'll get in the Fifteen, I'll get in the Eleven, I'll ... I'll take a scholarship to Oxford. I could sit for it four years from now. Four years . . . is that right? Nineteen-twenty-two — twenty-three — twenty-four — twenty-five . . .

(*Fade up Choir — 'The Song is Ended' — peak, and out*)

MOTHER Oh dear! Tom's getting so difficult.

FATHER Clever boys always are, dear. Awkward age, seventeen.

MOTHER Well, I wish he wasn't so clever. Seen this last letter of his? No? Well, here you are.

FATHER Thank you, Constance. (*Reading*) 'Dear Mum: If you and Dad really want me to get a scholarship at Oxford, I suppose I can go and get one — ' Modest young man! 'But I'd like you to know for my part, I think it a waste of time. Everyone knows that Oxford and Cambridge are backwaters. In the modern world — '

MOTHER You see? Pompous isn't the word for it. And what does Tom know about the modern world?

FATHER What do *we* know, for that matter? Changes all the time. Look at that skirt you're wearing.

MOTHER I know, dear, but — one can't look frumpish. But Tom . . . ? Shall I write back, or you?

FATHER I'd better, I think.

MOTHER But what will you say, Ned?

FATHER Oh, I'll say something like this: 'Dear Tom, Don't be an ass. We're not *forcing* you to go to Oxford; we just think that having a brain you might as well take the chance to develop it. If however you prefer to go straight from school to an office in London or a job in the Colonies — '

MOTHER Maybe he *would* prefer that?

FATHER Not him, my dear. Not him! Young people now seem to think it's smart to be cynical but they're all romantics underneath. Old Arnold's dreaming spires haven't lost their magic yet, you know.

(*Fade up Oxford bell and to background*)

TERRY Coming out, Varney?

TOM All right.

TERRY Got your gown?

TOM Here.

TERRY Oh, so you're a scholar?

TOM So they tell me.

TERRY That mean you're going to work a lot?

TOM Work?

TERRY 'Work' I said. W–O–R–K.

TOM Work? . . . Work! Good Lord, no!

　　(*Fade out bell*)

FATHER Bad news, Constance.

MOTHER What, dear?

FATHER They've fixed a General Strike for May the third.

MOTHER A general — I don't believe it!

FATHER I'm afraid it's true, my dear. The Trade Union Congress has —

MOTHER If it's true, I've never heard anything so . . . so . . . so . . . so unspeakable!

TERRY Tom, you old Stephen Dedalus, I've never heard anything so priceless.

TOM What, Terry? This strike, you mean? Why, it's just politics, isn't it?

TERRY You don't get the point. We can all get permission to go off.

TOM Go off where, Terry?

TERRY Anywhere you like. To drive buses and trains and things. The transport workers will be out, so we'll have the field to ourselves. Isn't it heaven?

TOM You mean you and I'll be allowed to go driving trains?

TERRY Allowed? My dear Tom, we'll be begged to. In the cause of the nation of course.

TOM Oh drat the cause of the nation. But I *would* like to drive a train.

　　(*Fade up Choir* — '*Bye, Bye, Blackbird*' — *mix with trains and lose behind*)

MOTHER Ned, isn't it wonderful? Tom dropped in this afternoon.

FATHER Tom! Where on earth from?

MOTHER He's turned out trumps, Ned darling. He's driving a railway engine. And you just should have seen how grimy he looked.

FATHER Grimy? I bet he's grimy. I told you he'd grow up soon. But you're quite right, dear; it's wonderful.

(*Fade up Tom whistling 'Bye, Bye, Blackbird'*)

STRIKER You seems happy, mate.

(*Whistling out*)

TOM Happy? Yes. I've had a pretty good day.

STRIKER You've had a pretty good day? Let's see if I can guess why. Do you usually wear them clothes?

TOM Well, I have for the last three days.

STRIKER Kind of fancy dress, eh, chum?

TOM Fancy dress? Don't be funny, you're wearing the same yourself. Only *you've* got quite a clean face.

STRIKER Yes, I have for once. And *you* know why, don't you? Because I'm out on strike. And *you're* one of the blokes what's trying to break that strike.

TOM Well, yes, I suppose I am. No ill-feeling, though?

STRIKER 'No ill-feeling'! Tell me, mister, you ever been hungry?

TOM Well, I —

STRIKER You ever been down a coal mine?

TOM No, I —

STRIKER You ever been inside of a miner's cottage?

TOM Well, as a matter of —

STRIKER No, you ain't. You're just plumb ignorant. You don't know your ABC.

TOM Ah, there you're wrong. When it comes to the English alphabet —

STRIKER You can spell, can you?

TOM Middling well. Yes.

STRIKER All right. See what this spells then. S . . . C . . . A . . . B . . . S–C–A–B. Scab! That's what you are. Goodnight.

(*Fade up Choir — 'I Can't Give You Anything But Love' — and lose behind*)

MOTHER Very nice letter from Tom. You know, Ned, for two years now — ever since that strike in fact — he seems to have got more serious.

FATHER Um. Must have worked quite hard to get that First in Mods. Wonder how he'll do in Greats.

MOTHER I'm sure he'll try his best, Ned. Why do they call it Greats?

FATHER Because it's the greatest bore of any exam in the world. Or perhaps that's a little unfair, I'm prejudiced against philosophy. Being a doctor, you know. Still I dare say it's good for the mind.

MOTHER It's mostly philosophy, is it?

FATHER Oh yes, yes; terribly dry stuff too. You wouldn't like it, Constance. Quite inhuman, you know. Talk a language of their own.

(*Oxford bell; then knock on door*)

TUTOR (*off*) Come in! Come in! (*Door opening*)

Ah, Mr Varney. Sit down over there by that pretence of a fire. Now what's our essay today?

TOM The Syllogism, sir.

TUTOR Yes, yes, yes, the syllogism. A very pregnant subject. Fire ahead, Mr Varney.

TOM (*reading mechanically*) Mill begins his account of the syllogism by an assault on the usefulness of the dictum 'de omni et nullo', a survival, he thinks, from the age of darkness when men believed in universals and failed to see that 'the class is nothing but the objects contained in it' ...

(*Fade up whistling — 'I Can't Give You Anything But Love'*)

TERRY Stop whistling out of tune, Jane dear, and listen to a modest proposal.

JANE Modest? From *you*, Terry?

TERRY You know my friend Tom Varney?

JANE Only from your accounts of him.

TERRY Well, I think it's time you met him. I think you'd be rather good for him.

JANE Why?

TERRY Well, you see, he used to be very amusing but now he does nothing but work. I think a flirtation with *you*, Jane —

JANE Thank you very much. How do you know I'll like your Mr Varney?

TERRY Well, you might or you mightn't.

(*Fade up Tom reading fast and mechanically*)

TOM 'Condillac, says Mill, is sadly wrong. For first you know your subject, then you name it. Your knowledge is precise and particular, the name is approximate and conventional. Here there is suggested an ingenuous process of weakening reality: first the thing, then the idea of the thing, then the name of the idea. Which is a vicious dissociation, for the name, though avowedly a symbol, is not so much a label as an emanation or expression of the idea and the idea *is* the thing' . . .

    (*His reading has been drowned in the ripple and splash of water; this to background*)

JANE Isn't it ravishing, here on the river? . . . Tom?

TOM Yes, Jane, yes. It's a . . . kind of timeless feeling.

JANE Well, don't sound so solemn — or is it the effect of punting?

TOM Oh that's no effort, I'm a born punter. I'm trying to remember a poem. It's an early Elizabethan —

JANE Look out, Tom! That willow-branch! (*Crash-cum-splash*) You *are* a fool! Now we're — all tangled up.

TOM Well . . . Let's stay tangled a bit.

JANE No, Tom, no . . . You can't go kissing girls on a public river like that.

TOM This is our river now. And look, I've remembered that poem. 'In a harbour green' — very appropriate too, harbour means arbour — all these willow branches,

   'In a harbour green asleep whereas I lay
   The birdés sang sweet in the middés of the day;
   I dreaméd fast of mirth and play.
    In youth is pleasure, in youth is pleasure.'

JANE That all?

TOM No, but I can't quite remember . . . and I think the rest's rather sad.

JANE Then don't let's have it. Not today, Tom . . . No!

TUTOR Fire ahead, Mr Varney, fire ahead. Your essays are improving. If you keep it up — well, I don't like to prophesy — but I think you might possibly — possibly, I say, not probably — figure quite well in the Class List.

JANE (*faded up*) He loves me — he loves me not — he loves me — he loves me not — he loves me — he —

TERRY Hullo, Jane. Day-dreaming?

JANE Yes, Terry.

TERRY Jane, I want to talk to you.

JANE Yes, Terry. About Tom, I suppose?

TERRY Yes, Jane.

JANE Awkward for you. Who was it first introduced us?

TERRY I know, I know, but how could I tell you'd fall in love with him?

JANE Well, *you're* not in love with me —

TERRY Of course not, I've known you too long. But seriously, Jane, you can't go falling in love with people like Tom.

JANE I thought you liked him.

TERRY I do — but he's mad.

JANE How do you mean: 'mad'?

TERRY Remember the General Strike?

JANE Well, I was at school —

TERRY Well, Tom and I were up, in our first year, and we both took emergency jobs. Strike-breaking, you know. Tom drove a railway engine —

JANE What fun for him.

TERRY Yes but wait. When we got back here to Oxford Tom went into a gloom. And then one night he got tight and made a sort of public confession.

JANE Public confession of what?

TERRY Of the part he'd played in the strike. He said he felt like a swine. And all because of something some striker had said at a coffee stall.

JANE Well?

TERRY Well?

JANE Well, I think that's rather sympathetic.

TERRY Maybe — but it's unbalanced. You never know what he'll do next.

JANE I know what he's doing next. He's just going to get a First. And then he'll get a wonderful job. And then . . .

TERRY Then I suppose you'll marry him. Wait till he gets his First.

JANE You don't think he will, do you? I do. Look, I'll prove it to you by petals.

TERRY Childish you are, Jane!

JANE He *will* get a First — he *won't* get a First — he *will* get a First . . .
     (*and continues so behind the next sequence*)

TOM My subject today, sir, is — er — Error.

TUTOR Error? Very nice too. Fire ahead, Mr Varney, fire ahead.

TOM (*reading*) Roughly speaking, Error can be reduced to one of two categories: One — Chaos; or Two — a subspecies of knowledge.
     One: Error as chaos.

Error — on the subject side — corresponds to Nothing — on the object side — meaning by 'nothing' what is completely indeterminate. This will mean that in so far as there is a positive element in error . . .

(*Fade up Jane's voice*)

JANE He *will* get a First — he *won't* get a First — he *will* get a First — he —

TOM Hullo, darling. Daydreaming?

JANE Extraordinary. That's just what Terry said to —

TOM I want to talk to you, Jane.

JANE *And* he said that too.

TOM I don't care what he said. This is important.

JANE Don't bluster so, darling. Look at that extraordinary plum-coloured light on the chapel —

TOM Jane, I'm clearing out.

JANE What?

TOM I'm clearing out.

JANE What are you talking about?

TOM I'm going down. Going away from Oxford.

JANE When?

TOM Now.

JANE Tom! What are you talking about?

TOM I'll tell you. I was reading old Baldy an essay on Error and something annoyed him at the end of it. Sort of contempt of court idea . . .

TUTOR Is that all, Mr Varney?

TOM Yes, sir.

TUTOR Would you kindly read me that last sentence again?

TOM Yes, sir. 'As the sentence in Plato's "Sophist" suggests, it is all fable — muthos — and we had better judge our philosophers according to their capacity for story-telling.'

TUTOR Story-telling? Hm. A rather distasteful word.

TOM Why, sir? I can't see that really —

TUTOR When a man is described as a story-teller, it often means he is a liar. Of course, I know you didn't mean that. Or did you?

TOM Or did I?

TUTOR Well, make up your mind. If all philosophers are liars and all philosophy is lies, it would seem rather perverse in you to study it.

TOM Yes, rather perverse . . . Sir?

TUTOR Yes?

TOM I wonder if I'm not really rather perverse. To be taking Greats and all. I mean it doesn't seem to have much connection with . . .

TUTOR With what?

TOM Well . . . with the Slump, for instance.

TUTOR The Slump? Do you belong to the University Labour Club?

TOM No, sir, I don't belong to any clubs.

TUTOR 'm? Well, where did you pick up these sceptical notions of yours?

TOM I don't really know. But it has been sort of dawning on me lately that . . . that Oxford philosophy is really rather a . . .

TUTOR A what? A parlour game?

TOM Yes, sir. I know that sounds impertinent but —

TUTOR I've thought so myself at times. In my weaker moments. Still, now you've gone as far as this — well, I mean, there's no *harm* in taking an Honours degree. Then once you've got your Second — or even, it's possible, your First — you are perfectly free to imitate Prospero and take the *Critique of Pure Reason* and the *Nichomachean Ethics* and all your old lecture-notes and essays and drown the whole lot in the Isis.

TOM I wonder if there *is* no harm in it.

TUTOR In what? In having a degree? Why, a First in Greats — or even a Second for that matter — well, it is at least an asset when you're looking for a job.

TOM That's what I mean; it might make things almost too easy. I'm sorry, sir — I'm afraid this must sound priggish — but it might make me take the wrong job.

TUTOR Nonsense; you're a free agent. And really, these qualms of yours — well, they may be perfectly natural — but after all you're a scholar, the College have put their money on you. If you were a commoner now — but I think you know what I mean?

TOM Yes, sir, I know what you mean. I do owe the College a lot but . . . well, it's a conflict of loyalties.

TUTOR Loyalties? And who, may I ask, will benefit if you don't take your degree? Wall Street? The Unemployed?

TOM I might benefit myself. I might get more sort of straightened out, I —

TUTOR Oh you introspective generation! (*Clock strikes*) There, our time seems to be up. Now what's the essay for next week?

TOM The essay? Er, Kant's er, Kant's er — No, sir, I can't face it.

TUTOR Can't face next week's essay?

TOM I can't face Greats, sir. I'm serious.

TUTOR Serious?

TOM I want to go down, sir. Now.

TUTOR Sit down again. The last man who talked like this to me, I remember exactly what happened. He went out and got drunk and next day he'd changed his mind and now in fact he's a Don. Now I know you'll change your mind too but if I may advise you ... .

JANE You *will* change your mind, Tom, won't you?

TOM What do you think I am, Jane?

JANE So you're really going to go down? Without a degree?

TOM Yes, of course I am.

JANE But what will you do, darling? How will you *live*?

TOM How does anyone live?

JANE No, Tom, but you must be reasonable, you must be reasonable . . .

MOTHER You *must* be reasonable, Tom. What's the good of your education if —

FATHER You've had every chance, Tom. Everything's been done for you.

TOM That's just why I'm sick of it. I'm going off to get a job.

FATHER Don't be a fool. What sort of a job can you get?

TOM I haven't decided yet. Something that brings me in touch with people. Real people, I mean. I haven't met many yet.

(*Fade up Choir: 'Where the Blue of the Night' and lose behind*)

TERRY Jane!

JANE Terry!

TERRY I thought you were abroad.

JANE Just back. Isn't this country green?

TERRY Is it? Jane, you look frightfully elegant.

JANE *You* look very grown-up.

TERRY Ah, that's big business, my dear. I went in my old man's firm as soon as I came down from Oxford.

JANE What's everyone else doing? I've lost touch, you know.

TERRY Everyone else? Well ... Jim got a Fellowship at All Souls. Tony's gone on the stage —

JANE Can't act, can he?

TERRY Of course not. But to continue: Evelyn's in ICI; Hamish — this shook us a bit — Hamish got into the FO; Brian's eating his dinners or whatever they call it in Gray's Inn; Peter's on the BBC; George is in Kenya administrating or something. And Paul is running a too, too arty bookshop.

JANE And Tom?

TERRY Oh Tom? I thought you'd have heard from him.

JANE Not a line. Not for two years in fact.

TERRY Well, he did do a vanishing act. But rumour has it he's somewhere in the provinces, working on an evening newspaper. Cub reporter, you know.

JANE Rather a big cub. How does he like it?

TERRY I don't really know, Jane dear. Three pound ten a week or so, and seeing how he always detested the telephone —

(*Telephone rings*)

TOM Hullo, Hullo! That the City Police? Tom Varney here. Anything doing?

CITY POLICEMAN No, lad. We've had nobody in.

TOM Well, can you ring DO, please?

(*Telephone rings*)

TOM Hullo! Detective Wimbush in? Speaking? Look, this is Varney —

DETECTIVE No good, Tom. Nobody in today.

(*Telephone rings*)

TOM Hullo! County Police? Varney here.

COUNTY POLICEMAN Nothing doing today, sir.

TOM Nothing again. Why don't you close up shop? (*Telephone rings off*) Crime seems off for today. What *is* on the menu? Disease?

(*Telephone rings*)

TOM Hullo! That the Central Hospital? That you, Elsie? Anything come in?

ELSIE Well, Tom, there *is* a case of food poi — Sorry, I can't talk now; Matron's near the door of the switch; I'll give you a ring back.

(*Telephone rings off*)

FATHER Constance, I think I've fixed it.

MOTHER That job you mentioned for Tom?

FATHER If he wants it, he can have it. But maybe he won't want it.

MOTHER Don't be silly, Ned. Tom must be sick to death of that frightful town by now. And the frightful people he meets —

FATHER May I quote what he said in his last letter but one? 'My colleagues here just don't believe in anything. That's what I like about them. It makes such a good starting point. We live in a whirl of facts and we . . .'

(*Fade up typewriters and chatter, and behind*)

TOM We live in a whirl of facts and we take them for what they are worth.

(*Typewriters and chatter out*)

After the Police Court the Sale of Work — the Allotments Society Show — check on the alleged Van Dyck in the junk shop — evening the female Liberals, pick-ups the Local Philharmonic and, of course, the Four Square Gospellists. That was yesterday. And today the Hodgson funeral. Local worthy; bricklayer; Royal Antediluvian Order of Buffaloes. Met the boys in the Coach and Horses — who was to cover what? Tim the wreaths in the cemetery, Bill the door of the church, me the wreaths in the house. *And* I got a look at the corpse. Then back to the Coach and Horses — the same again please, Miss, we've got to check their initials.

(*Fade up typewriters and chatter behind*)

So here I am with my story.

CHIEF REPORTER Tom! Hey, come here. The Old Man wants to see you.

TOM What!

CHIEF REPORTER You're for it, lad. That pick-up of yours last night.

TOM The Four Square Gos —

CHIEF REPORTER No, the Philharmonic. You never went there, did you?

TOM No but I —

CHIEF REPORTER You wrote that Miss Delia Brown was weak in her upper register.

TOM She always is.

CHIEF REPORTER When she's there, she is.

TOM She was billed, Albert.

CHIEF REPORTER Aye but she never appeared. She got held up in a car-smash.

TOM Injured?

CHIEF REPORTER Dead. Ha! Ha! Call yourself a reporter! Too bad, Tom. Well, the Old Man's waiting.

(*Fade out typewriters and chatter, then knock — pause — second knock*)

EDITOR (*off*) Come in!

(*Door opens; Tom coughs three times*)

TOM I was told you wanted to see me, sir.

(*Pause, Tom coughs*)

EDITOR What did you say?

TOM I was told you wanted to see me.

EDITOR Very odd thing for me to want. (*Pause*) Well, when are you going to explain yourself?

TOM About that concert, sir? I got held up in —

EDITOR I don't care where you got held up. You're fired. This paper's got a reputation for accuracy. Or, if you prefer it, truth. That's what I want, 'Mister' Varney, truth at all costs.

TOM Truth at all costs? Right, Mr Shepherd, you've asked for it. This paper of yours that I've had the honour to work on, sir, is stupid to the point of imbecility. It's only good to wrap fish in. But not the best fish; *oh* no! I went to a funeral today, sir; I had a good look at the corpse; its name was Hodgson, remember? Well, I wrote you a piece to requirements saying Hodgson was one of the chief ornaments of the city. With a face like that, sir? *Oh* no! Oh no, no, no, *no*!

(*Pause*)

FATHER 'My dear Father' — Father? Why not Dad? — 'It is handsome of you to find me such a nice fat comfortable job; I'm afraid I can't accept it. I have just been fired from my paper, so I think I shall join the unemployed. As there are now over two million of the same, I ought not to feel too lonely. Besides, it will give me time to catch up with my reading — ' I give up. 'Catch up with his reading'!

(*Fade up Tom's voice reading to himself*)

TOM 'The monopoly of capital' — yes, this is the page — 'the monopoly of capital becomes a fetter upon the mode of production' — um, um, um, um, um — 'incompatible with their capitalist integument. This integument is burst asunder. The knell of capitalist private property — '

MARY Will you put that book down — or do you intend to buy it?

TOM My dear young lady, as I've been coming to this shop for longer than you've been serving in it —

MARY Och away! That's nothing to do with it. If your hands werena so dirty —

TOM Dirty? . . . Yes, that's car oil.

MARY Car-oil? Do you want that book or don't you?

TOM I've got it at home, Miss; I don't want to buy it again. But if you're set on selling me something today, where's that book I ordered — that History of Trade Unionism?

MARY It's no come in yet. No great loss, I would say.

TOM You don't approve of Trade Unions?

MARY I was in one once. In a factory. They made me join.

TOM You were in a factory?

MARY Two years — and I never want to go back to it.

TOM You prefer selling people books. Fond of books?

MARY No. I'm no much of a reader.

TOM Then why do you —

MARY I feel independent in this wee shop. It's only twenty-five bob, but —

TOM Twenty-five — that's not much. More than I'm getting though.

MARY You? But you're on the News.

TOM No, my dear. I've been sacked.

MARY Sacked! . . . That's awful hard on you.

TOM You think so? (*Pause*) Look, Miss, I don't know your name, I'm afraid —

MARY You don't have to.

TOM Well, Miss You-Don't-Have-To, what about going to the pictures this evening?

MARY Well, I never! I'd like you to know that I'm not in the custom —

TOM Of going to the pictures with wicked young men whose names you don't even know.

MARY Oh, I know *your* name; it's on our books. Mr T. Varney — £3-17-6.

TOM You know me only too well then. What do you want to see? Harold Lloyd?

MARY I told you I'm not in the cus — No, I've seen Harold Lloyd. I'd like to go to that drama. *You* know the one I mean.

TOM Of course I do. You mean the one that ends happily?

MARY That's it.

TOM Fine. I'll meet you at six o'clock and off we'll go and end happily.

(*Fade up Wedding March on piano with one finger, break off, pause, then knock*)

ANNIE A telegram, Ma'am.

(*Pause*)

MOTHER Oh, my *dear*!

ANNIE It's not bad news, is it?

MOTHER Bad news? ... Ask the Master to come here, please.

ANNIE Yes, Ma'am.

MOTHER I don't believe it! Who on earth can she be? Why, it's completely absurd. If Tom had only — Ned, come here at once.

FATHER Don't hurry me, dear. I'm not feeling well today.

MOTHER Nor am I — since I got this telegram. Look! (*Pause*) Well?

FATHER Well, that's that, isn't it?

MOTHER And what are they going to live on?

FATHER Air, I suppose. The traditional diet for people who marry like that.

MOTHER Ned, don't be so flippant. Can't you see —

FATHER Yes, darling, but don't take it so hard. She may be an excellent girl.

MOTHER I don't believe Tom would choose an excellent girl.

FATHER You're getting too hard on Tom —

MOTHER Yes, I dare say I am but — we just don't speak the same language.

FATHER It's the same for me, you know. Tom and I — it's years since we've talked to each other — really talked, I mean.

MOTHER Do you ... think ... it's our fault?

FATHER A bit, perhaps. It's chiefly the time we live in.

ANNIE I'm sorry; I couldn't help hearing. Has Master Tom got married?

MOTHER Yes, Annie. Very sudden, isn't it?

ANNIE The sudden weddings are the best, they say. And Master Tom's just of an age to marry.

MOTHER (*to self*) Just of an *age*? ... But that's not the only qualification.

MARY (*singing softly*)
  'Glorious things of thee are spoken,

Zion, City of our God . . .'

TOM For God's sake, stop singing that blasted tune!

MARY Tom, don't talk like that. Blasted tune? It's a hymn tune!

TOM It's also the anthem of Nazi Germany. Where've you put the matches?

MARY They're there on the arm of your chair. Tom, are the Nazis really all that bad?

TOM Mary, how long have we been married now? Oh well, never mind; some people never learn.

MARY I dinna see why I should bother about what goes on in Germany.

TOM Why does anyone ever bother about anything?

MARY Well, *I* bother about *you*, but *you*, sometimes, Tom —

TOM *I* know, *I* know. It's not your fault you can't think. And it's not my fault I can.

MARY You may be able to think but you never make any money. Look at this room we're in —

TOM Mary, you're just a little bourgeois. I sometimes wish —
      (*Doorbell*)

MARY That'll be another bill. All right, I'll go. (*Pause*) No. It's a telegram for you, Tom.
      (*Pause*)

TOM Another bill, did you say?

MARY What is it, Tom?

TOM My father's died.

MARY Oh Tom!

TOM Look, Mary dear, don't talk to me for a little. No, don't go away, just sit over there, will you, Mary. Just let me think to myself. I didn't expect this. (*To self*) No, I didn't expect it; I ought to have seen him again. But we didn't speak the same language. Mary speaks more of his language; oddly enough. I ought to have taken her to see him. Too late now; that Jack-in-the-Box again. But Mary can meet Mum. That's the next thing I'll do. Before that creature bobs up again. Out of the night. Grinning. Another bill. And there'll be more to come.
      (*Pause*)

DUNCAN (*singing*)
      Oh no, oh no, ma brither dear,
      Oh no, this maunna be!
      Ye'll tak your broad sword in your hand
      And ye'll gang in wi me!

(*Hums refrain till interrupted*)

NEWSBOY Paper, chum?

DUNCAN I don't know. What's in it?

NEWSBOY Oh, nothing much. Civil War in Spain.

DUNCAN Och, take it away.

(*Sings the same verse as above; fade out. Then crash of glass or china*)

MARY Tom! You've broken the vase. The one your mother sent me.

TOM Sorry.

MARY What made you jerk up your arm like that?

TOM Nerves, I expect. You see, Mary, I've just — er — come to a decision.

MARY You're going to get a job!

TOM No. At least *you* wouldn't call it that.

MARY Och, dinna be so mysterious.

TOM Well, Mary, what I'm going to tell you — well, I'm afraid you may not like it very much.

MARY Well, tell me.

TOM Mary, I've often been not very nice to you — selfish in fact — but this time it isn't really selfish; only I'm afraid you'll think it is.

MARY Go on, Tom.

TOM Well, Mary, I'm nearly thirty now and do you know — I've never yet been abroad. Well, I'm going abroad now.

MARY Where?

TOM Spain.

MARY Spain! Why?

TOM There's a war in Spain.

MARY Oh, that Civil War of theirs.

TOM A civil war of ours.

MARY I don't understand you, Tom. Why do you want to go there? Are you going to report on the war?

TOM No, I'm going to fight in it.

MARY But Tom! . . . You can't do that. What about me?

TOM I'd try to explain but you wouldn't understand.

MARY No, I dare say I wouldn't. And I dinna believe it anyway. You'll never go to Spain.

TOM Mary —

MARY It's just all talk as usual. Dinna be daft, Tom; I dinna believe what you say. And I won't believe you until —

TOM Until that telephone rings from a London station and my voice tells you I'm off.

MARY Tom, you're cruel. I dinna believe you anyway; you wouldna leave me like that. People don't go to wars unless they have to. I dinna believe you, Tom . . .

(*Telephone rings*)

MARY Hullo! Who's that? You, Tom! Where *are* you? Victoria! Oh!

(*Telephone rings off*)

So he did do it. Well, I hate him for doing it. Why, he might be killed out there. Oh God . . . please look after him. Tom . . . Tom . . .

(*Pause, then café chatter and to background. Clap of hands*)

TOM That right?

AMERICAN No, sir. No Spanish waiter would respond to that. Look, do it like this. (*Claps hands and shouts*) Camarero! You see. Now you do the rest. Practise the lingo while you can.

TOM Camarero! Dos café con leche.

WAITER Con leche? Si, señor.

AMERICAN Easy, isn't it? Not a bad accent, though, if you've never been here before. You sure picked a queer time to come.

TOM You been long in Spain?

AMERICAN Oh, I come and go. Representing my firm, see. But now with this war, business is so darn bad . . .

TOM How's the war going, would you say?

AMERICAN I don't know. No, sir, and I don't care. I figure it's none of my business. It's a local squabble, see, and neither side's much good.

TOM A local squabble. But the issues surely are —

AMERICAN You don't know these Spaniards; their politics don't make sense. All these goldarn initials — UGT, CNT — they're fighting each other as much as they're fighting Franco. Yeah and they're childish too; look at these rich men here all going round in overalls. No, sir —

TOM Here comes our coffee. What do I say when I pay for it?

AMERICAN Pay for it at the end.

TOM But what do I say at the end?

AMERICAN You say: 'Cuanto cuesta?'

TOM Cuanta cuesta. Good.

AMERICAN Learning your phrases, huh? Going to stay long here?

TOM I think so. Not here though. Madrid.

AMERICAN Madrid! Say, it's none of my business but – Madrid's just about to fall.

TOM So they tell me.

AMERICAN You don't believe it?

TOM No-o.

AMERICAN You don't, huh? . . . So you're really going to Madrid?

TOM Yes.

AMERICAN Then it's not much good your learning to say 'Cuanto cuesta'. There's nothing to buy in Madrid. No, you'll want some other phrase there.

TOM What phrase do you suggest?

AMERICAN Oh, I don't know. 'Cuidado' might be useful.

TOM 'Cuidado'? What does that mean?

AMERICAN Mean buddy? It means take cover.

LOUD VOICE Cuidado! Cuidado! Protenjanse!
　　(*Then babble of exclamations*)

CROWD Attento! Salva! Salva!
　Achtung! Achtung!
　Prends garde! (*etc*).
　　(*Up machine gun*)

1ST FOREIGN VOICE Keep down your head, Comrade Tom. To sit by the window so, it is not healthy.

2ND FOREIGN VOICE You must make more high your books. Look, I bring you more. On the shelves here is plenty.
　　(*Noise of falling books*)
　El gusto es mio. Nice barricade, eh?

TOM Yes, a nice barricade. But don't make it so high, I can't get my rifle out. (*to self*) Books! Ha! I never somehow imagined a barricade made of books. And I never imagined a Front as being like this. Crouching in a great big echoing building with silk curtains and falling plaster. Outside the window a scraggy donkey grazing beside the corpse of a Fascist. University City, Madrid. Faculty of Philosophy and Letters. Quite like Oxford, in fact. (*mortar and debris*) Or not . . . quite like Oxford? How would old Baldy like this?

2ND FOREIGN VOICE More books, Comrade.

TOM Hey! Enough, genug, basta. Phe-e-ew, look at these books – Hegel, Kant, Spinoza. Yes, Baldy *would* be all right here. Well, I'd better reload. Awful old rifle this. No importo nada. This is the country of Don Quixote.

(*Fade up Himno de Riego, peak, and fade out*)

MARY I hate him, I hate him ... writing to me like that, telling me he's happier there with his International Brigade than he ever has been with me or anyone else. I'll light the fire with his letter. (*strikes match*) There! And tomorrow I'll go back to Scotland.

(*Fade up Himno de Riego, peak, and fade out*)

COMPANY COMMANDER Camerados! Men of my company. You know why now I wish to speak to you. For two years you and I are fighting in Spain. We came to Spain to kill Fascists. Well, camerados, we *have* killed Fascists — plenty! (*cheering*) But now it has been arranged — over our heads, my soldiers — that we can fight no more. The International Brigade is dismissed. That is what we regret. But we do not regret this — that we have come here. Many of you — as I — have been in the concentration camp; we have no home to return to. But we do not give up, camerados; there will be other battlefields. And those of you who have homes, even when you return to friends, to comfort, to safety, you will remember Spain. You will remember Spain and what this conflict meant. And you will be proud of your record.

(*Fade up Himno de Riego and behind*)

TOM Proud of our record? ... We were, but that record's running down again.

(*Disc runs down and stops; pause. Fade up Tom whistling same tune*)

MOTHER What's that tune, Tom?

TOM (*whistling*) Oh, just something I picked up.

MOTHER Funny boy you are. Tom! I can't believe you're really here.

TOM I am, Mum — like it or not. (*Whistles a phrase*) Er ... Mum, what am I to do about Mary? She said in her letter she'd gone to Scotland for good.

MOTHER That's nonsense of course. Write to her.

TOM Write to her? ... No, I can't. We don't understand each other. And so many things have happened since we were — since I left England.

MOTHER Yes, indeed. If you'd been here in September, Tom!

TOM Munich, you mean?

MOTHER We all thought it was War, you know. And then how thankful we were!

TOM Umm.

MOTHER I suppose you didn't see any of the English papers?

TOM No, thank God —

MOTHER I've got all the cuttings in my album, here. Now ... here are the ones from the Times.

TOM September 30th: 'Agreement Reached at Munich Today. Enthusiastic Welcome for Mr Chamberlain.' um ... um ... um ... ' "Everything is all right" he said to the journalists awaiting him' ... Umph. October the first ... um ... 'the drive to London began to the singing of "For he's a jolly good fellow" ...' This must be the main page. Lord, what headlines — 'Declaration of Peace at Munich — Ovation in London — Joy in Berlin — Group at the Palace — Depression at Prague.' That tells a story, doesn't it?

MOTHER Yes, dear. I don't mind saying I knelt down in this room and I thanked God for our Prime Minister. For bringing us peace in our time. And then when I saw him on the news-reel and heard him recounting ...

TOM It hasn't occurred to you, has it ...

MOTHER What?

TOM Well, I don't want to depress you, Mum, but some day, even this year perhaps, you may switch on that little set there and that same voice will tell you that we are at war.

MOTHER You don't believe that, Tom? But Tom, surely — I mean, Tom — Tom, if one thinks it over — why do you think that's likely?

(Fade up behind previous speech Chamberlain on disc, and fade out)

MARY *(slow)* Dear Tom, I have not written you lately because I can't. But now that war is declared I am writing to wish you good luck, Tom. I wonder if you will join up. I have gone back in the factory, it is hard work but I felt I ought to. I suppose I will stay here until the war's over. After that I don't know, Tom.

TOM She felt she ought to. Like I felt about Spain. And I felt *right*, damn it — even if some of my swans did turn out to be geese. That was my war. But this? Is this my war or not?

DUNCAN (*singing*)
   'Oh no, oh no, ma brither dear – '
Where's this damn recruiting office?
   'Oh no, this maunna be!
   Ye'll tak your broad sword in your hand – '
Ah, here's the bloody place. No red carpets, I see. Here, don't you
shove in front of me.
VOLUNTEER I wasn't shoving.
DUNCAN 'Ye'll tak your broad sword in your hand – '
VOLUNTEER Eh?
DUNCAN 'And ye'll gang in wi' me!'
   (*Hums chorus; fade out*)

OBSERVER (*on distort*) Hullo control! . . . Hullo control! . . . Bandits
approaching! . . . Bandits approaching!
TOM So this is the Battle of Britain?
TERRY 'So this is the Forest of Arden'.
TOM 'm, Terry?
TERRY I was just a bit tickled by your intonation. You might just as
well have been in Arden.
TOM I might. I'm certainly not in the battle. And I'm getting tired of
doing nothing, Terry.
TERRY So am I, old boy, so am I.
TOM But you're in the –
TERRY Yes, yes, yes, I know I'm a buckshee captain but I just sit on
my behind.
TOM I just sit on the fence, I suppose.
TERRY Don't mortify yourself so. What can we do to cheer you up? I
know. Saturday evening I'm having a dinner with Jane.
TOM Jane?
TERRY Yes. You bring along someone else and –
TOM Saturday's the seventh, isn't it?
TERRY That's right. September the seventh. And that reminds me. I
promised Jane that first I'd take her to Lord's – Lord's Eleven v.
Middlesex Eleven. Well, I've just remembered I can't, you'd better
go and stand in for me.
TOM But, Terry, I haven't seen Jane for –
TERRY Don't be silly, *she* won't bite you. She's divorced by the way.
You knew that?
TOM No, I didn't.

TERRY Same as you?

TOM No.

TERRY No? Sorry, somebody told me — Well, anyway, you take Jane along to Lord's. I think I can get there later — round about five.

TOM Round about five?

TERRY Yes, that's a date. Round about five or soon after.

(*Fade up open-air crowd, laughter*)

1ST SPECTATOR Blimey! That ain't Hendren bowling?

2ND SPECTATOR Hendren? That's right. Good old Patsy.

1ST SPECTATOR But *he* can't bowl for — (*Applause*)

2ND SPECTATOR Smith seems to know what to do with 'em.

1ST SPECTATOR I said he couldn't bowl for nuts. He can still bat all right though. See him this morning?

2ND SPECTATOR No. What did he make?

1ST SPECTATOR Well, he had bad luck — forty-five.

2ND SPECTATOR Missed his fifty, eh?

(*Sudden laughter from Jane, close*)

TOM What are you laughing at?

JANE I don't know, Tom . . . Life.

TOM Always a subject for laughter.

JANE Your life and mine especially.

(*Applause*)

1ST SPECTATOR There he goes again — run, rabbit, run!

JANE It doesn't seem to make much sense.

TOM Do you think what . . . do you think what I suggested just now makes sense?

JANE In the tea interval? . . . Yes. (*Hums 'I Can't Give You Anything But Love', and breaks off*) Remember that tune?

TOM Yes. Punting. On the Cherwell. 'That's the only thing I've plenty of . . . baby.' Not that I've ever had plenty of it.

JANE You will. From now on, Tom.

(*Applause*)

1ST SPECTATOR There he goes again.

2ND SPECTATOR Why don't Hendren come off?

JANE Nice here in Lord's. A harbour green. Do you remember that too?

TOM 'In a harbour green whereas I lay
The birdés sang sweet — '

(*Sudden murmur of crowd*)

What's that? Another boundary?

JANE Can't be. They're changing ends. What's the crowd standing up for?

VOICES Look, look! Right up there in the sky.

... eight, nine, ten, eleven, twelve, thirteen, fourteen ...

Another lot behind them.

Blimey, that's the Luftwaffe. (*etc.*)

TOM This is what people call *it*, Jane.

JANE The Luftwaffe! But they look so tiny, they —

WARDEN (*off*) I say, you people, I say, you people —

JANE Who's that comic little man in the tin hat and plus-fours?

TOM Armlet too. A warden.

WARDEN (*approaching*) I say, you people, do take cover. You can't stand around like this — unnecessary risks — most embarrassing for me. You must take cover, you people —

TERRY (*approaching*) Hullo, Jane darling. Hullo, Tom. What's going on round here?

TOM Hullo, Terry. The beginning of the end, it looks like.

TERRY You're damn right. Look over there. East.

2ND SPECTATOR Oy! Look at that there pillar of smoke.

JANE Where can that be? East End?

TOM Docks probably.

1ST SPECTATOR Here comes more of 'em.

WARDEN I say, you people, you must take cover. I mean, it's your duty, I mean. If you won't co-operate, I mean, how shall we ever get anywhere?

TOM Come on, Jane, I think we'd better move off.

JANE Why? I'm still watching those —

TERRY Come on, Jane, don't be a silly. Why, even the chaps have stopped play. Look, I'll go ahead and see if I can pick up a taxi ...

WARDEN I say, you people, you're making this awfully awkward. Play the game, you people, I mean you must take cover.

TOM (*to self*) Take cover? Cuidado! Protenjanse! Why, I'd almost forgotten.

2ND SPECTATOR Well, one thing about it: Hendren's come off now.

WARDEN Hurry up, my good man, get a move on. Take cover, take cover.

JANE Terry's having difficulty scrounging a taxi.

TOM Er ... Sorry?

JANE Terry, I said — What's wrong with you, Tom?

TOM Jane.

JANE Yes.

TOM The Tea Interval ... Remember what we agreed?

JANE Remember! Don't be so silly.

TOM Well ... I'm afraid it's no go.

JANE No go?

TOM No, Jane darling. I think I'm going to join up.

TERRY (*calling off*) Hullo, children, come on. Taxi!

JANE So he *has* got one.

TOM What? Oh, a taxi. Look, Jane, about that harbour green. Ten minutes ago I still thought it was feasible —

TERRY (*off*) Come on there, duckies, there's a war on!

TOM But it's not — no more than in the poem. It was a dream there too.

JANE Oh ... I see, Tom ... Yes, of course I see. But why should joining up make a difference? Couldn't we all the same —

TOM No, darling.

TERRY Come on, Terry's impatient. He's very fond of his skin.

JANE (*calling*) Com-ing!

TOM The second verse I don't think I ever told you —
'I dreamed I walked still to and fro
And from her company I did not go
And when I waked it was not so —
    In youth is pleasure, in youth is pleasure.'

(*Fade up factory noises and to background*)

FOREMAN Morning, Mary. How are you feeling, lass?

MARY Well, Mr Higgs, I'm tired after the Blitz but — I've just had a letter from my husband.

FOREMAN Oh? Good news?

MARY Yes! He's joined the Navy!
    (*Fade up factory noises and fade out*)

MOTHER What are you waiting for, Annie?

ANNIE Excuse me, Ma'am, I was just wondering —

MOTHER What was in Master Tom's letter? You *are* a faithful old thing. Well, he's finished his training, Annie, and he's just been assigned to a ship.

ANNIE Oh, aren't you proud? When he came home this last time,

Master Tom looked so handsome. Those bell bottoms suit him, don't they, Ma'am?

MOTHER Yes, Annie, I think they do. But I hope he'll get out of them soon.

(*Fade up factory noises and to background*)

MARY Yes, indeed, Mr Higgs. He's been a whole year now at sea. He likes it, you know.

FOREMAN That's nice. Is he going up for a commission, lass?

MARY I'm sure they'll ask him to. Tom would make a lovely officer.

(*Fade out factory noises*)

DIVVY OFFICER Varney.

TOM Here, sir.

DIVVY OFFICER I wanted to ... er ... discuss something with you. I don't know how you'll feel about it but I'm thinking of starting a white paper for you.

TOM You mean, sir, you want me to go up for a commission?

DIVVY OFFICER Well, with your background, you know — How would you like to be an officer? Well, Varney?

TOM Well, sir, I think I'd rather not.

DIVVY OFFICER You'd rather not? Why, man? The Service is in need of good officers. What've you got up your sleeve, Varney?

TOM Well, sir, it's just that ... er ... the lower deck suits me, sir.

DIVVY OFFICER That's not the point. Now a chap like yourself with an Oxford degree —

TOM Oh I never took my degree, sir.

DIVVY OFFICER Why, did they plough you?

TOM No, sir, I just didn't want a degree.

DIVVY OFFICER And now you don't want a commission?

TOM No, sir.

DIVVY OFFICER You're due for leave, aren't you, Varney?

TOM Yes, sir.

DIVVY OFFICER Well, think it over on your leave and if you change your mind — *if* you change your mind ...

(*Fade up Tom whistling Himno de Riego*)

MOTHER Happy, Tom?

TOM Yes, Mum.

MOTHER I thought you must be, whistling like that. You're a changed man, you know, Tom.

TOM Am I? Perhaps I am, Mum. I feel as if I'd . . . found something or other.

MOTHER You like the Navy, don't you?

TOM More than that, Mum. I couldn't say so on board though; with all us jolly matelots the order of the day is dripping.

MOTHER Dripping?

TOM No, not that stuff Mary always gave me on bread. She's coming down this weekend, you know.

MOTHER You've told me that several times already. Friday or Saturday, Tommy?

TOM I've got a date with her Saturday. They won't let her off before.

MOTHER You haven't seen her, have you, since . . .

TOM No, Mum.

MOTHER What is it, Annie?

ANNIE A telegram for Master Tom.

 (*Pause*)

TOM Damn!

MOTHER What is it?

TOM Got to report back at once.

ANNIE At once! Now isn't that a shame!

TOM Five days more by rights but — Well, that's the Service. I must send a wire to Mary.

MOTHER Mary? Poor Mary.

 (*Fade up factory noise to background*)

MARY On Saturday Tom has a date with me, a date with me, a date with me,

 On Saturday Tom has a date with me and I have a date with Tom!

 (*Fade out factory noise, pause, then fade up chatter and clatter of lower deck mess*)

1ST SAILOR Oy, oy, oy, 'oo's took my padlock?

DUNCAN Och, man, ye never had a padlock.

1ST SAILOR Oh, yes, I did – a green padlock it was.

2ND SAILOR Eh, lad, mind my foot.

1ST SAILOR Ginger, hey, let me tell you — smashing big eats I had yesterday.

2ND SAILOR I had big eats in Liverpool. Little fish and chip shop — a proper treat it was.

1ST SAILOR Garn! Look, chums, what's the buzz?

2ND SAILOR Eh, if you used your loaf...

DUNCAN What do ye mean, man?

2ND SAILOR Eh, I know summat — but I'm not lettin' on, y'know.

1ST SAILOR That's right. This here trip is special.

DUNCAN That's what *I* think. I've got a premonition that —

TOM (*approaching*) Duncan!

DUNCAN Hullo, Tom.

VOICES Hullo, Tom.

TOM Duncan, come over here. I've got something to show you. Here's that lighter I promised you.

DUNCAN Ah, that's grand. Thank you, Tom. (*beginning to sing*)
'Oh no, oh no, ma brither dear — '

TOM It's not 'oh no! oh no!', it's 'oh yes! oh yes!', you've got a bloody good lighter. And anyway, Duncan, we're getting tired of that song.

DUNCAN It's an old ballad, Tom.

TOM Well, don't you know any other old ballads?

DUNCAN I do but I don't know the tunes. 'Yestreen I dreamed' — no, I don't know the tune.

TOM Yestreen what? Recite it.

DUNCAN 'Yestreen I dreamed a dreary dream
  Beyond the Isle of Skye;
 I saw a dead man win a fight
  And I think that man was I.'

TOM 'Yestreen I — '? That's rather good. Say it again, will you, Duncan.

DUNCAN 'Yestreen I dreamed a dreary dream
  Beyond the Isle of Skye;
 I saw a dead man win a fight
  And I think that man was I.'

(*Fade up factory noise, mix with choir — 'You Are My Sunshine' — and behind*)

FOREMAN There you are, lass! We've got it installed at last. Music While You Work! How do you like it?

MARY It's all right.

FOREMAN Eh, Mary, what's wrong with you this morning?

MARY I'm sorry, Mr Higgs, I —

FOREMAN Headache or summat?

MARY No, Mr Higgs, it's just I'm disappointed. I had a date today but
. . . Och well, that's just life.

> (*Lose factory noises, bring up choir, then fade out slowly*)

TOM Track in the water on port bow, sir, approaching.

OFFICER OF WATCH What bearing? . . . Hell! It's a torpedo. Hard to
port!

VOICE Hard to port!

TOM (*to self*) What bearing, eh? This time I needn't answer. Here it
comes, this is the end, Tom Varney. The tin fish, the old black
Jack-in-the-Box. And then the drums of blindness. Not that *we'll* hear
the explosion.

> (*Pause, bring in disc of 'Rockabye Baby', and to background*)

I *didn't* hear the explosion. This must be death, I take it. Weight of
water without any surface. Down, down and down, no object for the
eyes. But in my ears are voices.

MOTHER Tommy! I've told you already. You're not to go out on that
rock!

UNCLE DES My word, Tommy, you've grown.

FLAHERTY Och, stamp yer feet. Class dismissed. I'm quittin'.

STRIKER See what this spells then. S . . . C . . . A . . . B . . .

JANE Look out, Tom! That willow-branch!

TUTOR Fire ahead, Mr Varney, fire ahead.

FATHER You've had every chance, Tom. Everything's been done for
you.

EDITOR That's what I want, Mr Varney. Truth at all costs.

MARY Oh, I know your name. It's on our books.

AMERICAN There's nothing to buy in Madrid. No, you'll want some
other phrase there.

COMPANY COMMANDER Well, camerados, we *have* killed Fascists —
plenty.

JANE Nice here in Lord's. A harbour green. Do you remember that
too?

WARDEN I say, you people, you *must* take cover.

TERRY Come on there, duckies, there's a war on!

DIVVY OFFICER Well, with your background, you know —

MOTHER You're a changed man, you know, Tom.

TOM A changed man, Mum? You're right.

DUNCAN 'Yestreen I dreamed a dreary dream
　　Beyond the Isle of Skye;
　I saw a dead man win a fight
　And I think that man was I.'

OFFICER OF WATCH Give the correct bearing without me having to ask you.

TOM The correct bearing? ... Aye, aye, sir.
　　(*Fade up disc to end*)

MOTHER Ah, he's asleep at last.

TOM I am asleep at last. The Japanese flower opened in water. It did not open fully, the bearing was ... not quite right. Was I a misfit? Maybe. I hurt my mother, my father, I hurt Jane and Mary. And I leave nothing behind me — child, work, or deed to remember. But I tried, you know, I tried. Believe it or not, I did have ideals of a sort. But I could not quite get the bearing. Now let me sleep; I'm tired.
　　(*Fade up disc of 'Rockabye Baby', and to close*)

THE DARK TOWER

a radio parable play

MacNeice gave his *The Dark Tower* three distinct productions in his lifetime – first broadcast 21 January 1946; second production of 30 January
1950 with many small revisions and some expansions; third version of
14 May 1956 with further minor changes – all productions on the Home
Service and repeated on the Third Programme. This, MacNeice's most
celebrated and produced play, a considerable accomplishment in verse, written at the end of the war and out of war experience, was suggested by
a well-known nightmare-poem of Browning's, with Roland as a reluctant
quest-hero, more like the changeable Tom Varney (of *He Had a Date*) than
the strong-willed Columbus. Roland is educated for a parabolic quest he
believes in only spasmodically; he is led astray many times, but finally faces
absolute evil. In the two productions of 1946 and 1950 Cyril Cusack played
Roland; in 1950 Mary Wimbush played Neaera and Dylan Thomas the
Raven. For a BBC Festival of Radio Drama in 1956 Richard Burton played
Roland and Hedli Anderson Neaera. Benjamin Britten composed 'special
music' used in all productions. The play, dedicated to Britten, was published
by Faber with several other MacNeice radio scripts in May 1947, and
reissued by itself in November 1964, i.e. posthumously, and unfortunately
without MacNeice's final version being used. For his book of 1947 Mac-
Neice wrote a 'General Introduction' which is a forthright statement about
radio drama, included as Appendix 2 of this volume. The text of the play
used here is that of the third and last version of 1956 (latest in MacNeice's
lifetime), from a copy of the script held in the Berg Collection in the New
York Public Library.

The Dark Tower is a parable play, belonging to that wide class of writings which includes *Everyman*, *The Faerie Queene*, and *The Pilgrim's Progress*. Though under the name of allegory this kind of writing is sometimes dismissed as outmoded, the clothed as distinct from the naked allegory is in fact very much alive. Obvious examples are *Peer Gynt* and the stories of Kafka but also in such books as *The Magic Mountain* by Thomas Mann, where the disguise of 'realism' is maintained and nothing happens that is quite inconceivable in life, it is still the symbolic core which makes the work important. My own impression is that pure 'realism' is in our time almost played out, though most works of fiction of course will remain realistic *on the surface*. The single-track mind and the single-plane novel or play are almost bound to falsify the world in which we live. The fact that there is method in madness and the fact that there is fact in fantasy (and equally fantasy in 'fact') have been brought home to us not only by Freud and other psychologists but by events themselves. This being so, reportage can no longer masquerade as art. So the novelist, abandoning the 'straight' method of photography, is likely to resort once more not only to the twist of plot but to all kinds of other twists which may help him to do justice to the world's complexity. Some element of parable therefore, far from making a work thinner and more abstract, ought to make it more concrete. Man does after all live by symbols.

The dual-plane work will not normally be allegory in the algebraic sense; i.e. it will not be desirable or even possible to equate each of the outward and visible signs with a precise or rational inner meaning. Thus *The Dark Tower* was suggested to me by Browning's poem 'Childe Roland to the Dark Tower came', a work which does not admit of a completely rational analysis and still less adds up to any clear moral or message. This poem has the solidity of a dream; the writer of such a poem, though he may be aware of the 'meanings' implicit in his dream, must not take the dream to pieces, must present his characters concretely, must allow the story to persist as a story and not dwindle into a diagram. While I could therefore have offered here an explicit summary of those implicit 'meanings' in *The Dark Tower* of which I myself was conscious, I·am not doing so, because it might impair the impact of the play. I would merely say — for the benefit of people like the *Daily Worker*'s critic, who found the programme pointless and depressing — that in my opinion it is neither. *The Faerie Queene*, *The Pilgrim's Progress*,

Piers Plowman, and the early Moralities could not have been written by men without any beliefs. In an age which precludes the simple and militant faith of a Bunyan, belief (whether consciously formulated or not) still remains a *sine qua non* of the creative writer. I have my beliefs and they permeate *The Dark Tower*. But do not ask me what Ism it illustrates or what Solution it offers. You do not normally ask for such things in the single-plane work; why should they be forced upon something much more complex? 'Why, look you now, how unworthy a thing you make of me!' What is life *useful* for anyway?

Comments on points of detail will be found at the end of this book. [See pp. 410–11 below.] The best in this kind are but shadows and in print they are shadows of shadows. To help the reader to *hear* this piece, I will therefore add this: in production I got the actors to play their parts 'straight', i.e. like flesh and blood (in dreams the characters are usually like flesh and blood too). Out of an excellent cast I am particularly grateful to Cyril Cusack for his most sensitive rendering of 'Roland'. And Benjamin Britten provided this programme with music which is, I think, the best I have heard in a radio play. Without his music *The Dark Tower* lacks a dimension.

CHARACTERS

SERGEANT-TRUMPETER

GAVIN

ROLAND

MOTHER

TUTOR

SYLVIE

BLIND PETER

SOAK

BARMAID

STENTOR

CROWD

TICKET COLLECTOR

STEWARD

OFFICER

NEAERA

1ST PASSENGER

HIS WIFE

2ND PASSENGER

VOICE

TOUT

PRIEST

FATHER'S VOICE

PARROT

RAVEN

CLOCK VOICE

CHILD'S VOICE

THE DARK TOWER

ANNOUNCER 'The Dark Tower' by Louis MacNeice — a new production of the programme which was first broadcast in 1946. Though this programme appears to be attached to no particular time or place, it was largely inspired by World War II. And, though it is on the surface a fantasy, it is concerned with very real questions of faith and doubt, of doom and free will, of temptation and self-sacrifice.

READER The Programme which follows is a parable play — suggested by Robert Browning's poem 'Childe Roland to the Dark Tower came'. The theme is the ancient but ever-green theme of the Quest — the dedicated adventure; the manner of presentation is that of a dream — but a dream that is full of meaning. Browning's poem ends with a challenge blown on a trumpet:

> 'And yet
> Dauntless the slughorn to my lips I set
> And blew. "*Childe Roland to the Dark Tower came*".'

Note well the words '*And yet*'. Roland did not have to — he did not wish to — and yet in the end he came to: — The Dark Tower.

(*A trumpet plays through the Challenge Call*)
SERGEANT-TRUMPETER
There now, that's the challenge. And mark this:
Always hold the note at the end.
GAVIN Yes, Sergeant-Trumpeter, yes.
ROLAND (*as a boy*)[1] Why need Gavin hold the note at the end?
SERGEANT-TRUMPETER
Ach, ye're too young to know. It's all tradition.
ROLAND What's tradition, Sergeant-Trumpeter?
GAVIN Ask Mother that one. She knows.
SERGEANT-TRUMPETER Aye, *she* knows.
But run along, sonny. Leave your brother to practise.
(*The trumpet begins — but breaks off*)
SERGEANT-TRUMPETER No. Again.
(*The trumpet re-begins — breaks off*)

118 LOUIS MACNEICE

SERGEANT-TRUMPETER Again.
(*The trumpet begins and is sustained*)
SERGEANT-TRUMPETER
That's it now. But hold that last note — hold it!
(*On the long last note the trumpet fades into the distance*)

ROLAND Mother! What's tradition?
MOTHER Hand me that album. No — the black one.
ROLAND Not the locked one!
MOTHER Yes, the locked one. I have the key.
Now, Roland, sit here by me on the sofa.
We'll look at them backwards.
ROLAND Why must we look at them backwards?
MOTHER Because then you may recognize —
Now! You know who this is?
ROLAND Why, that's my brother Michael.
And here's my brother Henry!
Michael and Henry and Denis and Roger and John!
Do you keep this album locked because they're dead?
MOTHER No . . . not exactly.
Now — can you guess who this is?
ROLAND That's someone I saw in a dream once.
MOTHER It must have been in a dream.
He left this house three months before you were born.
ROLAND Is it . . . is it my father?
MOTHER
Yes. And this is your grandfather. And this is *his* father —
For the time being you needn't look at the rest;
This book goes back through seven long generations,
As far as George the founder of the family.
ROLAND And did they all die the same way?
MOTHER They did, Roland. And now I've answered your question.
ROLAND Question . . . ? What question, Mother?
(*The trumpet call is heard in the distance and held behind*)
Ah, there's Gavin practising.
He's got it right at last.
(*The trumpet call sounds, still distant, and closes*)
GAVIN Mother! I know the challenge. When can I leave?
Tomorrow?
MOTHER Why not today, Gavin?

GAVIN Today! But I haven't yet checked my equipment;
  I mean — for such a long journey I —
MOTHER You will travel light, my son.
GAVIN Well, yes ... of course ... today then.
ROLAND Where are you going, Gavin?
GAVIN Why, surely you know; I'm —
MOTHER Hsh!
ROLAND I know where he's going. Across the sea like Michael.
GAVIN That's right, Roland. Across the big, bad sea.
  Like Michael and Henry and Denis and Roger and John.
  And after that through the Forest.
  And after that through the Desert —
ROLAND What's the Desert made of?
GAVIN Well ... I've never been there.
  Some deserts are made of sand and some are made of grit but —
MOTHER This one is made of doubts and dried-up hopes.
ROLAND And what do you find at the other end of the desert?
GAVIN Well, I ... well...
MOTHER You can tell him.
GAVIN I find the Dark Tower.
    (*The 'Dark Tower' theme fades up and then fades to close behind*)

TUTOR
  Now, Master Roland, as this is our first day of lessons
  I trust I shall find you as willing a pupil
  As your six brothers before you.
ROLAND Did you like teaching my brothers?
TUTOR Like it? It was an honour.
  It was teaching to some purpose.
ROLAND When's my brother Gavin coming back?
TUTOR What!
ROLAND Gavin. When's he coming back?
TUTOR Roland! ...
  I see I must start from the beginning.
  I thought your mother'd have told you but maybe being the
    youngest —
ROLAND What would my mother have told me?
TUTOR You ask when your brother Gavin is coming back?
  You must get this straight from the start:
  Your family never come back.

Now, now, now, don't let me scare you.
Sit down on that stool and I'll try to explain.
Now, Roland —
I said that to teach your brothers was an honour.
Before your mother engaged me to tutor John
I was an usher in a great city,
I taught two dozen lads in a class —
The sons of careerists — salesmen, middlemen, half-men,
Governed by greed and caution; it was my job
To teach them enough — and only enough —
To fit them for making money. Means to an end.

ROLAND My family don't make money?

TUTOR They make history.

ROLAND And what do you mean by an end?

TUTOR I mean — surely they told you?
I mean: the Dark Tower.

ROLAND Will *I* ever go to the Dark Tower?

TUTOR Of course you will. That is why I am here.

ROLAND (*gaily*) Oh well! That's different.

TUTOR It is.

ROLAND And that means I'll fight the Dragon?

TUTOR Yes — but let me tell you:
We call it the Dragon for short, it is a nameless force
Hard to define — for no one who has seen it,
Apart from those who have seen its handiwork,
Has returned to give an account of it.
All that we know is there is something there
Which makes the Dark Tower dark and is the source
Of evil through the world. It is immortal
But men must try to kill it — and keep on trying
So long as we would be human.

ROLAND What would happen
If we just let it alone?

TUTOR Well . . . some of us would live longer; all of us
Would lead a degraded life, for the Dragon would be supreme
Over our minds as well as our bodies. Gavin —
And Michael and Henry and Denis and Roger and John —
Might still be here — perhaps your father too,
He would be seventy-five — but mark this well:
They would not be themselves. Do you understand?

ROLAND I'm not quite sure, I . . .

TUTOR You are still small. We'll talk of the Dragon later.
Now come to the blackboard and we'll try some Latin.
You see this sentence?
ROLAND Per ardua...
TUTOR Per ardua ad astra.
ROLAND What does it mean?
TUTOR It does not go very well in a modern language.
We had a word 'honour' — but it is obsolete.
Try the word 'duty'; and there's another word — 'Necessity'.
ROLAND Necessity! That's a bit hard to spell.
TUTOR
You'll have to spell it, I fear. Repeat this after me:
N —
ROLAND N —
TUTOR E —
ROLAND E —

(*Their voices dwindle away and a tolling bell*[2] *grows up out of the distance, with orchestra, and is held behind*)

SERGEANT-TRUMPETER Ah God, there's the bell for Gavin.
He had the greatest power to his lungs of the lot of them
And now he's another name in the roll of honour
Where Michael's is still new gold. Five years it is —
Or would it be more like six — since we tolled for Michael?
Bells and trumpets, trumpets and bells,
I'll have to be learning the young one next;
Then he'll be away too and my lady will have no more.
MOTHER No more children, Sergeant-Trumpeter?
SERGEANT-TRUMPETER Ach, I beg your pardon. I didn't see you.
MOTHER No matter. But know this:
I have one more child to bear.
No, I'm not mad; you needn't stare at me, Sergeant.
This is a child of stone.[3]
SERGEANT-TRUMPETER A child of...
MOTHER Stone. To be born on my death-bed.
No matter. I'm speaking in metaphor.
SERGEANT-TRUMPETER That's all right then. How's young Roland
Making out at his lessons?
MOTHER I don't know.
Roland lacks concentration; he's not like my other sons,

He's almost flippant, he's always asking questions —
SERGEANT-TRUMPETER Ach, he's young yet.
MOTHER Gavin was his age once.
    So were Michael and Henry and Denis and Roger and John.
    They never forgot what they learnt. And they asked no questions.
SERGEANT-TRUMPETER
    Ah well — by the time that Roland comes to me
    When he's had his fill of theory and is all set for action,
    In another half dozen years when he comes to learn the trumpet
      call —
MOTHER Hsh, don't talk of it now.
    Let one bell toll at a time.
        (*The bell recedes into nothing*)

TUTOR So ends our course on ethics. Thank you, Roland;
    After all these years our syllabus is concluded.
    You have a brain; what remains to be tried is your will.
    Remember our point today: the sensitive man
    Is the more exposed to seduction. In six years
    I have come to know you; you have a warm heart —
    It is perhaps too warm for a man with your commission,
    Therefore be careful. Keep to your one resolve,
    Your single code of conduct, listen to no one
    Who doubts your values — and above all, Roland,
    Never fall in love — That is not for you.
    If ever a hint of love should enter your heart,
    You must arise and go.... That's it: Go!
    Yes, Roland my son. Go quickly.

SYLVIE
    But why must you go so quickly?[4] Now that the sun's come out.
ROLAND (*adult*) I have my lesson to learn.
SYLVIE You're always learning lessons!
    I'll begin to think you prefer your books to me.
ROLAND Oh, but Sylvie, this isn't books any more.
SYLVIE Not books? Then —
ROLAND I'm learning to play the trumpet.
SYLVIE Whatever for? Roland, you make me laugh.
    Is this another idea of your mother's?

ROLAND Sylvie, I —
SYLVIE I needn't ask. What's all this leading to?
ROLAND I could tell you, darling. But not today.
   Today is a thing in itself — apart from the future.
   Whatever follows, I will remember this tree
   With this dazzle of sun and shadow — and I will remember
   The mayflies jigging above us in the delight
   Of the dying instant — and I'll remember *you*
   With the bronze lights in your hair.
SYLVIE Yes, darling; but why so sad?
   There will be other trees and —
ROLAND Each tree is itself, each moment is itself,
   Inviolable gifts of time — of God —
   But you cannot take them with you.
SYLVIE Take them with you where?
ROLAND Kiss me, Sylvie. I'm keeping my teacher waiting.

    (*The Challenge Call is played through once*)
SERGEANT-TRUMPETER Nicely blown! Nicely blown!
   You've graduated, my lad.
   But remember — when I'm not here — hold the note at the end.
ROLAND You mean when *I'm* not here.
SERGEANT-TRUMPETER
   Aye, you're right. But you are my last pupil,
   I'll be shutting up shop, I want you to do me credit.
   When you've crossed the sea and the desert and come to the place
     itself
   I want you to do me credit when you unsling that horn.
ROLAND I hope I will.
SERGEANT-TRUMPETER I'm sure ye will. D'ye know
   Ye've caught me accent during these last lessons —
ROLAND Have I?
SERGEANT-TRUMPETER
   Ye have. And if ye're after catching me accent
   Maybe ye've also caught a touch of me spirit.
ROLAND (*slightly forced laugh; pause*) Sergeant?
SERGEANT-TRUMPETER Eh?
ROLAND Do you believe in all this?
SERGEANT-TRUMPETER All what?
ROLAND Do you think that there really is any dragon to fight?

SERGEANT-TRUMPETER
   What are you saying! What was it killed Gavin?
   And Michael and Henry and Denis and Roger and John?
   And your father himself and his father before him and all of them
      back to George!
ROLAND I don't know but . . . nobody's *seen* this dragon.
SERGEANT-TRUMPETER Seen him? They've seen what he's done!
   Have you never talked to Blind Peter?
ROLAND No, I —
SERGEANT-TRUMPETER
   I thought not. Cooped up here in the castle —
   Inside this big black ring of smothering yew-trees —
   You never mixed with the folk.
   But before you leave — if you want a reason for leaving —
   I recommend that you pay a call on Peter.
   And his house is low; mind your head as you enter.

BLIND PETER That's right, sir; mind your head as you enter.
   Now take that chair, it's the only one with springs,
   I saved it from my hey-day. Well now, sir,
   It's kind of you to visit me. I can tell
   By your voice alone that you're your father's son;
   Your handshake's not so strong though.
ROLAND Why, was my father —
BLIND PETER He had a grip of iron.
   And what's more, sir, he had a will of iron.
   And what's still more again, he had a conscience —
   Which is something we all need. *I* should know!
ROLAND Why?
BLIND PETER Why what?
ROLAND
   Why do you sound so sad when you talk about having a conscience?
BLIND PETER
   Because his conscience is something a man can lose.
   It's cold in here, I'll make a long story short.
   Fifty years ago when I had my sight —
   But the Dragon was loose at the time —
ROLAND The Drag —
BLIND PETER I had a job and a wife and a new-born child
   And I believed in God. Until one day

I told you the Dragon was loose at the time,
No one had challenged him lately, so he came out from his den —
What some people call the Tower — and creeping around
He got to our part of the world; nobody saw him of course,
There was just a kind of a bad smell in the air
And everything went sour; people's mouths and eyes
Changed their look overnight — and the government changed too —
And as for me I woke up feeling different
And when I looked in the mirror that first morning
The mirror said 'Informer'!

ROLAND Informer?

BLIND PETER Yes, sir. My new role.
They passed a pack of laws forbidding this and that
And anyone breaking 'em the penalty was death.
I grew quite rich sending men to their death.
The last I sent was my wife's father.

ROLAND But ... but did you believe in these laws?

BLIND PETER Believe? Aha! Did I believe in anything?
God had gone round the corner. I was acquiring riches.
But to make a long story short —
When they hanged my wife's father my wife took poison,
So I was left with the child. Then the child took ill —
Scared me stiff — so I sent for all the doctors,
I could afford 'em then — but they couldn't discover
Anything wrong in its body, it was more as if its soul
Was set on quitting — and indeed why not?
To be a human being, people agree, is difficult.

ROLAND Then the child ...?

BLIND PETER Quit.
Yes; she quit — but slowly.
I watched it happen. That's why now I'm blind.

ROLAND Why? You don't mean that you yourself —

BLIND PETER
When you've seen certain things, you don't want to see no more.
Tell me, sir. Are people's faces nowadays
As ugly as they were? You know what I mean: evil?

ROLAND No, not most of them. *Some*, I suppose —

BLIND PETER Those ones belong to the Dragon.

ROLAND Why put the blame of everything on the Dragon?
Men have free choice, haven't they?
Free choice of good or evil —

BLIND PETER That's just it —
  And the evil choice is the Dragon!
  But I needn't explain it to you, sir; *you've* made up your mind,
  You're like your father — one of the dedicated
  Whose life is a quest, whose death is a victory.
  Yes! God bless you! *You've* made up your mind!
ROLAND But have I, Peter? Have I?

SYLVIE Have you, Roland dearest? Really made up your mind?
ROLAND I go away today.
SYLVIE That's no answer.
  You go away because they tell you to.
  Because your mother's brought you up on nothing
  But out-of-date beliefs and mock heroics.
  It's easy enough for her —
ROLAND Easy for her?
  Who's given her flesh and blood — and I'm the seventh son!
SYLVIE I've heard all that. They call it sacrifice
  But each new death is a stone in a necklace to her.
  Your mother, Roland, is mad.
ROLAND The world is mad.
SYLVIE Not all of it, my love. Those who have power
  Are mad enough but there *are* people, Roland,
  Who keep themselves to themselves or rather to each other,
  Living a sane and gentle life in a forest nook or a hill pocket,
  Perpetuating their kind and their kindness, keeping
  Their hands clean and their eyes keen, at one with
  Themselves, each other and nature. I had thought
  That you and I perhaps —
ROLAND   There is no perhaps
  In my tradition, Sylvie.
SYLVIE You mean in your family's.
  Isn't it time you saw that you were different?
  You're no knight errant, Roland.
ROLAND No, I'm not.
  But there is a word 'Necessity' —
SYLVIE Necessity? You mean your mother's orders.
ROLAND Not quite. But apart from that,
  I saw a man today — they call him Blind Peter —
SYLVIE Leave the blind to mislead the blind. That Peter

Is where he is because of his own weakness;
You can't help him, Roland.

ROLAND Maybe not —
But maybe I can do something to prevent
A recurrence of Blind Peters.

SYLVIE Imagination!

ROLAND Imagination? ... That things can be bettered?
That action can be worth while? That there are ends
Which, even if not reached, are worth approaching?
Imagination? Yes, I wish I had it —
I have a little — You should support that little
And not support my doubts.

    (*A drum-roll is heard behind*)

ROLAND Listen; there is the drum.
They are waiting for me at the gate.
Sylvie, I —

SYLVIE Kiss me at least.

    (*Pause*)

ROLAND I shall never —

SYLVIE See me again?
You will, Roland, you will.
I know you. You will set out but you won't go on,
Your common sense will triumph, you'll come back.
And your love for me will triumph and in the end —

ROLAND This is the end. Goodbye.

    (*The drum swells and ends on a peak*)

TUTOR To you, Roland, my last message:
For seven years I have been your tutor.
You have worked hard on the whole but whether really
You have grasped the point of it all remains to be seen.
A man lives on a sliding staircase —
Sliding downwards, remember; to be a man
He has to climb against it, keeping level
Or even ascending slightly; he will not reach
The top — if there is a top — and when he dies
He will slump and go down regardless. All the same
While he lives he must climb. Remember that.
And I thank you for your attention. Goodbye, Roland.

SERGEANT-TRUMPETER To you, Roland, my last message:

You are off now on the Quest like your brothers before you
To take a slap at the Evil that never dies.
Well, here's this trumpet; sling it around your waist
And keep it bright and clean till the time comes
When you have to sound the challenge — the first and the last
  time —
And I trust you will do your old instructor credit
And put the fear of God — or of Man — into that Dragon.
That's all now. God bless you. But remember —
Hold that note at the end.

MOTHER To you, Roland, my last message:
Here is a ring with a blood-red stone. So long as
This stone retains its colour, it means that I
Retain my purpose in sending you on the Quest.
I put it now on your finger.

ROLAND Mother! It burns.

MOTHER
That is the heat in the stone. So long as the stone is red
The ring will burn and that small circle of fire
Around your little finger will be also
The circle of my will around your mind.
I gave a ring like this to your father, Roland,
And to John and Roger and Denis and Henry and Michael
And to Gavin the last before you. My will was around and behind
  them.
Should ever you doubt or waver, look at this ring —
And feel it burn — and go on.

ROLAND Mother! Before I go —

MOTHER No more words. Go!
Turn your face to the sea. Open the gates there!
The March of Departure, Sergeant.
Let my son go out — my last. And make the music gay!
    (*A drum roll, followed by the March at full volume, then gradually*
    dwindles)

ROLAND Forgive me stopping you, sir —

SOAK⁵ Forgive you? Certainly not.
I'm on my way to the Tavern.

ROLAND
I'm on my way to the quays. Is it this turning or next?

SOAK
    Any turning you like. Look down these stinking streets —
    There's sea at the end of each of 'em.
    Yes, young man, but what's at the end of the sea?
    Never believe what they said when you booked your passage.

ROLAND But I haven't booked it yet.

SOAK
    Not booked your passage yet! Why, then there's no need to hurry.
    You come with me to the Tavern; it's only a step.

ROLAND I cannot spare a step.

SOAK All right, all right;
    If you won't come to the Tavern, the Tavern must come to you.
    Ho there, music!
        (*The orchestra strikes up raggedly — continuing while he speaks*)

SOAK That's the idea. Music does wonders, young man.
    Music can build a palace, let alone a pub.
    Come on, you masons of the Muses, swing it,
    Fling me up four walls. Now, now, don't drop your tempo;
    Easy with those hods. All right; four walls.
    Now benches — tables — No! No doors or windows;
    What drunk wants daylight? But you've left out the bar.
    Come on — 'Cellos! Percussion! All of you! A bar!
    That's right. Dismiss!
        (*The music overruns and ends*)

SOAK Barmaid.

BARMAID Yes, sir?

SOAK Give us whatever you have and make it triple.

ROLAND Just a small one for me, please.

SOAK Oh don't be so objective. One would think,
    Looking at your long face, that there's a war on.

ROLAND But —

SOAK There is no war on — and you have no face.
    Drink up. Don't be objective.

ROLAND What in the name of —

BARMAID Look, dearie; don't mind *him*.
    He always talks like that. You take my tip:
    You're new here and this town is a sea-port,
    The tone is rather ... You go somewhere inland.

ROLAND But how can I?
    I have to go to sea.

BARMAID The sea out there leads nowhere.

SOAK Come, sweetheart, the same again.

BARMAID Nowhere, I've warned you. As for our friend here,
Don't stay too long in his company.

SOAK What's that? Don't stay too long in my what?

BARMAID Company was the word.

SOAK Company? I have none. Why, how could I?
There's never anyone around where I am.
I exist for myself and all the rest is projection.
Come on, projection, drink! Dance on your strings and drink!

BARMAID Oblige him, dearie, oblige him.

SOAK There! My projection drinks.
I wrote this farce before I was born, you know —
This puppet play. In my mother's womb, dear boy —
I have never abdicated the life of the womb.
Watch, Mabel: my new puppet drinks again —
A pretty boy but I've given him no more lines.
Have I, young man? (*Pause*)
You see, he cannot speak.
All he can do henceforward is to drink —
Look! A pull on the wire — the elbow lifts.
Give him the same again.

BARMAID Well . . .

SOAK There is no well about it. Except the well
That has no bottom and that fills the world.
Triplets, I said. Where are those damned musicians?
Buck up, you puppets! Play!
     (*The orchestra strikes up a lullaby, continued behind his speech*)

SOAK Good. Serenade me now till I fall asleep
And all the notes are one — and all the sounds are silence.
Unity, Mabel, unity is my motto.
The end of drink is a whole without any parts —
A great black sponge of night that fills the world
And when you squeeze it, Mabel, it drips inwards.
D'you want me to squeeze it? Right. Piano there.
Piano — I must sleep. Didn't you hear me?
Piano, puppets. All right, pianissimo.
Nissimo . . . nissimo . . . issimo . . .
     (*The music ends and only his snoring is heard*)

ROLAND A puppet? . . . A projection? . . . How he lies!
And yet I've sometimes thought the same, you know —
The same but the other way round.

There is no evidence for anything
Except my own existence — he says his.
But he's wrong anyway — look at him snoring there.
If I were something existing in his mind
How could I go on now that he's asleep?
SOAK (*muffled*) Because I'm dreaming you.[6]
ROLAND Dreaming?
BARMAID Yes, sir.
He does have curious dreams.
SOAK Yes, and the curious thing about my dreams
Is that they always have an unhappy ending
For all except the dreamer. Thus at the moment
You'd never guess, young man, what role I've cast you for —
ROLAND What the —
BARMAID Never mind, dear.
Tomorrow he'll wake up.
ROLAND Tomorrow *he'll* wake up?
And I — shall I wake up? Perhaps to find
That this whole Quest is a dream. Perhaps I'm still at home
In my bed by the window looking across the valley
Between the yew-trees to where Sylvie lives
Not among yews but apples —
STENTOR All Aboard![7]
ROLAND What's that?
STENTOR All Aboard!
SOAK You'd never guess
What happens in my dream . . .
STENTOR All Aboard! All Aboard!
        (*The noise of the crowd materializes, increasing behind*)
Come along there, young man — unless you want to be left.
All aboard for the Further Side of the Sea,
For the Dead End of the World and the Bourne of No Return!
All Aboard, ladies and gents, knaves and fools, babes and sucklings,
Philistines, pharisees, parasites, pimps,
Nymphos and dipsos — All Aboard!
Lost souls and broken bodies; make it snappy.
That's right, folks. Mind your feet on the gangway.
        (*The noise of the crowd peaks*)
TICKET COLLECTOR
Ticket? Thank you . . . Ticket? Thank you . . .
Ticket? Thank you . . . Ticket? Thank you.

(*The crowd noises peak; the ship's siren sounds and then the crowd
noises fade out*)

STEWARD This way, sir. Let me show you your state room.
   Hot and cold and a blue light over the bed.
   Ring once for a drink, twice for an aspirin.
   Now if you want anything else — a manicure, for example —
ROLAND No, steward. A sleeping draught.
STEWARD Sir! In the morning?
ROLAND Morning be damned. My head aches.
STEWARD Drinking last night, sir?
ROLAND Thinking.
STEWARD Thinking? That's too bad, sir.
   But you'll soon get over that, sir.
   In this ship nobody thinks, sir.
   Why should they? They're at sea, sir.
   So their brains must be at sea, sir . . .
   And if your brain's at sea, sir —
ROLAND Listen! I want a sleeping draught.
   How many times do I have to ring for that?
STEWARD As many times as you like, sir.
   If you can keep awake, sir.
   But talking of sleeping draughts, sir,
   Do you hear that lady playing the fiddle?
ROLAND Fiddle? No. I don't.
STEWARD Ah, that's because she plays it in her head.
   But she's a very nice lady, sir.
   Her name, sir, is Neaera.
ROLAND Why should I care what her name is?
   I tell you, steward —
STEWARD Of course if you'd rather play tombola —
ROLAND Tombola?
STEWARD Game of chance, sir. They call out numbers.
   Kills the time, sir. Rather like life, sir.
   You can buy your tickets now in the lounge.
   The ship's started, you know, sir.
ROLAND Oh, so the ship's started?
   But I can't hear the engines.
STEWARD Can't you, sir? I was right then.
ROLAND Right? What do you mean?
STEWARD I thought so the moment I saw you.
   You don't, sir; of course you don't.

ROLAND Don't what, damn you? Don't what?

STEWARD *You* don't know where you're going, sir.

(*Pause. The ship's engines are heard on the orchestra; from them emerges the chatter of the lounge with the banal laughter of tombola players*)

OFFICER Clickety-click: sixty-six . . .

Kelly's Eye: Number One . . .

And we —

CROWD (*raggedly*) Shake the Bag!

(*The orchestral engines give place to a solo violin*)

NEAERA . . . Andantino . . . rallentando . . . adagio —

(*Her violin playing breaks off*)

My God! You startled me.

ROLAND I'm sorry, I —

NEAERA Do sit down. So you're going Nowhere too?

ROLAND On the contrary, madam —

NEAERA Call me Neaera.

ROLAND But —

NEAERA And I'll call you Roland.

ROLAND How do you know my name?

NEAERA A little bird told me. A swan, if you want to know;

He sang your name and he died.

That's right, sit down. I've seen your dossier too.

ROLAND Seen my —

NEAERA Oh yes, chéri. In the Captain's cabin.

ROLAND But how can I have a dossier? I've done nothing.

NEAERA That's just it. It's dull.

But the future part amuses me.

Oh yes, my dear, this dossier includes the future —

And you don't come out of it well.

ROLAND What do you mean?

NEAERA You never believed in this Quest of yours, you see —

The Dark Tower — the Dragon — all this blague.

That's why you were so easy to seduce

In the idle days at sea — the days that are just beginning.

(*Her violin begins again, then gives way to crowd chatter in the lounge*)

OFFICER Key of the Door: Twenty-One!

Eleventh Hour: Eleven!

Ten Commandments: Nine!

Kelly's Eye: Number One!

And we —

VOICES Shake the Bag!
> (*The violin re-emerges, held behind*)

NEAERA ... Lento ... accelerando ... presto ... calando ...
morendo ...
> (*The violin fades away*)

STEWARD Well, sir? So the lady is still practising.
Golden days, sir, golden days.
At sea, sir, have you noticed
One doesn't notice time?
You probably feel you just came on board yesterday
And yet you got your sea-legs weeks ago, sir.

ROLAND Sea-legs? Why, this trip has been so calm
I've never felt —

STEWARD That's right, sir; never feel.
There's nothing in life but profit and pleasure.
Allegro assai — some people plump for pleasure
But I now fancy the profit —
Ah thank you, sir, thank you.
The sea today[8] in the sun, sir, looks like what shall I say, sir?

ROLAND The sea today? A dance of golden sovereigns.

NEAERA The sea today is adagios of doves.

ROLAND The sea today is gulls and dolphins.

NEAERA The sea today is noughts and crosses.

OFFICER And we —

CROWD Shake the Bag!

NEAERA The sea today, Roland, is crystal.

ROLAND The sea today, Neaera, is timeless.

NEAERA The sea today is drums and fifes.

ROLAND The sea today is broken bottles.

NEAERA The sea today is snakes and ladders.

OFFICER Especially snakes!

CROWD Especially snakes!

NEAERA
Roland, what's that ring? I've never seen one like it.

ROLAND There is no other ring like it.

NEAERA A strange ring for a man ...
My colour, you know — that red ...
Why do you twitch your finger?

ROLAND Because it burns.

NEAERA It burns?
Like tingling ears perhaps? Someone is thinking of you.

ROLAND What? ... I hope not.
  Come, darling, let's have a drink.
OFFICER And we —
CROWD Shake the Bag!
ROLAND The sea today is drunken marble.
NEAERA The sea today is silver stallions.
ROLAND The sea today is — Tell me, steward:
  Where's all this floating seaweed come from?
STEWARD I imagine, sir — forgive me mentioning it —
  That we are approaching land.
ROLAND Land!
STEWARD Yes, sir — but *you* won't be landing of course.
  The best people never land, sir.
ROLAND No? ... I suppose not.
          (*Neaera's violin is heard again, held behind*)
NEAERA
  ... piu sonoro ... con forza ... accelerando ... crescendo ...
          (*The violin ends on a crashing chord and at once we hear the hubbub
          of the crowd on deck with steps on gangway, held behind*)
STENTOR Any more for the shore? Any more for the shore?
  Line up there on the forward deck
  All what wants to chance their neck!
  Any more for the shore?
TICKET COLLECTOR This way: thank you — This way: thank you —
  This way: thank you — This way: thank you.
STENTOR Anyone more? Hurry up please!
  But remember this: Once you're off
  You can't come back not ever on board.
  We leave at once. At once!
TICKET COLLECTOR This way: thank you — This way: thank you —
  This way: thank you — This way: thank you.
1ST PASSENGER
  Here, here, who're you shoving? What's the blinking hurry?
HIS WIFE That's right.
1ST PASSENGER
  Some people seem very keen to land in the future.
  Can't use their eyes — if you ask me!
HIS WIFE That's right. Look at them vicious rocks.
1ST PASSENGER
  And that tumble-down shack what thinks it's a Customs House.
HIS WIFE And them horrible mountains behind it.

2ND PASSENGER You'd think this country was uninhabited.

TICKET COLLECTOR

This way: thank you — This way: thank you — This way: thank *you*!
  (*The crowd noise fades out*)
OK, sir. That's the lot.

STENTOR Gangway up! Gangway up!
Clear away there. Mind your heads!

NEAERA What are you staring at, Roland?
Come away, chéri; the show's over.
There goes the gangway; we're moving out now.
What *are* you staring at, darling?

ROLAND (*to self*)
Was that . . . was that . . . I couldn't see in the face of the sun but —
Steward, you've sharp eyes.
Did you see over there on the quay, sitting on a rusty bollard —

STEWARD Hsh, sir, Neaera will hear you.
Yes, sir; a very nice piece.
She was looking at you, sir, too — staring in fact, one might say,
Seems to be staring still — but what's she doing now?
Climbing up on the bollard?
Good Lord, sir, that's bad form; she's making gestures.

SYLVIE (*distant cry*) Roland! . . . Roland! . . .

ROLAND Sylvie!
I knew it. Out of my way there!
  (*The orchestra is brought in behind*)

STENTOR Here, here, here! Stop him!
Man gone mad there! Don't let him jump!

NEAERA Roland! Come back!
  (*A loud splash from the orchestra, which continues behind*)

STENTOR Man overboard! Man overboard!
  (*The crowd reacts excitedly*)
Lifebuoy! Where's a lifebuoy?

VOICE Garn! This here ship don't carry no lifebuoys.
Nor he won't need one. Look! He's climbing up on the quay.

OFFICER And we —

CROWD Shake the Bag!

NEAERA Well, James . . . that's that.

STEWARD Yes, madam.

NEAERA You can drop the madam now.

STEWARD Yes, Neaera — my sweetie-pie.

NEAERA That's more like it, James, my great big he-man,

Come to my cabin now; we'll count the takings.
    (*Orchestra and ship's siren fade out*)

ROLAND There she goes now.
SYLVIE There she goes now...
    Roland, you are a hypocrite!
ROLAND No, Sylvie; merely a sleep-walker.
    Ugh! (*Shivers*)
SYLVIE The sea must have been cold. Come, let's walk.
ROLAND How did you get here, Sylvie?
SYLVIE I followed you — but not on a luxury liner.
    Mine was a cargo boat, its limit was seven knots.
ROLAND And yet you got here first.
    And now I suppose you regret it.
    Are you going to leave me, Sylvie?
SYLVIE How can I? We're marooned here.
    This is a desolate land. I suggest we keep together.
ROLAND You have the gift of forgiveness.
SYLVIE I have the gift of common sense.
    As you're bound to be seduced from your so-called Quest,
    In future, Roland, leave the seducing to me.
    Or can't I, perhaps, compete with your ladies of pleasure?
ROLAND Pleasure? That was not pleasure.
SYLVIE It was. But it was not happiness.
ROLAND And *you* offer me happiness?
SYLVIE You doubt that I have it to offer?
ROLAND No, I don't doubt that. But my tutor always said
    Happiness cannot be taken as a present.
SYLVIE Forget your tutor. This is a foreign land
    Where no one will interfere with us.
ROLAND No one? No *man* perhaps.
SYLVIE What do you mean by that?
ROLAND Look round you, Sylvie. See the deserted port,
    The ruined shacks, the slag-heaps covered with lichen
    And behind it all the frown and fear of the forest.
    This is the Dragon's demesne.
SYLVIE Roland, how childish you are.
ROLAND You think so? Look at this notice
    That flaps here on the hoarding —
    And this one and this one and this one.

SYLVIE

'Wanted for Murder' . . . 'Wanted for Murder' . . . 'Wanted' . . .

ROLAND

You're reading the words wrong. Not 'for', Sylvie, 'to'!

SYLVIE 'Wanted to Murder'. You're right.

But what does it mean?

ROLAND It means we are on a soil where murder pays.

SYLVIE It pays in many places.

ROLAND Yes, but here

The paymaster is the government — and pay-day

Is every day of the week.

The Dragon's doing, I tell you.

SYLVIE Well, if it is, *you* can't cure it.

At the best you can cure yourself —

And that only through love.

ROLAND Love?

SYLVIE Through me, Roland, through me.

(*Pause*)

ROLAND Yes, I think you're right.

Sylvie, take this ring; I cannot wear it now,

I have failed this ring — but this ring will not fail you.

SYLVIE You mean . . . ?

ROLAND Yes. Let me put it on your finger.

SYLVIE Not yet, Roland. That must be done in a church.

ROLAND And where can we find a church round here?

SYLVIE What a strange colour. Like the blood of a child.

ROLAND

I repeat! Where can we find a church or a chapel here?

TOUT 'Scusa. Lady and gentleman want guide to chapel?

ROLAND God! Where did this come from?

TOUT Me? Me come from sewer.

Me accredited guide — very good, very funny.

Lady and gentleman see chapel today?

ROLAND Where is this chapel of yours?

TOUT Chapel not mine, chapel belong to God.

Me take you there up this road, see.

Me tell you history, very much history, cheap.

(*Distant chapel bell and orchestra, held behind*)

TOUT That chapel bell, tee-hee!

Ting-a-ling for the wedding!

ROLAND What wedding?

TOUT Me not know. No, sir, nobody know.

    Happy pair not come yet.

SYLVIE Roland, this is a sign.

    Tell him to show us the way.

TOUT Me show you the way sure.

    Beautiful lady put best feet first.

    Chapel up there in forest.

ROLAND In the forest?

TOUT Sure, boss. Chapel old.

    Chapel in forest before forest grew.

    But needs repairs now bad.

    Haunted too — tee-hee!

ROLAND Haunted!

TOUT Sure, boss.

    Plenty ghosts — tu-whit, tu-whoo.

    Me need bonus for them ghosts.

ROLAND You'll have your bonus. Only get us there quick.

    Sylvie, we will exorcise these ghosts.

    You know how, my dearest?

SYLVIE I know how.

       (*The bell continues but is gradually submerged by orchestral chapel music, swelling to a close*)

PRIEST You have the ring? Good.

    Before I complete this ceremony making you man and wife

    I must deliver a warning.

    The original sin is doubt.

    And in these days of contempt for the individual

    It is also the topical sin.

    So if either of you have doubts of the holiness of marriage

    Or if either of you has doubts of the other

    And can conceive a time when he or she

    Will think again and wish this thing undone,

    Now is your time to speak. (*Pause*)

    Good. So you have no doubts. There is one other formality.

    Although there is no congregation present,

    Although apart from ourselves and a few sparrows and fieldmice

    This chapel is now empty, I must still put the question:

    If anyone here know just cause or impediment —

BLIND PETER'S VOICE I do!

GAVIN'S VOICE I do!

FATHER'S VOICE I do!

BLIND PETER'S VOICE This young man who's come to you to get
  married
  Promised me when he left, a week before I died,
  As he would avenge my blindness and bring it about
  How no one should go the way I went in future.
  Well, has he done it? No, and he'll never do it
  Not if you splice him up to that poor simple girl
  Who only dreams how he and she will be happy.
GAVIN'S VOICE No, Roland, my brother; Blind Peter is right.
  Forget your dreams of a home. You can never be happy
  If you forsake the Quest. And if you could —
  Happiness is not all. You must go on —
  Turn your back on this chapel, go on through the forest,
  Alone, always alone, and then across the desert,
  And at the other end of that desert —
FATHER'S VOICE You will find what I found, Roland.
ROLAND You?
FATHER'S VOICE
  You should know my voice though you never heard it.
  Though you had not seen me, you knew my portrait.
ROLAND My father?
FATHER'S VOICE I am still waiting to be your father.
  While you malinger, you are no son of mine.
  Well?
ROLAND Sylvie . . .
SYLVIE I know what you want . . . your ring.
  There . . . back on your finger.
  Look how it glows in this darkness.
ROLAND Glows? It will burn me up.
SYLVIE Roland, before we part —
PRIEST This chapel is now closed. I am sorry.
  Goodbye, my daughter; your way lies back,
  Back by the road you came over the hopeless sea,
  Back to your little house and your apple orchard
  And there you must marry one of your own kind
  And spray the trees in spring and raise the ladders in autumn
  And spread the shining crop on the spare-room floor and —
ROLAND Sylvie, before we part —
PRIEST This chapel is now closed. I am sorry.
  Goodbye, my son; your way lies forward,
  Forward through the gibbering guile of the forest,

Forward through the silent doubt of the desert.
And here let me warn you: if in the forest
You hear any voices call from the trees,
Pay no attention, Roland, pay no attention —
    (*Long bird screech leading into 'forest' music, held behind*)
PARROT Pretty Polly! Pretty Polly!
  Who's this coming now?
RAVEN Caw-caw! Caw-caw!
  Who's a-walkin' in *my* forest?
PARROT Pretty Polly! The leaves have fallen.
RAVEN Caw-caw! He's walking late.
PARROT Pretty Polly! He's looking pale.
RAVEN Caw-caw! His bones will be paler.
PARROT Pretty Polly! Here he comes.
RAVEN Caw-caw! Greet him!
PARROT Where are you going, Roland, so fast?
RAVEN Roland, running away from your past?
PARROT } You can't do that! You can't do that!
RAVEN
PARROT Still on the road? Still on the Quest?
RAVEN None achieve it but the best.
PARROT } You're not the sort. You're not the sort.
RAVEN
PARROT Why not stop, my dear young man?
RAVEN Let heroes die as heroes can.
PARROT } *You* must *live!* *You* must *live!*
RAVEN
    (*The 'forest' music swells up, held behind*)
PARROT Pretty Polly! He's passed us by.
RAVEN Caw-caw! The devil take him.
PARROT Pretty Polly! The devil will.
    (*The 'forest' music gives place to 'desert' music, brought to close*)
ROLAND Oh this desert!
  The forest was bad enough but this beats all.
    (*The music ends*)
  When my tutor described it to me, it sounded strange
  But now I am here, with the grit of it filling my shoes,
  I find that the worst thing about it is this:
  The desert is something familiar.
  And with no end — no end.
CLOCK VOICE Tick Tock, Tick Tock,

Sand and grit, bones and waste,
A million hours — all the same,
A million minutes — each an hour,
And nothing stops for nothing starts
But the hands move, the dead hands move,
The desert is the only clock —
Tick Tock, Tick Tock,
Tick Tock, Tick Tock . . .

ROLAND Flat — no shape — no colour — only here and there
A mirage of the past — something I've met before —
Figures arising from dust, repeating themselves,
Telling me things that I have no wish to remember.
Mirage . . . mirage . . . mirage . . .[9]

CLOCK VOICE Tick Tock, Tick Tock (*etc.*)

SOAK A pretty boy — but I've given him no more lines.
He'd never guess what happens in my dream.
Look — pull on the wire, his feet move forward.
Left Right, Left Right . . .
    (*He synchronizes with the Clock Voice*)

CLOCK VOICE ⎱Tick Tock (*etc.*)
SOAK   ⎰Left Right (*etc.*)

STEWARD Golden days, sir, golden days.
In the desert sir, have you noticed
One doesn't notice time?
But I thought so the moment I saw you:
You don't know where you're going.
Golden days, golden days . . .
    (*He synchronizes with the Clock Voice and Soak*)

CLOCK VOICE ⎞Tick Tock (*etc.*)
SOAK   ⎟Left Right (*etc.*)
STEWARD ⎠Golden Days (*etc.*)

NEAERA . . . adagio . . . rallentando . . .
This dossier includes your future —
You don't come out of it well.
But kiss me, Roland, kiss me.
Kiss me, kiss me . . .
    (*Synchronizes*)

CLOCK VOICE ⎞Tick Tock (*etc.*)
SOAK   ⎟Left Right (*etc.*)
STEWARD ⎟Golden Days (*etc.*)
NEAERA   ⎠Kiss me (*etc.*)

SYLVIE But why must you go so quickly?
Now that the sun's come out.
You, Roland — you're no knight errant.
Your love for me will triumph, you'll come back,
Then you and I, you and I . . .
        (*Synchronizes*)

CLOCK VOICE	Tick Tock (*etc.*)
SOAK	Left Right (*etc.*)
STEWARD	Golden days (*etc.*)
NEAERA	Kiss me (*etc.*)
SYLVIE	You and I (*etc.*)

ROLAND No!
        (*The voices break off; then 'desert' music which ends*)
Shapes of dust and fancy! Unreal voices!
But where is the voice that launched me on my road?
Where is the shape the first that I remember?
Why doesn't *she* appear — even in fancy?
It is the least she could — Mother, where are you?
Yes, you; I'm calling you — my mother who sent me forth —
It was all your doing. But for you
I who had no beliefs of my own,
I who had no will of my own,
Should not be here today pursuing
A dark tower that is only dark
Because it does not exist. And Mother!
It is only your will that drives me still
As signified in the blood-red stone
I wear on my finger under my glove
Which burns me like a living weal.
. . . Burns me? . . . Burns me? . . . It always has —
But have I gone numb? I can feel nothing.
Off with this glove! I *can't* believe that —
        (*A chord from the orchestra*)
The ring! The ring!
The colour is gone; the blood has gone out of it.
But that must mean . . . that means . . .
MOTHER'S VOICE It means, my son, that I want you back.
ROLAND And the Quest then?
MOTHER'S VOICE Lapses.
On my deathbed I have changed my mind;
I am bearing now a child of stone.

He can go on the Quest. But you, Roland — come back!

ROLAND The ring ... is always right.

Recall! Reprieve! A thousand years of sunshine!
And the apples will be in bloom round Sylvie's house.
Was that my mother's voice? Look at the ring.
It is pale as death, there is no more breach of duty,
Her will is not behind me. Breach of duty?
If she is dying, *there* is the breach of duty —
Not to be there. Mother, you sent me out
And I went out. Now that you call me back
I will come back! The desert take this ring —
It serves no further purpose!
(*An orchestral clink*)
What was that?
It must have struck something hard. That's the first
Sound I've heard in the desert. Where did I throw that ring?
A stone? But a carved stone! Looks like a milestone.
As if the desert had any use for milestones!
How many miles to Babylon? Let's see now;
These letters are choked with sand. 'To Those ... To Those ...'
(*Reading*) 'To Those Who Did Not Go Back —
Whose Bones being Nowhere, their signature is for All Men —
Who went to their Death of their own Free Will
Bequeathing Free Will to Others.'

PARROT Pretty Polly! A tall story!

RAVEN Caw-caw! And not so new!

PARROT Pretty Polly! Unknown warriors!

RAVEN Caw-caw! Nobody cares!

PARROT 'Who went to their death'! — Pretty Polly!

RAVEN 'Of their own free will'! — Caw-caw!

ROLAND Of their own free will? It wasn't like that with me.
It was my mother pushed me to this point
And now she pulls me back. Let's see this ring —
Where's it fallen? Hm. Yes, there's no mistake,
Red no longer: my mother wants me back
And indeed it is high time; this desert has no end
Nor even any contour, the blank horizon
Retreats and yet retreats; without either rise or fall
Repeats, retreats, defeats; there is no sign of a tower —
You could see a tower for miles; there is not even a knoll,
Flatness is all — and nothing. Own free will!

As if I Roland had ever ... Tutors, trumpeters, women,
Old soaks and crooked stewards, everyone I have met
Has played his music on me. Own free will!
Three words not one of which I understand!
All right, mother dear, I'm coming.
    (*'Desert' music sounds and ends*)
Now ... Where are my footsteps? Better follow them back.
Back to the forest and through it and so to the shore of the sea.
Are these my footsteps? But how small they look!
Well, you're a small man, Roland — Better admit it —
You'll be still smaller now ... But are these my footsteps?
They are so near together — and I thought
I was walking with great strides! O Roland, Roland,
You thought yourself a hero and you walked
With little steps like that! Now you must watch
These niggling foot-prints all your return journey
To underline your shame. What's shame to me
Who never had free will? ... 'Their own free will
Bequeathing free will to others.' Others indeed!
I begin to think my drunken friend was right
In his subjective tavern; there are no others
Apart from the projections of my mind
And, once that mind is empty, man's a desert.
Others! Who are these others! Where can I find them?
CHILD'S VOICE Nowhere, Roland. Nowhere.
ROLAND There! What did I say? There *are* no others —
CHILD'S VOICE You will never find us if you go forward —
    For you will be dead before we are born.
    You will never find us if you go back —
    For you will have killed us in the womb.
ROLAND What! So I'm an infanticide now?
CHILD'S VOICE Not yet. But if you go back.
ROLAND Who said I was going back?
CHILD'S VOICE I thought you had made up your mind.
ROLAND I never make up my mind!
    Didn't I say that my mother — Look, I'll leave it to chance;
    Chance is as good an arbiter as any.
    Watch me, you unborn children. See this tiny cactus?
    I will strip it leaf by leaf — let that decide —
    This Year, Next Year, Eena-Meena — *you* know the game, you unborn
      children.

Now.

Forward — back; forward — back; forward — back — forward;
Back — forward; back — forward; back — forward — BACK!
There! The voice of chance. The oracle of the cactus.
Back! Back! That's what the cactus says.
But *I'm* — hold it, you unborn children!
Do you think that I'll let a cactus dictate to me?
'Back!' says my love and my frailty but *I'm* —
No, no, Mother, don't pull on the string;
Free will or no, I must pay my debts —
The debts I incurred the hour I was born.
'Back!' says the cactus but *I'm* ... going forward![10]
Mother, don't pull on the string; you must die alone.
Forgive me, dear, but — I tell you I'm going forward.
Forward, Roland ... into the empty desert.
Where all is flat and colourless and silent.

> (*He pauses; the orchestra creeps in with a heartbeat rhythm, held behind*)

Silent? ... Then what's this?
Something new! A *sound*! But a sound of what?
Don't say that it's my heart! Why, Roland you poor fool,
Who would think you had one? You must be afraid;
It is fear reveals the heart.

> (*Heartbeat louder*)

Aha, you piece of clockwork —
Trying to have your little say while you can!
Before your wheels run down here in the empty desert.

> (*Sudden chord; heartbeat continues behind*)[11]

Empty? ... Where have those mountains come from?
Closing round in a ring. Hump-backed horrors
That want to be in at the death. And where's the horizon?
A moment ago this was level. What's the game?
A confidence trick? A trap! I am cooped in.
A circle of ugly cliffs — a lobster-pot of rock!
Silence, my stupid heart! This looks like ... looks like what?
This looks like the great circus in Ancient Rome,
Only there is no audience — and no lions.
No audience did I say?

> (*Chord; heartbeat behind — and steadily increasing*)

No audience! Why, that's Gavin on top of that peak!
And Michael and Denis and Henry and Roger and John!

And men that I've never seen — in outlandish clothes,
Some of them even in armour. And there's Blind Peter —
With sight in his eyes, for he's pointing —
And my father too — I remember him from the album —
And my tutor — he must be dead — looking graver than ever
And — well to the front of course — my dear old Sergeant-Trumpeter.
    (*Figure in the music*)

SERGEANT-TRUMPETER Roland! Hold the note at the end.

GAVIN Be ready, old boy. This is it!

BLIND PETER Strike a good blow to avenge Blind Peter.

FATHER Your heritage, my son. You were born to fight.

ROLAND Fight? Fight whom? This circus has no lions.

TUTOR No lions, Roland? Have you forgotten your lessons?
    I never mentioned lions; it was a dragon —
    And only that for lack of a better name.

ROLAND
    Yes, yes, dragon of course — but you told me, my good tutor,
    The Dragon would not appear until I came to the Tower
    And until I had blown my blast — Well, there is no Tower!

GAVIN That fooled me, Roland my brother.

FATHER Look over there, Roland my son.

ROLAND Where? . . . Oh *that* little thing?
    Like a wart coming out of the ground!

FATHER It's growing, Roland, it's growing.

TUTOR You should recognize it from my lectures.

BLIND PETER That's the joker all right.
    (*Figure in the music*)

GAVIN The tower! The Dark Tower!

SERGEANT-TRUMPETER Quick now, my lad. Unsling your trumpet.

ROLAND But —

FATHER It's growing, my son; waste no time.

ROLAND It's growing; yes, it's growing.

CHILD'S VOICE Growing! Ooh! Look at it.
    Strike a good blow for us unborn children.

MOTHER And strike a blow for all dead mothers.

GAVIN Jump to it, Roland.

FATHER Waste no time.

SERGEANT-TRUMPETER Remember that challenge call.
    Blow it the way I taught you.

ROLAND
    Yes, dear friends, I will blow it the way you taught me.

I Roland, the black sheep, the unbeliever —
Who never did anything of his own free will —
Will do this now to bequeath free will to others.
Ahoy there, tower, Dark Tower, you're getting big,
Your shadow is cold upon me. What of that?
And you, you Dragon or whatever you are
Who make men beasts, come out — here is a man;
Come out and do your worst.
    (*Orchestra ends*)

ROLAND Wrist be steady
As I raise the trumpet so — now fill my lungs —
    (*Challenge Call rings out — with orchestra; Sergeant-Trumpeter
    speaks as the last long note is reached*)

SERGEANT-TRUMPETER
Good lad, Roland. Hold that note at the end.
    (*The trumpet holds it, to close*)

PRISONER'S PROGRESS

a radio parable play

Prisoner's Progress (broadcast 27 April 1954 on the Third Programme) was a BBC entry for the Italia Prize 1954. (The play won the Premio Italiano, the second prize, while Dylan Thomas's *Under Milk Wood* won the Italia Prize itself.) This parable play universalizes the situation of prisoner-of-war camps in World War II and desperate escape attempts — here ending in death for the unheroic hero, Thomas Waters, played by Anthony Jacobs, and heroine Alison, played by Cecile Chevreau. The accordionist Toralf Tollefsen played and sang ballads and nursery songs, improvising along the way. The copytext used here is the prize entry text, preserved (along with a parallel translation into French) at the Humanities Research Center of the University of Texas at Austin, which makes cuts or condensations of the original typescript — most changes anticipated in the broadcasting text as used in the studio during rehearsal and production.

Prisoner's Progress, like two earlier programmes of mine, *The Dark Tower* and *One Eye Wild*, is a parable play. The hero of each of the three is to some extent a lost soul and, on the surface at least, an unheroic figure. But in each case the hero finds himself at the end. All three programmes present types and moods and problems of our time, but whereas *The Dark Tower* is unabashed fantasy and, in spite of medieval trimmings, not to be pigeon-holed in any particular period or place, the other two are more obviously topical in detail and far more naturalistic in treatment, the symbolical or fantastic or 'poetic' elements being brought in by sleight of hand.

In *One Eye Wild* this is achieved by a trick similar to that in *The Private Life of Walter Mitty*; in *Prisoner's Progress* it is largely done by quotation. Since I was treating my characters naturalistically, I could not endow them with an unnatural eloquence, so instead I gave them naturalistic opportunities to draw upon: the Bible, *The Ancient Mariner*, the ballad of True Thomas, etc. Similarly with the music, which is limited to voice and accordion. The nursery rhyme tunes and popular songs like 'Comin' Round the Mountain' are always introduced for the first time naturalistically, but the words were chosen for their double meanings and the tunes reappear later with significant variations (brilliantly improvised by Toralf Tollefsen) to underline the changes of mood and situation.

The whole point about *Prisoner's Progress* is that it exists on two planes. The prisoner-of-war camp is closely based upon real camps in World War II as described to me by René Cutforth,[2] who also helped me very much by analysing the varying emotional reactions to such camps of different types of prisoner. But, in order not to confuse the issue, I avoided any mention of Germans or British and supposed a war between two unspecified forces known as the Browns and the Greys (both colours being intentionally sombre).

Nothing happens in the programme which could not happen in a twentieth-century war, but certain things such as the escape through the neolithic passage tomb, while not impossible, may seem improbable (though I am told that certain prisoners in North Africa did make their escape through an ancient Roman underground gallery). Of course the whole business of tunnelling and, still more, the intrusion of the Stone Age, give an obvious chance for double meanings. And both the imprisonment and the escape in *Prisoner's Progress* are intended to stand for all kinds of imprisonment and escape — moral, intellectual, spiritual. Here again there is a parallel with *The Dark Tower* in which the Desert stands for a spiritual or inner desert. And just as Roland's chief complaint about the Desert is that it 'is something familiar', so Waters's chief complaint about his prison camp is that 'I have been here before'.

CHARACTERS

CATSMEAT, a coloured cook
EMSLEY, an effeminate athlete
PUBLIC ADDRESS (MALE)
THE COMMANDANT
SENIOR GREY OFFICER (SGO)
THE PADRE
CANFORD, officer on the Escape Committee
VOICE
WATERS, the hero
POTTER, a very ordinary officer
BATTY DE VERE, a prisoner obsessed by time
MACGREGOR (MAC), a Scottish officer on the escape team
GUGGENHEIM, a woman archaeologist
DIANA, a good-time girl
ALISON, the heroine
PUBLIC ADDRESS (FEMALE)
REGAN, an Irish bomber pilot
GUARD
THE UPLAND WOMAN

PRISONER'S PROGRESS

NARRATOR The programme which follows is a fable of imprisonment and of escape. While it is loosely based upon data from World War Two, it makes no claim to be documentary.

There is a war going on between the Greys and the Browns. The Greys are on our side, the Browns are the enemy, but the programme is focused not on the war itself but simply on one or two prisoners — who are prisoners in more senses than one.

(*Fade up accordion playing 'Comin' Round the Mountain'; then Catsmeat joins in singing*)

CATSMEAT (*singing*) She'll be comin' round the mountain when she comes,

She'll be comin' round the mountain when she comes,

She'll be comin' round the mountain, comin' round the —

EMSLEY Catsmeat! Stop that! (*Song and accordion break off*) I really loathe that song.

CATSMEAT Anything I can do for you, Mr Emsley?

EMSLEY Why sing about mountains when we've got one here on our doorstep?

CATSMEAT Yes, Mr Emsley. Mighty big mountain too. Need to be a mighty big lady to come round that one.

EMSLEY Catsmeat! How is the oil situation?

CATSMEAT Not too good, Mr Emsley. Nothing but machine oil now.

EMSLEY Yes, but how much of it?

CATSMEAT Maybe half a pint till the parcels come.

EMSLEY Oh, till the parcels come!

CATSMEAT Yes, half a pint at the most. Makes cooking kind of difficult.

EMSLEY Could you spare me a spoonful or two?

CATSMEAT Oh Lord, not two, Mr Emsley.

EMSLEY One spoonful then. Dessert spoon.

CATSMEAT Dessert spoon? That would be four cigarettes.

EMSLEY Four? It used to be one.

CATSMEAT Times is hard, Mr Emsley.

EMSLEY Catsmeat, you're just a Jew.

CATSMEAT No, Mr Emsley, I'm a Negro. And the white world owes me a living. Besides, Mr Emsley, I'm a cook, my business is gentlemen's stomachs. You don't want oil for your stomach, you just want it for massage. Now I can't call that priority.

EMSLEY Two cigarettes.

CATSMEAT No, sir. It ain't priority.

EMSLEY Of course it's priority. You know very well I'm a sprinter. When this war started I was almost Olympic class.

CATSMEAT When this war started ... maybe. Four cigarettes or nothing.

EMSLEY Two cigarettes.

CATSMEAT No, sir.

EMSLEY Three cigarettes.

CATSMEAT Four.

EMSLEY I haven't got four.

CATSMEAT You have.

EMSLEY Three cigarettes.

> (*Catsmeat chuckles and begins to hum 'Comin' Round the Mountain'; he is interrupted by an army whistle*)

CATSMEAT What's that?

EMSLEY Parcels!

CATSMEAT Parcels comin' round the mountain.

EMSLEY Oh dear God, send me a big one. (*Whistle repeated*) Do you really think it is? Look, take your four cigarettes.

CATSMEAT Thank you, Mr Emsley.

PUBLIC ADDRESS (MALE) Attention everyone. Attention everyone. Announcing the arrival of a new batch of prisoners.

CATSMEAT Prisoners!

EMSLEY Here! Give me back my cigarettes.

PUBLIC ADDRESS All officers will assemble at once on the parade ground.

CATSMEAT Too late, Mr Emsley. Here's your oil.

EMSLEY Now let me tell you what I think of you, you filthy black thief, you capitalist, you —

CATSMEAT Too late, Mr Emsley. Don't keep the Commandant waiting. Thank the Lord I ain't an officer.

> (*The scene changes to the parade ground*)

COMMANDANT For prisoners newly arrived and as remembrance to all there is this which clear must be made.

So. This is a prisoner-of-war camp. Here man has guards, man has wire, here all the night man has searchlights. Therefore man here must be happy.

For prisoners newly arrived a pleasant surprise this comes but here must you run your own business.

And now I am overhanding you to your own Senior Officer. How man must be happy he also to you explain will.

(*Pause*)

SENIOR GREY OFFICER Gentlemen, I propose to be brief; most of you know all this already. You heard what the Commandant said. We do in fact more or less run our own show in this camp. And that being so, there's one thing I want to emphasize. You see that mountain. The nearest Grey troops who're not prisoners are several hundred miles beyond it. But in the shadow of that mountain we've made ourselves a little Grey island. An island of civilization. An island, I may add, of discipline. And so long as I'm here, that discipline will not be relaxed. Which reminds me: this is for the new arrivals. You see over there beyond the wire a very high fence of corrugated iron. That is put there for an object. Beyond that fence is another compound, a compound for female prisoners. Like us those women are Greys, but officers, for their own good, will kindly forget their existence. That is an order.

The Chaplain would now like to speak to you.

PADRE Well, chaps; I just wanted to welcome the newcomers and to tell them this place isn't really as bad as it looks. There's one thing about Camp Malcanto 22 and that is we have lots of fun here. And if any of you new boys are keen on theatricals, well, that's my special domain.

Just one other point. If any of you have your little problems — and they do crop up even here at times — just drop round to my office at the end of Hut Five F. It's only 8 feet by 6 but I call it Liberty Hall. So please do remember that, chaps.

Now here's Major Canford to talk to you.

CANFORD Gentlemen, there's one thing about Malcanto 22 and that, I'm proud to say, is our study groups. I'm Supplies Officer here but I also organize the courses. We've got courses by now in nearly every-thing. Languages, accountancy, advertising, poultry-farming — we have to imagine the poultry — everything you'll need if and when this damned war's over —

VOICE *If* and when, sir?

CANFORD Everything you'll need on return to civilian life. By the way, any of you newcomers ever hold a teaching job? (*Pause*) No?

WATERS Yes, sir.

CANFORD Name and rank?

WATERS Waters, sir. Second lieutenant.

CANFORD University lecturer?

WATERS No, sir. Schoolmaster.

CANFORD Public school?

WATERS Grammar school, sir.

CANFORD Oh. Subjects?

WATERS Pretty well everything, sir.

CANFORD Special subjects?

WATERS Special er . . . ? English and history.

CANFORD Oh. As a matter of fact we don't have courses in those. Could have, I suppose, but not very functional.

WATERS As a matter of fact, sir, I'm not awfully good at teaching.

CANFORD Aren't you? Any other academics here?

POTTER Yes, sir.

CANFORD Name and rank?

POTTER Potter. Lieutenant. *I* taught in a public school, sir.

CANFORD Good man. What did you teach?

POTTER PT, sir. And boxing and things.

CANFORD Oh. Excellent, but that's not quite my province. You'd better talk to Mr Emsley about that afterwards. He's our athletics organizer. You'll find him, I expect, in the ping-pong room.

(*The scene changes to the ping-pong room. Fade up ping-pong and crowd background*)

EMSLEY Yes, my dear, I'm Emsley. And you really ran at the White City? Oh, I'm so glad they brought you to Malcanto 22. How were you captured by the way?

POTTER Oh it was quite a party. But I can't tell you all that much about it because I was knocked out so early on. Waters might tell you more details. He has the platoon on my right.

EMSLEY Waters?

POTTER Haven't you met him yet? Well, maybe you haven't missed much. Very strange bird indeed. Still, he might remember some details.

(*Fade up ping-pong and background then fade out*)

EMSLEY Waters, my dear, how did you land in the bag?

WATERS Me? Oh it started long ago. I was a bastard, you see.

EMSLEY Oh don't. I'm sure you weren't.

WATERS Literally, I mean. Illegitimate. And I never met my father till just before this war. So that was why I joined up.

EMSLEY Why, was he nasty?

WATERS No, he was terribly nice but he made a pass at my wife.

EMSLEY Oh, so you're married?

WATERS Not now. What's the name of that mountain?

EMSLEY Oh everyone calls it the mountain. If you wanted to escape from here, that's what you'd have to get over.

WATERS Does anyone ever escape?

EMSLEY No, but they're always trying. To overstep the trip wire man shall be shot. And to overclimb that mountain, man, I should think, must be crazy.

WATERS Lies south, doesn't it?

EMSLEY Yes, it cuts off the sun a lot. It's horribly cold here in winter; one needs lots of newspaper underclothes.

WATERS You've been here long?

EMSLEY Ages. Absolute ages. Still, I contrive to keep fit. Ever do any running yourself?

WATERS Running? Yes. How can one avoid it in the Army?

EMSLEY No, I mean real running. Hundred yards, the quarter, the mile —

WATERS Oh no, nothing like that. I'm just a bastard, you see; I never went in for sport much. Except, of course, for mountaineering.

EMSLEY Really, my dear? Mountaineering?

(*Fade up accordion — 'Comin' Round the Mountain' — with chatter and accordion behind*)

BATTY Excuse me, my dear fellow, do you know the time?

MAC 10.45. But what does it matter?

BATTY No, no, I mean the day.

EMSLEY Wednesday, I think. Yes, bridge night.

BATTY No, my dear fellow, I'm sorry. I mean the day of the month.

EMSLEY That's a poser.

MAC Twenty-first or twenty-second.

BATTY Thank you so much. Which month?

WATERS Oh God! One might be back at school. Not a corner to oneself — except in one's mind. And that's a corner and a half. Full of little ifs — if onlies.

If only they hadn't moved us to that sector.

If only I hadn't gone up for a commission.

If only I hadn't joined up in the first place.

If only I hadn't married Vera.

If only I hadn't met my father.
If only *he'd* not met my mother.
If only ... if only ... if only.

BATTY Excuse me, Waters my dear fellow, can you tell me what year we're in?

WATERS Year? ... Year?

PUBLIC ADDRESS Attention everyone! Bridge for tonight has been cancelled. (*Crowd reactions*) I repeat: Bridge for tonight has been cancelled. As a result of this, the Chaplain will be in his office should anyone wish to consult him.

(*Fade out accordion. The scene changes to the Chaplain's office*)

PADRE So you have a little problem, Waters?

WATERS Well, no, Padre ... Rather a big one.

PADRE Could you speak up? I'm a little deaf, you know. Perforated eardrum. Hazards of war, as they say.

WATERS I said rather a big one.

PADRE Rather a big what?

WATERS Problem.

PADRE Sex?

WATERS No, not really.

PADRE It wouldn't be religion, would it?

WATERS Well, er, no. I suppose it's really psychological.

PADRE What's that?

WATERS Psychological.

PADRE Oh, psychological. Well, we've no trick cyclists here, so *I'll* have to do my little best for you. Now what exactly is the trouble?

WATERS The whole point is that it's *not* exact. I don't quite know how to put it. You see, this camp, this whole inane insane muddle of bits and pieces, this make-believe work and make-believe play and make-believe quarrels and intrigues and friendships, this averagely odd and oddly average community, misers and morons and scapegoats and scavengers, snow-blind, sand-happy, punch-drunk, thought-shy with the enemy's wire and our own red tape all round us, with the snoopers and the searchlights and the rollcalls — oh well, what do you expect.

PADRE It must still seem strange to you of course.

WATERS No, that's the point, it doesn't. Padre, I've been here before.

PADRE What's that?

WATERS I've been here before.

PADRE I assure you you're mistaken. I'm about the oldest inhabitant here, I can tell you exactly when Malcanto Twenty-Two was started.

WATERS No, no, I mean before that. I've been here long, long, before — almost before I can remember. And what's more, I've never really left here. That mountain up there, it's always been between me and the sun.

PADRE Let me see. How long have you been here?

WATERS Three months.

PADRE How long?

WATERS Three months.

PADRE Oh it's still early days then. Three months more and you'll feel different. Tell you what. Ever gone in for theatricals?

WATERS Theatricals?

PADRE Drama.

WATERS Drama? . . . When I came in and found him kissing her . . . the photograph of my mother, she'd been dead just a year you know, it was the only thing on the mantelpiece . . . I took it in my hands and went up to him and . . . it was the only one I had too —

PADRE What play was this?

WATERS Play? It was the only thing on the mantelpiece. The only photo I had. And after that I had nothing. So that was why I joined up.

PADRE Our next show, you know, is *The Importance of Being Earnest*; I'm trying to cast it at the moment. Well, it might take your mind off things if . . . Let's see, we haven't got Chasuble cast. Or Merriman either, I think. Not to mention Cecily Cardew. You know the play, of course?

WATERS What play?

PADRE What?

WATERS What play?

PADRE I've told you. *The Importance of Being Earnest*.

WATERS

'I never met a man who looked
    With such a wistful eye
Upon that little tent of blue
    Which prisoners call the sky
And at every drifting cloud that went
    With sails of silver by.'

PADRE Sorry, old man, what's all that about?

WATERS Same author.

PADRE Oh. Well, if you know him all that well . . . I'm wondering if you'd be better as Merriman or Chasuble.

WATERS Padre, does anyone ever escape from here?

PADRE What's that?

WATERS Does anyone ever escape from here?

PADRE Escape? What made you think of that? No, no one's brought it off yet. Of course there's an Escape Committee; extremely thorough, I'm told. But to get back to the show —

WATERS It involves climbing that mountain?

PADRE Only way to go, I believe. But don't start thinking on those lines. They've a long waiting list, you know. Even if they put you on it, you might have to wait for years.

WATERS But I *have* been waiting for years.

PADRE Now, now, old chap, cut it out. And these tunnels of theirs, they're always discovered, I assure you.

WATERS If I really wanted to escape ... But how can one tell what one wants?

PADRE Look, *I've* a suggestion — and please don't let it embarrass you. I don't know if you're a believer — lots of the boys here aren't — but still they quite often find it soothing. Like me to read you the Gospel?

WATERS I'd rather have the Old Testament.

PADRE Which Testament?

WATERS The *Old* Testament.

PADRE Oh, the Old Testament? That's not quite as soothing, you know.

WATERS I'll find you the passage. You read it.

(*Fade up air-raid siren and behind*)

PADRE Oh, air raids again? Haven't had one of those for months.

WATERS There you are. The Book of Job.

PADRE Oh. Starting here? Right.
'After this opened Job his mouth and cursed his day.'
They don't bomb *us*, you know — except by mistake of course. They're after that big Brown air base.
'And Job spake and said: Let the day perish in which I was born, and the night in which it was said: There is a man child conceived.'
Hope they knock the daylights out of them.
'Let that day be darkness; let not God — '
You know, Waters, I'm not dead sure that Job is quite the thing for you. I know it's beautiful English but —

WATERS 'Let darkness and the shadow of death stain it; let a cloud dwell upon it; let the blackness of the day terrify it.'

PADRE My word! So you know it by heart!

WATERS 'Why died I not from the womb? Why did I not give up the ghost when I came out of the belly?'

PADRE Er ... You seem to have skipped something.

WATERS 'For now should I have lain still and been quiet, I should have slept: then had I been at rest' — How does it go on?

PADRE Can't hear our planes. Hope to goodness that wasn't a false alarm.

WATERS 'Or as an untimely hidden birth I had not been; as infants which never saw light. There the wicked cease from troubling and there the weary be at rest.

For the thing which I greatly feared is come upon me' —

PADRE Skipped again, I'm afraid.

WATERS 'And that which I was afraid of is come unto me. I was not in safety, neither had I rest, neither was I quiet; yet trouble came.'

(*Shutting of heavy book*)

PADRE Bravo, Waters! Never mind the slips, I can see you've an actor's memory. Chasuble, we'll have you as Chasuble.

WATERS No really, Padre, I don't want to.

PADRE Yes, you'll be excellent as Chasuble. But what's puzzling me is: where are those blasted planes of ours? False alarm, I suppose. Oh well, well, not every alarm bears fruit.

(*Pause; the scene changes. Catsmeat with accordion*)

CATSMEAT

I had a little nut tree,
    Nothing would it bear
But a silver nutmeg
    And a golden pear;
The King of Spain's daughter (*breaks off*)
Oh sorry, Mr Waters, I didn't see you. Anything I can do for you?

WATERS Where did you learn that song?

CATSMEAT I just picked it up. Why?

WATERS Sing it again, will you?

CATSMEAT Sure, Mr Waters. With pleasure. (*Sings*)

I had a little nut tree —

WATERS Slower.

CATSMEAT Slower? Sure. (*Sings*)

I had a little nut tree,
    Nothing would it bear
But a silver nutmeg
    And a golden pear;
The King of Spain's daughter

    Came to visit me,
  And all for the sake
    Of my little nut tree.

WATERS
  And all for the sake
    Of my little nut tree.
    (*Pause*)
The tree of the knowledge of good and evil.

CATSMEAT Oh no, Mr Waters. That was an apple tree.

WATERS The King of Spain's daughter ... I suppose she was a brunette.

CATSMEAT Sure thing, Mr Waters. And she played the castanets.

WATERS She played the piano. Badly.
    (*Pause*)

CATSMEAT Mr Waters?

WATERS Yes?

CATSMEAT You broods too much.

WATERS I always have. Don't you?

CATSMEAT Got no time. I cook.
    (*Sings with accordion*)
Oh what have you got for dinner, Mrs Bond?
There's beef in the larder and ducks in the pond.
Dilly, dilly, dilly, come to be killed,
For you must be stuffed and my customers filled.
My customers filled — that's my job.

WATERS Come to be killed — that's mine. Tell me, Catsmeat, what do you think about women?

CATSMEAT I think a heap — but I suppresses it. Like a cigarette, Mr Waters?

WATERS What do you want for it?

CATSMEAT Couple of vouchers will do. That's to you, Mr Waters. If it was anyone else —

WATERS OK, couple of vouchers. You must be getting quite rich here.

CATSMEAT The white world owes me a living. I came to this camp as a batman, mighty little future in that. But there sure is a future in cooking.
    (*Hums 'Mrs Bond', then breaks off*)
Mr Waters?

WATERS What?

CATSMEAT *The Importance of Being Earnest.*

WATERS What about it?

CATSMEAT The Padre wants you for it. He was looking for you half an hour ago.

WATERS Well, he's not going to get me. Why, even the name puts me off.

(*The scene changes to the rehearsal room*)

PADRE *The Importance of Being Earnest*! I know you voted for a leg-show but perhaps you'd not read this play then. Take it from me, there's a laugh in every line. And as for the leg-show, please don't blame me for that, it was the SGO banned it.

MAC That man would ban the Song of Solomon.

EMSLEY Hsh, my dear. Even these walls have ears.

MAC Brown ears, perhaps. Not Grey ones.

PADRE Come on, chaps, let's get cracking. Now we've got nearly all the cast here; I'm sorry Waters hasn't shown up for Chasuble, but I'll get him for our second rehearsal. And we're also shy of a woman.

MAC Shy of a woman? Plenty of women next door.

EMSLEY Now, now, Mac my dear, really — !

MAC That female compound! The discoveries one might make there! The discoveries, man, the discoveries!

(*The scene changes to the women's compound*)

GUGGENHEIM Diana! Come here at once. I've made a fantastic discovery.

DIANA What is it? The Stone Age again?

GUGGENHEIM Please call it the New Stone Age. Yes, it is something neolithic. I knew this was a site as soon as I picked up that arrowhead. But you will not guess what I picked up this time. Go on, Diana dear; guess.

DIANA How can I? *I'm* not an archaeologist.

ALISON Hello, Guggenheim. Why are you looking so flushed?

DIANA She's found something again.

ALISON Nice bit of flint to cut up our Sunday horsemeat?

DIANA No, no, Alison, something much more shattering. Hurry up, Guggenheim. Tell us.

GUGGENHEIM Well, I was down below the floor of our hut again —

DIANA Regular old mole, isn't she?

GUGGENHEIM If I am telling you, please do not interrupt. I go down there to hide my diary, you know there is three foot of space beneath the floorboards —

ALISON Can't say I've ever been down there.

GUGGENHEIM And this time I thought I will do a little crawl. I had my torch with me of course —

DIANA How that battery never runs out I —

GUGGENHEIM Please do not interrupt. I crawl so far as I can go and just at the end what do you think I find? A great stone sticking up edgeways.

DIANA Is that all?

GUGGENHEIM All? But this is a worked stone. It even has geometric carvings on it. You see such at New Grange in Ireland.

ALISON And what is New Grange in Ireland?

GUGGENHEIM You do not know? A world-famous neolithic monument. What we call a passage-grave. Well, my dears, this stone is dislodged from the roof of a passage-grave. And so, what next?

ALISON What next?

GUGGENHEIM It follows as the night the day. That passage-grave itself must lie just beneath our hut.

DIANA I always thought that hut smelt even worse than the others.

GUGGENHEIM But do not you see? Now we must all of us excavate.

DIANA All of us? Thank you very much dear. And what exactly are we looking for?

GUGGENHEIM We want to get into that grave.

PUBLIC ADDRESS (FEMALE) Attention everyone! By order of the Commandant an indoctrination course for women will commence tomorrow at eighteen hundred hours in Hut Ten. Attendance entirely voluntary but absentees will be noted.

ALISON But what the — Indoctrination Course! I thought the Commandant's line was to leave us alone.

DIANA That's just his cunning, dear. Bore us first and —

GUGGENHEIM My theory is that, since this stone is dislodged, there may be a hole beneath it.

ALISON Look, dear, we're not navvies. Diana, are you going to this course?

DIANA Absentees will be noted. Besides, it might give us a laugh.

GUGGENHEIM Then, when we get down into the grave, who knows what we shall find?

ALISON It'll give us a laugh if the Commandant speaks himself. On the values of civilization.

(The scene changes to Hut Ten)

COMMANDANT Civilization! What is civilization? To tell you a secret the time is arrived. Therefore I start this course for you. And another course for the men. Civilization — this is my secret, ladies — civilization is something that we have invented.

PUBLIC ADDRESS (MALE) Attention everyone! By order of the Commandant an indoctrination course for men will commence tomorrow at fifteen hundred hours on the parade ground. Attendance entirely voluntary but absentees will be noted.

EMSLEY But my dear!

PUBLIC ADDRESS (MALE) Attention everyone! By order of the SGO a deindoctrination course will commence tomorrow at seventeen hundred hours sharp in the gymnasium. Attendance compulsory.

(The scene changes to the gymnasium)

SENIOR GREY OFFICER Gentlemen, two hours ago you heard the Commandant. He mounted an assault on your minds. He urged you to open your minds. I must now urge you to close them. He spoke about Brown ideology. Brown ideology's bunk. So in fact is all ideology. We here, as I said, are on an island. An island of common sense in an endless ocean of madness. We're completely cut off from our homes, we hear no news of the war. But when peace comes, I should say when victory comes, when our great Grey armies come pouring down over that mountain, as we all have no doubt will happen, however long it may take . . .

(Fade up accordion — 'Comin' Round the Mountain'. Peak and fade out slowly. Pause. The scene changes to a spot behind the latrines)

EMSLEY Waters, my dear! What a place for a sunbath!

WATERS Had to get away from all the babble.

EMSLEY But the smell, my dear, the smell! I know one can hanker for solitude but really, to pick the one spot that's bang up against the latrines —

WATERS It's the only place that's not crowded.

EMSLEY Not crowded, my dear? Can you wonder! Well, well, I'll leave you to it.

(Pause)

WATERS Leave me to it? Yes. Leave me to it for ever.

Indoctrination ... deindoctrination ... self-accusation ... mortification ... But now I don't mind any more – as long as I get out of the babble. Everything's equally real. And/or equally unreal. How fakirs feel, I suppose, yogis, people like that. If I wait long enough, the sun will just reach that flower. A weed I suppose it is really. A poor thing but mine own.

'To see a world in a grain of sand,
And heaven in a wild flower,
Hold infinity in the palm of your hand – '

But is this the palm of my hand? Doesn't somehow seem to belong to me. Dirty too. Hand of a tramp, a beggar.

'And Eternity in an hour.'

CANFORD (*off*) Waters! Waters!

WATERS Oh, hell!

CANFORD Ah, there you are, Waters. How can you bear this stink? The SGO wants to see you.

WATERS The SGO? What about?

CANFORD Somebody's told him you're a climber. Well, he wants you to climb something.

    (*Fade up accordion, then Catsmeat singing:*)

CATSMEAT

Lavender's blue, diddle, diddle,
Lavender's green;
When I am king, diddle, diddle,
You shall be queen...

    (*Fade out accordion. The scene changes to the SGO's office*)

SGO You realize, Waters, if you're caught doing this, you'll get solitary confinement for weeks. You'll just have to gauge your time between the searchlights; and don't start till after midnight. But we know it can be done, we had a chap here once who did it, he was an Alpinist too. And we must have news of the war.

WATERS About twenty foot that tower, sir?

SGO Just about, I should say. And then you drop in at the skylight. And we'll hope this air force bloke's vocal.

CANFORD That's hoping rather a lot, I fear.

WATERS Do they always shut them up there, sir?

SGO Airmen? Yes. Keep them there till they're transferred.

WATERS What about the guards, sir? Won't they come popping in?

SGO Not very likely after midnight. Anyhow you'd hear them on the stairs. Anyhow we'll stage a diversion. So take your time and just pump this airman good and proper. It's our very first chance for months to even get a clue how the war's going.

(*The scene changes to the room in the tower*)

REGAN How the war's going? D'you know, as I've said already, I'm afraid I just can't tell you. I suppose it's going to plan.

WATERS You don't even know if the Southern Front is —

REGAN Sure I've never been near it. I don't read the papers at all. I keep my mind on my job, you see.

WATERS But the war in general —

REGAN Och, I just can't think of things in general. I could tell you about my last flight. I was only just back from my leave, I spent it fishing the Corrib —

WATERS But you don't even know if we're winning or losing?

REGAN I imagine it's a kind of stalemate. But now this last flight of mine —

WATERS Don't you think you should lower your voice?

REGAN I'm sorry. I suppose you'd be punished if they caught you up here in this tower?

WATERS I should.

REGAN Then maybe you ought to go now. I'm afraid that's all I can tell you. I'm only a dumb pilot.

WATERS Why did you join the air force?

REGAN Why not?

WATERS Well, aren't you a neutral?

REGAN What's that got to do with it? And you? Were you a volunteer or a conscript?

WATERS Believe it or not, a volunteer. But I feel we're all of us conscripts.

REGAN You're right. It's the world we live in.

WATERS You call it a world? You flatter it. This mad machine we all live in — it's something too absurd to make fun of, something so frightening we can't feel frightened any more. People making rules — for what purpose? People seeking power — for what purpose? People making wars — for what purpose? These half-wits who run our lives, they only try to run our lives because they can't run their own. Experts! Experts in idiocy! No, I don't believe in any of it.

REGAN What do you believe in then? Psychoanalysis?
WATERS Don't make me laugh;
    'Other maps are such shapes, with their islands and capes!
    But we've got our brave Captain to thank'
    (So the crew would protest) 'that he's brought us the best —
    A perfect and absolute blank!'
A perfect and absolute blank — that's your psychologist's ideal, the
end of the perfect analysis. Give me my islands and capes! But what
do *you* believe in anyway?
REGAN Me? In having a good time.
WATERS And so you became a bomber pilot.
REGAN Och, there's good times and good times. Sorry I couldn't help
you more. About the war, I mean. But tell your SGO it's going
according to plan.
WATERS Meaning it's not?
REGAN Meaning: according to plan.

      (*The scene changes back to the SGO's office*)
SGO According to plan! What the devil does that mean?
WATERS He didn't seem strong on the details, sir.
SGO Well, I take it he means we're winning.
WATERS I suppose he does, sir.
SGO I suppose! You sound like two birds of a feather. If you're as vague
as all that, perhaps I've made the wrong decision.
WATERS The wrong decision?
SGO I'll risk it. What do you think, Canford?
CANFORD I'd risk it.
SGO Waters, I want you to join the Escape Team.
WATERS Join the —!
SGO One thing you've proved at least. You proved last night you can
climb. Well, I need a professional climber to lead the chaps over the
mountain. You're on for escaping, I take it?
WATERS Yes, sir.
SGO Then listen. You probably know that we have a tunnel on hand.
Mac and some others have been working on it for months. They're
running it at a new angle — out towards the women's compound.
Well, as you're now on the team, you're naturally in on the digging.
Mac will take you down there tomorrow. In the meantime I hear the
Chaplain's been trying to get you for his show.
WATERS Yes, sir, but I told him I couldn't.

SGO Well, I'm telling you now you can. You'll report for rehearsal tonight.

WATERS But, sir, I —

SGO Are you an imbecile, Waters? All of our escape teams have to have cover activities. Divert suspicion, can't you see?

WATERS Yes, sir.

SGO Right. Tonight you report to the Chaplain.

(*The scene changes to the rehearsal room*)

PADRE No, no, no, Waters, stop! I'm sorry but this won't do. Waters, old chap, we're delighted to have you with us, but you're reading the part, you're reading it.

WATERS I know I'm reading the part.

PADRE I don't mean that; of course I'm not asking you to know it yet. I want you to read the lines and appear *not* to be reading them.

WATERS Sorry, Padre. I missed that.

PADRE What? Speak up.

WATERS I missed that. Could you say it again?

PADRE Waters, do try to concentrate. I know it's your first rehearsal but I want you inside this part. Right into it, old boy. Right in as far as you can go.

(*The scene changes to the tunnel*)

MAC Well, that is as far as you can go. Find it hot?

WATERS Damned hot. Sort of tingling and prickling all over.

MAC Right. Now you start working. You pass back the earth between your legs and I'll pass it back to Bouncer. Ready?

WATERS Ready.

(*Effects and grunts*)

MAC Hard work, isn't it?

WATERS Bloody hard.

MAC You'll get used to it. I find it helps to keep a sort of slow rhythm in one's head.

(*Effects and grunts*)

WATERS A sort of ... slow ... rhythm a ... sort of a slow ... slow ... ache and a ... (*Shower of earth*)

MAC OK Waters. Take a rest. I've got a wee earth-fall here behind you. Just got to tidy it up a bit. You know where we are now, don't you?

WATERS No. Do you?

MAC Just about under the wire. Heading towards the women's compound. Soon we'll be changing our course.

WATERS Under the wire, did you say?

MAC Just about, by my reckoning.

WATERS (*to himself*) The wire that has always been round my life.

MAC Never can be sure of these things, though. No, you never can be sure.

(*The scene changes*)

EMSLEY Good evening, my dear. I hear you've been digging. Tired?

WATERS Tired?

EMSLEY Never mind, we've got a surprise for you. Look who's here.

WATERS Regan! . . . But why did they let you join us?

REGAN I gather they thought I was harmless. After a day's interrogation.

EMSLEY Interrogation, my dear? Wait till you have indoctrination.

REGAN Indoctrination?

(*The scene changes to the women's compound*)

PUBLIC ADDRESS (FEMALE) Attention everyone. The nineteenth indoctrination class will take place at eighteen hundred hours tomorrow.

GUGGENHEIM Indoctrination? What can be more tiring?

DIANA One thing, my dear. Excavation.

GUGGENHEIM But you must not say that. Why, we have found the hole.

DIANA I can't call something a hole when it's still all bung-full of earth.

GUGGENHEIM We are making good progress. Soon we shall be in the passage.

DIANA And if we get into this passage, what do we do with it? It's not as if it led anywhere.

GUGGENHEIM It leads to a tomb, I have told you.

DIANA What's the good of that? If it only led out into the open, then perhaps we could escape by it.

GUGGENHEIM Escape? Do not talk such nonsense. This passage will lead to a tomb and there is an end of it. Apart from that, escaping is not for women.

DIANA I wouldn't mind having a try. Nor would Alison, I bet.

ALISON Nor, as you say, would Alison.

GUGGENHEIM You are very, very foolish girls. Suppose you did escape from this camp, what would remain for you then? You would have to go over the mountain.

(*Fade up accordion — 'Comin' Round the Mountain' — then fade out*)

REGAN Waters! I've something to tell you. Or do you know it already?

WATERS What is it?

REGAN The SGO's co-opting me on to your escape team.

WATERS Really? I'm very glad. By the way, why's he co-opted you?

REGAN He seems to think that back home pilots are becoming a scarcity.

WATERS How does he know?

REGAN He doesn't. That's what I told him. Thinking of myself as usual.

WATERS Thinking of yourself?

REGAN Naturally.

WATERS Regan, when you think of yourself . . .

REGAN Go on.

WATERS What exactly do you think of?

REGAN What's that?

WATERS I call myself I. Granted? But you call yourself I too. Then what is either of us meaning? Do I really know who 'I' am? Do *you* really know —

REGAN I do. I know I'm not anyone else.

WATERS That's just the snag. One isn't anyone else and one never will be. So one never can know what it's like to be anyone else. And that's why nothing one does can ever matter a damn.

REGAN I don't quite follow you there.

WATERS Whatever one does, there's no need to feel any shame. Look, let me put it like this. Supposing I was a hunchback, well, I'd never know what it meant not to be born a hunchback. So whatever I did or said or felt or thought, would always be all of a piece, all of a piece with my hump. And that goes for everyone, Regan. Whoever you are, you're conditioned to be what you are and you can't be anyone else. So you never need feel ashamed.

REGAN But you do feel ashamed sometimes, don't you?

WATERS Sometimes, damn you? All the time. But I've got no right to feel ashamed.

REGAN Would this be what you mean? Because you're conditioned to do whatever you do, therefore you can do no wrong. So if you feel ashamed, you're being untrue to yourself and therefore you *are* doing wrong. Because you're just kidding yourself into thinking you *have* done wrong. I suppose that could go on for ever. Feeling ashamed of feeling ashamed of feeling ashamed of — Och, my dear man, if the two of us now were in a bar —

WATERS In a bar? Tomorrow you and I'll be in a tunnel.

(*The scene changes to the tunnel*)

REGAN Oh, the fearful heat of this tunnel! Is this how it feels to be a tapeworm?

MAC Shut up, Regan. Waters, tell him to shut up.

WATERS Regan. Mac says shut up.

REGAN All right. I was only observing in passing —

MAC For God's sake will you shut up there!

WATERS Anything wrong, Mac?

MAC Yes, there is. Bloody great rock in my way. Send Regan back for a crowbar. There's one in the entrance.

WATERS Regan, can you go back and get the crowbar?

REGAN All right.

MAC That would be our luck! First thing I've met of the sort in the whole sweating length of this tunnel.

WATERS Well, why can't we go round it?

MAC That's probably what we'll have to do. It's only — Listen to this.
(*Chink of small instrument on rock*)
Hear nothing odd about that? Of course you're new to tunnelling. To my ear that sounds hollow.

WATERS Hollow?

MAC But if it is, then where in hell have we got to?

REGAN Here's your crowbar.

WATERS Thank you. Here's the crowbar, Mac.

MAC All right. Move back and give me room. Now then.
(*Crowbar on rock*)
It is!
(*Second blow*)
Yes, my God, it's hollow.
(*Third blow*)
And what's more — it seems to be loose! Well, what do we do now?

WATERS I suppose you go on and loosen it.

MAC And tumble right out into the Commandant's lap or somewhere.

WATERS But, he said we were right out beyond the wire.

MAC I know we're beyond the wire; I shouldn't be surprised if we're near that corrugated fence. And we also ought to be well beneath the surface. Unless my reckoning's haywire. After all, this tunnel's been kept dead level. I think I'll take a chance on it. Move back again, Waters, will you?

REGAN What's he up to?

WATERS Hsh!

(*Several blows of crowbar*)

MAC It's moving, my God, it's moving! (*Repeat crowbar*) Oy! There's a light through there! Yes, a light! Get back, both of you! That's torn it, this damned stone's going!

(*Large stone falling into gallery; pause*)

DIANA (*off*) Hullo there! Come on in! (*Pause*) I said come on in. Don't be shy. We're all Grey girls in here.

MAC Grey girls? Girls?

DIANA And we know you're Grey, too. We can hear you.

MAC Mad! Stark staring mad! I'm going in to see.

(*Effect of dropping body*)

DIANA Careful there! Wait till I shine my torch.

MAC Well, I'll be damned. What's this place? Who are you?

DIANA I'm from the women's compound, my name's Diana. And this place, if you want to know, is a bonafide neolithic passage.

MAC A bonafide what? You mean we're under your compound?

GUGGENHEIM (*off*) Diana! Who are you talking to?

DIANA A man. Believe it or not.

GUGGENHEIM (*off*) A man?

(*Dropping body*)

DIANA And here comes another one.

MAC Come over here, Waters. Where does this passage lead to?

DIANA Guggenheim — here she comes now — says it's exceptionally long.

MAC I asked you: where does it lead to?

DIANA Don't be so brusque; you hardly know me. It leads to a tomb of course.

MAC A tomb?

WATERS A tomb?

(*Dropping body*)

REGAN What's going on in here?

GUGGENHEIM Diana! Who are these men?

DIANA Some of our neighbours who've just broken into the passage.

GUGGENHEIM Broken in?

DIANA Look!

GUGGENHEIM How dare they?

REGAN Would you please keep that torch off me, dear? I don't feel quite fit for a spotlight.

GUGGENHEIM You mean to say it is you knocked that large stone out of the roof and —

MAC Shut up! Is there any way out of this passage?

DIANA Only back into our compound. Up there to the right. Terminus is under the floorboards.

MAC Then what's that light along there, the other direction?

DIANA Oh, that's our tomb. There's no way out of that.

MAC What's the light, I asked you.

DIANA Oh, that's just Alison. Looking for Stone Age ornaments.

MAC Waters, we'll go along and check.

GUGGENHEIM I would like to point out —

MAC Point out anything you like but not to me. Regan, you stay here and talk to her. And you, Miss, since you've got a torch —

DIANA Don't call me Miss!

MAC Diana then. Perhaps you will light us to this tomb of yours, Diana.

GUGGENHEIM Before you invade my tomb —

MAC No, no, tell it to Regan.

REGAN Look, ma'am, take it easy; we never meant to intrude on you, we're only planning to escape.

GUGGENHEIM You cannot escape by this passage.

REGAN Ah, that remains to be seen.

GUGGENHEIM You do not understand. This is a neolithic monument. And I have a proprietary right on it.

REGAN Now that sheds a different light on things. If light's the right word down here. I'm sorry but I didn't catch your name.

GUGGENHEIM Guggenheim.

REGAN Well now, Dr Guggenheim —

GUGGENHEIM I am not a doctor — perhaps I should be.

REGAN Ah, indeed you should. The coincidence is, Dr Guggenheim, I fancy the Stone Age myself.

GUGGENHEIM Then let me tell you. You have been to New Grange in County Meath?

REGAN Oh, repeatedly. Repeatedly.

GUGGENHEIM Of course. Well this is in the same class. And the entrance passage here is considerably longer. As for the grave itself, it's a megalithic circular chamber. In a state of perfect preservation.

MAC Well, Waters? (*Tap on rock*) Seems bloody solid, doesn't it?

WATERS Can't see any way out of it. Unless one blasted it of course.

MAC Oh, blasting's out of the question. Anyhow we don't know where we are. If this damn tomb's in the middle of the female compound ... we'll just have to make exact measurements.

DIANA Our archaeological expert's measured it all already.

ALISON Not only measured it. She's got a whole set of plans of it.

MAC Oh, has she indeed? Would you mind lighting me back to her?

DIANA It will be a pleasure, Mr Onetrack.

MAC Right. Waters, you might finish checking the walls of this tomb.

WATERS OK, but I haven't a torch.

ALISON I'll switch on mine again.

WATERS Thank you.

(*Pause*)

ALISON Not very talkative, are you?

WATERS This is a job.

ALISON Some people talk at their jobs.

WATERS Women do: yes.

ALISON I see you don't like the sex.

WATERS Haven't met any for some time.

ALISON But you don't like them all that much, do you?

WATERS Well ... I happen to know them.

ALISON How do you mean you know them? (*Pause*) Married?

WATERS Have been.

ALISON Divorced?

WATERS Yes.

ALISON Same here.

WATERS Then perhaps you don't like men?

ALISON Oh, I like some of them vastly.

(*Pause*)

WATERS 'M. All solid rock.

ALISON I could have told you that.

WATERS And was this place really a tomb?

ALISON We've told you that over and over.

WATERS With a body in it and everything?

ALISON I don't know what you mean, everything. No, we didn't find the body. Guggenheim said if we had, it would be in the foetal position. You know, like in the womb.

WATERS I know what foetal means.

ALISON But we did find one thing: ear-rings.

WATERS Stone Age ear-rings?

ALISON Guggenheim says so. Here. Like to have a look at them? Five thousand years old, she says.

WATERS Could you shine your torch on them please? 'M. What are they made of?

ALISON Why, can't you guess? Gold.

WATERS Gold?

ALISON 'Gold? Yellow glittering precious gold?'

WATERS   'No, gods,
  I am no idle votarist — '

BOTH   'Roots, you clear heavens!'

WATERS Are you a Shakespearean actress or something?

ALISON No. Only read Eng. Lit. at Girton.

WATERS Did you? I used to teach Eng. Lit.

ALISON Did you like that?

WATERS No. What class did you get?

ALISON A rather poor second. All I had was a memory.

WATERS Really good memory?

ALISON Quote me some verse and I'll cap it.

WATERS Quote you some verse ... All right then.
  'Alone, alone, all, all alone,
  Alone on a wide wide sea!
  And never a saint took pity on
  My soul in agony.'

ALISON
  'The many men so beautiful
  And they all dead did lie:
  And a thousand thousand slimy things — '

WATERS
  'Lived on and so did I.'

ALISON Really, that was too easy.

MAC (off) Waters! Waters! Where are you?

WATERS Here.

MAC Hurry up! Come and look at these plans.

WATERS Coming. Could you light me along please?

ALISON Of course. Just a little lady with a lamp.

WATERS Thank you. What's your name?

ALISON Alison. What's yours?

WATERS Waters.

ALISON I told you my christian name.

WATERS I never tell anyone my christian name.

ALISON Why, is it something —

MAC Ah, there you are, Waters. Look, this woman's a genius.

REGAN And not just a common or garden one.

GUGGENHEIM I am flattered, gentlemen, I —

MAC Miss Guggenheim, could I borrow these plans for the night?

GUGGENHEIM Well, I don't know. If you're still thinking about escape —

REGAN Och, we've put that out of our heads. This is just pure archaeology.

GUGGENHEIM Well, I don't know. There might be an air-raid tonight.

MAC If there's an air-raid, Miss Guggenheim, I promise you these will be safe.

GUGGENHEIM You promise?

MAC I'll return them to you tomorrow. Will you promise me one thing too? Don't tell anyone you met us.

GUGGENHEIM Of course not.

MAC Right. We'll be seeing you tomorrow.

(Pause. The scene changes to the men's compound. Air raid sirens)

REGAN Isn't that a coincidence? Your Miss Guggenheim will have a fit.

MAC Let her. I must copy these plans. It looks to me, Regan, we'll have to break out from the tomb.

REGAN How?

MAC That's just what I'm trying to think.

REGAN And what will you tell the SGO?

MAC Nothing for the moment. Nothing.

REGAN Not even about the passage?

MAC No.

REGAN Let alone the women.

MAC The women. He'd have a fit. *(Fade up ack-ack)* Come on, Catsmeat! Give us your air-raid song.
      (Fade up accordion, then Catsmeat singing)

CATSMEAT Ten green bottles hanging on the wall . . .
      (Crowd join in. Add air raid noises, then bomb again)

REGAN Wasn't that rather close?

MAC It was. And it gives me an idea.
      (Second bomb close)

REGAN An idea?

MAC Waters suggested blasting a hole in the tomb. I told him we couldn't because of the noise. But we could under cover of a raid.
      (Third bomb close)

REGAN You mean no one would notice?

MAC That's what I mean; precisely. When I've been down there again tomorrow and sized it up with these plans I'll moot it to the SGO.

(Peak song plus air raid, then fade out. The scene changes to the SGO's office)

SGO Damn queer story this, Mac. You say you've run slap into the Stone Age? All right, all right, I accept it. Just like the Browns to set up a camp in a graveyard. But what's all this about gelignite?

MAC I think it's our only way out, sir.

SGO And the noise?

MAC We could do it under cover of an air raid.

SGO 'M. Just possible. But where do you get your gelignite?

CANFORD I think I might fix that, sir.

SGO How?

CANFORD As Supplies Officer it's just about time for me to throw another scrounging expedition. The Commandant, as you know, sir, seems always quite ready to permit that. Well, sir, as you also know, within two miles from here there's quarrying work going on. And the workers are foreign conscripts.

SGO Yes, yes, I know all that but you can't contact them, Canford.

CANFORD No, but our good friend the cook can.

SGO That cheating budmash!

CANFORD Yes, sir; his cheating's an asset. Those wops in the quarries would sell their souls for cigarettes.

SGO I see. You obtain a permit from the Commandant, sally from the camp with Catsmeat, Catsmeat is stacked with cigarettes . . .

CANFORD And then we return with the gelignite.

SGO All right, but it's damn risky.

(Fade up accordion — 'Mrs Bond' — and fade out)

SGO Any luck, Canford?

CANFORD No, sir. Catsmeat was watched all the time. Couldn't get near a quarryman.

SGO Then you'd better make another expedition in a fortnight.

CANFORD Three weeks would look less suspicious.

SGO All right, three weeks — though it's dangerous this delay. The guards are too zealous these days. Probing around with their listening sticks. Better put the tunnel out of bounds.

CANFORD I've done that already sir. After all, till we get the gelignite, there's nothing more to be done there.

SGO To be done there! Stone Age tomb! Of course there's nothing to be done there!

(*The scene changes to the tomb*)

DIANA Really, Mac, my sweetie, come to think of it!

MAC Come to think of what?

DIANA This! It's such an odd place for it.

MAC It's better since you brought the blankets.

DIANA Wish I could bring a spring mattress.

MAC What would your friend Miss Guggenheim think?

DIANA Oh, she'll be asleep by now. Dreaming of dolmens and things.

GUGGENHEIM We came into our own about six thousand BC. Before that it was a man's world.

DIANA And what would *your* friends think?

MAC Oh, they'll be asleep too. Regan will be dreaming of . . .

REGAN Bomb doors open. Strike! Give him more line now. Didn't I tell you they'd take the Black Hackle today?

MAC And God knows what Waters will be dreaming of.

WATERS The photograph was on the mantelpiece. And there was my father kissing her. If only he'd not been my father. Or if Vera'd not been my wife. If only . . . if only . . . if only . . .

MAC If only that nigger'd get cracking and fetch us the plastic.

DIANA Plastic?

MAC Gelignite, love.

DIANA And then you escape? Just like that.

MAC I don't know about 'just like that', but we'll do our damndest.

DIANA And what about me, Mac dear?

MAC You? What about you, love?

DIANA Why don't you take me with you?

MAC What! Don't be daft.

DIANA I'm perfectly able-bodied.

MAC But you're a woman, damn it!

DIANA I could pass as a man all right. I've got a workman's dungarees.

MAC It's absolutely impossible. Come on, Diana, snuggle down.

(*The scene changes; fade up accordion, joined by Catsmeat, singing*)

CATSMEAT

Lavender's blue, diddle, diddle,
Lavender's green;

When I am king, diddle, diddle,
You shall be queen.

(*Fade out accordion. The scene changes*)

CANFORD Good evening, sir.

SGO You look pleased.

CANFORD Yes, sir. We've got the gelignite.

SGO Jolly good show. Then all we need now is an air-raid.

CANFORD Bouncer's dropped out by the way.

SGO Why?

CANFORD Gone to hospital. Bit late to brief anyone else.

SGO That'll leave four in the team. Yes. Seeing what a gamble it is I suggest we leave it at that. Very unlikely all four will get over the mountain. If Mac doesn't blow them up first of course.

CANFORD He's taking every precaution. They'll take cover in the tunnel, you see, their own tunnel, that is. He's shoring it up with props just where it runs into the passage.

SGO He's doing that now?

CANFORD Yes, this moment. He's down there now with Waters and Regan.

(*The scene changes to the passage-grave*)

MAC Waters! Regan! There's something I want to ask you.

REGAN Go on and ask it then.

MAC This is in strict confidence.

REGAN All right.

MAC All right, Waters?

WATERS Naturally.

MAC Well, you know that Bouncer's in hospital and Griffiths has now got dysentery.

REGAN I didn't know about Griffiths.

MAC So that leaves three of us.
    (*Pause*)

REGAN Well?

MAC We'll be ready by tomorrow night, you know. We could even manage it tonight but I do want to get these props in.
    (*Pause*)

WATERS Well?

MAC This is in confidence, mind.

REGAN Och, we know it's in confidence.

MAC There's someone I want to co-opt.

(*Pause*)

REGAN Who?

MAC Diana.

REGAN Diana! You're mad.

MAC I'm not.

WATERS Anyhow it's impossible.

MAC It's not.

WATERS Look, we know what you've been up to in the tomb but —

REGAN Steady, Waters, steady. After all, I don't see why it's impossible. A woman's got as much right to escape as we have.

WATERS She hasn't. Anyhow I'm not going climbing with women.

MAC Listen, Waters, I'm running this show —

WATERS Subject to the SGO.

MAC I made this proposal in confidence.

WATERS Confidence be damned, I —

GUGGENHEIM Excuse me. Excuse me. I must speak to you.

MAC Miss Guggenheim!

GUGGENHEIM What is this that I hear? I have been ill. No one told me.

MAC What do you mean?

GUGGENHEIM You're planning to destroy my tomb.

MAC We are planning to escape, Miss Guggenheim.

GUGGENHEIM Escape! Escape! Not through my tomb. Far from it.

MAC Nobody is going to stop us.

GUGGENHEIM The Commandant will stop you. When I tell him.

MAC What! You're a damned traitor.

GUGGENHEIM Traitor? I'm an archaeologist.

(*The scene changes to the men's compound, then fade up accordion and crowd*)

SINGERS She'll be comin' round the mountain . . . (*etc. and refrain to close*)

POTTER What shall we have next?

BATTY Just a moment, please. Anyone know the time?

EMSLEY Time for bombs, my dear.

BATTY But the planes haven't come over yet.

EMSLEY No, they get later and later.

POTTER They're not late. Where's Regan? He's the expert.

VOICE Is there a Regan in the house?

EMSLEY No Regan — and, my God, no Waters, no Mac. Canford, they're not doing it tonight are they?

CANFORD Shut up! There's been a snag. You didn't see the Commandant today, did you?

EMSLEY Why?

CANFORD Honestly, I don't know. But old Mac was in a shocking flap and kept asking if we'd seen the Commandant.
  (*Fade up ack-ack*)

CANFORD Well, here we go. Music! (*Fade up accordion and crowd singing 'Ten Green Bottles', then bombs*) 'M. Quite a raid tonight.
  (*Explosion*)

EMSLEY That was an odd noise.

CANFORD Yes, wasn't it? Did you hear it whistle?

EMSLEY No.

CANFORD Nor did I. I wonder ... I wonder ...
  (*Fade up song and then behind*)

EMSLEY You don't think they've done it, do you?

CANFORD Shut up! (*Fade up song, then automatic rifle fire*) Yes, my God! They've done it! Go on singing there! Cross your fingers, Emsley. Sing, chaps! Make all the noise you can!
  (*Fade up song, then door flung open*)

EMSLEY My dear! Here come the bloody guards.

GUARD Silence! Silence there! (*Singers stop, except Catsmeat*) You there! Nigger! Stop that!

CATSMEAT (*breaking off song*) I ain't a nigger. I'm a Negro. (*Continues song*)

GUARD I order you. Stop, or I shoot.

CATSMEAT 'And if one green bottle should accidentally fall — '
  (*Shot on last word, falling body and discord from accordion*)

EMSLEY You bastard!

GUARD Stand back or I shoot you, too. Stand to attention. All of you.

BATTY Does anyone know what time it is?

GUARD Silence! Silence for the Commandant!
  (*Door opens*)

COMMANDANT Prisoners! Guilty men! I am here a roll-call to make.

CANFORD Well, there's one on the floor you needn't count.

COMMANDANT Silence! Often have I told you that here must man be happy. And that from here no escape is. But now you have our contract broken. To escape has been tried — and defeated. Shot. All have been shot.

(*The scene changes to a pine wood*)

WATERS Regan? That you?

REGAN Yes.

WATERS Can you crawl over here?

REGAN Coming. (*Pause*) Where are you? Ah — isn't it dark?

WATERS What happened to Mac?

REGAN Don't know. But I guess he went back down the passage.

WATERS Looking for that bitch?

REGAN I suppose she got cold feet.

WATERS Hsh!

REGAN What was that?

(*Pause*)

WATERS Nothing. I think we ought to get weaving. Still too near that damned camp.

REGAN Well, thank God for this forest. We're a couple of needles in a haystack.

WATERS Don't speak too soon. Come on.

(*Pause, with breathing*)

REGAN How far would you say we've got now?

WATERS A good three miles.

REGAN Do I see a light in the distance? Ahead of us, over to the left.

WATERS I spotted that some time ago. I think it's that house on the map. That last house all by itself at the head of the glen.

REGAN Let's give it a nice wide berth then.

WATERS I'm steering half a mile west of it.

REGAN Half a mile west of it, is it?

(*Effects*)

WATERS Now! Let's have a breather.

REGAN Suits me. And we might have a snack while we're about it. God! I seem to have dropped my rations.

WATERS You're welcome to dig into mine. Oh no, I'm sorry, you're not.

REGAN Sure, that's all right. They were only enough for one.

WATERS That's not what I mean. I forgot them in the rush. When Mac brought the operation forward.

REGAN That was old Guggenheim's fault. But what are we going to do now?

WATERS We can't climb that mountain without food. There's only one thing we can do. Go and steal food from that house.

REGAN All right.

WATERS We'll be there in ten minutes.

(Pause)

There!

REGAN Why did this pinewood choose to stop just here? That's a hundred yards open space. And their light's on still, worse luck.

WATERS Now you stay here and —

REGAN How do you mean I stay here?

WATERS Well, there's no point in us both going. I think we'd better toss for it.

REGAN Just as you say. The one who calls right starts his career as a burglar.

WATERS OK, you call.

REGAN Tails.

WATERS Tails it is. But be careful.

REGAN Careful's the word. See you in a jiffy.

WATERS Good luck, Regan.

REGAN Goodbye now.

(Long pause, then revolver shot)

WATERS God! Do I go and see? Or wait? Better wait. They might have missed him. And then if he doesn't come back? Don't panic. Count to a hundred.

ALISON Hullo.

WATERS What?

ALISON It's me.

WATERS Who're you?

ALISON Alison.

WATERS Alison?

ALISON Guess how I got here.

WATERS Shut up! Something's happened.

ALISON What?

WATERS I think they've got Regan. In that house.

ALISON Oh, Regan?

WATERS I'm going over there to find out.

ALISON Then I'm coming too.

WATERS You're not.

ALISON I am. And you know why?

WATERS There's no possible reason why. You oughtn't to be here anyway. And if you think I'm prepared to take *you* up this mountain —

ALISON For God's sake listen a moment. I'm going to that house because I'm a woman. Because I happen to know that there's no one there but a woman. Because her husband's one of the guards in our compound. A guard that we got to talk.

WATERS That true?

ALISON Yes.

WATERS Well, even so —

ALISON Wait; that's not all. She's not only a woman all on her own in a house. She's also a Grey. That is, she was a Grey some twenty years back or so.

WATERS What's your proposal?

ALISON I propose to visit her. Alone. Even if she shot your friend, she's not very likely to shoot me. Not if I come by the front door.

WATERS You will do no such thing!

ALISON Oh won't I! Want me to scream?

WATERS I'll meet you half way. We'll toss for it. If you call right, you go.

ALISON OK. Toss then. Tails.

WATERS Tails it is.

ALISON I always call right. Goodbye for the moment. When it's safe for you to come, I'll whistle. The V-sign three times over. Agreed?

WATERS Agreed. Good luck. (*Pause*)

One–two–three — at any rate she's got guts — four–five — but why's it her and not Mac's girl? — seven–eight — she'll damn well have to go back though — nine–ten–eleven — how on earth did she get here so quickly? — twelve–thirteen–fourteen–

(*Fade out Waters. Pause; knock on door*)

UPLAND WOMAN (*off*) Who's there?

ALISON A friend.

UPLAND WOMAN A woman?

ALISON A woman. Could you let me in please.

UPLAND WOMAN Then stand back from the door.

ALISON Right. I'm standing back.

(*Door opens*)

UPLAND WOMAN Put your hands above your head. Come in. (*Door closes*) Stand over there against the wall. No; keep your hands up. Now then, tell me who you are.

ALISON I'm an escaped prisoner from the woman's compound down the valley.

UPLAND WOMAN Another escaped prisoner!

ALISON Another?

UPLAND WOMAN The first one's lying in the larder.

ALISON Dead?

UPLAND WOMAN I was brought up to shoot thieves.

ALISON I believe you were brought up Grey.

UPLAND WOMAN Who told you that?

ALISON Your husband.

UPLAND WOMAN My husband?

ALISON He talked; he responds to blackmail. He could be punished
for that.

UPLAND WOMAN Yes, I was brought up Grey. But I have no love for
the Greys.

ALISON Why not?

UPLAND WOMAN The Browns have a good way of life, the Greys have
a bad one.

ALISON Are you sure about that?

UPLAND WOMAN And besides, the Greys killed my two sons.

ALISON How?

UPLAND WOMAN In a battle.

ALISON People do get killed in battles.

UPLAND WOMAN Killing is something I hate.

ALISON And yet . . . ?

UPLAND WOMAN I know what you mean. He had broken into my
house.

ALISON And what about me?

UPLAND WOMAN I shall hand you over. Naturally.

ALISON Why naturally?

UPLAND WOMAN You can drop your hands now. Sit down there at
the table. But remember I've got this gun on you.

ALISON I couldn't very well forget it.

UPLAND WOMAN Are you hungry?

ALISON Not at the moment.

UPLAND WOMAN Then I will talk to you. Yes, I was brought up Grey.
In a seaport. That's where I met my husband; he was then a merchant
seaman. He was different from the local men, he had far more of . . .
ideas. And besides, he was a man!

ALISON He's still very much a 'man', you know.

UPLAND WOMAN What do you mean?

ALISON There are women employed in our compound, women of this
country, this country which you've adopted, who are looking around
for men.

UPLAND WOMAN Be careful what you say.

ALISON Look, we're both women. We've both, I take it, got womanly intuition. I know that your husband's unfaithful to you. And you know it too.

(*Pause*)

UPLAND WOMAN Yes, I know it. But that's no reason for me to betray my country...

ALISON No, but there *is* a reason. And that is: it's not your country. You're still one of us at heart.

UPLAND WOMAN I deny that.

ALISON Did you marry your husband because of his ideas? Or was it because he was a 'man'?

UPLAND WOMAN You will leave my husband out of this!

ALISON All right. What's that picture over your mantelpiece? (*Pause*) If you won't tell me, I'll guess. I've never been there but I think it's that seaport you came from.

UPLAND WOMAN You are quite clever.

ALISON And you keep that picture on the wall because you'd like to be back there. Now shall I make some more guesses!

UPLAND WOMAN What could I care what you guess!

ALISON In that case I won't. Would *you* like to guess for a change? I've got some pictures too. Snapshots. Here. Guess what this first one is.

UPLAND WOMAN Your home, I suppose.

ALISON And the second?

UPLAND WOMAN Presumably your baby.

ALISON Correct. My baby. And he's dead.

UPLAND WOMAN Dead?

ALISON I'd like you to guess how he died.

UPLAND WOMAN I'm sorry he's dead. I can't guess.

ALISON He was killed by a bomb. Whose bomb? (*Pause*) Well, make a guess. Make a guess...

(*The scene changes. Whistle; V-sign once*)

WATERS My God! She must have fixed it!

(*Repeat V-sign twice, fading; pause. The scene changes back to the camp*)

PUBLIC ADDRESS (MALE) Attention everyone! The funeral of Captain MacGregor will take place this afternoon at fourteen-thirty hours.

EMSLEY Poor Mac! It seems the whole roof fell in on him.

BATTY Emsley, my dear fellow. Do you know the —

EMSLEY No! The time, what's the time to you? Time is just something we die in. Four of us died yesterday. Catsmeat and Mac and Regan and Waters — or perhaps not Regan and Waters, we've only the Commandant's word for it.

PUBLIC ADDRESS (MALE) Attention everyone! *The Importance of Being Earnest.* The Chaplain has decided to cancel tonight's rehearsal. I will repeat that. *The Importance of Being Earnest* . . .

(*The scene changes back to the mountain*)

ALISON Waters! Now that we're resting . . . can't we talk?

WATERS We oughtn't to rest very long. Good thing we got a night's sleep. For which I must thank you. But I wonder if that woman will rat on us.

ALISON Rat on us?

WATERS Tip off the Browns. Why did you want to escape?

ALISON It's obvious, isn't it?

WATERS No. But I like this here and now, I like this act of escaping.

ALISON Even with a female encumbrance?

WATERS You've earned your passage. But I still don't know why it's you. I was against all girls but I thought it was going to be Mac's girl.

ALISON I can see you're against all girls. Well, it was a last-minute change. Diana twisted her ankle struggling with Guggenheim.

WATERS *Did* Guggenheim go to the Commandant?

ALISON Diana prevented her. So, seeing she had everything ready, dungarees and the rest, I just stepped into her shoes.

WATERS But you didn't get out by yourself?

ALISON No, Mac gave me a leg up. He was still waiting for Diana, I had to explain she'd dropped out.

WATERS And Mac? Did he come out after you?

ALISON I just don't know; I was running like hell, you see. What hope have we really of making it?

WATERS Hope? Hope? We've got a good start. If you can keep up the pace.

ALISON I'll try.

'Does the road wind uphill all the way?'

WATERS 'Yes, to the very end.'

No, that's too easy. Try this one.

'Oh wearisome condition of humanity!'

Born under one law, to another bound' —

ALISON

'Vainly begot and yet forbidden vanity,
Created sick, commanded to be sound.'
A favourite of yours, I take it?

WATERS Yes. How did you guess?

ALISON A strange little bird told me.

WATERS A bird in your head?

ALISON In *your* head.

WATERS No, you don't know me that well.

ALISON You'd be surprised how —

WATERS It's no reflection on you. One can't really know other people.
Everyone's really so lonely.

ALISON That's just it. The lonelinesses can meet, you see.

WATERS Are you lonely yourself?

ALISON You just said everyone was. I wish I had a needle and thread
on me.

WATERS Why?

ALISON Well, look at these dungarees.

WATERS I could give you a poem for that.

ALISON Which one?

WATERS No, we should be going.

ALISON Just let's have the poem first.

WATERS Well, I —

ALISON Go on!

WATERS 'A sweet disorder in the dress'

ALISON 'Kindles in clothes a wantonness — '
        (*She breaks into laughter*)

WATERS Now you've interrupted. I've lost it.

ALISON I'm sorry but — what a poem to choose at this altitude! Do
you know, I think you're human after all.

WATERS Thank you. I mean it. Thank you. I feel we ought to go on
now. We must reach the col before dark. Pretty rough going the next
bit. Let's hope the rain holds off.
        (*Pause; fade up wind and rain, and behind*)
Look! We can shelter in here. We've not got as far as we should
though.

ALISON Then let's go on.

WATERS No; no point in getting drenched. Besides, the light's getting
bad. Besides, you're exhausted, Alison. Come on; you clamber in first.
        (*Rock effects*)

ALISON Handy little cave. Cavelet. Don't straggle out in the rain though. That's better. Plenty of room for all. What was that you said about other people?

WATERS Other people?

ALISON You've always felt kind of cut off?

WATERS Always? No, not quite always. When I was married, for a bit — Look, I think you should try and get some sleep. If the rain stops and provided the moon comes out, we could climb a bit further later.

ALISON (*yawning*) Sleep? . . . No . . . Don't really think I could . . . I mean how could I . . . how could I? . . .

WATERS But she *is* asleep. Out like a light. Wish I could. Not really safe though; they're after us. Ten-to-one they're after us. (*Pause*) Out like a light. Like the light of her eyes. Don't be silly.

ALISON (*in her sleep*) Oh!

WATERS What is it?

ALISON The house! The house! My baby! Where is he? Where is he?

WATERS Wake up! Alison, wake up!

ALISON Oh! Where was I?

WATERS Having a nightmare, I think.

ALISON How did you know?

WATERS You were talking in your sleep.

ALISON Was I? What about?

WATERS A house . . . and a baby.

ALISON Yes. I lost him in an air-raid. No, don't say anything about it. I've had all that. I'm adjusted.

WATERS I think you *are* another person. Both another and a person. Alison, I'd like to ask —

ALISON No, don't. Let's both keep silent for a bit.

    (*Pause; then fade up distant accordion 'Lavender's Blue', then behind*)

WATERS Alison? Do you hear anything?

ALISON No. Do you?

WATERS Yes. I hear an accordion.

ALISON What! (*Pause*) You're hearing things, dear.

WATERS I told you I'm hearing things. It's what Catsmeat used to play.

ALISON Catsmeat?

WATERS (*in time to music*)
    Lavender's blue, diddle, diddle,
    Lavender's green;
    When I am king, diddle, diddle,
    You shall be queen.

(Accordion out)

If we ever get home ...

ALISON What?

WATERS She should be queen.

ALISON May I feel your forehead? ... Yes, you're fevered.

WATERS I'm not fevered; I always feel fine on mountains. I say, the rain is stopping. Now if only the moon would come up —

ALISON Well, relax till it does, my dear. And don't go hearing accordions.

(Pause; then accordion distant, 'Little Nut Tree')

WATERS Nothing would it bear ... *(Fade out accordion)* By God, the moon! Let's go.

ALISON How far is it up to the col?

WATERS Couple of hours I should think. We'll rest every half hour. Let's see, what's the time now. Five past eleven. We'll rest at 11.35. *(Pause)* 11.35. No, it's 34. One minute more, dear.

ALISON Pedant!

WATERS There!

ALISON Lord, I'm tired! I say, we seem to be getting away with it.

WATERS Don't speak too soon. If and when we get over this mountain, our problems are only beginning.

ALISON If problems ever *begin*.

WATERS Meaning?

ALISON I think they've been here from always.

(Pause)

WATERS Do you know ... ?

ALISON Yes?

WATERS I think you're rather like me. Except that you said you're adjusted.

ALISON That wasn't entirely true. Yes, I am a little bit like you. That's why we'd never get on. There'd be no future in it.

WATERS Get on? ... get on? ... We'd better. Next stop five past midnight.

(Fade up tick-tock increasing in volume behind)

ALISON Your wrist-watch sounds very loud.

WATERS My wrist-watch doesn't sound at all. It's you who're hearing things now.

(Fade up tick-tock)

ALISON I'm so tired, Waters. Can't we stop?

WATERS Just another minute or two. (*Tick-tock to peak*) OK. Now we
can stop.

    (*Cut tick-tock*)

ALISON And it's stopped too.

WATERS What has?

    (*Pause*)

ALISON Why don't you tell me your christian name?

WATERS Because I don't like it.

ALISON Why? (*Pause*) Is it something very extraordinary?

WATERS No ... just Thomas.

ALISON Thomas? What's wrong with that?

WATERS They called him doubting Thomas.

    (*Pause*)

ALISON I like the name. Thomas, will you kiss me, please.

WATERS Why?

ALISON Because I'm cold and afraid. And because I think you want to.
(*Pause*) Am I right?

WATERS Yes, you're right.

    (*Pause*)

ALISON But you know, Thomas ... there'd be no future in it.

WATERS You said that before. And she wonders I'm Doubting Thomas!

ALISON There was also one called True Thomas.

    'Light down, light down now, true Thomas,
      And lean your head upon my knee;
    Abide you there a little space,
      And I will show you ferlies three.

    O see ye not yon narrow road,
      So thick beset wi' thorns and briers?
    That is the Path of Righteousness,
      Though after it but few enquires.

    And see ye not yon braid, braid road
      That lies across the lily leven?
    That is the Path of Wickedness,
      Though some call it the road to Heaven.'

WATERS Alison!

ALISON

    'And see ye not yon bonny road
      That winds about the fernie brae?
    That is the Road to fair Elfland,
      Where thou and I this night maun gae.'

WATERS 'Where thou and I this night maun gae.'
  Come on, time's up. Next stop 12.35.
    (*Fade up tick-tock and behind*)
ALISON Thomas! It must be 12.35 now.
WATERS As a matter of fact it is. As a matter of fact it's 12.45.
    (*Cut tick-tock*)
ALISON Bastard!
WATERS Don't say that. Please.
ALISON I don't think, Thomas, I can go on any more.
WATERS Just the last lap to the col.
ALISON Does it make any difference?
WATERS Then we can look down the other side.
    (*Distant barking of dogs*)
ALISON What's that?
WATERS I don't hear anything.
ALISON Dogs.
WATERS OK Alison, dear. I hear accordions and you hear dogs — and
  wrist-watches.
ALISON You mean there are no dogs?
WATERS No. (*Barking of dogs, still distant*) No dogs at all. Wait till we
  get to the col.
ALISON You want to look down the other side?
WATERS I want to get up on the sky-line. Listen. I bet you can't cap
  this one. I'll give you the first verse; you give me the last.
  'My love is of a birth as rare
  As 'tis for object strange and high:
  It was begotten by despair
  Upon Impossibility.'
ALISON Of course I can cap that. I've known it since my teens.
WATERS Have you really? So have I. All right, my dearest, go on.
ALISON 'Therefore . . . therefore . . .' therefore something or other —
WATERS 'Therefore the love which' — !
ALISON
  'Therefore the love which us doth bind,
  But Fate so enviously debars,
  Is the Conjunction of the Mind,
  And Opposition of the Stars.'
WATERS The stars? The stars! Look up at them. Look at them staring
  at us.
    (*Dogs barking — nearer*)
ALISON Listen! Can't you hear them now?

WATERS Yes. I can hear them — now. Yes; the opposition of the stars.

ALISON Meaning dogs?

WATERS Meaning dogs.

ALISON Meaning dogs on our trail?

WATERS Meaning dogs — and stars — on our trail. Come on, my dearest, let's go.

(*Montage of dogs and tick-tock; then cut*)

There! We've made it. The col!

ALISON And you're right. We can see down beyond it. Freedom is somewhere over there.

WATERS Freedom? You said there's no future there.

ALISON No future for you and me. I wasn't talking of freedom.

WATERS What were you talking of?

ALISON Let's call it the conjunction of the mind.

WATERS Alison! For once and for good, there's something I — What's that light? Look back, my darling! Down there.

ALISON Lights . . . several lights. And they're moving. Moving searchlights.

(*Fade up dogs, nearer*)

WATERS Searchlights and dogs! They're after us. And not a spot of cover in sight.

ALISON What's that sort of dark thing there?

WATERS That? Looks like a cairn. All right; it's the best we can do.

(*Build dogs, and spasmodically behind*)

Right. Kneel down, Alison. Kneel close to me. No one can see us from here.

ALISON Yes, but they're still coming up.

WATERS Oh, to hell with their dogs and searchlights!

ALISON If they capture us here . . . it would mean return to camp?

WATERS Return to . . . ? No!

ALISON Couldn't we run for it, Thomas?

WATERS With all that open ground? And look over there — on that ridge.

ALISON I can't see anything there.

WATERS I thought I saw moving figures. Yes, I'm right; they've a light. Another damn portable searchlight. Look, they're moving it this way. Fifteen yards from this cairn and they'd have us bang in their sights.

ALISON So what do you propose we do? Stay here and be captured?

WATERS I propose no such thing. It's all up to you now, Alison.

(*Fade up dogs and behind*)

ALISON Well, if it's up to me — listen to those damned dogs — I propose that you and I run for it. I suppose we've a chance in a hundred.

WATERS Chance in a thousand, darling.

ALISON All right, then. Let's run for it.

WATERS Pretty well suicide.

ALISON Maybe. With a joy of life thrown in.

WATERS A joy of —

ALISON And something else.

WATERS What else?

ALISON L–o–v–e.

WATERS Love? You mean that?

ALISON I mean it.

> (*Fade up dogs and behind*)

And now no more poetry. Give me your hand and we'll run for it.

WATERS For 'it'? . . . Do you know, I feel happy. I haven't felt that for years.

ALISON Nor have I. But let's count one, two, three, and —

WATERS Just one more bit of poetry. The same again, I'm afraid.
'My love is of a birth as rare —

> (*Alison joins in*)

BOTH

'As 'tis for object strange and high.
It was begotten by despair
Upon Impossibility.'

> (*Pause; fade up dogs*)

WATERS Give me your hand. We've not time to lose. One!

BOTH Two! Three and — GO!

> (*Pause. Automatic rifle fire; silence*)

> (*Fade up accordion 'Lavender's Blue' — once through, then Catsmeat's voice joins in*)

CATSMEAT (*singing*)

Lavender's blue, diddle diddle,
Lavender's green;
When I am king, diddle, diddle,
You shall be queen.

> (*Accordion pianissimo to close*)

ONE FOR THE GRAVE

a modern morality play

One for the Grave was written for the stage 1958–9 and left in draft, unrevised, in 1960–1, with the note 'probably many alterations to come', two years before MacNeice's death. (Earlier titles on the draft were: 'Every Man Meets It', 'The Benefit of the Doubt', and 'One for the Dead', under which last title it was published in the *Massachusetts Review*, winter 1967.) The world première, under the direction of Frank Dermody, was held at the Abbey Theatre during the Dublin Theatre Festival, October 1966. The settings were by Liam Miller, the music by Gerard Victory. The play was published as a book by Faber in January 1968. Quite openly based on the late medieval morality play *Everyman* and just as openly satirizing crass commercialism and television-in-production (after MacNeice's bitter experience as a radio man urged to practise in the television medium and doing so without conviction), *One for the Grave* attempts to encompass in parabolic and abbreviated form as many details and universals of MacNeice's generation as he could think of introducing within the limits of the central idea: an ordinary and unheroic man called to account for his life at the time of his death – on a live television programme. MacNeice's notes precede the play and Hedli Anderson's notes on the first production follow it (p. 259 below). The text used here is that of the holograph manuscript in the Berg Collection, New York Public Library.

AUTHOR'S NOTES

1. NB This is still very much a *draft*, to which much could be added and/or subtracted. Indeed this piece should always remain to *some* extent elastic if only in order to stay up to date; unlike its medieval model, the topical allusions are important.

2. The basic pattern, however, the story line, follows that of the medieval *Everyman* and must on no account be sacrificed. This means that in production a very delicate balance must be preserved between its primary content, which is serious, and the revue or music-hall elements (sometimes pretty near slapstick) which are introduced not primarily for their own sake but for satirical purposes, the modern Everyman's world being one which cannot be properly treated *without* satire.

3. This being so, the whole device of the Television Studio (where the floor represents the Earth and the production gallery Heaven) is very much more than a gimmick. Because it is the fate of the Twentieth-Century Everyman to live in a world of mass media. Similarly, the Admom sequence is not just there for comic relief.

4. As regards casting: the actor playing Everyman must obviously be extremely plastic, changing tint at the drop of a hat. The Son and Daughter must also be versatile. The Floor Manager should superficially resemble a quite usual type of suave (perhaps slightly Americanized) light entertainment FM, but with an undertone of sinister authority. As for the Director, his face must never be seen and he should move as little as possible, except perhaps for the well-known flick of thumb and fingers when ordering a cut. He requires a deep and dominating voice.

5. Acting: Obviously the style will vary between the naturalistic flashback scenes and the stylized ones. In the latter, especially during musical numbers, the various stage-hands etc. on the studio floor should, in grouping and movement, be treated like the rank-and-file members of a revue.

6. Spectacle: This obviously depends on (*a*) the size of stage and (*b*) what funds are available. While the play *could* be done in a token way, the more the production can suggest the bustle of a real TV studio with its crowds of personnel and clutter of machines (e.g. the boom — a most spectacular prop) the better. By the way, the audience represents an invited *television* audience.

7. Music: At the moment many of the lyrics are set to traditional tunes; I should like this kept in most cases but all such should be arranged and, if necessary, modernized by the same hand that sets the

deliberately modern numbers. Some could be unaccompanied but a small (modern) ensemble or, at any rate, one or two *popular* instruments will be required for others. If necessary, the choirs off could be canned.

CHARACTERS

THE FLOOR MANAGER	THE MOTHER
THE DIRECTOR	THE VISION MIXER
HIS SECRETARY	SACRIFICE
THE DESIGNER	PATRIA
THE CROONER	ADMOM
A CAMERAMAN	THE ELECTRONIC BRAIN
JIMMY, a props man	SEAN BULL
EVERYMAN	THE COMEDIAN
MAGGIE	FREE WILL
ELEANOR	THE ANALYST
HER LOVER	THE MARXIST
CAREER	THE SCIENTIST
A CADDY	A SINGER
CONSCIENCE	LIL, a dresser
LUCRE	THE GRAVEDIGGER
BELLBOY	THE DOCTOR OF MED
COMMON SENSE	THE DOCTOR OF DIV
THE SON	CAMERAMAN NO. I
THE DAUGHTER	CAMERAMAN NO. 2
DOREEN	BOOM OPERATOR
MARY	STUDIO HAND
FORGETFULNESS	THREE POP SINGERS

Also as many stage-hands, members of camera crews, wardrobe and make-up types, etc., as can be afforded and accommodated on the stage. Also voices off — both speaking and singing.

Note: a number of the above could easily be doubled, e.g. The Crooner with Sean Bull, Maggie (or Eleanor) with Doreen or Mary, Conscience with the Mother, Lucre with the Doctor of Med (or Div) — and so on and so on. Thanks to the set-up it won't matter if those doubling are recognizable.

ONE FOR THE GRAVE

ACT ONE

(Lights up on front of empty stage, which represents a television studio. On stage a token tracking camera on wheels with a small platform which ideally should be able to be raised or lowered for cameraman, and a rail behind for one man to push it. Also, ideally, a boom — which again would involve two men — but this is not strictly necessary. Upstage — but, ideally, more or less blacked out to start with — three small shallow sets of TV type, numbering One to Three from Stage Left to Right, with red lights over them spelling EXIT. Upstage on an upper level or bridge — but blacked-out to start with — the Production Gallery — ?screened by gauze — where the Director and his assistants sit with their backs to the audience; facing the audience there should be a suggestion of a line of monitors.

When the lights are fully up, the Floor Manager's voice is heard shouting, off)

FLOOR MANAGER Come on, chaps! Get on the floor! The audience is waiting.

(From both entrances there pour in a number of technicians, studio hands, etc., who take up their respective positions. The Floor Manager follows, in a dinner jacket with headphones draped round his neck and comes downstage to address the audience)

FLOOR MANAGER Ladies and gentlemen, good evening! Welcome to our theatre! I'm glad to see you all looking so fit. You'll need to be for this show.

DIRECTOR'S VOICE Get on with it, Morty. Cut the wisecracks.

FLOOR MANAGER Sorry, chief.

Well, ladies and gentlemen, I expect most of you have been in a television theatre before, but for the benefit of those who haven't let me just put you in the picture.

(Stamps)

This . . . is the floor of the studio and I am the floor manager. Familiarly called the FM. Or, putting it another way, I always have my feet on the earth. But, to put out a show, we need more than the earth — the floor. We need the powers up above.

(*Light up Production Gallery, showing back of Director seated between two or more figures — ?dummies — whom he should overtop*)

Look up there. That is the Production Gallery. That's where the Director sits.

(*Director raises his hand in backward salute*)

With him are his Secretary, his Vision Mixer and others. The whole show is controlled from that gallery and the Director's word is absolute.

DIRECTOR'S VOICE When it can be heard, Morty.

FLOOR MANAGER He said 'when it can be heard'. The Director has a sense of humour.

Well, there you have it; the Gallery up there in Olympian remoteness —

(*Blackout Gallery*)

and the Floor down here where we all have our feet on the earth: camera crews, props men, all of us — and of course the artists. But no doubt you're wondering how the floor and the gallery keep in touch? It's simple.

(*Puts on headphones*)

You see these headphones — or cans as we call them in the trade? Through these I can hear whatever the Director says. Like this. Hullo, Chief! Can you hear me?

DIRECTOR'S VOICE What was that, Morty?

FLOOR MANAGER Sorry, Chief; can't hear you.

DIRECTOR'S VOICE I said: What was that?

FLOOR MANAGER I only said: Can't you hear me?

DIRECTOR'S VOICE Only just. You'll have to speak up.

FLOOR MANAGER OK Chief.

I told you it was simple, didn't I? The Director up there speaks into a talkback and I hear what he says on these cans and I pass on his orders to the studio. Though, as you'll have noticed, there are one or two other people who also wear cans — like our Number One cameraman there and that other chap up there with that thing like a giant steel fishing rod; that's what we call the boom, it's got a mike on the end of it. To both those chaps the Director can speak direct but to most of the others he has to speak through me. And it's I who keep them on their toes.

Well, now I think I've put you in the picture but, before we start the show, I'd just like to ask you all a favour. This is an actuality show and our leading actor is an amateur, so when you're watching it please don't only watch it entertainmentwise; please watch it also imaginationwise. Point taken? Excellent.

(*He turns away*)

DIRECTOR'S VOICE Morty! You've forgotten Admom.

(*Floor Manager turns back to audience*)

FLOOR MANAGER Ladies and gentlemen, I'm terribly sorry. Before the show starts I want to introduce to you one of your favourite artists, who will entertain you at the interval. You all must have seen her many times; to some of you she's a mother, to some of you she's a sweetheart, to some of you she's no less than a great big guardian angel.

(*He cues towards the nearer entrance*)

Ladies and gentlemen, your very own Admom!

(*Admom enters, to fanfare. Flashy middle-aged glamour — blend of brass and sugar. She blows kisses to audience*)

She's saving her voice for later, but you see what a treat's in store for you.

OK, Chief.

Blackout the studio!

(*Blackout stage; light Gallery*)

DIRECTOR What's wrong, Pam?

SECRETARY (*facing him and audience*) This script.

DIRECTOR Well, what about it?

SECRETARY It's blank. Not a line of dialogue in it.

DIRECTOR Pam dear! How long have you been my secretary? Haven't you taken in yet we're not televising a play! This show is pure actuality.

SECRETARY Then I don't have to call the shots?

DIRECTOR Of course not. Just sit in your place and take any notes I give you.

(*She sits beside him*)

Now where's that designer?

SECRETARY He was down on the floor just now putting some last minute touches —

(*Designer comes in, facing audience*)

DIRECTOR Ah there you are, Julian!

DESIGNER Sorry if I've held things up. Some of the props were wrong, as usual. They'd delivered a lot of medieval ones. Memento mori stuff.

DIRECTOR Oh these wretched supply departments! When it *was* the Middle Ages, they were always sending us shooting sticks.

DESIGNER And sten guns sometimes.

DIRECTOR And sten guns.

OK, Morty! Ready in the studio?

FLOOR MANAGER (*on distort, from darkness*) We're ready. Camerawise, lightingwise, boomwise, artwise, lifewise, and deathwise.

DIRECTOR Good. Then we'll go from the top. Silence in the studio.
> (*Blackout Gallery; light Studio*)

FLOOR MANAGER Silence in the studio! Stop that damned racket! We're going from the top.

Jimmy, bring that mike further down.
> (*A studio hand brings handmike down stage. Floor Manager cues the nearer entrance. Crooner comes in and advances briskly to mike*)

CROONER (*crooning*) On earth —

For what it's worth —

We meet

And part —

Oh my babyblue blushpink battleship-grey life!

We meet

In the street,

We part

In the cart,

We live

Like a spiv,

We die

Like a fly,

For what it's all consumerwise actionwise inactionwise bodywise brainwise heartwise soulwise creationwise damnationwise worth —

On earth . . .

For what it's worth.

DIRECTOR'S VOICE Come on; grams there! Clapping!
> (*Clapping on disc; Crooner bows and goes off*)

That could have been smoother but we can't go back on it. Can't go back on anything tonight.

They all know that, don't they, in the studio?

FLOOR MANAGER The boys all know it. Perhaps I ought to tell the audience.
> (*Comes downstage*)

Ladies and gentlemen, before our leading actor comes on, perhaps there's one more thing I should explain to you.

This is really a very peculiar sort of show because it's not a finished product — and never will be. In fact it's really a rehearsal but it's not a typical rehearsal because . . . well, there's only one of it.

It's a sort of do-it-yourself job and the man who does it is Everyman. And now I'm going to cue him.

DIRECTOR'S VOICE Hold it, Morty!

Camera One, are you focused on that entrance?

(*Cameraman holds up hand in assent*)

What lens angle are you on?

CAMERAMAN Zero.

DIRECTOR OK. It's yours, Morty.

(*Floor Manager cues. Everyman enters, bang opposite camera. He is middling well dressed and might come from any sphere of society. Floor Manager cues him again. He does not speak*)

FLOOR MANAGER Come on, come on! Your lines!

EVERYMAN But I haven't learnt them.

FLOOR MANAGER Boy! You've left it late!

EVERYMAN They told me this was actuality. I thought it must be some sort of quiz programme.

FLOOR MANAGER Everyman, you're right there. Only this is a universal quiz.

EVERYMAN Universal?

FLOOR MANAGER Any time, any place, common or garden, ultimate. After all, my dear fellow, this is a mass medium.

Look, I'll brief you quickly. The Director of this show is high up there — you can't see him — so it's I that relays his directions to the artists.

EVERYMAN But I'm not an artist; I've never even been in a studio before.

FLOOR MANAGER In *this* studio you have. Light up that first set!

(*Light up Set One — a token luxury flat with sofa and academic pictures. It is empty*)

FLOOR MANAGER Remember that room?

EVERYMAN Oh yes . . . yes . . . But I've just come from there. Eleanor was sitting on that very sofa beside me. But where's she gone?

FLOOR MANAGER It's *you* who've gone.

OK. Set Two.

(*Blackout Set One; light Two — a mean little office with a typewriter on the desk and a sheet of paper protruding from it*)

EVERYMAN But I've just come from there too! I was typing a memo, I think. Only what was it about? It's funny, I —

FLOOR MANAGER Bring it over here, Bill.

(*Bill extracts memo and brings it downstage to Floor Manager*)
'm . . . You've never finished it. Shall I jog your memory? The last sentence begins:

(*reads*) 'In view of the above considerations and particularly this matter of my failing health I feel reluctantly compelled, in spite of my loyalty to the firm or perhaps I should say because of it, to tender my . . .' That's where you stuck. I presume you meant 'resignation'.

EVERYMAN Did I? Nonsense! I never meant to resign.

FLOOR MANAGER No? Set Three!

(*Blackout Set Two, light Three — a slum bedroom*)

EVERYMAN (*with changed accent*) Oh there? Never want to go there again!

(*A woman half rises from the bedclothes*)

MAGGIE Evvy! Is that you? Come back at once!

FLOOR MANAGER Quick change here. Wardrobe!

(*Wardrobe whips off Everyman's jacket and tie*)
Up you go! She needs you.

(*Everyman, as if doped, goes upstage on to Set Three and sits gingerly on a cane chair*)

MAGGIE No. Evvy! Closer.

(*He shuffles chair up to bed*)
Well, can't you kiss your own wife?

EVERYMAN No, Maggie, I can't.

MAGGIE Course you can't! You feel too guilty.

(*Silence*)
Not much to say for yourself, have you?

EVERYMAN What have you to say for *me*?

FLOOR MANAGER Right cue for once. Tell him.

MAGGIE Why should I say anything for him?

FLOOR MANAGER Because he's about to die.

MAGGIE Oh is he indeed! Well, before he dies, here's an earful for him.

EVERYMAN Who said I was about to —

MAGGIE Shut up! You know what you done to me, Evvy. Married me on false pretences and dragged me down and down. Oh it wasn't just you called yourself a clerk when you was only common working class. And it wasn't just the horses and the drink and the tarts —

EVERYMAN There wasn't no tarts.

MAGGIE Oh wasn't there! But it wasn't just the debts all them things led to, it was the way you withered. And withered me up along with you. When I think of that first time as you took me out to the flicks and your eyes had a lovelight in 'em as good as what was on the screen like and when I compares you then with what you become now —

EVERYMAN It was your fault just as much as mine.

FLOOR MANAGER Wrong answer!

(*Gong. Blackout Set Three*)

FLOOR MANAGER Wardrobe! His jacket and tie.

(*They are carried upstage*)

DIRECTOR'S VOICE Nice work there, all the cameras.

(*Cameraman raises hand. Everyman returns downstage in jacket and tie, bemused*)

FLOOR MANAGER Ready to go on?

EVERYMAN No. What was that Maggie said? About me dying?

FLOOR MANAGER I said it.

EVERYMAN But only in the play?

FLOOR MANAGER I've told you it isn't a play.

EVERYMAN Anyway that wasn't me. (*Changes accent*) The real me was over there. (*Points*)

FLOOR MANAGER Set One!

(*Light Set One — Eleanor on sofa, weeping*)

EVERYMAN Eleanor! But why's she crying?

FLOOR MANAGER For you — we must assume.

(*Eleanor's lover comes in, kisses her and sits down close to her*)

LOVER Not still crying, darling? But you know you didn't love him.

ELEANOR No . . . but I was fond of him.

LOVER Of course you were. However, now we can get married.

ELEANOR I know; it's freedom for both of us. But if only it had come a shade . . .

LOVER Sooner?

ELEANOR Later. Look, darling, I'll be candid; it's a sordid matter of death duties. He knew he had a heart, you see, so he made a settlement in my favour — one of those five years arrangements. Well, this is the fifth year but there still are two months to run.

(*The Lover draws away from her*)

Damn him, damn him, damn him! Why did he always bungle everything?

(*Blackout Set Three*)

FLOOR MANAGER You see? You're damned there too.

(*Looks at wristwatch*)

'm. We're running a shade slow.

EVERYMAN No, there was never any future in it; I must have known that all along. Still, I didn't know she had a lover.

FLOOR MANAGER No future in it, did you say? You don't mean a future life?

EVERYMAN I don't know anything about that.

FLOOR MANAGER Don't you?

EVERYMAN Do *you*?

FLOOR MANAGER I'm not here to answer questions; I'm here in charge of this studio. It's you who must answer any questions there are. And I tell you time's running short.

EVERYMAN I think my life here is possibly the only one.

FLOOR MANAGER Possibly?

EVERYMAN Probably.

FLOOR MANAGER Not 'certainly'?

EVERYMAN Probably.

FLOOR MANAGER Then let's assume it is the only one. In that case, has it been worth while?

EVERYMAN Of course it's been worth while.

MAGGIE'S VOICE (*from darkness*) Liar!

EVERYMAN Don't listen to her. I told you that wasn't me.

ELEANOR'S VOICE (*from darkness*) Liar!

EVERYMAN Don't listen to her either. You can't pin me down like this. After all I'm Everyman. I've had wives and lives by the million, I've had every sort of career, I've —

DIRECTOR'S VOICE Cue Career!

Camera One, stand by for a two-shot.

(*Floor Manager cues. Career enters, dressed like a Civil Servant, attended by a caddy with a large golf bag full of various implements*)

EVERYMAN Career! Just the chap I wanted to see!

I need your help in a new transaction;

I'm relying on you to guarantee —

CAREER Guarantee what exactly?

EVERYMAN   Me!

CAREER You, my dear Everyman? Well, it depends

Whether you're talking of means or ends —

FLOOR MANAGER Make it the singular; call it 'end'.

EVERYMAN Help me, Career. Look, you're my friend —

CAREER Yes, but I have to know in advance

What it is you propose to do:

(*very fast*) To build a new town or destroy an old

Or found a college or a zoo

Or turn a screw or dissect a mouse
Or launch a rocket or sell a pup
Or breed a rose or delouse a louse
Or train a team for the Davis Cup
Or chart the stars on screen or sky
Or manage a bank or write an ad
Or cook an account or an oyster pie
Or make a film of The Shropshire Lad
Or gather plankton from the brine
Or drill for oil or lift a face
Or start one more uranium mine
Or operate on a hopeless case
Or conduct a bus or a five-piece band
Or design a dam or an atom pile —
For any of these I'm here at hand,
Ready to help you with a smile.

EVERYMAN Thank you, Career. I must reply
It's none of these — and you know why?
What I propose to do is die.

CAREER Then I can't help you.

EVERYMAN   But you can!
You are Career and I am man.
I call upon you to confirm
That I was worth that waste of sperm
And that this curious thing we call
Life was a good thing after all.
Therefore, before I keep my date
With tight-lipped and tight-fisted Fate,
I ask you to corroborate
That here on earth I pulled my weight.

CAREER Caddy! The putter!

> (*Caddy hands Everyman a putter*)

Your weight with this?

> (*Everyman makes a feeble stroke with it, towards audience, at an invisible ball; then with an air of despondency hands it to a stage hand. Career takes telescope from caddy and hands it to Everyman*)

Or this?

> (*Everyman looks through telescope over audience, shakes his head sadly and hands it over. Career hands him a sten gun*)

Or this?

> (*Everyman passes it on hastily. Career hands him a set of sweep's rods*)

Or this?

(Everyman tries to fit them together, makes an upward lunge — and they fall apart. He hands them over. Career hands him a bishop's crozier)

Or this?

(Everyman holds it in his left hand, makes as if to bless audience with his right, then shakes his head and hands it over. Career hands him a bass clarinet)

Or this?

(Everyman puts his mouth to it and with great effort produces one hideous sound. He passes it on. Career hands him a rolled umbrella)

Or this?

(Everyman for some time examines umbrella as if he didn't know what it was, then suddenly smiles a smile of recognition, unrolls it very deliberately, puts it up and stands under it)

CAREER Why are you silent, Everyman?

FLOOR MANAGER Strike that umbrella. His face is not in camera.

(A stage hand removes the umbrella)

Well? He asked you why are you silent.

EVERYMAN Then I ask *him*. All these and more
I used in life, but let *him* tell —
Tell them, Career — I used them well.

CAREER Oh yes, at times — at others not.
You used them certainly — but for what?

(A pansy male figure, Lucre, and a female figure, Conscience, have suddenly appeared)

For which of these? For him? For her?

EVERYMAN These two? They're two I've never met.

CONSCIENCE You have met *me*. Can you forget!
When you were young and first began
To work, whatever work it was,
You yearned to prove yourself a man
Or else to help your fellow men
Or both perhaps at once, because
You had some inkling of me then.

EVERYMAN I'm sorry — but I have none now.

(Gong)

FLOOR MANAGER Point taken. Tell him why and how.

CONSCIENCE My name is Conscience. You, when young,
Knew me a little — not for long —
And then you met this fellow here

Who called your tune for many a year.

EVERYMAN He certainly didn't!

LUCRE   Yes, I did.

Don't you remember in Madrid
Turning your coat in '36
And not because of politics —
Oh no, my dear, because of me.
And don't you remember other years
In other countries, other spheres —
The League of Nations, the TUC,
In art or sport or God knows what
Selling the pass, selling the lot,
And at a bargain — you agree?
Since what you lost was only she
And what you won was none but me.

EVERYMAN Then you are...?

LUCRE Lucre!

(*Gong*)

EVERYMAN Lucre!

LUCRE Yes, my dear, they call me 'filthy' — but that's only their fun, you know.

(*He takes out a compact and powders his nose. A bellboy comes in with a cablegram on a salver*)

BELLBOY Paging Filthy Lucre! Paging Filthy Lucre!

LUCRE Here I am!

(*Opens cablegram*)

I must fly! They want me at a summit conference.

(*Goes out*)

CONSCIENCE And me? Who wants me?

DIRECTOR'S VOICE Morty! Get her off.

(*Floor Manager cues Conscience to exit*)

And Career too.

(*Floor Manager cues Career*)

CAREER Goodbye, Everyman.

EVERYMAN Wait a minute.

CAREER I can't.

EVERYMAN Just a minute.

CAREER (*indicating Floor Manager*) He won't let me.

(*He goes out*)

FLOOR MANAGER Over to you, Everyman. He let you down, didn't he. Better try another witness.

EVERYMAN (*northern accent, ponderingly*) Anuther witness? Where's my thinking cap?

FLOOR MANAGER Wardrobe.

(*Wardrobe puts cloth cap on Everyman*)

EVERYMAN Nay, Career were no cop. Ah'd trust my Common Sense though. Where is t'lass?

(*Floor Manager cues into wings. A female figure enters, plainly and severely dressed, wearing secretarial glasses*)

Hullo, luv. Ah knew tha'd come on tick.

COMMON SENSE Everyman, what's wrong now?

EVERYMAN Wrong! Nowt's reet. Ah'm on spot, luv.

COMMON SENSE What spot?

EVERYMAN Ah'm due for coffin.

COMMON SENSE Well, don't let them charge you too much for it.

EVERYMAN That's not what ah mean. Ah want thy services as witness for defence.

COMMON SENSE Do you indeed? What do you expect me to say?

EVERYMAN Summat like this. Ah want thee to say ah always used thee proper and followed all thy advice in matters both great and small —

COMMON SENSE I'll say nothing of the sort. Followed my advice indeed! When I warned you not to waste so much time on whippets and racing pigeons. When I warned you against the Never-Never system — that television set, that refrigerator. When I warned you —

EVERYMAN But tha never did, luv! Tha encouraged me.

COMMON SENSE You only heard me say what you wanted me to say. You dressed me up in your thoughts as Common Sense. At the same time you asked me to let my hair down.

(*With one movement she releases a fall of hair. Then takes off her glasses and throws them to him*)

Here. Catch!

Yes, you dressed me up as Common Sense. But underneath of course . . .

(*With one movement she unzips her frock and steps out of it, revealing very fancy bra and panties*)

I was your Wishful Thinking.

(*She dances round Everyman*)

EVERYMAN My wishful thinking? My dream lass!

(*He makes a grab at her; she eludes him*)

COMMON SENSE Everyman! That's no behaviour for somebody who's dying.

EVERYMAN But ah've been coortin thee for years, luv. Isn't it time thee and me did summat practical about it?

COMMON SENSE Time? Certainly not. No one can do those practical things with me. That is my nature, Everyman.

(*Gong. Everyman pursues Common Sense round stage — ?to music — and all but catches her*)

DIRECTOR'S VOICE Hold it!

FLOOR MANAGER Hold it, both of you.

(*Everyman and Common Sense freeze in their tracks, he with his arms stretched towards her. Floor Manager approaches them*)

I'm afraid that's not allowed in this studio. Not while *I'm* Floor Manager.

(*He points to Exit. Common Sense goes out*)

FLOOR MANAGER (*to Everyman*) You're forgetting this is a public entertainment. It's being watched by millions.

Right. Ready to go on?

EVERYMAN Go on? Where to?

FLOOR MANAGER Alex! Light Set One.

(*The luxury flat is lit up*)

Jimmy, strike that picture. The one over the mantelpiece. Put the Picasso there instead of it.

JIMMY The what, Morty?

FLOOR MANAGER That picture leaning against the flat.

(*Jimmy holds it up*)

JIMMY This?

FLOOR MANAGER That.

(*Jimmy hangs it on set*)

And now that lump of stone with the hole in it, put it camera right. On that table.

(*Jimmy does so*)

FLOOR MANAGER (*to Everyman*) Take off that cap.

(*Everyman takes it off. Wardrobe comes up and removes it*)

EVERYMAN Eee, lad, what dost want with me?

FLOOR MANAGER You can take off that accent too.

EVERYMAN Anything you say. What am I to play now?

FLOOR MANAGER You're to play with your children, Everyman.

EVERYMAN But which children? I've millions.

FLOOR MANAGER Get on Set One.

(*He points. Everyman goes upstage*)

Now sit in that chair. Cross your legs and try to look rich.

(*Everyman does so. Floor Manager cues Son and Daughter, both expensively dressed, who come on and enter set*)

EVERYMAN Oh it's you!

(*Uncrosses legs*)

You're too old to play with now.

SON We were once too young to play with.

DAUGHTER You *never* played with us, Daddy.

EVERYMAN Absolute rubbish. I indulged your every whim.

SON We didn't want them indulged. Why did you never thrash me?

DAUGHTER Why did you tell me I had talent when I hadn't?

EVERYMAN Talent for what?

DAUGHTER For painting?

EVERYMAN But I thought you had.

DAUGHTER Well, I hadn't. And you told me I didn't need training. You just threw that at my head.

(*She points at the Picasso*)

SON Why did you let me come down after my first year at Oxford?

EVERYMAN Because you wanted to.

SON (*bitterly*) Wanted to!

DAUGHTER Why, when I was through with painting, did you let me go on the stage?

EVERYMAN Well, you weren't on it very long, darling.

DAUGHTER Naturally not. I was too bad.

SON Why did you give me all that money when I came of age? That's why I never got anywhere.

DAUGHTER Why did you consent to my marriage?

EVERYMAN I couldn't have stopped you.

DAUGHTER You encouraged me. And, since he was your junior partner, you must have known what he was.

EVERYMAN I didn't, I didn't, I didn't!

SON No, you never knew anything.

DAUGHTER Which is why we don't know anything.

SON We're out of touch with everything.

DAUGHTER Even including ourselves.

EVERYMAN I can't bear it. You're lying. My God, I did all I could for you.

(*He rushes on to Set Two, which is still blacked out*)

FLOOR MANAGER Wardrobe!

(*A dresser dresses Son and Daughter in mackintoshes*)

Set Two!

(Set Two is lit up. Everyman is sitting at desk. Son and Daughter come in)

EVERYMAN What do you mean? Coming into my office like this!

SON This is the showdown, Father.

DAUGHTER Yes, Father. This is it.

SON I must have more money.

DAUGHTER So must I.

EVERYMAN But you've both got good jobs.

SON I'm sacked.

DAUGHTER I've turned in my chips.

EVERYMAN It's not true!

DAUGHTER It is.

SON It is.

EVERYMAN After all the education I've given you!

SON *You've* given us! State scholarships.

DAUGHTER And a fat lot of good they've done us.

SON You promised us a brave new world —

EVERYMAN It wasn't me; it was the State. You just said yourself it was.

DAUGHTER I'd rather have left school at fourteen.

SON So would I. I'd be somewhere by now. Instead of competing with the nobs —

DAUGHTER And you can't compete with them anyway.

EVERYMAN Look, it's nothing to do with me —

SON That's just the point.

DAUGHTER It never was.

SON And that's why we want some dough from you.

DAUGHTER It's the only reason we're here.

EVERYMAN But . . . all this has happened before. *You* were sacked from *your* job, *you* resigned from *yours* — and you both came in here to dun me, wearing those very same mackintoshes. And I gave you a hundred quid each. Why put the clock back like this?

SON Whose clock, Father? Yours — or ours?

DAUGHTER We know about yours. It's stopping.

(Everyman runs on to Set Three)

FLOOR MANAGER Dresser! Those teddy costumes. Quick.

(Son and Daughter are assisted in a quick change)

DIRECTOR'S VOICE Camera One!

CAMERAMAN Boss?

DIRECTOR'S VOICE Track in on Set Three. Be ready for a tight three-shot.

(Cameraman raises hand and is pushed in towards set)

FLOOR MANAGER Jimmy, got that cracked mirror in position?

JIMMY Yeah, Morty.

FLOOR MANAGER And what about the flick-knife?

JIMMY He's got it.

FLOOR MANAGER And she's got the lipstick?

JIMMY Sure, Morty.

FLOOR MANAGER OK. Set Three!

> (*Set Three is lit up. Everyman is in bed under the bedclothes with only one shirtsleeved arm hanging out*)

DIRECTOR'S VOICE Hold it, Morty, till I tell you. Don't cue too soon.

FLOOR MANAGER No, chief.

DIRECTOR'S VOICE Grams! Put on that clock.

> (*Heavy clock ticking on disc*)

Try playing it faster.

> (*Speed increased*)

OK.

Right, Morty. Cue them.

> (*Floor Manager cues. Son and Daughter enter Set Three. Daughter goes up to bed and peers*)

SON Ain't 'e croaked yet?

> (*She shakes her head*)

Bleedin' old crumb! See if 'is pocket-book's under the pillow as usual.

DAUGHTER See for yourself.

SON Do as I tell you! You don't want the busies to catch us 'ere.

> (*She puts her hand under pillow. Everyman grips her wrist and sits up*)

DAUGHTER Let go of me, you bleedin' old punk!

> (*Son comes up and flashes flick-knife*)

SON Let go of her, pop, or . . .

> (*Everyman drops her wrist*)

That's more sensible. 'And me 'is pocket book.

> (*She does so. He inspects it*)

Yeah. That'll get us out of London.

EVERYMAN So you'd rob your own father!

SON You don't need it no more. We do. The busies is after us.

EVERYMAN Why, what you done this time?

SON Done up an old party comin' out of the Ladies in the High Street.

DAUGHTER The bitch! She must have spent 'er last penny down there. Nothing in 'er bleedin' 'andbag but a bleedin' lipstick.

> (*She takes it out of her pocket*)

Not such a bad one though.

(*She starts to make up her mouth in mirror*)

SON Come on, Sis. You can do that later.

DAUGHTER Trouble with you is you're yellow.

DIRECTOR'S VOICE Track in, One. Track in.

(*Camera moves in*)

EVERYMAN 'Alf a tick. Leave me ten bob.

SON Oh no we don't; you're dying. It's you what ought to be leavin' things.

EVERYMAN There's one thing I'll leave you. My curse.

(*Gong*)

You brought nothing on me but disgrace. Pair of 'alf-baked delinquents.

SON And 'oo was the one what 'alf-baked us. 'Oo was it failed to bring us up like?

DAUGHTER 'Oo was it told us everything was a racket? 'Oo was it told us to see to ourselves — once Ma died?

DIRECTOR'S VOICE Track in still further, One.

(*Camera pushes in*)

EVERYMAN It wasn't my fault she died.

SON I'm not so sure of that neither. But we ain't got time to argue that now.

(*Knocking by spot boy*)

DAUGHTER Schtum! The busies!

(*Spot boy opens spot door. Son and Daughter swing round to face camera*)

FLOOR MANAGER Hands up, kids.

(*They both put up hands*)

DIRECTOR'S VOICE Very nice shot, One. I'll just hold that a few seconds.

(*Pause*)

OK. Cut!

(*Set Three is blacked out*)

FLOOR MANAGER Elsie! Everyman's jacket!

Jimmy! Rearrange that bed. And bring on the rocking chair.

(*Turns to audience*)

Well, ladies and gentlemen, I hope you're enjoying the show. I am anyway, even if you're not. Of course for me it's an ever-present problem; for you it's only a future problem. Talking of the future, have you heard the one about the three men in the crematorium? An Englishman, an Irishman, and a Jew. The argument was: who should be cremated first.

(He is interrupted by Everyman, staggering downstage)

EVERYMAN The dice are loaded! The dice are loaded!

FLOOR MANAGER Wait for your cue for speech.

EVERYMAN I won't wait, I can't. I've got free will, haven't I?

FLOOR MANAGER Not in this studio, chum.

EVERYMAN But I'm Everyman; I've had millions of children. Those three pairs weren't typical. Think of John and Mary, Jean et Marie, Giovanni e Maria, Johann und Maria, Ivan and Marya, Sean agus Maire, Junior and Shirley. Think of all those Christmas stockings and yo-yos and Davy Crockett hats and toy pistols and national savings certificates and white mice and pop records and higher education and hula hoops. Yes, more often than not I've been an excellent parent. Heaven knows that's true.

FLOOR MANAGER *Heaven* knows?

Eric! Move that boom over here.

(Eric swings the mike towards him)

FLOOR MANAGER *(into mike)* Hullo there! Can you hear me? Only just? Then I'll raise my voice. Everyman — all right, I'll spell it. E for earth, V for virus, E for evil, R for ruin, Y for yellow, M for misfit, A for anguish, N for nobody ... That's right, Everyman. Well, Everyman claims he's been an excellent parent ... Excellent what? I'll spell it. P for pap, A for ashes, R for rot, E for envy, N for nonsense, T for torture: Parent. Everyman claims he's —

(He is cut off by a burst of laughter through distort)

FLOOR MANAGER *(as laughter subsides)* There you are, Everyman. That's your answer.

EVERYMAN My answer? It's faked. Faked like everything else between these four walls. I'm walking out here and now.

(He moves towards one of the doors marked 'Exit' in lights but as he reaches it, the two letters 'No' flash up to form the phrase 'No Exit'. He moves towards the other door, with the same result. All those in the studio burst into laughter)

DIRECTOR'S VOICE Grams! Back up that laughter.

(Add laughter on disc)

EVERYMAN *(coming downstage again)* Stop it! Stop it! Stop it!

(He puts his hands to his ears)

DIRECTOR'S VOICE OK. Grams out.

(The grams are cut)

FLOOR MANAGER Stop laughing, chaps.

(They stop. He goes up to Everyman and gently removes his hands from his ears)

Look, my dear fellow —

EVERYMAN Take your hands off me. They're like ice.

FLOOR MANAGER So are yours, my dear fellow. Not surprisingly.

(*He looks at his wrist-watch*)

Well, who's your next witness?

EVERYMAN I've got no time for your so-called witnesses.

FLOOR MANAGER Oh but you have. Though only a little time. Look, let me give you a tip. You're Everyman; it's in your character to get corrupted with the years. By the time you come on this floor you've forgotten the meaning of innocence. Suppose we go back to your youth?

EVERYMAN Yes. I was innocent then.

FLOOR MANAGER Whom can you call on to prove it?

EVERYMAN I know! My first love.

FLOOR MANAGER Which of them?

EVERYMAN Almost any of them would do. Jane, Joanna, Margot, Rosalind, Peggy, Patricia, Trixy, Sue; Annchen, Gretchen, Gretel, Greta; Ginette, Ninette, Babette, Colette; Francesca, Giovanna, Teresa, Lucrezia —

FLOOR MANAGER OK, OK; point taken. Which do you choose?

EVERYMAN Which . . . I leave it to you. First love is always genuine.

FLOOR MANAGER All right then. Set Three!

(*Set Three is lit up. The bed has been converted into a settee with cheap cushions. A working-class girl sits in a rocking chair, singing softly 'Rockabye Baby'. The dresser puts a cloth cap on Everyman*)

EVERYMAN Doreen!

(*Everyman goes up on to set*)

Whatever were you singing that for?

DOREEN I was looking ahead, Evvy, to when you and me get married.

EVERYMAN Married?! . . . I'll have to wait for a rise.

DOREEN Oh Evvy! You said last week —

EVERYMAN I've thought it over since then. You see, Doreen —

DOREEN I see only too well. It's that Connie with her perm and her giggle and —

EVERYMAN It's not a bloody perm, it's natural.

DOREEN So it *is* Connie! I knew it.

(*She takes off a ring and hands it to him*)

Here, Evvy, take this back. It's cheap, it should just suit Connie.

EVERYMAN But Doreen darling —

DOREEN Don't darling me! There's the door; you needn't come darkening it again.

(*Everyman hesitates, then goes downstage. Doreen begins to sing again; her voice cracks as the lights dim. Set Three is blacked out. The voice tails off, as the dresser removes Everyman's cloth cap and throws a college scarf round his neck. Mary comes downstage in a straw hat and a summer frock c.1930. She approaches Everyman from behind and tugs his scarf*)

EVERYMAN (*turning*) Who's that? Oh Mary darling!

(*He pushes back her hat and they kiss*)

MARY What a wonderful day! I feel they've laid it on specially. Specially for you and me.

EVERYMAN Who have?

MARY Why Those Ones. (*She points upward*) Let's go and sit on the bank of the river.

(*They come right downstage and sit on floor facing the audience*)

EVERYMAN Look at all those mayflies. To think they live one day only!

MARY (*dreamily*) On a day like this . . . it might be worth it. I wonder . . . do mayflies have a love-life?

EVERYMAN Of course they do. That's why they dance in the air so.

MARY Everything's dancing today. Look at that ripple over there. And those willows going white in the sudden gust of wind. And that field of hay over there.

EVERYMAN It isn't hay, silly; it's wheat.

MARY Well, whatever it is, I shall never forget it. And why you should wear a scarf when the sun's as warm as this — !

(*She removes his scarf and toys with it*)

That couple in the punt, do you think they're like us?

EVERYMAN Certainly not. No one in the world's like us.

MARY No one has the same world *we* have.

EVERYMAN And no one has the same day we have.

MARY No, I'll never forget this day.

EVERYMAN I'll never forget how the sun at this moment brings out the lights in your hair.

MARY Have you a hanky?

(*He shakes his head*)

Pity. I was going to tie a knot in it. Never mind; this is even better.

(*She ties a knot in his scarf*)

There! That's to remind you.

EVERYMAN Of what?

MARY Of me.

EVERYMAN Oh you mug!

(*They embrace, then lie down interclasped*)

DIRECTOR'S VOICE Cue Forgetfulness. Track in Camera One.

(*Floor Manager cues. A female figure, wearing dark glasses, comes in and stands behind the couple, looking down on them*)

DIRECTOR'S VOICE A narrower lens, One . . . Thank you. Nice composition.

(*Forgetfulness taps first Everyman, then Mary, on their shoulders*)

FORGETFULNESS (*sadly*) Break it up, children; break it up.

(*They draw apart and stand up with their backs to each other*)

MARY (*as if doped*) Where was I?

FORGETFULNESS You were dreaming.

(*She points to an Exit. Mary walks out as if sleep-walking*)

EVERYMAN I've been asleep. Was anyone here?

FORGETFULNESS No one.

EVERYMAN That's funny. I thought for a moment . . .

(*He notices his scarf on the ground, picks it up and slowly unties the knot, then puts it around his neck*)

What a horrible day! It's cold.

(*Gong. Everyman turns towards audience*)

And what am I doing by this river? Is it the Isis or the Avon or possibly even the Ouse or —

FORGETFULNESS Its name is Lethe, Everyman.

(*She goes out while he stands gazing over audience*)

FLOOR MANAGER Innocence, eh? You'd better go further back still.

DIRECTOR'S VOICE That's right, Morty. Set up the Mother scene. Is she ready for her cue?

FLOOR MANAGER She's been ready since we started.

DIRECTOR'S VOICE Then cue her when you're set.

FLOOR MANAGER OK. I'll just check the props.

Jimmy! Has she got the chocolates?

JIMMY No Morty. She hasn't.

FLOOR MANAGER Then why the hell not? Give her those chocolates at once.

JIMMY I can't. Somebody's eaten 'em.

FLOOR MANAGER I'll talk to *him* later. What about the box?

JIMMY Oh the box is OK.

FLOOR MANAGER Then tie it up neatly with its ribbon. A big symmetrical bow, mind.

Now where's that kiddy stool? You there, bring it down here.

(*A stagehand brings down a very small stool*)

DIRECTOR'S VOICE Two, can you hear me?

VOICE OFF (*on distort*) Yeah, boss.

DIRECTOR'S VOICE In this scene you get an over-the-shoulder of Everyman. Three over-the-shoulder of the Mother. One does the two-shots. Clear?

(*Cameraman raises hand. Floor Manager points to stool*)

FLOOR MANAGER Everyman! Sit there.

EVERYMAN It's too small.

FLOOR MANAGER I want it small. You're small too in this scene.

(*Everyman perches very awkwardly on stool*)

OK. Look expectant. I'm going to cue your mother.

(*He raises his hand and, after a pause, drops it. The Mother comes in and rushes to Everyman whom she embraces; she is wearing Edwardian dress and carries a large box of chocolates and a book wrapped up in brown paper*)

MOTHER Evvy, my darling, my pet! Here's Mummy, back from her rest cure.

EVERYMAN Oh lovely, lovely Mummy! It's been ages, it's been awful! Are you quite, quite better now?

MOTHER 'Quite' perhaps, darling; not 'quite, quite'. But Evvy needn't worry; Mummy'll be 'quite, quite' soon. And she's brought some presents for Evvy. She got them the moment she left the rest cure place. First, there's this nice big book —

EVERYMAN What's in that box, Mummy?

MOTHER First there's this nice big book. (*She tears off the wrapping*) I know my Evvy can't read yet so I got him a book full of pictures. There are stories in it too of course. They were written by a man called Hans Andersen.

(*Everyman takes the book and turns the pages*)

EVERYMAN Ooh what's this? A Christmas tree!

MOTHER That's right — but that's a sad story.

EVERYMAN Why, what's sad about Christmas trees? Oh here's a great big bird — it's a swan.

MOTHER That's called the Ugly Duckling.

EVERYMAN Why's it called a duckling if it's a swan? Ooh, I don't like this one! A little girl without any feet and her shoes are running away on their own.

MOTHER That's another sad story. She was too fond of dancing.

EVERYMAN But *you're* fond of dancing, Mummy.

MOTHER Mummy won't dance again for some time, I fear. Ah that's a man who lost his shadow.

And this is a story called The Nightingale.

EVERYMAN Who's that ugly big man looking over the end of the bed?

MOTHER That's supposed to be Death. But don't be frightened; they sent him away.

EVERYMAN Can anyone send Death away, Mummy?

DIRECTOR'S VOICE Morty! You're in shot.

FLOOR MANAGER Sorry, chief.

(*Having sidled in between the Mother and the camera, he now withdraws*)

EVERYMAN (*shutting book*) Mummy, I don't like this book. Can I see what's in the box now?

MOTHER Don't be impatient, my pet. I give you three guesses.

EVERYMAN Chockies!

MOTHER What a clever little boy my Evvy is. Yes, this box is chock-full of chockies as . . . as Mummy's heart is full of love for her baby.

EVERYMAN And Evvy's heart's full of love for his Mummy.

(*He embraces her and eagerly opens the box, which holds nothing but empty chocolate papers. As he drops them one by one on the floor, the lights dim gradually to blackout. A gong*)

DIRECTOR'S VOICE Hold that blackout. Let her get off.

FLOOR MANAGER (*in darkness*) This way, Madam. Come with me.

(*In the darkness, off, a child's voice is heard singing a hymn as far as the lines:*
    'Teach me to live that I may dread
    The grave as little as my bed . . .'
The voice is cut as the lights come up. Everyman is still sitting on the kiddy stool as if in a trance)

EVERYMAN The grave . . . as little . . . as my bed?

(*He slumps on to floor, in crumpled position, with face towards audience*)

DIRECTOR'S VOICE One, track in. And from above. Hold that shot. It's excellent.

(*Blackout stage and light up production gallery*)

DIRECTOR Excellent, isn't it, Pam?

SECRETARY (*in profile*) Yes, I think it's lovely.

DIRECTOR And you, Julian?

DESIGNER (*in profile*) Beautiful foetal position. I'm sorry about the stool though.

DIRECTOR Why, what's wrong with it?

DESIGNER I specified something smaller.

DIRECTOR Don't be perfectionist, Julian. That's a fault *I* grew out of long ago.

VISION MIXER (*in profile*) Shall I cut now?

DIRECTOR No, hold it.

(*On distort*) Morty! What about Sacrifice?

FLOOR MANAGER'S VOICE (*distant, on distort*) Sacrifice? She's just come in from make-up.

DIRECTOR (*on distort*) OK. Stand by to cue her. But first get Everyman off that stool and strike it.

One, get focused on that entrance. Sacrifice will walk into camera. We'll lose Everyman for the moment.

VISION MIXER You'll tell me when to cut?

DIRECTOR The moment I say Cue.

(*On distort*) Ready, Morty?

FLOOR MANAGER (*on distort*) Ready.

DIRECTOR Here we go then. Cue!

> (*Blackout gallery, light stage. Everyman is hidden behind a flat. Sacrifice enters, dressed something between a nurse and a nun. She stands upstage and looks around*)

SACRIFICE I am Sacrifice. Does anyone want me?

> (*Silence*)

If nobody wants me, I will go back where I came from.

EVERYMAN (*rushing out*) No, no, no, don't go! You're my best witness — *my* Sacrifice.

SACRIFICE You? Who are you?

EVERYMAN (*turning to audience*) Don't pay no heed to her, she's kidding. She knows me backwards same as I know her. Yes, she's the one'll speak up for me. Why, I've been in both her wars and not a conscript neither. (*Dropping voice*) Or sometimes I *have* been a conscript.

> (*Dresser puts on his head a World War I military cap*)

DIRECTOR'S VOICE Morty, cue Patria too.

> (*Floor Manager cues. Patria enters, dressed like a synthesis of the Women's Auxiliary Forces. She stands beside Sacrifice*)

EVERYMAN Yes, I was at Mons, Gallipoli, the Somme, Passchendaele, the lot.

DIRECTOR'S VOICE Come in, Grams.

> (*'Tipperary' is heard off stage. Everyman begins to march around stage, Sacrifice following him*)

EVERYMAN I'm following you, Sacrifice, I'm following you.

SACRIFICE Are you, Everyman?

EVERYMAN (*still marching*) Only trouble is I can't see you. Which means I can't see the sense of you.

DIRECTOR'S VOICE Cut grams!

> (*'Tipperary' ends abruptly. Everyman comes to attention, facing Patria*)

PATRIA Everyman! Stand at ease.
(*He does so*)
You know who I am?

EVERYMAN (*cockney*) 'Dulce et decorum est pro patria mori'.

PATRIA Ten out of ten.
Next question: Why did you join up?

EVERYMAN Because Kitchener pointed 'is bloody great finger at me.

SACRIFICE You were patriotic in fact? You were true to *her*?

EVERYMAN That's right. And true to you too, ma'am. My Kitchener
and country (*jerks thumb at Patria*) wanted me, and my sacrifice (*jerks
thumb at Sacrifice*) — you was supreme!

PATRIA You're lying, Everyman.

SACRIFICE You're lying.
(*Patria removes his hat and extracts a large white feather*)

PATRIA *That* was why you joined up.

EVERYMAN (*to Floor Manager*) Now look 'ere, you're riggin' it again.
I'm Everyman, I been millions o' different soldiers — not to mention
sailors and airmen and Civil Defence and flamin' old National Fire
Service.

FLOOR MANAGER Dresser! Beret!
(*The dresser hands him a World War II beret*)

DIRECTOR'S VOICE Grams!
(*Air-raid siren on disc: the 'Alert'*)

EVERYMAN (*educated voice*) Yes, World War Two. Dunkirk, Alamein,
Anzio, Burma, Arnhem, what-have you. In infantry, artillery, para-
troops, tanks; in aircraft-carriers, submarines, corvettes, and mine-
sweepers; as fighter pilot, navigator, rear-gunner, ground staff.

DIRECTOR'S VOICE Wind him up, Morty.
(*Floor Manager makes winding-up movement*)

EVERYMAN But what's much more important than that —
(*He notices Floor Manager and breaks off*)

DIRECTOR'S VOICE That'll do, Grams. Lose it.
(*The 'Alert' fades*)

PATRIA Everyman! 'Shun!
(*Everyman comes to attention*)
Why did you join up this time? For me again?

EVERYMAN No, not this time; of course not. The issues this time were
international. King and country didn't come into it. All through the
'Thirties I'd been antifascist and —

DIRECTOR'S VOICE Hold it! Get Patria off.
(*Floor Manager cues Patria. She exits*)

SACRIFICE You were saying?

EVERYMAN I thought this last war was a just one. I entered it for an ideal. And you, my Sacrifice, I thought you would be worth it.

SACRIFICE And was I?

(*A pause; then the 'All Clear' is heard on grams. Everyman throws his beret on the ground*)

Was I?

EVERYMAN (*more to self*) All Clear they called it ... Nothing's clear.

(*Sacrifice shakes her head sadly and moves slowly towards Exit*)

DIRECTOR'S VOICE Camera One! Hold Everyman, lose Sacrifice.

(*The All Clear fades out as Sacrifice goes off*)

Fine!

Now, Morty, I think we'll have a break for tea.

FLOOR MANAGER Relax all of you. We're giving you a break.

EVERYMAN (*cockney again*) Giving me a break, Guv? A break! When this whole flamin' show's been fixed and rigged and –

FLOOR MANAGER Of course it's been fixed. It's a *permanent* fixture; it's popular. And there are plenty of people over there who'd be proud to be in your shoes. And, proud or not, they *will* be. Besides, I only meant a tea-break.

(*To studio crew*) Now listen, chaps, you've done pretty well so far but in the second half I want you all really on your toes.

(*To audience*) Ladies and gentlemen, we now have an interval. And I'd just like to remind you that after the interval we start with a few minutes' advertising. This will be in charge of the lovely little lady whom I introduced to you earlier.

(*Everyman begins to light a cigarette; Floor Manager rounds on him*)

Sorry, chum. (*He takes cigarette and stamps on it*) Smoking forbidden in the studio – except when it's part of the action. And while I'm in charge of this floor – and I am and always shall be –

(*He turns to audience*)

and that goes for all of you too – well, just remember I'm in charge. I cue you in and I cue you out.

(*He strikes an attitude and begins to sing to the tune of 'John Peel'*)

Oh I cue you in and I cue you out

And nobody knows what it's all about;

Though you start in hope you must end in doubt

  When I knock on your door in the morning.

(*The studio crew have formed up behind him to constitute a chorus*)

CHORUS

  Oh he cues you in and he cues you out

And nobody knows what it's all about;
Though you start in hope you must end in doubt
   When he knocks on your door in the morning.
      (*Blackout. INTERVAL*)

ACT TWO

(*Lights come up on an empty stage. Floor Manager walks on and blows whistle. The hands pour on, making an enormous racket*)

DIRECTOR'S VOICE Morty!

FLOOR MANAGER Chief?

DIRECTOR'S VOICE Stop that damned racket.

FLOOR MANAGER Silence in the studio!

(*Silence*)

DIRECTOR'S VOICE Got her chalk marks, Morty?

FLOOR MANAGER Chalk marks, Jimmy?

JIMMY (*pointing to floor*) Here, Morty. True to the centimetre.

FLOOR MANAGER They're OK, Chief.

DIRECTOR'S VOICE One on that entrance.

Right, Morty. Cue Admom.

FLOOR MANAGER Stand by all of you. The Admom cometh.

(*He raises his hand, then drops it. Admom enters to a fanfare, followed by a page carrying two hoops of different sizes — one for close-up and one for middle shots — each shaped and proportioned like a TV screen. Floor Manager points her to her chalk marks*)

ADMOM Good evening, chickabiddies. Here is your very own Admom fresh from Salt Lake City. And she's brought her depth probers with her.

(*She pulls out from her corsage two pencil-shaped surgical-looking instruments and points them playfully at audience*)

The very latest in motivational research.

(*She hands the probers to a stage hand*)

You know the old saying of the famous British poet, Rabbie Burns? 'A chiel's amang ye taking notes'. Well, I'm not exactly a chiel — a child to you Sassenachs — after all I'm 39–21–39 — but I certainly can take notes — *your* statistics are vital too — and I sure know my consumers. And talking of consumers, where's my little boyfriend Everyman?

(*Floor Manager cues in Everyman*)

Ah there you are, sweetie-pie! It seems an age since I told you about that cute new aperient. Has it had any effects yet?

(*Without waiting for an answer, she turns back to audience*)

What other old friends do I see here? . . . Oh you, honey! (*She waves towards back of audience*) I'm glad to see you're wearing that invisible hearing aid.

Well, you're certainly a peach of an audience — I only wish I could
eat you. Old friends or new, I feel I know you so well. With all your
little fads and human weaknesses — I guess it's because I'm maternal
but I just adore those weaknesses. You there, sir, for example —

(*She blows a kiss*)

I know what you were up to today. Buying exactly the same things
as usual — same brand of cigarettes, same brand of gin, same daily
newspaper, same brand of peptalk — as you did yesterday and the day
before yesterday and the day before the day before the day before
yesterday, as you will do tomorrow and the day after tomorrow and
the day after the day after the day after tomorrow, or to cut a long
story short what the dear old Romans called in perpetuum — and quite
right too, I'm all for brand-consciousness.

And you there, madam, I must congratulate you. You went to the
stores today, didn't you? What a fine example of impulse buying —
it should be a lesson to all of us. Do let me know — if ever you get
round to cooking it — what that canned nasturtium tastes like.

And now, before we get on to our teeny-tiny concert — and don't
expect any cha-cha, it will all be the dear old tunes that you learnt at
Grandma's knee — I've a special word for Everyman. Come here and
sit at my feet, honey.

(*He does so*)

Everyman, to me you're just my Everybaby. This is a mass medium
and you are my mass poppet. You are my litmus paper and I am your
acid or alkali. You are my hairy doormat and I am your highheeled
shoe. You are my raw cloth; I am your tailor and cutter. You are my
old flame; I am your brand-new bellows. You are my far-flung banner;
I am your strange device. You are my horsepower; I am your chassis.
You are my sweat-glands; I am your deodorant. You are my upper
crust; I am your detergent. You are my holy spot; I am your holy
spotlight. You are my stillborn child; I am your bottle of pickle.
You are my lovely corpse; I am your lovely casket. In fact I'm your
all-in-all — both tranquillizer and stimulant. You are my honey and I
am your money. You are my Admass and I your Admom!

(*She signals to page who hands her the smaller TV hoop which she
holds up to frame her face, and begins to sing to tune of 'Comin' Round
the Mountain'*)

Oh 'tis I'm your second momma, Ev-ry-man,

'Tis I'm your second momma, Ev-ry-man,

'Tis I'm your second momma, I'm your second momma, 'tis I'm your
    second momma, Ev-ry-man.

(The stage hands take up the chorus)

CHORUS Oh 'tis she's your second momma, Ev-ry-man, etc.

ADMOM Oh 'tis I can soothe your fever, Ev-ry-man, etc.

CHORUS On 'tis she etc.

ADMOM Oh 'tis I will gild your casket, Ev-ry-man, etc.

CHORUS Oh 'tis she etc.

DIRECTOR'S VOICE Grams!

> *(Outburst of clapping on disc)*

In over it!

> *(Floor Manager cues. A robot-like figure, like a deep-sea diver, dressed in steel, with a huge steel head, various protuberous knobs and levers, and dials let into his chest, enters and stands beside Admom. Or he could be wheeled in on a trolley. The clapping fades)*

ADMOM Now here's an answer to *all* your worries. Everyman all through history — and Everywoman more recently — have wasted far too much time in the cumbrous business of thinking. But you needn't bother any more. Here is the very latest in infallible mechanical computers. Why be your own egghead when you can use electronics?

> *(She holds up the hoop to frame the Electronic Brain in a middle close-up. It points a lobster-like claw at audience and sings — in a metallic voice)*

ELECTRONIC BRAIN *(singing)* The old grey matter it ain't what it used to be, ain't what it used to be, ain't what it used to be,

The old grey matter it ain't what it used to be

Many long years ago —

CHORUS Many long years ago *(etc.)*

ELECTRONIC BRAIN But I've taken over, I think on behalf of you, think on behalf of you, think on behalf of you,

I've taken over, I think on behalf of you

Now and for evermore.

CHORUS Now and for evermore, now and for evermore —

Oh he's taken over, he thinks on behalf of us, thinks on behalf of us, thinks on behalf of us,

He's taken over, he thinks on behalf of us

Now and for evermore.

ELECTRONIC BRAIN Oh Adam and Eve hadn't heard of uranium, heard of uranium, heard of uranium,

Adam and Eve hadn't heard of uranium

Many long years ago.

CHORUS *(repeats)*

ELECTRONIC BRAIN So Adam and Eve were thrown out of Paradise,
  thrown out of Paradise, thrown out of Paradise,
 Adam and Eve were thrown out of Paradise,
    Many long years ago.
CHORUS (*repeats*)
ELECTRONIC BRAIN But Science today is the high road to Paradise,
  high road to Paradise, high road to Paradise,
 Science today is the high road to Paradise,
    Now and till Kingdom Come.
CHORUS Now and till Kingdom Come, now and till Kingdom Come,
  Science today (*etc.*).
    Now and till Kingdom Come!
    (*Clapping on disc. The Electronic Brain takes a bow and walks off,
    crossing Sean Bull who briskly takes his place beside Admom*)
ADMOM And now — the famous Irish tenor, Sean Bull!
    (*She holds up the hoop to frame his face. He sings in a mock sugary
    brogue, third-rate MacCormack, to the tune of 'I'm sittin' by the stile,
    Mary'*)
SEAN BULL (*singing*)
 I'm sittin' on the fence, Mary,
    Where we sat side by side,
 When we did not know which way to go
    For both our hands were tied.

 Oh the trains I missed with you, Mary,
    The dates that made no sense!
 It all comes back to me today
    Still sittin' on the fence.
 (*Speaking, without brogue*) Buy Jedermann's supergalvanized fencing.
    It's unrustable, it's unbustable, it will save you hedging and trim-
    ming. All the top people use it. Jedermann's Super Fencing!
ADMOM Thank you, Sean Bull. And your next?
SEAN BULL (*singing, again in brogue*)
 Oh a power of black porter's flowed under the bridges
 Of Shannon and Lagan and Liffey and Lee
 Since Brian Boru slew the Danes in the ditches
 And the bould Finn McCool courted Mother Machree.
    But och the dear memories they rest evergreen
    With a harp in the hand and a jar of poteen.
CHORUS But och etc.
SEAN BULL
 The green moon is settin' beyond the dark pylon

But still in ould Ireland the whiskey flows free,
With all the colleens wearin' stockin's of nylon
And Father O'Flynn rollin' down to the sea.
  But och the dear memories they still linger on
  Of Cuchullain and Deirdre and Potstill and Conn.
(*Speaking, in brogue*) Dhrink Irish whiskey —
(*Speaking, in Scots*) when ye canny get Scotch.
    (*Clapping on disc*)
ADMOM Thank you, Sean Bull; that was sweet.
    (*Sean Bull takes a bow and goes off, crossing Comedian got up like the
    early Chaplin*)
And now — as your final titbit for tonight before I return you to your
Master of Ceremonies (*she looks at Floor Manager who bows*) — I have
the greatest pleasure in introducing to you one of the best-known
comedians of this country whose name is known to none of you for
the simple reason that he's never himself.
Tonight he is: Charles Chaplin.
    (*Clapping on disc and out*)
And, since he is the Chaplin of the early pictures, he does not speak
in his act. So on his behalf I will tell you his slogan. It is: 'Always
carry a supercharged walking stick'.
DIRECTOR'S VOICE Morty! Where *is* his walking stick?
FLOOR MANAGER Jimmy! Walking stick!
    (*Jimmy runs down and hands Comedian a white stick. Instruments off
    strike up tune of 'The Moon Shines Bright on Charlie Chaplin'. Com-
    edian twirls his stick and shuffle-dances while Admom holds the larger
    hoop in front of him*)
EVERYMAN Coo, this takes me back!
    (*Comedian suddenly falls down. Everyman runs up and assists him
    to his feet. Comedian bows gravely to him and hands him the white
    stick*)
COMEDIAN You need it more than I do.
    (*He bows to audience and walks off briskly. Everyman passes his hand
    over his eyes and starts probing about with stick*)
ADMOM Everyman, honey! Can't you see?
EVERYMAN No, Mom. Where are you?
ADMOM (*to audience*) Shows what suggestion can do.
    Everyman! Evvy! Come here.
EVERYMAN Coming, Mom.
    (*He stumbles in the wrong direction. She catches him up and steadies
    him*)

ADMOM What happened to you, Evvy?

EVERYMAN I was on the road to Damascus.

>   (*Pause*)

Or was it the Dardanelles?

>   (*He sings*)

'Oh the moon shines bright on Charlie Chaplin,
His boots are crackin'
For want of blackin'
And his little baggy trousers they want mendin'
Before we send him
To the Dardanelles.'

ADMOM Give me that stick.

>   (*He does so*)

Now open your eyes.

EVERYMAN But I can see!

>   (*She thrusts stick back into his hand*)

No, I can't see.

>   (*She takes stick away again*)

Yes, I can.

>   (*She thrusts it back*)

No, I can't.

>   (*He stands helplessly with both hands resting on top of stick. A dresser places on his head the Comedian's Chaplinesque hat which he had dropped in his fall*)

ADMOM (*to audience*) Nothing like a prop, is there? Which only goes to show that advertising's the eyesight of the nation. And your very own Admom here — why, she's also your very own optician. Not to mention a lot of things which rhyme with it. Your physician, your beautician —

>   (*Floor Manager makes winding-up sign*)

Thank you, Morty — and your mortician too.

Well, goodnight everyone, remember me in your dreams.

>   (*She starts moving off. Floor Manager snatches stick from Everyman*)

FLOOR MANAGER Here, take this with you. We want him to die with his eyes open.

>   (*She takes stick and walks to Exit, swaying her hips. Everyman fingers his eyes and addresses audience*)

EVERYMAN Who was that? I thought for a moment she was my mother.

>   (*Pause*)

But, if she was, the milk was from a bottle.

ADMOM (*from Exit*) You're wrong, honey. It was dried milk.

(*She goes out. Gong*)

FLOOR MANAGER Elsie! Take away that hat.

(*A dresser removes the Chaplin hat*)

Now let's get on with the action. Everyman, you're seeing all right again?

EVERYMAN Yes.

FLOOR MANAGER Sure?

EVERYMAN Sure.

FLOOR MANAGER Good. You'll need all the eyesight you've got. This is the green rub.

EVERYMAN What does that mean?

FLOOR MANAGER A naval expression; I learnt it off Singapore. The thin end of the wedge. You've still got to clear yourself, chum. Prove before you die that your life's been worth living. Prove that in your time you've not only taken but given. Prove that you've repaid your mother for her birth-pangs. Only this time perhaps you should choose your witnesses more carefully.

EVERYMAN But I didn't choose them. I tell you the whole thing's been rigged.

FLOOR MANAGER Did you hear that, Chief?

DIRECTOR'S VOICE I heard. Never mind; we shan't cast him again.

FLOOR MANAGER Everyman, get this straight. This is your only chance. And you ought to be proud that we gave you the chance. After all you're only an amateur.

EVERYMAN Amateur or not, I still say fair's fair. Why was I brought here in the first place if it's all a foregone conclusion?

DIRECTOR'S VOICE Tell him: because we needed him.

FLOOR MANAGER The Director says: because we needed you. He needed you—*and I* did.

EVERYMAN What for?

FLOOR MANAGER You must find that out yourself. I can't give you all the answers.

EVERYMAN (*suddenly cockney*) No, I should say you can't!

(*He walks downstage and addresses audience*)

Tell you what it is, they've given me answers enough. And they've cooked 'em, I know they've cooked 'em; they're trying to make me a puppet. But I'm damned if they'll make me a puppet. I got free will, ain't I? Same as Napoleon and Christopher Columbus and the blokes what keep swimming the Channel.

FLOOR MANAGER Who said they had free will?

DIRECTOR'S VOICE Morty! Cue Free Will.

(*Floor Manager cues. A serious-looking man enters, in an overcoat and Anthony Eden hat, carrying a briefcase*)

EVERYMAN So *you're* the joker? Speak up for me.

(*Silence*)

'Ere! Are you Free Will or ain't you?

FREE WILL I am — but you never made use of me.

EVERYMAN Oh didn't I! What about that time my dad ordered me into the factory and I ran away and got a job in a garage?

(*Free Will shakes head*)

What about the General Strike — in 1926, remember? — when I was a freshman at Oxford and I went against my class and served in a strikers' canteen?

(*Free Will shakes head*)

What about the time I offered a blood transfusion when the other chaps held back?

(*Free Will shakes head*)

And the time I refused to agree to a divorce since I knew she'd come round — and she did?

(*Free Will shakes head*)

And the time I refused the Party Whip?

(*Free Will shakes head*)

And the time what I volunteered for the NFS.

(*Free Will shakes head*)

And the time I stuck it out in the jury — four against eight we were but I swung 'em, my God, I swung 'em!

(*Free Will shakes head*)

Well, if all you can do is shake your head —

FREE WILL On none of those occasions can I remember that you called on me.

EVERYMAN No?! Then how do you explain that —

FREE WILL There are other people whose job it is to explain these things. Personally, I have another appointment. And I have to hurry; it's not on this planet.

(*He takes off his hat to the audience and goes out briskly*)

DIRECTOR'S VOICE Morty! Set One. The Analyst.

FLOOR MANAGER Eric! Set One.

(*Set One is lit up; it has been transformed into a psychoanalyst's consulting room. The Analyst is waiting*)

FLOOR MANAGER Everyman! Up you go. Lie on that couch.

(*The Analyst beckons. Everyman goes up and lies on couch*)

ANALYST That's right. Close your eyes.

DIRECTOR'S VOICE Track in, One, track in.

ANALYST Now what is all this about free will? Nonsense, my child, those were all conditioned responses. The Party Whip for instance — a simple Oedipus Complex.

EVERYMAN Why?

ANALYST Because you were in love with the Mother of Parliaments.

EVERYMAN And the blood transfusion.

ANALYST Oh blood! Blood for you represented the seminal fluid. In offering to give your blood to that man who'd just lost his legs, you were — in fact — committing an indecent assault on him.

EVERYMAN (*as if falling into trance*) Was I, father?

ANALYST Yes, my child.

EVERYMAN But the National Fire Service surely? I joined that simply because —

ANALYST Simply because you wanted to *play* with fire. Your mother had always forbidden it when you were little.

EVERYMAN So she had. There was the range in the kitchen and the open fire in the parlour — she put a big fender in front of that — and all of them lovely boxes of matches. Some of 'em had black heads and some had red but they all was out of my reach. And then there was spills for my father's pipe — the bastard!

ANALYST You see? So when the Blitz came no fender was big enough for that. Naturally you joined the Fire Service; it was like going to a brothel.

EVERYMAN Yes, I slid down the greasy pole and —

ANALYST Ah that's another nice point —

EVERYMAN And we drove on the bell and all the other bleeders made way for us. And the fires — the fires was so beautiful, jumping the streets like greyhounds and climbing the steeples like monkeys — and then there was all them miles of hosepipe —

ANALYST QED, my child; QED.

EVERYMAN I suppose so, father, but what about the jury? The time I swung them and got the chap acquitted.

ANALYST Acquitted of what?

EVERYMAN Funny. I can't remember.

ANALYST Of course you can't; you'd identified yourself with him. You knew he had done it, you see.

EVERYMAN Done what, father, done what?

ANALYST Done a little girl in the park. You were just becoming a dirty old man, so you couldn't convict a dirty old man.
No, no, my child, free will doesn't come into it.

EVERYMAN What does, then, father?

ANALYST I do.

> (*He places his hand on Everyman's forehead*)

And you know what I'm going to do now? I'm going to remove all these complexes of yours so that you can start again from scratch. With an absolutely clean sheet.

EVERYMAN A clean sheet?

ANALYST A blank mind.

EVERYMAN How long will it take?

ANALYST Depends on your resistance. Not less than three or four years; it might take ten or twelve. I'll have to go deep, you know.

EVERYMAN I can't spare the time. I can't spare the time. I'm dying.

> (*Set One is blacked out and Set Two lit up. It has now become a classroom. The Marxist places a blackboard on an easel and turns round, rapping on his desk with a pointer. Everyman comes in*)

MARXIST Comrade, you're late for my lecture.

EVERYMAN Why? I can't see anyone else here.

MARXIST Of course you can't, you're Everyman. You are everyone else.

DIRECTOR'S VOICE Camera One, a narrower lens. I want a close-up of the blackboard.

> (*Marxist indicates blackboard, which is blank, with pointer*)

MARXIST Now what does this represent?

EVERYMAN I can't see anything. It's blank.

MARXIST It's only blank to one of your bourgeois mentality. Follow my pointer.

> (*Without touching the board he describes a rapid complicated pattern just in front of it*)

That . . . is the dialectic!

EVERYMAN (*as if doped*) Oh the dialectic? Of course, comrade.

> (*The Marxist turns the blackboard round. Its other side is equally blank*)

MARXIST Now here are the axioms. Can you read them?

> (*Everyman stares blankly, then takes out spectacles and puts them on*)

What does it say here about freedom?

> (*Everyman takes off his spectacles and shuts his eyes*)

EVERYMAN (*patly*) Freedom is the recognition of necessity.

MARXIST You're coming on, comrade. That clause in our creed must never be forgotten. But how does it apply to you, comrade? Think of your past actions. What about that time you worked in the strikers' canteen?

EVERYMAN When was that?

MARXIST 1926.

EVERYMAN Oh yes, the General Strike; I was a freshman at Oxford. The other undergraduates I knew were helping to break the strike. They were true to their class in fact.

MARXIST While you . . . were untrue to your class?

EVERYMAN Yes.

MARXIST But why?

EVERYMAN (*parrotwise, with no expression*) I was untrue to my class, not because I really saw the light — I had not even read *Das Kapital* nor yet because I was in any way capable of choosing between good and evil — I mean revolution and reaction. It was merely that in me, or rather in my family and social background, the disease of capitalist morality had reached an even further point than in most of the other undergraduates. I was an Honourable, you see, while most of *them*, well, they weren't even Etonians. My heritage then was an abscess and as such it had to burst. I just *had* to throw in my lot with the strikers; I did so adore doing anything unconventional. Apart from that, of course, it was an absolute necessity.

MARXIST But you did not then recognize it as such?

EVERYMAN Didn't I, my dear fel —, comrade?

MARXIST When you went to serve in that canteen, you thought you were acting freely?

EVERYMAN Of course I did.

MARXIST So you weren't. You had been utterly conditioned by history, you just had no choice in the matter. If you had known you had no choice, then you'd have been free — one of us. But you thought you had a choice, so you weren't free. And, even though you joined us, you weren't one of us.

QED, comrade?

EVERYMAN QED, father.

MARXIST Right. Come up here. Take this chalk. I want you to draw a diagram.

EVERYMAN Diagram of what?

MARXIST Of the future.

EVERYMAN The future? I don't know what it's like.

MARXIST I said you weren't one of us! Give me back the chalk and I'll show you.

(*He draws a large circle on the blackboard*)

This is the earth.

(*He draws a hammer and sickle within the circle; then draws a smaller circle*)

This is the moon.

(*Everyman, in hypnotic excitement, snatches the chalk*)

EVERYMAN I get it! I get it!

(*He marks the moon with a hammer and sickle, then turns the blackboard round and draws a huge circle almost filling it*)

This ... is the sun!

(*He is about to draw in the hammer and sickle when the Scientist enters from Set Three*)

SCIENTIST Everyman! You're going too far. That's completely unscientific. You can't make the *sun* a satellite. Even your friend here can't. It's a contradiction in terms.

MARXIST Comrade, I'd thank you not to interrupt my lecture.

SCIENTIST A thousand apologies. I thought this was a séance.

MARXIST A séance?

SCIENTIST Well, you know; blackboard-turning. You've put Everyman there in a trance.

MARXIST He came to me in a trance.

(*Scientist looks at his watch*)

SCIENTIST Well, your time's up anyway. I'm taking over now. Come with me, Everyman.

(*He takes his arm*)

MARXIST How dare you! You rotten deviationist!

SCIENTIST Deviationist? No, comrade, Scientist.

MARXIST Then as a scientist you must know that you yourself are conditioned, that the whole of science is conditioned by —

(*The Scientist whips out a large syringe*)

SCIENTIST I'll condition you!

MARXIST (*backing away*) What's that?

SCIENTIST Just a little injection. To change your personality, comrade.

MARXIST But I haven't got a personality. The personal cult's been exploded.

SCIENTIST Never mind; this will change what you *have* got. You won't be a Marxist any more.

MARXIST (*appalled*) I won't be a ... ?!

SCIENTIST Certainly not. You'll be even more of an automaton. You think you're the master? I am!

(*He chases Marxist and jabs him in the behind*)

There!

MARXIST (*wailing*) Ooh! And my best trousers too! My best trousers!

(As he rubs his behind, his expression turns imbecile)

DIRECTOR'S VOICE Camera One! Lose Marxist. Follow the other two.

(Scientist conducts Everyman on to Set Three which has now become a lab; on a table is a large microscope)

SCIENTIST Now, Everyman. What is this?

EVERYMAN Looks like a microscope.

SCIENTIST Correct. Come over here. I'm going to put you under it.

EVERYMAN What!

SCIENTIST When I say 'you', the word 'you' of course is an abstraction. A convenient concept that has no basis in fact.

EVERYMAN You mean I've no basis in —

SCIENTIST The word 'you', the word 'I', all such words are meaningless. Why, you might as well start using a word like 'soul'.

EVERYMAN But I do use the word 'soul'.

SCIENTIST My dear fellow! We're not in the Middle Ages. Come on, it won't bite you, have a peep.

(Everyman looks into microscope)

Well, what do you see?

EVERYMAN A lot of raspberry jam. Only it's moving about.

SCIENTIST That's what you're made of, Everyman. Just a moment, I'll change the slide.

(He does so)

EVERYMAN Little things wriggling and squirming.

SCIENTIST That's what you came from, Everyman. And what your children all came from. In the bed you were thinking of 'love' — another meaningless word — but that's what it all was really.

Now let's go a little further.

(He changes slides again)

That is a cell.

EVERYMAN A prison cell?

SCIENTIST Yes, in a manner of speaking. There are millions on millions on millions of those inside you and yet Everyman himself, in a sense, is a prisoner in each of them.

(He changes slides)

That . . . is a gene. The primary living particle. That's what conditions Everyman's life — the long arm of heredity.

EVERYMAN It doesn't look like an arm; it looks like two spirals intertwining. How big is this thing really?

SCIENTIST We're down to molecular level. So are we here.

(Changes slide)

That is a virus. It has certain things in common with a gene.

EVERYMAN I thought a virus was a disease.

SCIENTIST If it is — so what? Maybe all life is a disease. After all think of a cancer. A cancer is a growth and life is a growth. On the other hand what you are looking at — and it's part of you, Everyman, it's part of you — may not be alive at all. The interesting thing about a virus, the fascinating thing, is this: we just don't know what it is. It may be a micro-organism, it may be merely a chemical. Though I should apologize for saying 'merely'; the organic world has no right to sneer at the inorganic; the minerals after all are the chaps that are going to outlast the lot of us. But to return to our virus: it seems to be somewhere on the border — the border of life and non-life. Which suggests of course that life can be reduced to non-life.

EVERYMAN You're telling *me*!

SCIENTIST *I'm* telling you.

DIRECTOR'S VOICE Morty! Get out of shot!

(*Floor Manager draws away from them in front of the camera*)

SCIENTIST And now for the next slide.

EVERYMAN You can keep your next slide; and you know what you can do with it!

(*He pushes the microscope over*)

SCIENTIST That will cost you —

EVERYMAN Send the bill to my undertaker. And as for your billions of cells, I'm going to break out of one and all of them. I'm not taking this lying down.

SCIENTIST You're going to lie down very soon.

EVERYMAN In the body maybe, but my soul —

SCIENTIST Oh that thing again!

EVERYMAN I believe in that thing, I tell you. Whatever you say, I am I. There *is* such a person as myself.

SCIENTIST Yourself? Well, go and look for it.

EVERYMAN I will.

(*He turns his back on the Scientist and strides downstage*)

DIRECTOR'S VOICE Fine so far. Hold it.

FLOOR MANAGER Hold it all of you. Very nice work, the three stooges; now we'll line up the musical. Bert, bring that stand-mike down.

(*Bert does so*)

OK. Downstage please the Scientist, the Marxist, the Analyst. Now you needn't use much voice. Just mind your diction.

(*The Three stand round the mike, ready to sing in turn. Floor Manager cues the Analyst*)

ANALYST (*singing*)
  I'm gonna probe probe probe your dark subliminals,
  Uproot each secret that the Censor hid,
  Gonna wean you clean from your own personality
  Gonna take away your Ego and leave you with your Id.
THE THREE Take away your Ego and leave you with your Id!
MARXIST I'm gonna lick lick liquidate your memory,
  Gonna save you from the sty of the bourgeois swine;
  You must change your old beliefs for a suit of dialecticals
  And hang out your washing on the Party Line.
THE THREE Hang out your washing on the Party Line!
SCIENTIST I'm gonna scroot scroot scrutinize your elements,
  Gonna take you, baby, cross the Great Divide
  Down among the molecules — for in the last analysis
  Life is just a drop of dirty water on a slide.
THE THREE Just a bloody drop of dirty water on a slide!
    (*Floor Manager joins them at the mike*)
FLOOR MANAGER I'm gonna cue cue cue you to your destiny,
  Gonna brief you and groom you to embrace your bride,
  But the wedding bed is narrow and smells of chrysanthemums
  And Everyman who gets there finds he's died.
THE FOUR All of you who get there will find you've died!
    (*Flourish on an instrument*)
EVERYMAN My self! My self! Where can I find my self?
    (*He roams round stage*)
VOICES OFF Not here, Everyman. Not through the microscope.
  Not through the telescope.
  Not through the spectroscope.
  Not on the highways or byways.
  Not in the dark of the womb.
  Not in the gaps in the galaxy.
ANALYST (*approaching Everyman*) Goodbye, my child.
MARXIST (*following*) Goodbye, comrade.
SCIENTIST (*following*) Goodbye, specimen.
    (*All three hold out their hands; Everyman refuses and turns his back
    on them*)
EVERYMAN I turn my back on the three of you — (*he looks at Floor
Manager*) and on you also. I will talk to my fellows who *don't* know
all the answers.
    (*He comes downstage and addresses audience*)
  'Moriturus te saluto'. That's what the doomed gladiators cried out in

Ancient Rome to the Emperor. 'I who am about to die salute you.' But in *this* arena I say it to you, to each of you. (*He looks searchingly in different directions over audience*) Moriturus te saluto. Moriturus te saluto. Moriturus te saluto. I did not choose to be put in this ring to fight, I did not ask to be born, but a babe in arms is in arms in more senses than one and since my birth I've been fighting. Conscript or volunteer — I just don't know which I am — and it may have been a losing battle but at least I've been in it, I've been in it. And now les jeux sont faits and rien ne va plus. To be a human being is a cause for grief — and for pride. Everyman must vindicate himself. In what he does, what he makes, what he is. Oh I know they say one has no choice in the matter, but I don't believe them. Do you?

Caddy! Where's that caddy?

(*The Caddy runs on with the huge golf-bag*)

My driver!

(*Caddy gives him a driver. He tees up an imaginary ball, takes a few practice swings, then drives it out over audience*)

There! I can't see if it's on the fairway or not but at least it carried, it carried.

(*He passes the driver to a stage hand*)

Now my sweep's rods.

(*Caddy hangs them over — a three-piece set. Everyman fits them together and lunges upwards*)

Yes, as I thought. A filthy chimney. I've been cleaning it as long as I remember, but the soot comes back again quickly. Compounded of doubts and megrims and all the malaise of our time.

(*He lunges upwards again, then ducks as if to avoid a fall of soot*)

Never mind, that's better. I've earned my sweep's wages, I think.

(*Same business*)

Next.

(*Caddy hands him a large stone-breaker's hammer*)

'm. Working on the roads again.

(*He takes a swing*)

Breaking stones — like when I came out of Eden.

(*Swings*)

There were no roads then. I had to start from scratch.

(*Swings*)

And then there was Stonehenge.

(*Swings*)

And Troy — and Memphis — and the roads of Rome.

(*He leans on the hammer*)

Stones! I've broken 'em by the million, but they've never broken me.

(*He hands over the hammer*)

CADDY And now, sir?

EVERYMAN Now ... my conductor's baton.

(*Caddy hands it to him*)

DIRECTOR'S VOICE Morty! Wind him up.

(*Morty makes winding-up sign. Everyman ignores him*)

EVERYMAN If I cannot conduct my life, at least I'll conduct my death. We'll start with the last movement.

(*He raises the baton*)

DIRECTOR'S VOICE Wind him up, I said.

FLOOR MANAGER Sorry, chief. He won't look at me.

(*Everyman begins conducting but is immediately interrupted by some stage hands who burst in, carrying a large rocket — Thor model perhaps — in three parts*)

DIRECTOR'S VOICE Hold it! Hold it! What's *that*?

FLOOR MANAGER Hold it all of you. I don't know, chief, I'll find out. What the hell sort of prop is that, chaps?

HAND A rocket of course. And it's practical. Easy there with the warhead.

FLOOR MANAGER He says it's a practical rocket.

DIRECTOR'S VOICE Well, I didn't order rockets. It must be for the show next door. They've got extra firemen laid on there.

FLOOR MANAGER Sorry, chaps; you're in the wrong studio. Take that pretty little toy next door. It's a show called 'No Man and his Future'. You know, just one more documentary.

HAND OK, Morty; sorry about the mistake. But I naturally thought, seeing *you* was the FM here —

FLOOR MANAGER Oh I'm the FM there too. It doesn't come on till tomorrow; get me?

HAND I get you, Morty. OK, chaps, take it away.

(*As they carry it out, the Crooner runs in and grabs the stand mike*)

CROONER I'm just a rock rock rocket in the dark,
Intercontinental!
Interplanetary!
Interuniversal!
Just a rock rock rocket that will pop pop pop!

CHORUS (*repeats. Then instrumental coda*)

DIRECTOR'S VOICE OK, Morty. Blackout while they strip him for action.

FLOOR MANAGER Action?

DIRECTOR'S VOICE His last.

FLOOR MANAGER Wardrobe! Make-up! On your toes! Quick change
here for Everyman. After that, duckies, you can relax.
OK. All lights out.

> (*Studio is blacked-out but Gallery is lit up dimly to show the backs of
> Director and his associates in black silhouette. None of them moves. A
> voice begins to sing from the darkness*)

SINGER There's a long long trail a-winding
To the land of the tomb
Where the mocking bird is singing
And the long shades loom,
Where your eyes all turn to blindness
And the world all turns to stone
And Everyman must walk along
That long long trail alone.

DISTANT CHORUS (*repeats. Then Gallery is blacked-out and lights come
up slowly on stage to show Everyman in loincloth, medievally emaciated;
make-up girl is putting last touches to his face*)

DIRECTOR'S VOICE One. Give me a close-up.
'm. Not enough sweat.

FLOOR MANAGER Lil, can you get him more sweaty?

LIL I'll try, Morty.

FLOOR MANAGER Cold sweat, remember. Deathbed stuff.

LIL That better?

FLOOR MANAGER That better, chief?

DIRECTOR'S VOICE Middling. Never mind, I'll close for it.
Right, we'll run the next sequence.

FLOOR MANAGER Stand by all of you. We're just about to —

DIRECTOR'S VOICE Hold it! Where's that damned tomb?

FLOOR MANAGER Jimmy! What the devil are you up to? We've not got
all night for this job. Bring on that tomb at once and —

JIMMY Not my fault, Morty. The painters are still finishing the graining of the marble —

FLOOR MANAGER To hell with the graining of the marble! We needn't
be all that naturalistic. Wheel the wretched thing on; can't you see
Everyman's shivering?

> (*The tomb is wheeled on upstage; it is in the form of an allegedly marble
> oblong box about three feet high with a footstone and a headstone. A
> stage hand slaps a 'sticker' marked 'Wet Paint' on the footstone and
> another, marked 'Vacant', on the headstone*)

DIRECTOR'S VOICE Looks all right; the viewers will think it's marble. OK, cue the Gravedigger.

(*Floor Manager cues. The Gravedigger enters, an impressive bearded figure, carrying a spade. He stands behind the headstone, resting his crossed arms on it*)

DIRECTOR'S VOICE Right. Now the guard of honour.

FLOOR MANAGER Bill! I can't see the chalk marks.

BILL Here they are, Morty.

(*Floor Manager traces to chalk marks, nose to ground*)

FLOOR MANAGER I see ... but why do they go zigzag?

BILL That's to allow time for the Recessional.

FLOOR MANAGER Bright boy.

(*He pats Bill on the head*)

Right. Now we line up the Guard of Honour.

In the following order. Career and Common Sense — there are your chalk marks.

(*Career and Common Sense take up their positions downstage facing each other*)

Sacrifice and Patria!

(*They do the same upstage from the first pair*)

The Comedian and the Brain!

(*Same business*)

And four volunteers, please.

(*Pause*)

Come on. Anyone who's got nothing better to do.

(*He beckons to some of the stage hands who come sheepishly forward. Gradually the complete guard of honour, in two rows of five couples each, is lined up, running diagonally upstage from Stage Left to Right*)

STAGE HAND (*from back of guard*) Don't we have no swords, Morty?

FLOOR MANAGER No, this isn't a wedding. But you're right, you've got to do something. Try this.

(*He holds up his arm in the Nazi salute. The guard of honour do likewise*)

Does that fill the bill, chief?

DIRECTOR'S VOICE No.

FLOOR MANAGER Try this then.

(*He raises the Communist clenched fist. Guard of Honour follows suit*)

DIRECTOR'S VOICE No, no, no —

FLOOR MANAGER What about this?

(*He extends his arms upwards and outwards, with palms together, in a praying gesture. The Guard of Honour do the same, suggesting an abortive arch)*

DIRECTOR'S VOICE 'm. That takes me back. OK, I'll close for that.

FLOOR MANAGER OK chaps, keep it like that. Now Everyman — Where have you got to?

(*He looks down. Everyman is lying at his feet*)

You've collapsed a shade too soon, chum. Can't you get up?

(*Everyman shakes his head*)

All right; do it on your belly then. And follow what I tell you. This is your Guard of Honour. Or, putting it another way, your Northwest Passage. You must pass up — crawl up — between these two ranks till you get to the bourne from which — you know the rest of the quotation?

EVERYMAN I won't. I'm not going!

FLOOR MANAGER No?

EVERYMAN No, I tell you. Never!

FLOOR MANAGER Never's the operative word. (*He points*) This is the *road* to Never. And I'm the Floor Manager here and I'm cueing you up that road.

(*He cues Everyman who, as if hypnotized, begins to crawl up the passage formed by the guard of honour. He crawls slowly, in stylized jerks in time with the music. When he reaches the end of the Guard they reform in a second diagonal running Stage Right to Left, and then in a third Left to Right which will bring him about to the tomb. Meanwhile the Recessional has been sung — tune 'Comin thro' the Rye', taken very slow, as a dirge, and possibly punctuated with a muffled drum or tubular bells*)

SINGERS 'Gin a body miss his body
Comin thro' the Rye,
Gin a body lose his body
Need a body die?

Oh Everyman he also ran
He also ran sae fast,
But when his ghost had reached the post
It found its chance was past.

Gin a body (*etc.*).

Oh a' ma life was storm and strife
And yet I lo'ed it well,
But what it meant or where it went
I fear I canna tell.

Gin a body miss his body
Comin thro' the Rye,
Gin a body lose his body
Need a body die?

(*A great bell tolls once. Everyman has emerged, still on his belly, from the passage formed by the Guard*)

FLOOR MANAGER Guard of Honour! Hands to your sides! Dismiss!

(*They march off. Simultaneously two professional-looking gentlemen, dressed alike as if they were twins, walk on from different sides and stand over Everyman. One is the Doctor of Med, one is the Doctor of Div*)

MED (*to Floor Manager*) Is this my patient?

(*Floor Manager nods*)

DIV My patient, you mean.

FLOOR MANAGER You can share him between you. Who will examine him first? The Doctor of Med or the Doctor of Div?

MED We'll toss. You call.

DIV No, I'll toss.

(*He spins a coin*)

MED Ladders.

DIV Snakes.

Everyman, get on your feet.

(*He helps him up*)

FLOOR MANAGER Chair, Jimmy.

(*Jimmy places chair on to which Everyman subsides*)

DIV Now to business. What is your name?

EVERYMAN M or N.

DIV Who gave you this name?

EVERYMAN Some bastard, I suppose, who'd come down from the trees.

DIV Did you have no name before that?

EVERYMAN Before what? When?

DIV Well, shall we say in the era of the giant reptiles. Dinosaur, diplodocus, ichthyosaurus, pterodactyl.

EVERYMAN I'm sorry . . . I can't remember.

DIV Or before that again? When everyone lived in the sea.

EVERYMAN (*dreamily*) Did I live in the sea? . . . Yes, of course I did. Things were much easier then.

DIV And who was it put you in the sea?

EVERYMAN Don't know.

(*Div pulls a bible from his pocket*)

DIV You don't know! Have you never read this?

EVERYMAN What is it? I'm blind.

DIV (*reads*) 'And the earth was without form, and void; and darkness was upon the face of the deep'.

EVERYMAN Yes. This is where I came in. 'Here beginneth the last lesson'. 'It is written . . . it is written – ' I can't remember.

DIV It is written: ye shall not grow young as angels and songs grow young. Nor shall the hand move back on the dial nor the cord that was cut be joined. For man is contracted to his doom as the lemming swimmeth to the west. And the ravens croak in Lover's Lane and the telephone is not answered.

EVERYMAN But after that?

DIV A board is raised with the words 'To Let' and the board is removed again and Everyman's place is filled and his latchkey changed and the papers in his desk skimmed through and thrown in the basket and burnt.

EVERYMAN And I myself?

DIV Have you faith?

EVERYMAN How can I tell?

DIV Then how can *I* tell either? *If* you had faith –

MED He hasn't? My turn now, my dear fellow.

DIV You're welcome. See you in the club.

    (*He walks off*)

MED Now, Everyman. I was going to say open your shirt but I see you haven't got one.

    (*He pulls out a stethoscope and examines him*)

Yes, indeed. As I thought. You're a walking hospital. You were always dead on the surface; now you're dying in the depths.

EVERYMAN I was always dead on the surface?

MED Of course; think of your skin. Everyman's skin is a dead rind. Which means that all we can see of him is dead. For his hair's dead too, you know.

    (*He picks up bible which Div had dropped, opens it absently, then closes it*)

It is written: What is man that the beasts should respect him save that he walketh upright, whereby his arches fall and the discs come loose in his spine and his guts press on his pelvis? And though he live longer than most – yet not so long as a tortoise – his bones grow brittle and his skin wizened and his arteries harden and his glands degenerate and his brain turns bad.

Yes, Everyman, you've not come to me one moment too soon.

EVERYMAN You mean you can save me?

(Gong)

MED Save you? Of course not. But I can start straight away to write your certificate.

EVERYMAN But can't you do anything for me? A blood transfusion? . . . A life transfusion?

MED A forlorn hope — but I'll check. There *might* be some life donors present. Don't die before I come back.

> *(He walks downstage looking towards audience and singing. This lyric should be set like a slow Negro Spiritual)*

MED *(singing)* Is there a life donor here,
Oh is there a life donor here,
Like Elijah was to the widow's child —
Is there a life donor here?

CHORUS No, there ain't no life donor here,
There ain't no life donor here,
We got enough to do to keep ourselves alive,
Oh there ain't no life donor here.

MED Is there a life donor here,
Is there a life donor here,
Like Ezekiel was in the valley of bones —
Oh is there a life donor here?

CHORUS No, there ain't no life donor here,
There ain't no life donor here,
Them bones gotta stay in the valley of bones,
For there ain't no life donor here.

MED Is there a life donor here,
Is there a life donor here,
Like Pasteur was when the rabies came —
Oh is there a life donor here?

CHORUS No, there ain't no life donor here,
There ain't no life donor here;
We'd give it away if we'd got it to give
But there ain't no life donor here,
(rallentando) There ain't no life donor here.

> *(Med has returned upstage to Everyman)*

MED I'm sorry. They're all the wrong group.

GRAVEDIGGER *(still leaning on headstone)* Come on, Everyman. I'm waiting.

MED Right. He's all yours.

> *(He walks off; at the same time Free Will and Conscience enter from opposite sides)*

GRAVEDIGGER Come on, Everyman.

EVERYMAN I can't. I'm blind. Where are you?

(*Free Will and Conscience take each an arm*)

CONSCIENCE Come with us.

EVERYMAN Who are you?

CONSCIENCE I am your conscience. I have returned to you.

EVERYMAN And you?

FREE WILL I am your free will.

EVERYMAN You exist then?

FREE WILL I do. Now let's go. One step at a time. That's the way.
Easy does it.

(*They take Everyman as far as the footstone*)

CONSCIENCE Lean on this.

EVERYMAN You're not leaving me?

FREE WILL Don't worry; you're in good hands.

EVERYMAN Whose hands?

GRAVEDIGGER Mine.

(*Free Will and Conscience stand aside, but stay watching*)

EVERYMAN Who are you? My father? You sound like him. Not entirely
though; you sound kinder.

GRAVEDIGGER Do I? Thank you.

EVERYMAN (*feeling footstone*) What's this? The foot of a bed?

GRAVEDIGGER Yes, the foot of a bed.

(*Children's voices, distant, are heard singing — without words — the
hymn-tune 'Teach me to live'*)

Everyman, time's nearly up. Before you get into bed would you like
to say your prayers.

EVERYMAN I would — but I can't remember any.

GRAVEDIGGER Supposing I help you?

(*The singing ends*)

Repeat the lines after me.

O Thou whoever Thou art —

EVERYMAN Thou whoever Thou art —

GRAVEDIGGER Whether Thou art or not —

EVERYMAN Whether Thou art or not —

GRAVEDIGGER To Thee I make mine avowal —

EVERYMAN To Thee I make mine avowal —

GRAVEDIGGER I, Everyman, stand here alone —

EVERYMAN I, Everyman, stand here alone —

GRAVEDIGGER Having sinned against life and myself —

EVERYMAN Having sinned against life and myself —

GRAVEDIGGER But before I leave this world —
EVERYMAN Before I leave this world —
GRAVEDIGGER O Thou whoever Thou art —
EVERYMAN Thou whoever Thou art —
GRAVEDIGGER I thank Thee for giving me the chance —
EVERYMAN I thank Thee for giving me the chance.
GRAVEDIGGER If I failed to use it, forgive me.
EVERYMAN If I failed to use it, forgive me.
GRAVEDIGGER And now: ten seconds silence.
FLOOR MANAGER Ten seconds silence in the studio.

> (*Silence. Then Floor Manager cues Gravedigger who comes and puts his arm round Everyman*)

GRAVEDIGGER Time for bed, Everyman. I'll help you in.
EVERYMAN But who *are* you?
GRAVEDIGGER Who am I? Most people think I'm the end but I am also the beginning. I was present when your mother bore you. Life goes on, you see. Can you feel how strong my arms are?

> (*He moves Everyman away from footstone*)

FLOOR MANAGER Everyman, don't hold your head up. You're supposed to be —
GRAVEDIGGER Stop it, Morty. You needn't listen to *him* any more. Every hour of your life he's been standing at your elbow and whispering, or breathing down your neck — and his breath has always been cold. But now at this hour of your death — that's right, hold your head up — it's I who call the tune. Everyman, here and now, I salute you in the name of Life.
EVERYMAN And *your* name?
GRAVEDIGGER I've just said it. And now, Everyman: relax.

> (*He lifts him and places him in the tomb. Blackout. Children's voices are heard singing, without words, the tune of 'Happy Birthday to You'. As they end, Director's Voice is heard*)

DIRECTOR'S VOICE OK, Morty. Lights!
FLOOR MANAGER Lights, Eric!

> (*The studio is lit up. The Gravedigger removes the label 'Vacant' from the headstone. Floor Manager comes downstage to address audience*)

FLOOR MANAGER Well, ladies and gentlemen, that's it. As I warned you, this show was really more like a rehearsal. For Everyman, for me — and for you. And Everyman, remember, was only an amateur. As I imagine most of you are. So please don't be too critical of his performance. If it were you in his place, well, I'm sure you'd like the benefit of the doubt.

That's all. Goodnight. Thank you.

> (*He turns and joins the Gravedigger and shakes hands with him; then gives him his headphones*)

There you are, chum. The next show's yours.

GRAVEDIGGER (*having put on the cans*) Hullo, Chief! Can you hear me?

DIRECTOR'S VOICE Perfectly. Your voice is clearer than Morty's. OK. Cue the Finale.

GRAVEDIGGER The 'Finale'?

DIRECTOR'S VOICE Call it anything you like. Call it a Prelude if you want to. But cue it, my dear fellow, cue it.

GRAVEDIGGER OK. Chorus formation! Stand by everyone – Everyman.

> (*He picks up baton and conducts, as the lights turn very dim*)

CHORUS (*to tune of 'Tannenbaum', slow*)
Oh Everyman, oh Everyman,
Behold we weep for Everyman.

SOLO So few the suns that rose and shone
Before the dark fates moved him on.

CHORUS Oh Everyman, oh Everyman,
We bid farewell to Everyman.

> (*The tune changes to 'The Road to the Isles'*)

SOLO The blind Fury is loose upon the land
And every man and woman is her slave,
The blind Fury 'tis she that holds our hand
As step we down the highroad to the Grave.

CHORUS
By Loch Failure and Loch Sorrow and Loch Evil we must go
Where the storm clouds are brooding on the wave
For whatever else we know not there is one sure thing we know:
We must all take the highroad to the Grave.

> (*The lights gradually get brighter and the tempo becomes much faster*)

SOLO The bright daylight is here for all to see
Whatever it may mean of storm and strife,
The new freedom we shall find when we are free
And the chance of each man's lifetime is his life.

CHORUS
By Loch Sunlight and Loch Moonlight and Loch Lovelight we may go,
And our heart beating fast as drum and fife,
For whatever else we know not there is one sure thing we know:

That the great chance of your lifetime's your life.
CHORUS Oh Everyman, oh Everyman,
We wish new joy to Everyman.
SOLO Joyful returns of life on earth,
Each day he lives a day of birth!
CHORUS Oh Everyman, oh Everyman,
A new day dawns for Everyman.
(Instrumental coda and blackout)

A FEW NOTES BASED ON THE FIRST PRODUCTION
AT THE ABBEY THEATRE, DUBLIN,
OCTOBER 1966

1. The first act should be played at the tempo of a revue, thus keeping up the element of surprise and effecting a contrast with the 2nd Act (though 'Admom' must also have the tempo of revue).

2. The first song 'On Earth for What It's Worth . . .' has no tune. A young actor at the Abbey, Des Cave, improvised one. All other tunes are traditional — English, Scottish, American, and Irish (except 'I'm just a rock rock rocket').

It is recommended when translating songs to set them to the traditional tunes of the country concerned, unless a tune is so well known as to be common property, e.g. 'O Tannenbaum'.

3. Page 248: 'Everyman begins conducting but is immediately interrupted by some stage hands who burst in, carrying a large rocket . . .'. At the Abbey this was accompanied by the Chorus dancing in and singing the Crooner's song 'I'm just a rock rock rocket in the dark' (Tune by Gerard Victory). It had the effect of speeding up the action and worked very well.

All songs were vamped with two electrical guitars and a drum ensemble.

HEDLI MACNEICE

THEY MET ON GOOD FRIDAY

a sceptical historical romance

They Met on Good Friday (first broadcast 8 December 1959 on the Third Programme and repeated twice in 1960) is a fine radio play based on the old Irish annals and Icelandic sagas which had been favourites of MacNeice from his boyhood. It intermixes strong poetic prose and epic or saga verse. The music was by Tristram Cary, from his electronic studio. The role of King Brian was effectively played by Patrick Magee; Mary Wimbush played Halgerda. 'This programme shows not only the result of the battle [of Clontarf, AD 1014], but its implications — the clash between rival cultures and contrasted mentalities, culminating in the rout of the Norsemen combined with the death of Brian, who was the only true High King of All Ireland in history and who was then very old.'[1] When the play was published by the BBC in a book of four MacNeice plays in 1969, the last few lines on the last page of the typescript were unfortunately deleted; here they are restored from the script in the Berg Collection in the New York Public Library, the text used here.

In Ireland we are brought up to think of Brian Boru as a mixture of King Arthur, Miltiades, Nelson, and Charlemagne, and are taught that the Battle of Clontarf was one of the 'decisive' battles of history. So it surprises me to find that few people in England have even heard of this battle which, according to Sir Thomas Kendrick, 'must be ranked as incomparably the most splendid uprising of a wrathful nation to resist the menace of the Vikings in all the history of these northern invaders'.[3]

Whether the word 'nation' should be used in this context is doubtful. The records show that there were Irishmen fighting on the Norse side and Norsemen on the Irish side; although Brian, as High King of Ireland, was the only one in history whose writ really ran throughout the country, regional jealousies still tended to outweigh 'patriotism'. And, contrary to tradition, this was not a straight fight between Christian and pagan; most of the Vikings had recently become at least nominally Christian.

When this battle was fought, on Good Friday AD 1014, the Vikings (who the year before had conquered England) had been raiding — and settling on — the coasts of Ireland for a couple of centuries; Dublin, which they founded, was a Norse fort and a very important market. Consequently we find mixed blood in some of the protagonists on both sides. The relationships are complicated. Thus the Lady Macbeth of the story, Gormflaith, divorced by Brian, her third husband, has by her first husband, a Norse King of Dublin, a son who is married to a daughter of Brian by one of his other wives; it was Gormflaith who engineered the great Viking invasion in 1014.

The picture, though confused in detail, is clear in its general outline. The two armies represented two very different cultures; neither of these, though Clontarf was an Irish victory, was fated to survive long.

I have tried (except for simplification) to keep to such hard facts as the Irish annalists and the Icelandic saga writers agree on, but at the same time I have retained some of the recorded stories which are obviously not history but legend; these, though not true in the letter, are true to the spirit of the times. So the pendulum in this programme keeps swinging between realism and romance and accordingly between a simple down-to-earth dialogue (suggested by that of the Icelandic sagas) and various types of lyrical stylization including imitations both of early Irish verse and Norse alliterative verse.

I have also introduced the *folk*, who are notably absent from the chronicles. The play has no one clear moral, unless it be *plus ça change*, but I hope it opens a window on to a strange world which yet in a way may seem familiar. At any rate I think it is a good story.

CHARACTERS

OLD WOMAN

CHILD

THORSTEIN

PAINTER

HERALD

EARL SIGURD

SIGTRYG

VOICE(S)

BISHOP

GORMLAI

KING BRIAN

HARPER

POET

MESSENGER

1ST DANE

2ND DANE

NORWEGIAN

FAROE MAN

HALGERDA

SLAVE GIRL

GRIM

BURNER

ETAIN

BRODIR

OSPAK

1ST VIKING

2ND VIKING

1ST CAITHNESS MAN

2ND CAITHNESS MAN

THE FATES

MURAGH

MAEL MORDHA

MAEL SEACHLAINN

TURLOUGH

TEIGUE

PLOUGHMAN

SKALD

HRAFN

1ST GUARD

CAPTAIN OF THE GUARD

2ND GUARD

3RD GUARD

HARECK

ATTENDANT

CROWD OF WOMEN

THEY MET ON GOOD FRIDAY

ANNOUNCER In the ninth and tenth centuries AD the Vikings exploded on Europe — nobody quite knows why. From Scandinavia they set out in their long ships to burn and loot, to ravish and murder, and sometimes even to colonize. They settled in the Scottish islands, in Iceland, and northern England; in AD 1013 they actually conquered England. In the following year, in Ireland — a country they had long been plundering and where they had founded several still famous cities — they fought their greatest battle and met their greatest defeat on 23 April, Good Friday, AD 1014. There were Norsemen fighting on the Irish side and Irishmen fighting on the Norse side and in several of the protagonists the blood of the two races was mingled. Still, the two armies stood for two different ways of life and thought no doubt they were deciding something when: They Met on Good Friday.

(Harp overture, leading into sea music and behind)

OLD WOMAN The horses of the sea ... the horses of the sea ... the black and whinnying horses of the sea ... Their manes are tangled and their teeth are long and their wind is long and their ears are back. And they never quit, they never quit.

CHILD They never quit?

OLD WOMAN Changing the coasts of Ireland. You see these pebbles, child? When I was your age, they were big stones. And you see this stone the size of a handmill? When I was your age it was a boulder. But the waves have whittled them down with their hoofs. No one can fight the sea.

CHILD Not even Cuchullain?

OLD WOMAN Aye, *he* fought the sea. But he lost.

CHILD Not even King Brian?

OLD WOMAN Listen. King Brian is my age. People speak well of him now but I know the things he has done. And I know the things he has not done. Put him out there and the horses would trample him under. And so would the dragons that follow the horses.

CHILD Dragons?

OLD WOMAN The dragon ships, child. The horses' jaws are yellow with foam but the dragons' jaws are red with blood. When I was your age there was an old woman who had been carried away by one of those slavering dragons, sixty years back when her cheeks still had colour. Carried away to some land of ice. But when her cheeks were losing their colour they sold her back to a Dublin merchant. Sold her back for a bundle of hides. And this will all happen again.

CHILD I don't understand.

OLD WOMAN Mark my words, a little bird told me. A wren in an ash tree, a crow on a grave — or ask those gulls, they know it surely. Not a few weeks from now the dragons will ride up this beach. For the spearmen death, for the virgins rape, for the monasteries fire, for King Brian defeat.

CHILD But —

OLD WOMAN You don't believe it. Nor do many. Mark my words: at this very moment they are pitching their timbers and painting their prows. To be strong for the brine, to be spruce for the kill.

(*Lose music*)

THORSTEIN Grey? Grey, you dauber! Why can't you use your red and your gold? Call yourself a ship's painter! Call that a dragon — it looks more like a lemming. Give me the brush; I'll teach you your trade.

PAINTER Lemmings go west too.

THORSTEIN Now ... gold for the scales.

PAINTER Lemmings go west and they drown. And no man, Thorstein, knows what drives them. Small foolish creatures; they swim out west till they drown. You're dipping too deep; you are blurring the outline.

THORSTEIN Hold your tongue or I'll knock your teeth out. Blurring the — Wait till we grapple them! The bay of Dublin will be blurred with blood and the outlines of Ireland drawn anew. The red paint? Where's the red?

PAINTER In front of you.

THORSTEIN Hold your tongue! Now for his eyes — make them blood-shot. As they were last year when we sailed for England. Landed at Gainsborough, soaked up Oxford and Winchester, Bath and London fell on their knees to us, the English King escaped to Normandy.

PAINTER I have never been to England.

THORSTEIN You have never been anywhere, oaf. Look at the grey sea yonder — What is it for? To take men — who call themselves men — to harry the coasts of the world. As it took our forebears to Lisbon

and Cadiz. As thirty years back it took Eric the Red to Greenland.
As thirty days on it will take this dragon to Orkney.

PAINTER Orkney? I thought you were going to Ireland.

THORSTEIN Orkney, fool, lies on the way to Ireland. It is there that
things shall be decided. Things, fool. Matters of history.

(*Music: Viking horn, used heraldically*)

HERALD Silence in the Earl's Hall! The meeting will now be resumed.
The word lies with Sigurd, Earl of Orkney.

SIGURD Sigtryg of the Silken Beard, I speak to you man to man. Your
mother is an Irish queen; I also had an Irish mother. Blood these days
keeps mingling — if not on the field, in the bed. You call me to Ireland
to lead the host of the Vikings. I know your reasons; you are in fear
of King Brian who was lately your Mother's husband — her third
husband, am I right?

SIGTRYG Earl Sigurd of Orkney, all her husbands were kings. Her first
was my father, Olaf, King of Dublin. Her second Mael Seachlainn,
once High King of Ireland —

SIGURD Who still lives?

SIGTRYG Who still lives. Her third Brian, now High King of Ireland.

SIGURD Who still lives. So far so good — or so bad. What about her
fourth?

SIGTRYG Her fourth?

SIGURD He should be a king too. If I do what you ask me to do, if I
come to Ireland and defeat King Brian, I demand in return the hand
of your mother Gormlai — and with it the throne of Dublin.
Well?

(*Pause*)

SIGTRYG The throne of Dublin is supposed to be mine.

SIGURD 'Supposed' to be? Yes. In the old days the Norsemen in Dublin
were free. You, Sigtryg of the Silken Beard, it is you who paid tribute
to Brian. And only last Christmas, when he laid siege to Dublin, it
was no thanks to you he withdrew. Had it not been that the winter
was cold and the Irish ran short of food, our chief Norse market in
the west would be lost; Dublin, the city which our fathers founded,
Dublin, that jewel of the Viking world, would no longer be Norse —
but Irish! And among its charred ruins there would squat a race of
beggars, their hair falling into their eyes, their fingers in bowls of
porridge, their tongues never still, back-biting each other and all men.
What do you say, Thorstein?

THORSTEIN I say that Sigtryg has forfeited his kingdom —

SIGTRYG Thorstein!

SIGURD Let him speak.

THORSTEIN He is not strong enough to hold our city of Dublin. His greatest asset is his mother Gormlai but to you she would be a far stronger asset. Besides, she is still beautiful.

SIGURD Yes, I have heard of the lady. But this time — no divorce.

SIGTRYG Does that mean, Earl Sigurd . . .

SIGURD Yes?

SIGTRYG Does that mean you are accepting my offer?

SIGURD Repeat your offer. We must have things clear.

SIGTRYG I, Sigtryg, the King of Dublin —

SIGURD At present King of Dublin.

SIGTRYG I, Sigtryg, at present King of Dublin, hereby invite Earl Sigurd of Orkney to rally the fighters of the Viking world — from Norway, from Denmark, from Ireland, the Hebrides, Orkney and Man, and from all parts whatever — and to lead the same against Ireland there to do battle with King Brian who has done such harm to our people. In return for which . . .

SIGURD Yes?

SIGTRYG When he has defeated Brian, I promise him the throne of Dublin — and the hand of my mother Gormlai.

    (*Pause*)

You accept my offer?

SIGURD You accept my conditions?

SIGTRYG I do.

SIGURD I accept your offer then.

VOICE Long live Sigurd Earl of Orkney!

THORSTEIN Long live Sigurd King of Dublin!

    (*Crowd cheers*)

SIGURD Well, my friend Thorstein, so far so good. I wonder what Gormlai will say to it.

THORSTEIN Gormlai has had three husbands — one Norse, two Irish. The Norse husband is dead. The Irish, though old, are still alive. She hates them both but most she hates Brian. She would like another Norseman under her wolfskin — not the least if he brought Brian's head with him.

BISHOP Queen Gormlai —

GORMLAI What is it now, my lord Bishop?

BISHOP Queen Gormlai, I beg you to listen. These heathen Norsemen that you have sent for —

GORMLAI What is this talk of heathen and Christian, Norseman and Irish, Gael and Gall? Was not my first husband Norse — and a Christian? Was not my second Irish — and *you* know what he did, my lord Bishop. He plundered the shrine of St Patrick.

BISHOP No more of that, Queen Gormlai.

GORMLAI No more of that certainly; that was his great mistake. Your archbishop at Armagh never forgave him. But my third husband, Brian, his rival, *he* gave ten pounds of gold to Armagh.

BISHOP He did — and God will reward him.

GORMLAI He has been rewarded already. Where is Mael Seachlainn now? He was as good as Brian — and younger and stronger, I of all people know that — but Brian sits on his throne and he is now Brian's henchman.

BISHOP They are united against the Norseman.

GORMLAI United! United by fear. And it never was Brian who hated the Norsemen most. Did he not sail with them up the Shannon, looting?

BISHOP There was a reason —

GORMLAI There are always reasons. Fear, greed, envy, power-lust. I am tired of Irish kings, I have shared my bed with two of them.

BISHOP So you would bring in the Foreigners?

GORMLAI The Foreigners? Who are the Foreigners? In this land of mists and cattle raids and bickerings, this land that is pinned together with thorn trees and still keeps falling apart, this land where you take one step and you sink in a bog or you take one glance at the sky and get lost in the clouds, was it not time for new blood, for men from the north and the east?

BISHOP They burnt Clonmacnois.

GORMLAI So did your Munstermen. But I grant you they burnt Clonmacnois. And they founded Waterford, Wexford, Anagassan, Limerick, Dublin. And they taught your metalworkers metalwork and your boatbuilders how to build boats. Yes, and they even gave you coinage.

BISHOP When you speak of the Irish, Queen Gormlai, why do you use the word 'you'?

GORMLAI Because I no longer am one of you. I have some Norse blood and my first husband was Norse. I shall find another of his kind.

BISHOP If you do that, let me warn you —

GORMLAI Warn yourself, my lord Bishop. You are here under safe conduct but that does not excuse bad manners. You are not in Ireland now. This is the fort of Dublin.

Go; go back to Brian — Brian with his old man's dreams and his cold knotty fingers and his cunning. Go and join the rest of his toadies — his harpers, his poets, his jesters, his cup-bearers. I have seen his favourite wine-cup — all gold and garnets, but it leaks. I have seen the harp of his harper — of Irish oak, well-carved, there are wolfhounds carved on the pillar, but the instrument is unlucky.

BISHOP Unlucky, Queen Gormlai?

GORMLAI It was made to be played at a wake. It is not a harp for the young.

(*Fade up harp, hold, and break off*)

BRIAN Why have you stopped?

HARPER It stopped of itself, King Brian.

POET How can a harp stop of itself?

BRIAN He means he is tired.

POET He means he is idle, King Brian.

BRIAN Hold your tongue. I give you both too much licence.

HARPER No, not tired nor idle. The harp stopped of itself.

BRIAN Silence! . . . Stopped of itself? . . . Who made that harp?

HARPER But you know, King Brian!

BRIAN I asked you who made it.

HARPER Colum the Dumb.

POET He was not born dumb; the Danes cut his tongue out.

HARPER Because he would not show them the monastery treasures.

POET He made that harp to atone for his tongue.

HARPER But when he had put in the last silver button and tuned the last string —

POET He died!

BRIAN Stop talking! Who told you to talk? I do not feed you and clothe you to hear your tattle. As if I did not know about Colum the Dumb! Yes, he died.

(*Pause*)

Well? Do what I keep you for. Make music, make poetry, work!

POET Give me the lead.

(*Snatch of harp*)

HARPER Right?

POET Right.

(*Harp with recitation*)

POET Once ere Brian took the throne
All this land was ache and moan;
Since he laid his peace on all
We can call our lives our own.

Once our petty kings pursued
Cattle raid and family feud;
Since our High King put them down
Through his crown is peace renewed.

BRIAN (*to self*) Mael Seachlainn? . . . Yes, I foxed him.

POET Law and order east and west:
Now a woman richly dressed
Dares to walk the roads alone —
None will scare her, none molest.

Those who late were forced to eat
Sloes and acorns live on meat;
Those who slept in sty and ditch
Now are rich and find it sweet.

Like the eagle in his nest
Brian lords it in the west;
Like a green and towering tree
It is he that tops the rest.

BRIAN (*to self*) No, not green, not green . . .

POET When the Vikings came ashore
Brian waded in their gore;
Let them come the more they would,
Brian stood and slew the more.

God is with him day and night,
All his angels in their might
Stand with flaming swords around,
Stand their ground to —

MESSENGER King Brian! King Brian!
  (*Poet and harp break off*)

BRIAN Where are you from, man?

MESSENGER Dublin: I went round the markets, heard the rumours.
Sigtryg is back from Orkney.

BRIAN Yes?

MESSENGER Do not strike me, King Brian. Earl Sigurd of Orkney is
coming. He took some persuading but Sigtryg persuaded him. He
has sent out a summons to the Viking world.

BRIAN (*more to self*) Sigurd of Orkney . . . a strong man, they tell me

... If I were forty years younger, I — What are the three of you staring at? You! send for my son, Muragh.

MESSENGER At once, King Brian.

BRIAN And my grandson Turlough with him. And you two leave me also. Take away your lies and your music! Leave me alone. I must think.

POET
HARPER } God be with you, King Brian.

(*Pause*)

BRIAN Sixty years of wars ... leading Munster against Leinster ... one day against Mael Seachlainn, the next day with him ... one day against the Foreigner but the next — well, it's the fall of the dice. Mary, Queen of the Angels, forgive me; if I gambled, at least I won. The first High King of Ireland whose height was beyond challenge. But those who take the sword shall — Was this the hand that took it? The veins so swollen and knotted it might be the map of my history. Or the map of this whole doomed island. I need not go to the door to see what my country looks like. The bog like a purple running sore, the wood like a web of false intrigue, the wind like a whisper of foul intent, the hills like the graves of enormous hopes, the clouds like a tent of despair and death. Despair? Who is Earl Sigurd to make me despair! Let him come to Ireland if he wants to! Let him summon them all to Ireland! I shall receive them.

(*Viking horn*)

SIGURD I, Sigurd, Earl of Orkney, having made a solemn undertaking with Sigtryg at present King of Dublin, hereby call on my brethren overseas to come with me to Dublin by Palm Sunday, there to defeat and slay Brian the High King of Ireland. And let me remind you there is still gold in Ireland. And fat cattle. And women. And let me remind you also: this war will be fought in the true manner of the Vikings. There shall be no words of fear or of quarrel. All loot that is taken shall be brought to the pole. No sword shall be longer than an ell. No wound shall be bound till the same hour next day. No prisoners shall be taken. Nor, in your voyage to Dublin, shall your sails be furled for the wind. This is my summons — and these are the lands I send it to. Denmark!

(*Viking horn*)

1ST DANE I think I will go. What do you say? After all, last year we conquered England.

2ND DANE Then, if you *must* cross the sea, why not go to England? It's nearer.

1ST DANE The loot is already shared out. Besides, the fighting is over there.

SIGURD Norway!

(*Horn*)

NORWEGIAN So Sigurd is a Christian? A pity. I know I too was baptized, like everyone else in this country. Herded like sheep to the font — but I never believed it. And it is the ruin of Norway. Look at us today — our land being grabbed by Danes and Swedes and all sorts. Ireland could not be worse. Yes, I think I will pay it a visit.

SIGURD The Faroes!

(*Horn*)

FAROE MAN Hm? An invitation to Ireland! They say it is a land full of salmon and honey. And one thing about it.

VOICE What?

FAROE MAN It's a larger island than this. I have long been yearning for elbow room.

SIGURD Iceland!

(*Horn*)

HALGERDA Come here, you Irish slut. Tell me about your country.

SLAVE GIRL I have nothing to tell. I have forgotten it. Slaves have no memory, Halgerda.

HALGERDA Is it true there is a woman there like me? Gormlai — is that her name?

SLAVE GIRL Gormlai is a traitress — and a whore.

HALGERDA I asked you: is she like me?

SLAVE GIRL That is for you to judge.

(*Slap*)

Thank you. She also had three husbands. But at least she did not murder them.

HALGERDA Grim! If a slap will not cure you, I must take further measures.

GRIM You called me, mistress?

HALGERDA Take this girl out and flog her.

SLAVE GIRL Oh no, no! Not again!

GRIM This way, little jewel of Ireland.

SLAVE GIRL No, no, no . . .

(*Laughter from Halgerda*)

BURNER Why are you laughing Halgerda?

HALGERDA Oh, the last of the burners! What cave have you been hiding in lately?

BURNER You are not grateful, are you? You hated Njal. We burnt him.

HALGERDA Gunnar my husband settled his debts with the sword.

BURNER And we know what you did to Gunnar.

HALGERDA You are not in a position to insult me in my house. When you burnt Njal and his household, you lit a fire that is not yet quenched. This land of ice is too hot for you.

BURNER That is why I am leaving it.

HALGERDA And a good riddance. But what do you want with me?

BURNER I want a loan for my voyage.

HALGERDA How far is your voyage?

BURNER To Ireland.

HALGERDA To Ireland? You! From all I have heard of King Brian, you cannot fight *him* with faggots. Why should I give you a loan?

BURNER Because I did you a good turn.

HALGERDA A good turn in an ill way. Tell me, do you know Ireland?

BURNER I have been there once. Good looting.

HALGERDA Did you see Queen Gormlai?

BURNER I did. Even then she was plotting against Brian.

HALGERDA They say she is tall and beautiful.

BURNER Not as tall as you, Halgerda.

HALGERDA Few women are.

BURNER Nor as beautiful.

HALGERDA You are doing well. Tell me more.

BURNER She has eyes like blue ice, I think she has Norse blood. And what she wants, she will get. And once she has got it, she will want more.

GORMLAI More, I tell you, more! You promise me Sigurd will be here by Palm Sunday, but he has not enough ships. There are thirty ships more lying west of Man this moment.

SIGTRYG Whose ships are they, mother?

GORMLAI Bridor's and Ospak's.

SIGTRYG Those two brothers! Their help would be help.

GORMLAI It is up to you to persuade them. Off to your ship! The Isle of Man is not far.

ETAIN I do not want him to go.

GORMLAI *You* do not want him to go! And who are you to have any opinion?

ETAIN I am your son's wife.

GORMLAI You are my son's enemy. I know you would wish King Brian to win.

ETAIN I am King Brian's daughter.

GORMLAI You must choose between father and husband. It says in the Gospel —

ETAIN So *you* quote the Gospel now!

SIGTRYG Be quiet! Mother, I shall go to Man. But how do I persuade Ospak and Brodir?

GORMLAI As you did with Earl Sigurd. The throne of Dublin and my hand in marriage.

SIGTRYG But Earl Sigurd —

GORMLAI He need not know.

SIGTRYG I will try then. But which of the brothers?

GORMLAI Ospak has ten ships, Brodir twenty. Make your offer to Brodir.

SIGTRYG But they say he is a heathen, a renegade — a man who was once a deacon.

GORMLAI They say his hair is so long he can tuck it under his belt. What they say does not matter. Both those brothers are heathen.

SIGTRYG Right. I will go to Brodir.

(*Viking horn, then 'sea-wash' behind*)

BRODIR Ha! Ha! Ha! Ha! Ha! So that is settled. I shall be in Dublin on Palm Sunday.

SIGTRYG And you, Ospak?

OSPAK No. I do not like double-dealing. Brian is a good king.

BRODIR Then get back to your own ship. You are my brother no longer.

OSPAK I never chose to be your brother, but let me warn you, Brodir. I, as you know, have the gift of foresight. I think you go to your death. And, as proof of this, this night in this ship you will see certain wonders. Or perhaps not see them — hear them and feel them. And in each of your twenty ships a man will be dead by morning.

BRODIR You forget I have magic too.

OSPAK You will need it, Brodir. And stop your ears with wax. Or else the noise may deafen you.

BRODIR Deafen me?

(*Cross into wild din and behind*)

Light! Light! Who has put out the light?

1ST VIKING Brodir! What is happening? Oh my face!

BRODIR Shields! Take your shields, fend them off.

2ND VIKING Thor god of battles! Their beaks are like iron. What are they?

BRODIR Ravens, only ravens. Use your shields.

1ST VIKING Ravens, Brodir? Demons!

BRODIR What do I care! Keep off there! Keep away, you fowls of hell!

(*Shouts and mixed noises, then a scream and falling body, then silence*)

There goes my one man dead. You will answer for this, brother Ospak. And unless you answer me truly —

OSPAK I will answer nothing till you pledge me peace.

(*Pause*)

Well?

BRODIR Right.

'As the meter meted and the teller told and the doomsman deemed and the givers gave — '

OSPAK No, not now. Wait till nightfall.

BRODIR Why?

OSPAK I know you, Brodir. You never kill men by night. So I shall tell you then.

I shall tell you now. What happened last night foretold your doom. Those ravens which attacked you are the demons you put your faith in. When you all are dead in a short time from now in Ireland, it is those black demons that will drag you down to hell.

BRODIR The raven is Odin's bird.

OSPAK True. Let Odin protect you then.

BRODIR He is your god too.

OSPAK No longer. I go to the god you forsook.

BRODIR You will take baptism?

OSPAK Yes.

BRODIR Then I shall not see you in Ireland.

OSPAK You *will* see me in Ireland. But in the ranks of King Brian. No, don't draw your sword. Remember your pledge. Besides, Brodir, it is night still.

BRODIR Night? Yes, black as a raven. Never mind, I will pray to the god of ravens. And you, you can pray to the man on the naked tree. But you do not know those prayers yet — the prayers that I have forgotten. They are more fit for old men like Brian. They will not get you to Valhalla.

BRIAN Deus meus adiuva me.

BISHOP Salus tua, Domine, sit semper nobiscum.

BRIAN Have mercy upon us, O God the Father Almighty,
BISHOP O beginning of all things,
BRIAN O true knowledge,
BISHOP O morning star,
BRIAN O tree of life,
BISHOP O lily of the valleys,
BRIAN O lion,
BISHOP O eagle,
BRIAN O Christ Crucified!
BISHOP Have mercy upon us.
BRIAN Have mercy upon us.

SLAVE GIRL Mary, Mother of God, Mother of the Golden Light, Mary greatest of Marys, heal the weals on my back, I cannot sleep for the pain of them. And Mary Queen of the Angels, Fountain of the Gardens, Star of the Sea, I pray you to raise the waves of the sea and sink all the ships of the Vikings before they make land in my country. But if they should reach my country, hear the prayer of a slave girl in Iceland far from her home; O Mary Queen of the Heavens, if those long evil ships with the round shields on their gunwales and the dragons' heads on their prows should come to the mouth of the Liffey —

OLD WOMAN There child, what did I tell you! The dragons are back from the north, they are hungry. Look how the sun glints on the shields on the gunwales. I have seen them often before, time and again I have seen them, but never so many as this; the whole of the bay is afroth with them. If I were King Brian I would hide in the woods. I am as old as he is, older maybe but I've no wish to die. He rests his head on a pillow of feathers, I have not even a pillow of chaff; for all that I sleep the sounder. And I sleep as sound as Queen Gormlai for all her gold and her lovers. These great folk are all the same. They do no good to us. They do no good to themselves. Gormlai! If I were her husband I would take my shield to bed with me.

GORMLAI Earl Sigurd, I welcome you to Dublin. You look as my son described you.
SIGURD Thank you, Queen Gormlai. You look more than he described you.
GORMLAI More what?

SIGURD Beautiful. Fierce.

GORMLAI Good. Bring us some wine there.

So you could not describe me, Sigtryg!

SIGTRYG Who could, mother, who could?

GORMLAI Yes. I am not dead yet.

You eat sucking pig, Earl Sigurd?

SIGURD When I can get it, Queen Gormlai.

GORMLAI I have killed a hundred for supper. It is an Irish delicacy.

SIGURD Ireland, I think, must be full of delicacies.

GORMLAI Ireland is full of good things — and bad things. When I lived with Brian — may he still sleep uneasy! — in Kincora, around our house was a great earth dyke with crab-apple trees and ashtrees. And the wind moaned in those trees while Brian moaned beside me. That old man talks in his sleep; the memories he has are too many and black.

ETAIN It is not true. I will not listen —

GORMLAI Who asked you to?

ETAIN Sigtryg! Tell her —

SIGTRYG My mother should know.

ETAIN King Brian has many memories but they are not black, they are golden.

SIGURD So you praise King Brian?

ETAIN He is my father.

SIGURD Your father! Whom then do you want to win?

ETAIN My father. I will go now.

GORMLAI Yes, Etain, go to your work-basket. Try a little embroidery. Why not embroider a shroud? That would be daughterly of you.

(*Laughter from crowd*)

SIGURD A girl of spirit.

GORMLAI You think so? Well, what was I saying? Yes, my life in Kincora away out there in the west. Round our house was a dyke and beyond that dyke was a bog, with stumps of grey bog-oak in it like the broken bones of giants. One night when I could not sleep I put on a thick woollen cloak and went to the edge of that bog and there was a will-o'-the-wisp. And I called to him 'What is your life?' You know what he answered?

SIGURD So he answered?

GORMLAI He answered by action; he vanished. And that, I thought, is the life of the people in Ireland. They dart here and there, they flicker and fade in the bogs — but for me, I want something more solid. That is why I sent for you. Was I right, Sigurd?

SIGURD I suppose I am more solid than a will-o'-the-wisp.

(*Laughter*)

GORMLAI What would you say was the difference between your people and the Irish?

SIGURD I think there are many differences. We have better aims. We build better ships. We talk less.

GORMLAI And you are more solid? Both in body and spirit. You are better fighters? And better lovers?

SIGURD That you must judge for yourself, Queen Gormlai.

GORMLAI I think you will win this battle.

SIGURD I think so too — but what will be will be.

GORMLAI What day is it set for?

SIGURD I have left that to Brodir.

GORMLAI Why to Brodir?

SIGURD He practises divination.

GORMLAI Divination! I should not have thought you cared for that. Well, has he done his divining?

SIGURD No, he would have told me. But I will encourage him. Brodir!

GORMLAI Why, is he here?

SIGURD Here he comes.

GORMLAI So his hair *is* as long as they say.

BRODIR Earl Sigurd?

SIGURD It is time you did your divining.

BRODIR I have done so, Earl Sigurd.

SIGURD Then why did you not tell me?

BRODIR Ill news keeps.

SIGURD Go on.

BRODIR If we fight before Good Friday, all of us shall fall.

SIGURD Then we do not fight before Good Friday.

BRODIR If we fight on Good Friday, Brian shall fall.

GORMLAI Good. Bring us more wine there!

BRODIR Brian shall fall — but he will win.

GORMLAI I do not believe you. If Brian falls, the rest of them will vanish like will-o'-the-wisps.

SIGURD Will-o'-the-wisps have a trick of reappearing.

GORMLAI *You* don't believe him, do you?

SIGURD Maybe I do, maybe not. No matter; we fight on Good Friday.

GORMLAI Sigurd, you disappoint me. A man of your strength should not meddle with omens.

BRODIR I think there will be more omens. Once Good Friday is with us. And good will be the wrong word.

(Fade up witch-weaving music and behind)

1ST CAITHNESS MAN Can you see in?

2ND CAITHNESS MAN No. Let me get on your shoulders.

1ST C. MAN I'd rather we went. There's something wrong about this.

2ND C. MAN What's wrong? They are only weaving. There are plenty of looms in Caithness.

1ST C. MAN Aye, but this barn they are weaving in — this barn was not here yesterday.

2ND C. MAN Are you sure?

1ST C. MAN I live half a mile from here. There is no such barn on this moor.

2ND C. MAN Come, let me get on your shoulders. That's it. Now raise yourself. Just a little higher and I'll get my eye to the window slit. St Michael and All Angels! Odin, Thor and Freya!

1ST C. MAN What is it?

2ND C. MAN Women — but they are not women. The light is dim but they are not women. And that loom, it's dripping with blood. Listen! Now they're singing.

THE FATES

This is our warp   this is our woof,
    The hot guts of heroes;
We weave we sisters   the sorrowful tale
    Of lives to be lost.

In this dark morning   we weave the doom
    Of bold men in battle
On a far shore   on this evil Friday
    We weave and we weave . . .

(Fade out loom music, fade up Brian)

BRIAN Hos omnes invoco in auxilium meum.

BISHOP Forty saints in Glendalough.

BRIAN Per Jesum.

BISHOP Four thousand monks with the grace of God in Bangor.

BRIAN Per Jesum.

BISHOP Twelve youths who went with Columcille on pilgrimage to Alba.

BRIAN Per Jesum.

BISHOP The hermit found by Brendan in the Land of Promise.

BRIAN Per Jesum.

BISHOP Seven holy bishops of the Church of the Yew Wood.

BRIAN Per Jesum.

BISHOP Seven holy bishops of Tuam in Galway.

BRIAN Per Jesum.

BISHOP Seven holy bishops of Donaghmore in Leitrim.

BRIAN Per Jesum.

BISHOP Seven holy bishops of Donaghmore in Limerick.

BRIAN Per Jesum.

BISHOP Seven holy bishops of —

MURAGH Father!

BRIAN Muragh! You should not enter this chapel like that. Take off your helmet.

MURAGH I am sorry, father, but time runs on. It will be dawn soon. They are all waiting for their orders.

BRIAN One moment.

O warrior Michael help me in the hour of my departing.

BISHOP Amen.

MURAGH Why that prayer, father?

BRIAN This night I heard the banshee. Today is my last. And, as I told you, I shall spend it in prayer.

MURAGH Here?

BRIAN On the fringe of the battle. They must set up my tent where I know what goes on. In Tomar's Wood. I will have the lad Teigue there with me; he will be company enough. And you, Muragh, the battle is yours. If you fall, the command goes to Turlough.

MURAGH Turlough is too young.

BRIAN He too has my blood in his veins. What my son can do, my grandson can do. Goodbye, my lord Bishop; I go to my conference.

BISHOP God be with you, King Brian.

BRIAN And with you too. And with all of us. Muragh, I am ready.

MURAGH It is time. I dare say Sigurd is holding his conference already. Those Vikings are early birds.

BRIAN The early bird is the one the worms eat first. God forgive me, I should not joke on Good Friday. Where is my crown?

MURAGH You are wearing it.

BRIAN Ha! It is time I died. Is Mael Seachlainn up?

MURAGH They are all up.

BRIAN And my harper too?

MURAGH And your harper.

BRIAN He too may fight if he wants to. I have not allowed it before but I shall not need him again. Let him play for me once before it starts. But, before that, some different music. Let them sound the handbells. Let my army know I am coming. Today will decide everything.

(Montage of handbells and fade slowly)

SIGURD That is all, fellow Vikings. Today will decide everything.

BRODIR Earl Sigurd?

SIGURD Yes, Brodir?

BRODIR Two miles, I think, is too wide a front.

SIGURD I do not think so. Is it two miles, Maelmordha? This is your country.

MAELMORDHA To Clontarf is more than two miles. It would be two miles between the Tolka and the Liffey.

BRODIR And you're posting me by the Tolka two miles from Dublin?

SIGURD Would you rather stay inside with Sigtryg?

BRODIR If that is an insult I ignore it. Everyone knows how I fight. But the whole of that ground is wet; we should not spread out too much.

SIGURD If we do not, they can outflank us and cut off our ships.

MAELMORDHA That is true, that is just what they would do. We Irish have a saying: a Viking without his ship is like an ox that's been hobbled.

BRODIR We Vikings have another saying: when an Irishman changes sides —

MAELMORDHA Norsemen change sides too. I hear you have a brother, Brodir.

BRODIR By Thor and his hammer —

SIGURD Silence! Norsemen or Irish, we are all against Brian.

MAELMORDHA Yes, we are all against Brian. In Leinster we do not like Munstermen.

SIGURD I am grateful to you Maelmordha, and all your Leinstermen with you. And let us have no more bickering. My orders stand: Brodir on the right by the Tolka, myself in the centre with Maelmordha on my left, and left of him again the Norseman from Dublin.

BRODIR The bridge will be handy if they run.

THORSTEIN But Sigtryg may not open the gate to them.

VOICE As a Dublin Norseman I resent that.

THORSTEIN On your own behalf or on Sigtryg's?

SIGURD Thorstein, your tongue is too rough.

THORSTEIN It's a way we have in Iceland. Maybe it comes from having no kings or earls there.

BRODIR Where will Ospak be stationed?

SIGURD How should I know? Can I read the mind of King Brian?

BRIAN And right of Mael Seachlainn comes Ospak. Ospak, you hold our right flank. That is all clear then? From left to right this is our order. My son Muragh, in command of the whole army. Next my grandson, Turlough. Then the main forces of Munster. Then Mael Seachlainn, we have often fought together.

MAEL SEACHLAINN Sometimes beside each other, sometimes against each other.

BRIAN What was that, Mael Seachlainn?

MAEL S. I said that you and I were like brother and brother.

OSPAK That proves nothing.

BRIAN Ospak! Where was I? Yes, with Mael Seachlainn. Ah, yes, on his right the Connaughtmen and right of them on the flank by the Liffey Ospak. Now I will shake you each by the hand. When you leave this tent, I shall not see you again.

MURAGH Do not speak like that, father. I have placed a strong guard round this tent, they will stand here shield to shield till the battle is over. Is that not so, Captain of the Guard?

CAPTAIN It is indeed, Prince Muragh. Why would the King be afraid —

BRIAN The King be afraid! Come here, oaf!

CAPTAIN I only meant afraid we would desert. We will stand round this tent like dolmens on the hillsides. We will stand like the Rock of Cashel —

BRIAN You need not go on. You will stand.

CAPTAIN Stand is the word. Stand like the cliffs of Moher. Stand like —

BRIAN Have you been drinking?

CAPTAIN No. I will drink tonight.

BRIAN At my wake, you mean. Give me your hand . . . Yes, you have a grip. Goodbye.

MURAGH To your post, Captain of the Guard.

BRIAN Ospak, your hand. I am glad you are with us.

OSPAK I am glad, King Brian, I have learnt the true faith. And today, if I meet my brother Brodir —

BRIAN I leave that to you. Goodbye.
Mael Seachlainn! Where are you?

MAEL S. But I'm here.

BRIAN My sight must be going. I am old.

MAEL S. I am old too. Sixty-five.

BRIAN That is nothing. And yet I beat you at times.

MAEL S. I beat you at times too.

BRIAN Still I won in the end. Who is the High King now?

MAEL S. You know why I yielded —

BRIAN Let bygones be bygones. You were High King fourteen years —

MAEL S. Nineteen.

BRIAN You are right. It is I have been High King fourteen. And now for some twelve hours more.

MAEL S. Do not say that, Brian.

BRIAN Goodbye, Mael Seachlainn.

MAEL S. Goodbye, Brian. God be with you.

BRIAN Muragh!

MURAGH Father?

BRIAN I will not delay you. You must fight your battle — my battle. Remember that some of these Vikings wear chain-mail.

MURAGH I have met Vikings before, father. Besides, it is only their leaders.

BRIAN You will be meeting their leaders. Well, God be with you. Goodbye, son.

MURAGH Goodbye, father. I will do what I can.

BRIAN Turlough!

TURLOUGH Grandfather!

BRIAN None of them believe me, do they?

TURLOUGH When you say what?

BRIAN When I say today is my last.

TURLOUGH I believe you. I heard the banshee too.

BRIAN *You* heard —! That is not good.

TURLOUGH Muragh heard it too.

BRIAN Muragh too? . . . So much for my family. But there's one missing. My daughter. Why is Etain not here to say goodbye to me?

TURLOUGH She is in Dublin. With Sigtryg.

BRIAN Ah yes of course. And with Gormlai?

TURLOUGH And with Gormlai.

BRIAN And they threw her down from the window and the dogs devoured her carcass. Gormlai! May she meet the fate of Jezebel!

TURLOUGH Grandfather, goodbye. The battle will be starting.

BRIAN The battle? To be sure. But I fear I shall not see it. My eyes are misting over. It is not so light as it was. Teigue!

TEIGUE King Brian?

BRIAN Hold back the flap of the tent there. It must be dawn by now.
Is it dawn, Turlough?

TURLOUGH It is.

BRIAN Are you holding back the flap of the tent?

TEIGUE I am so.

BRIAN How is the sky?

TEIGUE Red. The shepherd's warning.

BRIAN The shepherd's? Ha, ha, ha! Yes, I can see a red glow. Still it's
not so light as it was. Turlough!

> (*Pause*)

Turlough, answer.

TEIGUE King Brian, he went. He was late.

BRIAN Call him back. No. He is needed over there on the left. Where
is my harper?

HARPER Here, King Brian.

BRIAN And my poet?

POET Here too.

BRIAN Good. I want a new piece — a last piece. I want — what do they
call it — a swansong.

POET Give me the lead.

> (*Snatch of harp*)

HARPER Right?

POET Right.

> (*Harp with voice*)

POET In his tent sits Brian blind,
Visions blazing in his mind,
Lesser men may fight and see,
Only he must stay behind.

To the east towards Dublin Bay
Stand the Vikings in array,
Great fair men with eyes of blue —
Who knows who will win the day?

To the east the longships ride,
Painted dragons side by side;
From Clontarf to Liffey bank
Rank on rank the hosts abide.

On our left by Tolka weir
Muragh waits and twirls his spear,
Next him Turlough —

BRIAN Stop!

(Voice and harp break off)

BRIAN Muragh! Turlough! Why are you two not with them?

HARPER But, King Brian —

BRIAN Give me that harp.

POET It was your order that —

(Effect of smashing harp)

BRIAN There! This is no day for music. Only for prayer — and blood-shed. Off with you two to the battle.

POET God be with you, King Brian.

HARPER God be with you, King Brian.

    (Pause)

BRIAN Teigue, have you the psalter?

TEIGUE The psalter?

BRIAN The great book in the golden case. You will have to read it aloud to me. But first spread the wolfskin on the ground.

TEIGUE It is spread already. At your feet.

BRIAN Good. Help me down to kneel on it. A hundred and fifty psalms there are. That might see out the battle. Thank you, Teigue. How is the weather?

TEIGUE Sharp. Very sharp.

BRIAN Sharp? To be sure. Sharp as nails.

Right. Psalm One.

TEIGUE 'Blessed is the man that walketh not in the counsel of the ungodly; nor standeth in the way of sinners; nor sitteth in the seat of the scornful...'

SIGURD Good! Unfurl my banner!

THORSTEIN We know about that banner. Everyone dies who carries it.

SIGURD True — but a fine piece of needlework.

My mother made it. She was Irish.

There! Look at it.

VOICES *(cheering)* The raven! The raven!

    (Horns and handbells)

OLD WOMAN Look, man, look! They're swarming like fleas in a sheep-skin. We'll have a grand view from here. They'll be fighting any moment now.

PLOUGHMAN Let them fight! I have this field to plough. What are you doing here anyway?

OLD WOMAN You're late for ploughing — this is April. I've come to see the sport. There'll be great killing today.

PLOUGHMAN I have a brother down there. My twin — but a born fool.

They've put him to guard King Brian. He couldn't guard these oxen here!

OLD WOMAN Look, can't you! That big man by the banner.

SIGURD (*calling*) Brodir, can you hear me!

BRODIR (*calling*) Earl Sigurd?

SIGURD The honour is yours. Begin.

BRODIR Thank you, Earl Sigurd.

Sound the war-horn.

(*Challenge on horn*)

OLD WOMAN Who's that fellow just over the stream there stepping forward? With long black hair flowing down under his helmet.

BRODIR Muragh, son of Brian! Do you hear me?

MURAGH I hear you, Brodir. Come and meet me.

BRODIR I am coming, Muragh.

Draw your swords.

(*Up battle music, music with effects and shouting, and behind*)

MAELMORDHA Come on, Leinstermen! Down with those Munster upstarts!

(*Up music, then quickly to distance behind*)

GORMLAI There goes my brother. Look, the Irish are breaking.

SIGTRYG Brodir is doing well too. It is too far to see who is who but away over there to the north you can see the flow of the armies. And that flow is clearly westward; the Irish are giving ground fast. Brodir and Sigurd — which of them would you choose, mother?

GORMLAI Whichever of them survives. Yes, Brodir is driving back Muragh.

ETAIN Look a little nearer. Your Dublin Vikings are not finding it easy.

GORMLAI Etain! Back to your work-basket.

SIGTRYG Or else hold your tongue.

ETAIN Sigurd too is not finding it so easy —

SIGTRYG Etain, speaking as your husband and also as Sigurd's friend —

ETAIN How dare you speak as my husband? Still less as Sigurd's friend! If you are his friend, what are you doing here? Skulking in Dublin, perched on this watch-tower with the women —

GORMLAI (*laughs*) A hit, Etain, a hit! But stop squabbling. You see what's happening? Away over there, towards the Tolka, Brodir has broken them. And Leinster has broken Munster. The battle is boiling like a broth of leeks. But it's all but over, all but over.

(*Up music and effects and behind*)

MURAGH Stand, you weaklings! What's wrong with you!

BRODIR Freya, goddess of battles! Look at them running!

MAEL S. Michael, bring your angels or we're lost!

THORSTEIN Ha, Sigurd! Men will write verse about this.

    (*Fade out music and effects*)

SKALD

By the weir of the Tolka	warriors gathered
In evil April	on Irish marshland
Gael against Gall	on a grey morning
Close to Clontarf	clamped in death-grip
Havoc disturbed	the heron's fishing,
On Dublin's gates	they doubled the bars,
Sigtryg the coward	crouched behind them.
Then did Earl Sigurd	scythe the warfield,
The wizard Brodir	whittle their spearshafts,
Thorstein of Iceland	thrive in the swordplay.
Against them mustered	Muragh and Turlough
Shin deep in water	shining with bloodlust
Behind them Brian	bowed with years
Knelt in his tent	in Tomar's Wood.

    (*Fade up distant battle effects and behind*)

TEIGUE Here beginneth the twenty-second psalm.

'My God, my God, why hast thou forsaken me?

'Why art thou so far from helping me, and from the words of my roaring?'

BRIAN Roaring? *I* am not roaring. But my knees feel the damp of the ground under this wolf-skin.

TEIGUE 'Our fathers trusted in thee; they trusted and thou didst deliver them. They cried unto thee and were delivered; they trusted in thee and were not confounded.'

    (*Cross-fade Teigue into foreground battle music*)

SIGURD Resting, Thorstein?

THORSTEIN I'm reading a face, Earl Sigurd.

SIGURD Whose face?

THORSTEIN That one at my feet. I have just killed him. A moment ago he looked angry; now he looks only surprised.

SIGURD The dead look often surprised. But back to business, Thorstein. This is a great day for Orkney.

THORSTEIN A great day for Iceland too. A pity the people at home there cannot see how the battle goes.

SIGURD In Iceland! They'd need long sight.

    (*Fade out music and effects*)

SLAVE GIRL Here is your jewel box, Halgerda.

HALGERDA Good. Now what shall I choose? See this silver tortoise brooch? Made by the best silversmith in Norway. And this bracelet? It came from Constantinople. By the way, I want my red dress from the chest.

SLAVE GIRL I will fetch it. Are you expecting guests?

HALGERDA No; today I dress for myself. Today is a great day.

SLAVE GIRL Why?

HALGERDA Haven't you heard — even a slave must have heard — today is the day they fixed for the battle. In your country, hundreds of miles to the south. That red dress, I wore it the day my husband Gunnar came wooing me. It is also red for blood.

SLAVE GIRL Whose blood?

HALGERDA That of your people. They have no chance, you poor wretch.

SLAVE GIRL That is what you say.

HALGERDA Ha! Don't stare at me like that; I can outstare the world. Go and fetch me that dress and the bodice that goes with it.

(*Fade up battle music or effects, but keep distant behind*)

TEIGUE Here beginneth the sixty-ninth psalm.

'Save me, O God, for the waters are come in unto my soul. I sink in deep mire where there is no standing; I am come into deep waters where the floods overflow me. I am weary of my crying, I am dry in the throat; while I wait for my God my eyes fail me.'

(*Up battle music and effects and behind*)

MURAGH Brodir! Brodir you renegade! So it was not as easy as you thought! Yes, Brodir, the tide has turned. Come on, Brodir, and meet me! Ha! I might have guessed it.

(*Fade out music and effects*)

SKALD

How does Brodir	battered by Muragh
Take to his heels,	hide in a thorncopse;
Muragh's long sword	minces the remnant,
On his right young Turlough	ramps like a lion.
Yet does not Sigurd	yield to their onset,
Not for nothing	noted in Orkney;
Stout as an oak	he stands in the centre,
Rallies the Vikings	raises his war-cry.

SIGURD Christ and Valhalla!

(*Up battle music and effects and behind*)

THORSTEIN Earl Sigurd, your banner has fallen.

SIGURD Pick it up then. Who slew the bearer?

THORSTEIN Turlough, grandson of Brian. But to all who bear it that banner is death. I will not pick it up, Earl Sigurd.

SIGURD Hrafn the Red, bear you the banner.

HRAFN Bear your own devil yourself!

SIGURD Hm, so that is your tone now? Well, I suppose, the beggar must bear his own bag. I will take it from its staff and wear it like a cloak. Come, you old raven, in honour to my mother and her needle — There, let us cut our way through them.

THORSTEIN Inland? Away from the sea?

SIGURD What does it matter? Every man's last fight is a defeat. Coming, Thorstein?

THORSTEIN I'm coming.

(*Up battle music, then fade effects to distance behind*)

TEIGUE Here beginneth the hundred and twenty-fourth psalm. 'If it had not been the Lord who was on our side, if it had not been the Lord who was on our side when men rose up against us — '

BRIAN One moment, Teigue. Open the flap of the tent and see how the day goes.

(*To self*) If it had not been the Lord who was on my side . . . when I was young and I hid in the woods in North Munster, when I beat the Foreigners at Limerick, when my brother Mahon was murdered —

TEIGUE King Brian! King Brian! We have won!

BRIAN Already?

TEIGUE The Vikings are running like hares. There are only a few here and there still holding.

BRIAN God be praised — but what will follow will follow. Go on with your reading now, Teigue.

TEIGUE 'If it had not been the Lord who was on our side when men rose up against us, then they had swallowed us up quick when their wrath was kindled against us. Then the waters had overwhelmed us, the stream had gone over our soul . . .'

1ST GUARD Captain!

CAPTAIN What is it?

1ST GUARD The battle is over. What about loot?

CAPTAIN Our orders were to stay here and protect the King.

1ST GUARD Sure he needs no protecting now.

2ND GUARD That's true enough.

3RD GUARD True enough.

1ST GUARD If we wait till we're relieved, the pickings will be gone. I could do with a nice Viking helmet —

2ND GUARD Or one of their axes maybe.

CAPTAIN Yes, their arms are better than ours. But do you think he'd notice?

1ST GUARD Who? The King? Sure he won't, he's at his prayers.

2ND GUARD Authorize us, Captain, authorize us.

CAPTAIN Well now...

1ST GUARD They say some of those Vikings wear gold rings on their arms. Think what you'd get for one in ale.

CAPTAIN You're right. A power of ale. Very good, lads, let's go!
      (*Cheering of guards and fade; effects distant behind*)

OLD WOMAN Now isn't that a grand sight? But they're trying to cross the Tolka, I hope they don't come up here.

PLOUGHMAN Why would they come up here? They'll be veering off there to the bay. Well, I've some furrows more to plough before the light fails.

OLD WOMAN Wait now, wait, man; look at that.

PLOUGHMAN What?

OLD WOMAN A small group of Foreigners yonder, they've cut their way through, they're making for Tomar's Wood.

PLOUGHMAN Tomar's Wood? That's where King Brian is.

OLD WOMAN Is it now? With your brother guarding him.

PLOUGHMAN Ach, my brother! With his head as wooden as this plough. I wouldn't care about *him*.

OLD WOMAN Look, man, they're entering the wood now.

SIGURD So you've joined us again, Brodir.

BRODIR And why not, Earl Sigurd?

SIGURD I thought you had had your fill.

BRODIR I lost the head of my axe. I could not fight Muragh with the shaft.

THORSTEIN Whose axe is that then?

SIGURD Hsh. See that tent — further on in the wood there? Listen!

THORSTEIN Voices.

SIGURD Brodir, now you are armed again — and not so tired as the rest of us, perhaps you will go ahead and find who is there in that tent?

THORSTEIN I will go with him.

SIGURD Good.

TEIGUE Here beginneth the hundred and thirtieth —

BRIAN No, Teigue, that is enough. Besides, you are losing your voice. Keep quiet now; I have someone to talk to.

Tibi soli peccavi et omne malum coram te feci. Peccavi et multiplicata sunt peccata mea super numerum harene maris — more than the sands of the sea — et non sum dignus videre altitudinem celi — no, not worthy, not worthy — prae multitudine peccatorum meorum.

THORSTEIN A priest!

BRODIR In a crown?!

BRIAN Who's there?

BRODIR Your enemies, Brian. Stand up if you want to.

BRIAN No, I will meet my death kneeling.

THORSTEIN Wait, Brodir —

BRODIR Back! Thorstein! Give me room!

BRIAN Christus adjuva me.

    (*Effect*)

THORSTEIN You should not have done that.

BRODIR Should not have! Let the whole world know that Brodir killed Brian.

    (*Up music, then behind*)

SKALD

Thus falls Brian,   Brodir boasts:

BRODIR

Here lies Brian   High King of Ireland!

SKALD

No victory for that   the Vikings gain.

Few are they now,   and far from the sea.

Longsighted Sigurd   looks to the east

Shading his eyes —   his ships are distant;

His line of retreat   is lost to the Irish

And here come the Irish   hot for the kill,

Muragh and Turlough   mad for vengeance;

Muragh swabs   the sweat from his eyes

And looks for Brodir   to left and right

But Brodir himself   breaks to the front

And faces Muragh —

BRODIR

Muragh, son of Brian!   I have killed your father.

What is your answer?

MURAGH

This is my answer.

    (*Up music and effects of single combat*)

THORSTEIN Lay on, Brodir!

TURLOUGH Watch his axe!

THORSTEIN Brodir, keep your shield up!

TURLOUGH Muragh!

    (*Crash*)

  Well done, Muragh.

SIGURD Get your breath again, Muragh. I'm ready when you are.

MURAGH You are the Earl?

SIGURD I am the Earl — and this is my standard. My mother made it; she was Irish.

MURAGH Yes, the work in it looks Irish. I'm ready, Sigurd.

SIGURD Will you fight without shields?

    (*Effect of shield dropping*)

MURAGH There!

    (*Effect of shield dropping*)

SIGURD There! Now Muragh, son of Brian!

    (*Up single combat music and behind*)

SKALD

  Now it is come   combat between them

  Sigurd and Muragh   shieldless both —

TURLOUGH Muragh!

THORSTEIN   Sigurd!

SKALD   mad with war-hate,

  The odds are on Orkney —

TURLOUGH   Ireland!

THORSTEIN   Orkney!

SKALD

  Sigurd's sword   slips in his fingers

  Muragh snatches   the moment of luck,

  Pierces his guard,   the point goes home,

  But as Sigurd totters,   he too takes aim,

  With flagging strength   flails at the neck,

  This time for Muragh   a mortal blow,

  So both men fall   by friends regretted —

TURLOUGH

  Woe in Ireland!

THORSTEIN

                  Wonder in Orkney!

    (*Fade out music*)

HARECK Yonder! Do you see yonder?

ATTENDANT What, Hareck?

HARECK Those men on horseback.

ATTENDANT I see no such thing. No men. No horses —

HARECK It is the Earl. I know by his riding.

ATTENDANT You are mad, man. Earl Sigurd today is fighting in Ireland. How could he be here in Orkney?

HARECK It is Earl Sigurd, I tell you. Or can this mean, does it mean — ?

(Percussion effect, then battle music behind)

TURLOUGH What this means is: the Vikings are beaten. Sigurd is dead, there is no more resistance. After them, fast as you can! After, after, after, after, after!

(Rout music and behind)

SKALD

Now runs Gall,	Gael pursues him
Hacking his hams	hounding him south
To the brimming Liffey	the bridge to Dublin
But the town stands closed,	the two-faced merchants
Gather in counsel,	call on Gormlai,
Gormlai and Sigtryg	to salve their conscience.

(Fade out rout music)

SIGTRYG You are asking me, you merchants of Dublin —

GORMLAI I will speak, Sigtryg; from this day on, my son, no one in Ireland respects you.

ETAIN No one anywhere.

GORMLAI Etain!

Merchants of Dublin, you want my advice. Are we to open the gates to your fellows? Before I answer, there is something I must know. Is there anyone here from the battlefield?

BURNER I am.

GORMLAI Oh you? One of the Burners from Iceland! How did you get into Dublin?

BURNER I swam the Liffey and found a gap in the fence.

GORMLAI You Burners would find a gap in anything. No matter, I want some news. Is Earl Sigurd still alive?

BURNER He is dead.

GORMLAI And Brodir?

BURNER Dead too.

ETAIN So there you have it, Queen Gormlai!

GORMLAI Yes, as you say, there I have it. Either would have suited me. *And* made a good king of Dublin. Unlike my son here, your husband.

SIGTRYG Mother, I —

GORMLAI Merchants of Dublin! I can read your minds like a book — a book with sorry pictures in the margin. You do not want me to open the gates to your kinsmen. Well, nor do I; I have no love for runaways. Let the Irish hound them as they will.

(*Up rout music and behind*)

TURLOUGH After them! Give them no quarter! Kill every man of them —

God of Hosts! What are *you* doing?

THORSTEIN Tying my shoe.

TURLOUGH Why don't you run like the others?

THORSTEIN Turlough, I'm tying my shoe. Besides, I live in Iceland. However fast I might run, I shouldn't get home tonight.

(*Long laugh from Turlough*)

TURLOUGH All right. You may go. Good luck to you.

(*Up rout music and behind*)

SKALD

Now runs Gall,	Gael pursues him
North to the woeful	weir of Clontarf;
With blood they tarnish	Tolka's waters,
Foothold is faulty,	few get over,
Slipping in slime	they are slain in hundreds,
Food for fish	they falter and sink,
As they enter the water	the Irish strike them,
Sword on the flanks	flail on the neck
Spear in the kidneys,	they spit and vanish —
Vengeance for Brian,	victory for Turlough,
Brian is murdered,	Muragh his son
Dead in the turmoil,	Turlough his grandson —
Here he comes now	the High King's heir —
Here he comes now	to harass the Vikings,
To clinch the conflict,	cap the story,
The young man Turlough	yearning for vengeance.

(*Music and effects change to water theme*)

TURLOUGH You there!

CAPTAIN OF GUARD Is it me?

TURLOUGH Haven't I seen you before?

CAPTAIN No, Prince Turlough.

TURLOUGH Then how do you know me? You are the man who deserted his post.

CAPTAIN No, it was my twin.

TURLOUGH You have a twin? I suppose that could be true.

CAPTAIN It is. And he didn't want to leave his post. It was the others persuaded him. Loot, they kept saying, there'll be loot — grand Viking helmets and axes and golden arm rings would buy you a twelve months' drinking.

TURLOUGH So you can't even lie properly! How would you know what they said to your twin? Kneel down and say your prayers, man.

CAPTAIN Oh no, Prince Turlough, no! I didn't mean to, I didn't.

TURLOUGH Kneel down — and make them short.

(*Lose music, hold effects behind in distance*)

OLD WOMAN Ploughman, there's something strange going on now.

PLOUGHMAN Leave me alone. I must plough my last furrow.

OLD WOMAN There's a man down there — he looks somehow familiar — and he's kneeling on the bank of the Tolka.

Ploughman — Oh, so he's gone.

Kneeling ... seems to be praying. But who would that be standing over him — with a sword in his hand — but he's raising it. Mother of God!

(*Scream, distant*)

The murdering villain! To kill a man when he's praying. But look, that serves him right. Overbalanced as he struck him and fell himself in the Tolka — may the devil drag him down and drown him. Floundering about in the water now — can't find his feet, it's carrying him down towards the weir. There, he's hit his head on a post — he's under, will he come up again ... Will he come up again? ... No, lost in the lather and pother ... No, he's gone for good now ... Well, whoever he was, there's some justice in heaven.

(*Cross-effects into solo harp — a snatch of a lament — then silence*)

POET How does it compare, harper?

HARPER It's not like the one the king broke. But it will do. Are you ready?

POET Ready.

(*Harp and voice*)

POET Now Good Friday's light is spent,
Brian murdered in his tent,
Muragh dead and Turlough dead —
Rough and red the way they went.

Shattered lies the Viking host;
Deeds we wrought of which to boast,
Yet in Ireland never an eye
Can be dry from coast to coast.

Now that Brian to heaven is gone,
His two servants linger on,
He the harper, I the bard,
Hard we find it —

MAEL S. Hard you find it?

HARPER King Mael Seachlainn!

MAEL S. You are my servants now. I am taking you on.

POET We thank you for that.

MAEL S. And there is something else I am taking on — or back. The High Kingship of Ireland. But before I am crowned yet again, I will bury Brian at Armagh. It will be the greatest funeral ever yet seen in Ireland.

(*To self*) Yes, he did me much wrong but ... it will be the finest funeral.

(*Fade up crowd of women lamenting*)

CROWD Ochone! Ochone!

OLD WOMAN Why do you do that?

(*Lament breaks off*)

WOMAN We are mourning.

OLD WOMAN Mourning? Aha! They pay you for it.

WOMAN I know they pay us — but these tears are tears. May he have it easy on the road to Heaven. May the veils of fire and of ice that clash at the gate stand still for him. May he pass through the seven crystal walls and hear the birds that sing there.

WOMEN Ochone! Ochone!

OLD WOMAN So you're weeping for Brian? The last time I wept was for the murrain on the cattle. That makes more sense.

WOMAN Who are you? Where do you come from?

OLD WOMAN Dublin.

WOMAN Dublin.

OLD WOMAN On my two feet. But I wouldn't weep for his death; I am just here for the spectacle. Great folk give us little else but, when they get married or die, they give us a grand show. Or even when they are born; I know that well.

WOMAN Why?

OLD WOMAN I have been a midwife in the houses of kings — great big whitewashed houses with fires half the length of the hall and skins not only to sit on but skins to wrap round your feet — and the roof so high you would hardly see the swallows in the rafters.

WOMAN So you are a midwife?

OLD WOMAN I was, I got tired of the business. There are too many people born anyway. No, a birth is nothing to a death.

WOMAN Mary and the saints protect us! You had best move on, strange woman.

OLD WOMAN I am moving on but let me tell you this. You are mourning for Brian and thanking God for his victory. Is that so? Thanking God for it!

WOMAN We are thanking God indeed. That battle has settled matters.

OLD WOMAN That battle has settled nothing. Ask the people who know. Just ask the big people who know.

BISHOP You see this crozier in my hand? I held it in my hand on the morning of Good Friday. When I blessed King Brian before he went to the battle. And the blessing I gave him and the hopes we all placed on him are as dried up now as the sap in this crozier of yew wood. As the new High King well knows. Or should I say the old High King?

MAEL SEACHLAINN You see this sceptre? Once it was mine. Then it was Brian's and now it is mine again. And it all proves nothing, nothing. The men of Leinster are still disaffected and in Munster and Connaught they're lying low but they hate me, and as for the Norsemen they're still selling Irish slave girls in Dublin.

GORMLAI Brian is dead — that's one good thing. And it is a pity Sigurd is dead. But otherwise nothing has changed very much. Out there in Irish Ireland they're still tying rags on the briars by the holy wells and they still are scared of a lonely whitethorn. And I — who am lonely too — they still are scared of me. As for the Foreigners, they are still here. And if ever they go, there are others will succeed them. No, no, no! Nothing was decided at Clontarf.

    (Pause, then snatch of harp)

HARPER Does that suit you, poet?

POET Anything you choose, harper.

    (Longer stretch of harp, then break off)

HARPER Why are you not reciting? This is our farewell to Brian.

POET I am tired of words. I spoke my farewell on the battlefield. You are lucky, harper.

HARPER Why lucky?

POET Words must be true or false; what you say on those strings is
neither.

HARPER I must do it alone then? The Farewell.

POET My words might flatter the dead — or they might malign him.
Yes, my friend; this time you must do it alone.

    (*Harp finale*)

THE MAD ISLANDS

a radio parable play

The Mad Islands (broadcast on 4 April 1962, Third Programme) is a fantasy based on an ancient Irish legend 'The Voyage of Maelduín' — from *Old Celtic Romances* translated by P. W. Joyce (1879, 1961) — with some reference to Alwyn and Brinley Rees's *Celtic Heritage* (1961), which MacNeice had reviewed in the *Observer*, and to Tennyson's poem 'The Voyage of Mael-dune' (1880). Some characters of the old folk legend are retained (e.g. the Miller of Hell); others invented in keeping with the author's and the tale's Celticism (e.g. Skerrie the Seal-Woman), or to lighten its spirit with wit and humour (e.g. the Jester; the Funster) or to update the story (e.g. the Alchemist turned into the Inventor who becomes a mad nuclear scientist), even though by so doing MacNeice introduced anachronisms. This strange parable play is an example of a false or vain quest, a fantasy about frustration, 'meant to be both timeless and topical'.[1] At the end there is a positive resolution: after many trials and frustrations on his quest the hero loses his hatred and sets off again with renewed hope. Some time before his death MacNeice prepared it for publication (the printed text used here) together with *The Administrator*; the two plays appeared posthumously in 1964, with his 'Introduction' to both, published immediately below.

These two plays were both written for what some think an obsolescent medium. Obsolescent or not, sound radio, in Britain at least, is not the *mass* medium it used to be, television having stolen most of its public though it cannot take over most of its territory. Sound radio can do things no other medium can and if 'sound' dies, those things will not be done. So I offer these two plays in print not only as readable pieces (or I hope so) in their own right but also as specimens of a peculiar genus which may soon become a historical curiosity. In getting these pieces ready for print I have not altered the dialogue but have cut out the technical radio directions (the 'slow cross-fades', the 'hold behinds', etc.), and have substituted more intelligible signposts. On the other hand I have resisted the temptation to tag on many adverbial labels to the speeches, words like 'calmly', 'rapidly', 'disingenuously'; I like to think that these qualities are implicit in the lines. At the beginning of *The Mad Islands* I indicate that a harp was used: in fact it was used repeatedly throughout the production both to suggest changes of mood and place and to cover the passage of time; very often it was mixed with recorded effects, naturalistic or 'radiophonic', i.e. doctored.

The Administrator was written and broadcast in 1961, *The Mad Islands* in 1962. The two plays, though in many ways quite dissimilar, have certain things in common. First and most important, they are both essentially 'radio', i.e. with all their jumping about, whether in time or place and between the actual and the fantasy, they could not be anything else. Then they both, in a way, are studies in frustration. As regards the fantasy element, the dreams in *The Administrator* correspond to the islands in the other play. But here perhaps the difference between them is most important: the dreams in *The Administrator* are 'naturalistic' in that they are the kind those particular dreamers might have in 'real life'; they are also intended to throw light on both the characters and the pasts of the dreamers. In *The Mad Islands*, on the other hand, we never get *out* of fantasy and the 'characters' (see below) are barely charac-terized. But this does not mean (again see below) that *The Mad Islands* is a simple 'escapist' fairy story that has nothing to do with the world we live in.

Compared with plays written for the stage, works such as these may appear very bitty until you get used to them. I find myself that one of the attractions of radio is that you can move so fast, almost as fast as dreams do: this is why the medium is a good one for dealing with dreams and why, the other way round, a dream technique suits the medium. But a word of warning about 'symbolism', that old thing which makes so many people bristle: neither of these pieces is intended as *primarily* symbolic, at least in the narrow and *deliberate* sense (though in *The Mad Islands* certain hard-edged symbols are inherited), still less as allegorical, meaning one-for-one correspondence. But in both plays there is meant to be a good deal of *suggestion* and overlapping of references. Not only again is this very feasible in radio: as one's time is too often too limited, it *pays* to do several things at once.

The Administrator needs little comment: I had a compulsion to write it as this sort of painful choice seems endemic in our society. My chief trouble here was the ending. Originally I intended to end it with Jerry still not making up his mind but, being told that the listening public hated this, against my grain and the probability of his character made him follow his wife's wishes. I have now stood this decision on its head. *The Mad Islands* I wrote because I have always been addicted to the legendary Ancient Irish voyages which suggested it. In the original legend of Maelduín *thirty-one* islands were visited. Alwyn and Brinley Rees in their book *Celtic Heritage* observe that in these voyages (the Voyage of Bran is another one) 'our world as we know it seems to resolve itself into its components', e.g. in an Island of Laughter people do *nothing but* laugh. I used one or two of the original islands and invented the others, just as Tennyson did in his 'Voyage of Maeldune', which he wrote in 1881 after reading P. W. Joyce's *Old Celtic Romances*, where the story was first published in English. One original motif which Tennyson ignored and I jumped at is that of the Miller of Hell, who in Joyce's version describes himself thus: 'I am the miller of hell. All the corn and all the riches of the world that men are dissatisfied with ... are sent here to be ground, and also every precious article, and every kind of wealth, which men try to conceal from God. All these I grind in the Mill of Inver-tre-Kenand, and send them afterwards away to the west.'

Apart from adding and subtracting islands I also twisted the basic story-line: the vendetta is traditional but not my dénouement. And the seal-woman, though thoroughly Celtic and appearing repeatedly in Irish and Scottish folk-lore (see *The People of the Sea* by David Thomson), did not originally have anything to do with Maelduín: the taboos, on the other hand, are traditional. Going wider, I did not mean my play to be either essentially Irish (in spite of its somewhat stylized dialogue)

or consistently of the saga period. In fact half its point is its anachronisms. For this is something else that radio can get away with: a character
can slip in and out of different periods without any embarrassment to
himself or the listener. On the stage or the screen it would be highly
embarrassing and not only in the little matter of costume.

CHARACTERS

MULDOON, who has a quest

CORMAC, his foster-brother and friend

THE JESTER

MULDOON'S MOTHER

URSACH, the steersman

THE CREW

SKERRIE, the seal-woman

LIAM

THE FUNSTER

BRANWEN AND OLWEN, the rival sisters

THE MILLER OF HELL

THE MERCHANT

THE ONE-EYED MAN

THE BUSYBODY

THE DROWNED MAN

THE [THREE] TEMPTERS

THE QUEEN OF THE TWILIGHT

THE INVENTOR

THE SLAVE

THE [FIVE] BIDDERS

VOICE(S)

THE HERMIT

THE CROWD

THE PORTER

THE BOY

THE MAD ISLANDS

(The play begins with harp music. Two young men are playing chess in a big house in Ancient Ireland)

CORMAC Your move, Muldoon.

(Pause)

Your move I said, Muldoon.

MULDOON My move?

CORMAC Easy now — your king's in danger.

MULDOON I can't see that.

CORMAC Well, I've warned you.

(After a pause a chessman is moved. Another pause and another is moved)

CORMAC Check!

MULDOON Check?

JESTER And mate.

MULDOON Who asked you, fool?

JESTER I know a mate when I see one. As the black bull said when they offered him the nanny-goat.

MULDOON Is it mate, Cormac?

CORMAC It is, Muldoon.

MULDOON Why do I always lose at this game?

JESTER Because chess is like life.

CORMAC Quiet, fool!

JESTER Look at this board. He need never have lost the queen. The queen! Ha! Ha! The queen!

(Moving off) He could find her again if he wanted to.

MULDOON What did he mean by that?

CORMAC Nothing. Talking like a fool is his business.

MULDOON Why did you order him quiet then? I am of age now. Tell me.

CORMAC Yes, you are of age at last. All right then. I didn't tell you before because you're my foster-brother and I wouldn't be losing you yet.

MULDOON Why would you lose me at all? An orphan like me, I've nowhere to go.

CORMAC The queen that was lost is still on the board. But she lives far away. A black queen, I reckon, or a red one.

MULDOON Lay off the riddles.

CORMAC I'm talking about your mother. She's still alive. We lied to you.

MULDOON You lied! You all of you lied? My mother still alive! How do I know you're not lying now?

CORMAC It was your mother sent you here. I was an infant then too so I cannot tell you the why or the wherefore. But my parents, who were alive then, she made them promise not to tell you. Not till you came of age.

MULDOON Well, I am of age now.

CORMAC Yes, at last, and that is why I am telling you. It is your move now, Muldoon.

MULDOON Where does my mother live?

CORMAC Far up the board to the north. Her knights and her bishops have all run away and her ivory castles are chipped. And the square she has moved to is black.

MULDOON Do you know the way there?

CORMAC My fool knows the way. Fool! Fool! Where are you?

JESTER Yes, Cormac?

CORMAC I have told Muldoon. Now we must take him to his mother. We leave at once, you must show us the quickest way.

JESTER 'Never take a short cut', says the old proverb. And it's doubly true in a case like this. Bound for the heart of the blackest bogs of Ireland, running the gauntlet of the will-o'-wisps and the haunters, and then not knowing what we will meet at the end of it!

MULDOON We will meet music.

JESTER Meet what?

MULDOON A long-lost mother is music.

JESTER She might be. And she might not.

(*A great gong takes us to the long-lost mother*)

MOTHER There! I have only to strike this gong and you see how my whole house shakes. As if it would sink in the bog like the great beasts lived here once. But you — my only and long-lost son — am I not speaking for an hour and I have not shaken you at all!

MULDOON But you have, mother, you have!

MOTHER Then what are you waiting for? Why are you not on your way?

MULDOON You have not kissed me yet.

MOTHER I will — when you have done your mission. You say you have never been to sea?

MULDOON No, mother. Only in dreams.

MOTHER How do you mean 'only'? I have not seen the sea — or smelt it or felt it — for years. And yet once I lived in a castle with sea north, west, and south of it. Oh the braided brine and the grace-notes of the wind, the smell of the wrack and the company of gulls! But I could not go near the sea now, not while that man's alive and roving the western islands. Water is not like land, each drop links on to the next drop; there is never a break or a baulk in it. One driblet of foam on my foot or one wisp of spray in my face and I'd feel that murderer was touching me. So long as he is out there sailing it, the whole of that sea is defiled. It is for you to make it pure again.

MULDOON With blood you mean, mother?

MOTHER With blood. But, landlubber that you are, I will have to loan you a steersman.

(*She raps the gong twice, sharply*)

URSACH You sounded for me?

MOTHER I did. Ursach, I am sending you to sea again.

URSACH To sea?

MOTHER You do not look pleased.

URSACH My death will come from the sea.

MOTHER Is it worse than a damp bed with the rats scrabbling in the thatch? After all you are a steersman.

URSACH My hand and the tiller are long since parted.

MOTHER This is my son Muldoon.

URSACH Your son but —! Are you Muldoon?

MULDOON I am, Ursach, and I need you. Will you steer me around the western seas till . . .

URSACH Till what?

MOTHER Till you find the killer of his father.

URSACH Is it you have set him on, Finoola?

MOTHER Who else?

URSACH Who else! If you asked *me*, Muldoon —

MOTHER No one is asking you.

MULDOON I *am* asking him something. Is it true that he killed my father?

URSACH Oh, that part is true.

MULDOON Very good. Mother, that knife on the wall — may I have it from you as a keepsake?

MOTHER That was the knife that did it. I found him in the church
with that in his heart. Take it and make good use of it.

URSACH A knife gives a simple answer. Just one jab and it is tit-for-tat.
But when I try to weigh things up —

MOTHER Who asked you to weigh things up? Muldoon, repeat what
I have told you.

MULDOON My father, your husband, was murdered by his friend.
Stabbed in the back while he was praying in church. Just a day and
a night before I was born.

MOTHER And the name of the friend? The title, I should say.

MULDOON He is known as the Lord of Eskers. He is now a sea-rover
in the west. This being so, I must go to the Port of the Unwise and
build or buy me a boat which Ursach here will steer.

URSACH If I consent.

MOTHER You will.

MULDOON For this boat I will raise a crew, seventeen men neither
more nor less; one more or less and ill luck will follow. Cormac, will
you be one of them?

CORMAC What do you think?

MULDOON And you, fool?

JESTER I might as well. A fool is always at sea.

MULDOON Thank you. That is two. And you, Ursach?
        (*Pause*)

URSACH Make it three.

MOTHER I knew you were loyal, Ursach.

URSACH I am loyal to this man for the sake of his father. I would not
have him lost among the islands.

MULDOON Are there so many islands?

URSACH No man yet has counted them.

MOTHER But at one or the next you will find the Lord of the Eskers.
And when you have found him, what then?

MULDOON With this very knife that killed my father —

MOTHER You will strike him, my son. Like this!
        (*She strikes the gong very loudly. Its reverberations melt into the bustle
        of a quay. Muldoon is assembling his crew*)

MULDOON Ursach, how many have we now?

URSACH Sixteen. We need one more.

JESTER They may call this the Port of the Unwise but I think the
unwise men in it have all signed up already.

URSACH If we had the one more we could sail on the tide.

CORMAC Look, Muldoon! There's someone coming now. Coming

down over the slippery stones, moving like a dancer through the slime and the seaweed. There's great balance and poise for you.

MULDOON He's coming this way. Maybe he wants to join us.

URSACH He, Muldoon? It's a woman.

JESTER And a strange woman at that. Look at the round head on her and the way the hair lies close to it.

URSACH There'll be no women in *my* crew!

CREW No! That's right! A woman would bring bad luck.

(*Their anger and superstition simmer*)

MULDOON *Your* crew, Ursach? It's I give the orders here.

URSACH Then you can find another steersman.

(*The strange woman joins them, unperturbed by their threatening aspect*)

SKERRIE Good day to you all. I heard you were a man short.

MULDOON But you're not a man.

SKERRIE Nor quite a woman either.

MULDOON Meaning by that?

SKERRIE I leave you to guess.

URSACH Just leave us anyway!

(*The anger of the crew has now come to the boil*)

CREW That's right! Off with you! (*etc.*)

MULDOON Be quiet, all of you! What is your name?

SKERRIE Skerrie they call me.

MULDOON That's an odd name.

JESTER It goes with the big eyes on her.

URSACH There's a rock near Orkney called the Sule Skerry. It's known for the seals that breed there.

SKERRIE Aye, there are quite a few seals there. I come from those parts, you know. But I know these seas well too, I've been round a number of the islands; there's not one island among them the same as the one before or after. Now the first island we shall come to —

URSACH *We* shall come to!

SKERRIE The first island we shall come to is the Island of Foolish Laughter. But we must put out at once or we shall miss the tide.

URSACH It will mean bad luck if we take her.

CREW That's right. Bad luck! Bad luck!

URSACH Where does this island lie, woman?

SKERRIE West-north-west from the Rock of the Oratory. It is thirteen leagues and a bit. You cannot mistake it for the crowds of birds on it.

URSACH She does know these seas, it seems.

MULDOON Better than you do. We take her.

> (*They take her. And the sound of harp and oars takes all of them out to sea*)

SKERRIE Your steersman is still angry with me.

MULDOON He thinks you are not a right woman.

SKERRIE Has he never heard of the Children of Lochlann?

MULDOON I dare say not. I haven't myself.

SKERRIE To whom it is given that our land-longing shall be sea-longing and our sea-longing shall be land-longing. So that we are never satisfied.

MULDOON Why have you come with me, Skerrie?

SKERRIE I have not yet told myself why.

> (*The harp and oars cover a passage of time*)

LIAM Land! Land ahead! To starboard!

URSACH Land ahead, Muldoon!

MULDOON Is this right?

SKERRIE It is the island I told you of.

MULDOON Right, Ursach. Steer straight for it.

SKERRIE The Island of Foolish Laughter. Here you must go ashore and ask for the Lord of the Eskers.

MULDOON You will not come with me?

SKERRIE That is not allowed. Go only yourself and Cormac and the Jester.

MULDOON And who will I ask about the Lord of the Eskers?

SKERRIE There is only one man to ask. You see, Muldoon –

JESTER Muldoon! Muldoon! Will you look at that island! It's fly-blown!

SKERRIE Those are not flies.

JESTER What are they then?

SKERRIE Birds, man. Laughing birds.

> (*The harp gives way to a chorus of birds laughing*)

FUNSTER Thank you, my feathered friends. Now let me tell you another. A funny thing happened to me on my way to this island this evening.

> (*The birds laugh still more*)

MULDOON Forgive me. May I speak to you?

FUNSTER Not till I've finished my act.

> (*The birds continue laughing*)

On my way to this island this evening –

> (*The bird laughter increases again*)

I met a Gael and a Gall. The Gall said to the Gael 'How are you blowing, my lord?'

(*The birds are now laughing themselves silly*)

The Gael replied: 'My lord, I find your questions too galling.'

(*The birds think this the funniest thing ever but gradually their laughter subsides*)

Thank you, my feathered friends. You may have heard it before but it's none the worse for that.

JESTER I think it stinks.

FUNSTER Who are you, sir?

JESTER Just someone who knows about laughter.

FUNSTER In that case you are a trespasser. Have you a permit for laughter?

JESTER A permit?

FUNSTER A permit, a pass, a diploma —

JESTER I am a fool, like my father before me. And I got my first laugh when I was in the cradle.

FUNSTER Well, you won't get any laugh here.

MULDOON Stop this argument. What I want to ask is —

JESTER So I won't get a laugh here?

FUNSTER This audience has certain standards.

(*One or two birds squawk to show that they take the point*)

You can try though, if you like.

JESTER Thank you. I will. Watch me. Eagles, puffins and loons, razorbills, wild geese and kittiwakes, ravens, sea-ravens and cormorants — I am now going to make you laugh. If I don't you may give me the bird.

(*Silence*)

Oh. Well, let's try again. Ah, just the story for you lot. Once upon a time there was a wren, a robin and a Jew —

(*Silence*)

And they met in the middle of a holly-bush —

(*Silence*)

You can keep this audience. They're deaf.

FUNSTER Listen, my friend. If you want to make people laugh —

MULDOON Listen to *me*. It's a matter of life and death. You must see everyone that comes to this island?

FUNSTER Naturally.

MULDOON Then have you seen — or heard of — the Lord of the Eskers?

FUNSTER Is that a riddle? I know some too. What happens when you step on the horizon?

JESTER It's like putting your hand up a skirt. You know that you've gone too far.

FUNSTER What happens when you come to the end of a rainbow?

JESTER You meet the smiling face of the tax man.

FUNSTER What happens when you did up a fairy mound?

JESTER A fairy mound. Well, I hardly like to tell you —

MULDOON Stop wasting the time. The Lord of the Eskers?

FUNSTER Never heard of him. What's his speciality?

MULDOON He killed my father.

FUNSTER So that's his speciality. Did you hear that, my feathered friends? This gentleman's looking for someone who killed this gentleman's father.

(*The birds begin laughing again*)

That's what I said, my feathered friends. He killed this gentleman's father. Well, you can't go farther than that.

(*The birds once more laugh themselves sick; then their laughter dissolves into the harp and the sounds of a boat at sea*)

SKERRIE The next island is the Island of the Rival Beds.

MULDOON Whose rival beds?

SKERRIE Branwen's and Olwen's — they're sisters. And here you must be very careful. For here you must go ashore alone.

MULDOON Why must I go ashore at all?

SKERRIE The Lord of the Eskers is fond of women. Of all the islands he might well choose this one. But, when you meet these two sisters, be sure you do nothing but question them. Will you promise me that?

MULDOON I promise you.

(*The harp music fades and there is silence; and then the love-cry of a tom-cat*)

BRANWEN Conor! Out you go!

OLWEN That is no way to treat him.

BRANWEN I can't bear it when he stares at me like that.

OLWEN It reminds you, does it, Branwen?

BRANWEN He was a marvellous lover.

OLWEN I could have had him if I'd wanted.

BRANWEN You could not, Olwen. But I could have had your grey one there.

OLWEN That's not true; is it, Diarmid?

(*Diarmid miaws*)

OLWEN He says No, you see.

BRANWEN He says Yes — don't you, Diarmid?

OLWEN Hsh, there's someone coming.

BRANWEN It's a man!

OLWEN Yes, a man — for the moment, poor thing. What are you doing, slipping your dress off the shoulder?

BRANWEN And what are *you* doing, shaking out your hair like that?

OLWEN Hsh!

BRANWEN Hsh yourself!

MULDOON May I come in?

BRANWEN You are welcome.

OLWEN This is only a humble bower but —

MULDOON Are you Branwen and Olwen?

BRANWEN }
OLWEN   }We are.

OLWEN Let me give you some wine.

BRANWEN You are windblown. Let me comb your hair.

OLWEN You look tired. Come and sit beside me here.

MULDOON Thank you, but I'm in a hurry, I —

BRANWEN In a hurry, man? Shame!

OLWEN No one comes here in a hurry.

BRANWEN And no one leaves in a hurry. (*Laughs*)

OLWEN Good for you, Branwen. No one leaves in a hurry!
  (*Both laugh*)

MULDOON All I want to ask is —

BRANWEN Why is your hand bleeding?

MULDOON It was those cats outside.

BRANWEN The wicked things! They would be jealous.

OLWEN They ought to know better by now. We've tried to train them, you know, but —

MULDOON Have you see the Lord of the Eskers?

BRANWEN Yes, we've tried to train them, but, you see, they're Irish.

OLWEN We've only been here two years, you know.

BRANWEN And haven't we a nice crowd of cats to show for it?

OLWEN When we left the land of our fathers we meant to be back by sundown.

BRANWEN We had hired such a pretty little boat — they said it was suitable for ladies — but indeed we never meant to go farther than Anglesey.

OLWEN Suitable for ladies! We were carried away, man. Of course all our family have stormy natures.

BRANWEN That's what our stepfather said. He called it the weather in the soul.

OLWEN No, not the soul, the mind.

BRANWEN Or was it the heart?

OLWEN We're both wrong; it was the intestines.

BRANWEN No, that wasn't the word. I think it began with a 'w'.

OLWEN Or would it have been a 'v'? Well, never mind, we had a good blow for our money.

MULDOON I'm sorry to keep asking questions. Have you seen the Lord of the Eskers?

OLWEN You asked that already.

MULDOON But you didn't answer.

BRANWEN The Lord of the Eskers? What sort of man was he then?

OLWEN Was he ginger with a bull neck?

BRANWEN Was he wearing a furry grey cloak with black markings like a mackerel?

OLWEN Or a black jerkin with snow-white gloves and boots?

BRANWEN And what were his whiskers like? Did they stick out straight or did they droop?

MULDOON I have never met the man.

BRANWEN Well, when would he have been here?

MULDOON A week ago — a month — a year — I couldn't tell you for certain.

BRANWEN If you will come to my room, I will show you my list.

OLWEN Come to mine. My list is longer.

BRANWEN It is not.

OLWEN It is. And I have little bells on my bed.

BRANWEN She has too — but my bed is softer.

OLWEN Her bed may be softer. When it comes to other things —

BRANWEN Don't listen to her. The proof is in the meeting.

MULDOON All I want to know is: if the Lord of the Eskers was here, when did he leave?

BRANWEN Oh, he would not have left.

OLWEN How could he?

BRANWEN They never leave — and it costs us a fortune in milk.

OLWEN You have probably seen him already.

BRANWEN Maybe it was he that scratched you.

MULDOON If you mean what I think —

OLWEN You are very quick at guessing.

    (*Branwen and Olwen laugh*)

OLWEN Why did you want this Lord of the Eskers anyway?

MULDOON To kill him.

BRANWEN To kill him! Oh, you villain!

MULDOON And, if you have turned him to a cat, I shall kill him just the same.

BRANWEN You will do no such thing. We have never lost a cat yet.

OLWEN Anyway you'd never guess which he was.

MULDOON Make me a cat too and I'll soon know which he is.

OLWEN We will not make you a cat!

BRANWEN Quite right, Olwen. And we won't even let him go to bed with us.

OLWEN Certainly not. And what's more we'll deport him from the island.

BRANWEN Yes, that's what we'll do, we'll deport him! Brian, Fergus, Conor, the lot of you —

OLWEN Diarmid, Feargal, Stumpy-Tail, the lot of you —
      (*The cats begin gathering*)

BRANWEN Cats who used to have souls —

OLWEN Cats who used to wear jerkins and breeches —

BRANWEN Cats who used to go to church —

OLWEN Cats who used to go to bed —

BRANWEN Gather round all of you and out with your claws! Drive this man into the sea!
      (*The cats hiss, spit, scream and snarl*)

MULDOON Keep back! Keep away! Or I'll kill you!

OLWEN Look at him walking backwards, waving his little knife. He's afraid of our cats, Branwen.

BRANWEN And well he might be, Olwen. They were all great fighters in their time.

OLWEN Yes and they fought to kill. But the funny thing, Branwen, is this. This Lord of . . . Lord of . . .

BRANWEN The Eskers.

OLWEN He is one killer that never came here — worse luck.
      (*The cat noises fade and the harp comes back and Muldoon is out at sea again*)

SKERRIE It was my mistake, Muldoon. I was told so while you were on shore. The Lord of the Eskers never landed on that island. He was swept clean past it by a storm.

MULDOON Who told you that?

SKERRIE An old acquaintance of mine. He was just passing by.

MULDOON Rowing or sailing?

SKERRIE Swimming. And he told me the Lord of the Eskers is just one jump ahead of us. Maybe even at that next island we're coming to.

MULDOON Which island is that?

SKERRIE It belongs to the Miller of Hell.

> (*Out of nowhere comes the noise of a water mill, with a crowd swarming around it*)

MILLER (*stentorian*) One at a time there! One at a time! Rotten oats on the left, mildewed barley on the right! And mind you don't fall down the shaft with them! Come along there, walk up, I'll buy all your doubts and disappointments, your defeated hopes, your encumbrances, I'll buy all your chares and your chores, your backbitings and your second thoughts. Come on up there, shovel them in — your hypocrisies and mediocrities, your outmoded ornaments and armaments, your half-baked lumps of dough, your half-formed castles in the air, your stillborn babies, your unhappy pasts. Hurry up there, roll them all in, down the shaft with them, my mill's still hungry. Bring me your vows of eternal love, your oaths on the book, your questions of principle. Whatever you pretend to or no longer believe and whatever you believe mistakenly, whatever you have failed to do and whatever you have done to no purpose, whatever you think you are when you're not and whatever you are when you are — bring it all up and shovel it in, it's grist to my mill and to hell with it!

> (*Pause*)

You there! What have you in the sack?

MERCHANT Gold.

MILLER Pure gold?

MERCHANT Stolen gold.

MILLER That will do; tip it in. And what about you with the patch over your eye?

ONE-EYED MAN What about me?

MILLER What have you brought to be ground? Not a sack nor even a wallet, not a crate nor even a casket, not a sheaf of corn nor an ear of it —

ONE-EYED MAN The patch on my eye.

MILLER The patch? Is it no use to you?

ONE-EYED MAN No use at all. Nor the eye underneath it.

MILLER Then they're both for me — and my mill's still hungry. First the patch, my friend! That's the way. Now throw the eye after it. There! Don't you feel better? Now then! What about the other eye?

ONE-EYED MAN I can still see middling with it.

MILLER Only middling? Go on! Throw it in!

BUSYBODY You do what he says. He'll grind it up new for you.

ONE-EYED MAN Here goes then!

(*He screams in agony*)

BUSYBODY Did it hurt?

ONE-EYED MAN Oh the pain! The pain! And the darkness!

BUSYBODY You'll get them back, you know, both of them. Or I should say all three of them: the two eyes and the patch. Just wait till they've gone through the mill.

FUNSTER Make way there! Way for the lady! She has brought you something you'll like.

MILLER And what is it this time, lady? A broken promise, a lying letter, a stolen trinket, a cuckolded husband —

FUNSTER She's brought a cat in a bag.

MILLER What's wrong with your cat?

BRANWEN It's my sister's cat.

MILLER A tom cat?

BRANWEN Very much a tom cat.

(*The tom cat, from inside the bag, utters a muffled love call*)

MILLER Yes, I can hear he is. Very good, lady; down the shaft with him!

(*The love call changes to an anguished yelp*)

BRANWEN That will teach you to go to Olwen's room. Bells on her bed indeed! There'll be no more bells for you.

MILLER And you, sir? Anything to grind? Don't keep me waiting, my mill's still hungry. Come on, sir, I know who you are. Any bad jokes today, any dirty stories? I remember now you brought me some before —

FUNSTER No, nothing of that sort today. I am going the round of my properties. In fact I'm preparing for an auction.

MILLER I know your auctions. Anything you don't sell, just ship it back here to me.

FUNSTER I'll remember that but it may not take place for years. Time means nothing to me, you know.

MILLER It doesn't to me much either. But then I'm the Miller of Hell.

FUNSTER Well, come to my auction if you can. By the way, I saw two strangers round at the back by the mill race.

MILLER Two strangers round by the mill race! They're not going to bathe in it, are they?

FUNSTER If I were you, Miller, I'd go round and see.

MILLER I think I will. I will not have people bathing in my sewage.

(*Muldoon and Cormac go round to the back. There is no crowd here but the mill race is loud*)

CORMAC Will you look at that stream, Muldoon! Look at the scum there is in it. Where does it all go to?

MULDOON I can tell you one thing, Cormac: seeing where the sun is setting, all that muck's flowing west.

MILLER The sun here's always setting but you're right — it *is* flowing west. In fact it's flowing to hell and I am the Miller of Hell. But now I'll ask you two a question. What are you doing here, trespassing?

MULDOON We are no trespassers. All we want is news.

MILLER All news here is stale news. Can't you smell it?

CORMAC We can!

MILLER But, as stale news goes, I can offer you almost anything. Robbery, rape, arson, murder —

MULDOON That last is the word. Have you seen the Lord of the Eskers?

MILLER I have indeed. Not long ago.

MULDOON How long ago?

MILLER Five years maybe. Or again it might be ten or twenty.

MULDOON Ten or twenty! You said not long ago.

MILLER What is short to me might be long to you. I remember him well though; he brought me some stuff to grind.

MULDOON I can guess what manner of stuff. An evil conscience, treachery, hatred, blood-guilt —

MILLER No, nothing in that class at all. He brought me a woman's handkerchief — embroidered with flowers and small birds — and a woman's gold bracelet and a necklace.

MULDOON But I don't understand.

ONE-EYED MAN My eyes! Where are my eyes?

MILLER Eyes, man? What have you done with them?

ONE-EYED MAN I gave them to you to grind and make new.

MILLER You gave them to me to grind.

ONE-EYED MAN But where are they?

MILLER They've gone west, man.

ONE-EYED MAN But I don't understand; they were to come out new.

MILLER None of you understand. I am the Miller of Hell. What I take I take and it flows away west. To the west, to death, to hell. And none of it ever comes back again.

ONE-EYED MAN Oh, I'm blind! ... Blind! ... Blind!

> (*Out of the Dark Ages and the noise of the mill race come the noises of a modern factory*)

MILLER There! What did you expect? This mill is a going concern — expanding throughout the centuries. Come on up, bring it in by the crate, by the bale, by the waggon-load. I will need new docks on this island, I will need a dozen new docks. Come on, you fools of the future, bring in your shiploads of folly. All your bad debts and your crooked contracts, your election speeches and your changing maps, your mergers and treaties and dud manifestoes, your flashy red herring, your brand-new obsolescent weapons. Come on up, roll it in, let me grind it away to the west. Will you look at it now, my sewer's in spate, it's goodbye to you all and the toil of your hands, the filth in your guts and the fraud in your hearts, it's goodbye to you all and the seed of your loins. I will grind it away, grind it away, grind it away, grind it away . . .

> (*The Miller's voice, huge though it is, is drowned in hooters and sirens. Then these in their turn recede and the sea takes over again. It is colder now and no land in sight*)

SKERRIE We are coming now to more dangerous seas. One ship out of three gets lost in them.

MULDOON I cannot understand about the Lord of the Eskers. A woman's necklace and a woman's bracelet and a handkerchief embroidered with —

URSACH Birds and flowers.

MULDOON Ursach! How did *you* know?

URSACH A little bird told me — an embroidered one.

MULDOON Ursach, you're keeping things back from me.

CORMAC Easy, Muldoon. Let the man get on with his steering. Did you not hear what Skerrie said?

MULDOON What did she say?

SKERRIE I was only giving a warning.

> (*Seals are heard lamenting in the distance*)

MULDOON What's that noise ahead of us? Who are they keening?

SKERRIE I told you people get drowned here. They are keening no one but themselves.

JESTER It's a wet wake all right but the wetness is not of the best.

CORMAC How many seals are there huddled on the rock there?

MULDOON Steer in to that rock, Ursach.

URSACH And have me wreck the boat!

SKERRIE That rock goes down sheer. Let them all back water as they come to it.

> (*Ursach steers in, the seawash on the rock is heard*)

URSACH Back water now! Back water!

> (*The seawash on the rock is loud but the barking of the seals tops it*)

SKERRIE Do you hear them greeting us? Greetings to you too. Now be silent.

(*The seals are silent*)

Leave it to me now. I'll talk to them. You there. How long have you been drowned?

(*The first seal barks disyllabically*)

Ten years he says. And you?

(*A second seal barks keeping the rhythm of the words*)

'Twenty-one years come Easter.'

And you, old fellow with the limpets on your cheeks?

(*A third seal barks keeping the rhythm likewise*)

He says he can't remember; it was before Christianity.

MULDOON Why, there's a man among them. With his arms clasped round his knees. And shivering all the time, shivering. This is where I ask questions. Man, naked man, answer me! Why are you there among the seals?

DROWNED MAN Because this is where I belong. I have beeen drowned too.

MULDOON But you're not a seal.

DROWNED MAN Not yet. I have been drowned too recently.

MULDOON How recently?

DROWNED MAN Only yesterday. My captain threw me overboard.

MULDOON Why?

DROWNED MAN Just out of pique. I told him he still had an eye for the women. So he pitched me out of the stern and now I am cold till doom.

SKERRIE Not till doom. Once you are changed you will be warm again.

DROWNED MAN How do you know? Who are you?

SKERRIE Never mind who I am. I know.

DROWNED MAN I too had an eye for women but I never saw one like you.

MULDOON What was your captain's name?

DROWNED MAN If only I was warm I would take you walking on the sea. We would gather the flowers of the sea and —

SKERRIE You will be warm when you're changed.

MULDOON What was your captain's name?

DROWNED MAN My captain? Had I a captain?

MULDOON Was it the Lord of the Eskers?

DROWNED MAN I can't hear what you say.

SKERRIE Spare him. The change is beginning.

MULDOON Where was your captain bound for?

DROWNED MAN (*Shivers and groans*)

LIAM Saint Brendan protect us! Look at him!

CORMAC Look at his legs. They're flippers!

JESTER Look at his hands. They're flippers.

MULDOON Quick, before you go; answer me. Where was your captain bound for?

SKERRIE I will try for you. Where was your captain bound for?
(*The new seal barks*)
The Happy Island, he says.

JESTER The Happy — I'll believe it when I see it.

MULDOON Skerrie, ask him one last —

SKERRIE I will ask him no more at all. When this first happens they suffer.

CORMAC God between us and evil! Look at his eyes, he's weeping.

SKERRIE He makes a beautiful seal.

MULDOON Sit to your oars, all of you! Ursach!

URSACH Yes, Muldoon?

MULDOON Steer for the Happy Island!

SKERRIE Goodbye, drowned man, goodbye. You will be warm again soon.
(*They leave the seals behind and hold on their course*)

MULDOON Now tell me about this Happy Island.

SKERRIE It is not really happy. Yet no one who lands there wants to leave there.

MULDOON But I must land there.

SKERRIE You must. If that man's captain was the Lord of the Eskers, he should be now with the Queen of the Twilight.

MULDOON The Queen of —

SKERRIE She is the one you must call on. But the more of you go, the more will be tempted, so here once again you must travel alone. The Queen lives inland behind cobweb curtains. Pay no heed to the people on the way there and above all don't take anything they offer you. If you do, you will become like them.
(*The next thing we know, Muldoon is on the island being tempted*)

THE TEMPTERS You look tired, stranger. Will you take a rest?
You look hungry, stranger. Will you take an apple?
You look thirsty, stranger. Will you take some ale?

MULDOON I will not. Where has the sun gone?

TEMPTER Where has the what gone?

MULDOON The sun in the sky. It is morning.

THE TEMPTERS It is never morning here.

There is never a sun in the sky.
Our queen does not like sunlight.
MULDOON Your queen! Where is your queen?
THE TEMPTERS In the birch-grove there.
In her house with the cobweb curtains.
As you go through them, do not break them.
Her spiders took years to spin them.
They are very beautiful cobwebs.
Are you sure you will not take an apple?
Or a peach? Or a plum? Or a cherry?
Or ale? Or wine? Or sleep?
Never mind. Our queen will give him some.
      (*And so he moves on to face the Queen*)
QUEEN Have you ever seen an apple like this?
MULDOON I have not.
QUEEN Yet you still will not take it?
MULDOON I will not.
QUEEN But you will drink?
MULDOON I will not.
QUEEN Very well. We must make do with talk.
MULDOON What will we talk about?
QUEEN Me.
      (*She waits for him to speak*)
Well? Have you nothing to ask me?
MULDOON Have you always lived here?
QUEEN No.
MULDOON Where did you come from then?
QUEEN I have forgotten. But I remember one thing. Where I once
lived there was a horror in the sky.
MULDOON What kind of horror?
QUEEN Something that hurt the eyes. It would hide behind the horizon
and then it would jump up shouting and it would climb up the sky
and all the flowers would open. And the brittle little birds would
sing.
MULDOON Are there no birds here?
QUEEN They stay in their nests. And the flowers stay snug under-
ground. That is why everyone is happy.
MULDOON Because nothing ever happens?
QUEEN Nothing ever happens. So everyone who comes here stays here.
Just as you will, you know.
MULDOON I will not.

QUEEN You deceive yourself. Only one man came here who left again.

MULDOON And when was that?

QUEEN Just yesterday. Or was it the year before yesterday? But he was stronger than you.

MULDOON How do you know?

QUEEN He was the Lord of the Eskers.

MULDOON Who?

QUEEN Do you know him?

MULDOON He killed my father.

QUEEN I would have wished him to stay. He too liked the twilight.

MULDOON The twilight! Do you see this knife?

QUEEN Pretty. Where does it come from?

MULDOON Out of my father's heart.

QUEEN The nice thing about that Lord of the Eskers: he had neither past nor future.

MULDOON His past was this knife — and his future is this knife.

QUEEN He was happy while he was here. Did I offer you anything to drink?

MULDOON You did. I refused.

QUEEN That's funny. He refused too. But then he was stronger than you. So you really want to know where he has gone?

MULDOON I do.

QUEEN Then all you have to do is take this little apple —

MULDOON I can't.

QUEEN Just one little bite and I'll tell you.
   (*Pause*)
Just one little strip of the peel.

MULDOON And then you will tell me?

QUEEN Of course.

MULDOON If I thought I could trust you —

QUEEN But you can!

MULDOON In that case ... Hand me the apple.
   (*Out of the distance, all the way from the sea, comes the voice of Skerrie, but distorted now and harsh like that of a seal*)

SKERRIE (*calling*) Muldoon! Muldoon!

QUEEN What was that? That horrible noise!
   (*The distorted voice still penetrates*)

SKERRIE Muldoon! Come back to me! Come back!
   (*Muldoon suddenly realizes his danger*)

MULDOON (*calling back*) Skerrie! I'm coming! I'm coming!
   (*Pause*)

QUEEN He's gone. Two in two days! But look — he's torn my cobwebs! The webs it took years to spin! And what's that coming through my doorway? Stay away, stay away, keep out! No, don't come near me, don't touch me! I am the Queen of the Twilight, this is no place for you. This is my house, you can't come in here. Oh, it's coming, it's streaming in, it's flowing to my feet, it's probing — it will kill me, whatever it is — but I know what it is, I have met it before, it's the sun!

    (*Muldoon has rejoined his boat, which is again in mid-sea*)

MULDOON Why did you call me back then?

SKERRIE Muldoon! Look into my eyes.

MULDOON Your eyes are always so sad?

SKERRIE The tide in them stays at the full. There is only one element for people like me.

    (*They suddenly hear a foghorn*)

URSACH What is that noise? Did you ever hear the like of that?

CORMAC It must be some great sea-monster.

    (*The foghorn sounds again — nearer*)

JESTER He should be more careful of his vocal chords.

LIAM Yes, it's a monster all right.

SKERRIE It is not. It is a foghorn.

    (*The foghorn is joined by others. Soon there is a forest of foghorns*)

URSACH She's right. That fog came quickly.

MULDOON Easy now! Look out for rocks!

URSACH Slow there! Go slow! Your souls to the devil, we're aground.

SKERRIE It's only a sandy beach. What they call the Beach of the Crucibles.

MULDOON And the island itself?

SKERRIE The Island of Progress. The whole of it, heather and rock, belongs to one man; he's an alchemist. If the fog were not so thick, you could see the smoke from his chimney; there is no smoke like it in the world.

MULDOON He's the next I have to see, is he?

SKERRIE He lives behind bolt and bar; to enter you need the password.

MULDOON And what is the password?

SKERRIE Today it would be . . . Tetragrammaton.

MULDOON Tetra — what?

    (*The password itself jumps him on to the island and there is the Inventor asking for it*)

INVENTOR (*from behind*) The password! The password!

MULDOON (*outside*) Tetragrammaton.

INVENTOR Wait till I let you in.

> (*Bolts and bars are drawn back, a creaking door opens and closes: Muldoon enters the material laboratory*)

INVENTOR Now we haven't much time. Have you brought the ingredients?

MULDOON The ingredients?

INVENTOR Keep going over there with the bellows. As I said in my letter, I have plenty of mercury; also of sulphur and arsenic. But you know what I ordered: I have the list here. The gall bladder of a baboon, a quart of Dead Sea water, a sprig of withered mistletoe, and a pound of this new stuff — uranium.

MULDOON I think there must be some mistake.

INVENTOR Nonsense, I told you all this in my letter. I take it you *can* read Syriac?

MULDOON Syriac? I haven't a word of it.

INVENTOR Ah, that explains it. I wrote it in Syriac for safety. Everyone's so mad for gold, you know. But now that you're here you may as well see what goes on. Come and take a peep in the cauldron.

> (*The cauldron bubbles as a slave works the bellows*)

INVENTOR There! Pretty colour, isn't it?

MULDOON What colour do you call that?

INVENTOR Yellow.

MULDOON Would you now? I'd call it colourless.

INVENTOR Oh, nonsense, sir, you must be blind. You'll see what I mean if you taste it.

MULDOON But I can't, it's too hot, it's boiling.

INVENTOR Why, can't you drink things boiling? Then you'll have to take my word for it: it's almost *aurum potabile*. Almost but just not quite. It's potable already but not yet gold — not yet. When it is, I'll put up a notice: All Gold to be Consumed on the Premises. You know what the premises are, of course?

MULDOON Well, they seem rather draughty, or should I say monastic —

INVENTOR The first premiss is this: at the centre of everything is nothing. Take, for example, this block of granite; I lugged it all the way from the beach, I'll pop it in the cauldron shortly. Now you, being a layman, no doubt would call this stone solid.

MULDOON I might.

INVENTOR Well, it's nothing of the sort. There are more winds blowing through this single stone than you'd find in the whole cave of

Aeolus. Now these winds couldn't blow at all if they had no space to blow in. Space — room for experiment. But for what kind of experiment? You'll be surprised when I tell you. This could make or break the world.

(*Someone outside hammers on the iron door*)

Perhaps that will be the ingredients. Who's there?

MILLER (*outside*) A friend.

INVENTOR Password then, friend?

MILLER Tetragrammaton.

INVENTOR Right. I won't be a minute.

(*The great door opens and the Miller enters. Then the great door once more closes*)

MULDOON If it isn't the Miller of Hell again!

MILLER Are you the nuclear alchemist? I heard your soup wanted colouring.

INVENTOR It's not just the colour, you know; don't let us confuse cause and effect. Once we have achieved our transmutation of the primal matter —

MILLER I have brought you a gallon of my best.

INVENTOR Of your best what?

MILLER Never mind. Just pour the whole lot in your cauldron.

INVENTOR Take it, slave. Pour it in the cauldron.

(*The Slave takes it and pours it. The cauldron reacts like a geyser*)

SLAVE (*screams*) Oh, my foot! My foot!

INVENTOR The clumsy fellow! He's scalded himself. Why have you gone over there into the corner?

MULDOON I can't bear the smell.

INVENTOR But it's the smell of progress! And the colour's *really* changing this time. Yellow? It's as yellow as buttercups. Do just come and see what's happening in the cauldron.

(*Out of the bubbling of the cauldron come the tickings and hummings of modern technology*)

MULDOON I'm watching what's happening in your room. Your filthy, black walls turning white, lights in great tubes in the roof, everything polished and shining and purring, rows upon rows of discs of crystal — some green, some red, some blue, some purple — and in each of those discs a ticking needle — tick, tick, tick! — you can hear them growing. Growing! Growing like a cancer!

(*The tickings and hummings increase*)

INVENTOR News from the centre! Something out of nothing! I have split the stone and released the wind! I have split the wind and released the whirlwind. Aurum potabile! Look! Yellow — yellower — yellowest! Come over here, both of you!

(*The Slave groans and falls with a thud*)

MILLER What's wrong with your slave?

INVENTOR He's fainted. The fumes of the gold were too much for him.

MILLER Fainted, man? He's dead. Have you a large sack.

INVENTOR What for?

MILLER Why, to take him away.

(*There is a violent noise as the cauldron boils over*)

INVENTOR Oh, my God! The cauldron's boiling over.

(*And once again from the far distance is heard the strange cry, half seal, half human*)

SKERRIE (*calling*) Muldoon! Muldoon!

INVENTOR Don't open that door.

(*But he does. And, for the second time, he escapes like a flash*)

INVENTOR He's gone. And at such a moment! No interest in science. Just think what he's missing!

(*There is a violent explosion then the sound of falling debris: then silence*)

MILLER (*calmly*) 'Science'? More grist to my mill then. Now what did I do with that sack?

(*He prepares to dispose of the remains. But Muldoon, back at sea, sails on*)

SKERRIE So all that time you never put your question! You would not be forgetting your mission of vengeance?

MULDOON I would not.

SKERRIE If you only did . . .

(*Pause*)

MULDOON Did you say something?

SKERRIE When a man keeps his eyes on a target of hate the power to love goes out of him.

MULDOON Ursach! I think I see land.

URSACH You're right, Muldoon.

JESTER Just another barren island?

URSACH Not this time, fool. There's a big crowd of people there. All gathering outside a big building.

JESTER Needless to say they call at this island too. Just in time for an auction. The auctioneer is someone they have met before.

FUNSTER Thirty — I am offered thirty — thirty pieces of silver. Any advance on thirty? All done at thirty.

   (Gavel)

Sold for thirty pieces of silver. To the gentleman in the mask. Now my next lot, lot 99, is rather a mixed bag. I might call it a lot and a half or maybe a lot and a wife. It consists of the following items: one pillar of salt —

   (Laughter)

I thought I'd get a laugh on that. One pillar of salt, two turtle doves — No, I'm slipping, it's the other way round. Lot 99 consists of the following: *(sings)*

Twelve bulls a-roaring,
Eleven cows swooning,
Ten commandments missing,
Nine ninepins falling,
Eight pimps a-pimping,
Seven stars a-sinking,
Six days a-working,
Five gold teeth,
Four talking fish,
Three mocking birds,
Two turtle doves, and
An old salt in a night dress.

The reserve price is one mess of pottage.

BIDDER Two messes of pottage.

MILLER One pot of sewage.

CORMAC Him again!

OLWEN One black tom cat two hands high.

BRANWEN One black tom cat three hands high.

JESTER And them again!

BIDDERS One black wolfhound.

   One black wolf.

   One black gelding.

   One black stallion.

   One black centaur.

JESTER One black snowball.

   (Pause)

FUNSTER I am offered one black snowball. Any advance on one black snowball?

BIDDERS One pack of cards you cannot lose with.

   One great looking glass not to be looked in.

OLWEN One little bed with bells on it.

MILLER One great millstone to wear round your neck.

BIDDERS One book of truth — both home and foreign.

One book of lies — both black and white.

BRANWEN One book for bedtime.

JESTER One book of Kells.

FUNSTER One book of Kells. I am offered one book of Kells.

(*A tolling bell is heard*)

Excuse me, here we must break off for the nonce. The bidding for Lot 99 rests at ... one book of ... Kells. But the next lot, I fear, is priority. There are two kinds of auction, as you probably know, the common and the extreme. Lot 99 is an instance of common. Extreme auction is when someone's dying. This is the case with lot 100. Hand me my hat with the weepers. Thank you. Lot 100, ladies and gentlemen, is dying at this moment in the centre of Ireland. She is of advanced years but has been well preserved in hatred. She has not one grey hair on her head nor, even on her deathbed, one tear in her eye. She has caused in her time a great deal of trouble: an excellent collector's piece. Any offers — while there's time — to save this woman's life? One of the great ladies of our day — her name, I'm afraid, is a secret — and not a grey hair on her head. She has plenty of venom in her yet — prolong her life and add a chapter to the annals of Ireland. Any offers for this life which is ebbing away every second. The reserve price is the life of the bidder.

(*Pause*)

MULDOON What did you say her name is?

FUNSTER I am not allowed to tell you.

MULDOON And where did you say she lives?

FUNSTER In a bog in the centre of Ireland.

MULDOON And you really may not divulge her name?

FUNSTER No. But I can let you talk to her.

MULDOON Talk to her?

FUNSTER That's me. Always some new entertainment. Look behind you. See that little door in the rock?

MULDOON That looks as if it had never been opened?

FUNSTER It hasn't as yet. It leads to a small cold cell. There you will find a conch hanging from a golden rope. You must put that conch to your ear and wait till you hear what comes to you. Then speak into a hole you will see in the wall. Provided it's working, a voice should come back to you.

MULDOON Out of the conch?

FUNSTER Out of the centre of Ireland.

(*A familiar gong is heard, but distorted as though by a weird telephone*)

MOTHER Is there no one in this house? Answer me! Have you all run away the first time I really need you? Ursach! Where's Ursach? No; I sent him to sea with my son. It's so long ago I had forgotten. Me that had a hundred servants to die here alone among the rats!

MULDOON (*answering her from over the sea*) Mother! Can you hear me?

MOTHER Who's that? A ghost?

MULDOON Mother, this is me, Muldoon.

MOTHER Then you're the ghost of Muldoon.

MULDOON I am not, mother, I'm alive.

MOTHER Where are you then?

MULDOON On an island. And I can buy back your life.

MOTHER Buy back my life! With what?

MULDOON With my own life, mother.

MOTHER With your own? Have you killed the Lord of the Eskers?

MULDOON No, I have not yet found him.

MOTHER Not found him? After all this time?

MULDOON Mother, I will bid for your life.

MOTHER You will not. You still have your mission.

MULDOON You prefer that I live to kill him?

MOTHER Muldoon, my son, I am standing where you first saw me. The first and last time you saw me. I am standing unaided with the gong-stick in my hand. I have only the strength to strike it the once — Let the sound of it boom in your mind for ever. You have only one thing to do: find that man before he dies and, when you have found him, raise your right hand so and —

  (*He hears a great blow on gong; then silence*)

FUNSTER The blessing of God on the souls of the dead. And now to return to Lot 99 . . .

  (*On this note they leave the Island of the Auction. Back at sea, some spiritual stock-taking begins*)

JESTER The funny thing is: I don't own the Book of Kells.

URSACH It's a good thing he didn't bid for her. This story is twisted enough as it is.

CORMAC Stop muttering there. The wind's getting up. Muldoon, why don't you speak?

SKERRIE Leave him to me. Muldoon, you couldn't have saved her. As a person dies his nature comes uppermost. Your mother's nature was not to be saved. Can you knit a shirt of spindrift or scutch the Milky Way!

MULDOON My quest makes no more sense.

SKERRIE It never did. Are you tired of the mad islands?

MULDOON Tired!

SKERRIE Very well then. I know quite a different island —

MULDOON No, Skerrie, no! Don't tempt me. Your voice is a voice but it is not a gong.

SKERRIE Muldoon, before it's too late — I am losing the best of both worlds —

MULDOON Ursach! How are we doing?

URSACH We are in for a storm, Muldoon.

MULDOON Good. That suits my mood. Come on, you winds and waves!

SKERRIE Be careful; they might hear you.

MULDOON Come on, you endless waters! This is I, Muldoon, I dare you to drown me. Ha! You cannot drown me until I have killed. But where is the man I must kill? Where have you hidden him, winds and waters?

CORMAC Muldoon! Sit down; you will fall overboard. Grab hold of him, Liam. And you too, Eamonn.

LIAM Now then, Muldoon, if you'd just —

MULDOON Let go of me or by the children of Lir —

(In the struggle the two men fall overboard)

Goodbye, Liam! Goodbye, Eamonn! Does anyone else feel like a dip?

(The storm swells up. Somewhere a gong sounds through it)

MULDOON It sounds in my mind . . . in the ruin of my mind . . . It will sound for ever till that ruin falls.

(The storm, as quickly, dwindles away again. The gong is heard again but farther off. We now hear the anguish of a steamship: their craft has suffered a sea change)

CORMAC Am I imagining things or are we going much faster?

URSACH Full ahead both.

(Ting ting)

Starboard ten.

VOICE Starboard ten, sir.

URSACH Steer 268.

VOICE 268, sir.

JESTER Whether we're going faster or not, there's nothing, I always say, like a deckchair.

(Pause)

SKERRIE The wind's dropped.

MULDOON Everything's dropped. Who are you? Where are we going?

SKERRIE Who I am can wait. We're going to see a hermit. He lives on an island that's little more than a rock. He lives a life that is little more than a death. We must sound our siren to tell him we're coming. He is blind, you see, and all the great ocean is dark to him.

(*We now 'cut away' to this hermit*)

HERMIT Hos omnes invoco in auxilium meum. The twelve youths who went with Columkill to Alba. The seven holy bishops of the Church of the Yew Wood. The seven holy bishops of Tuam in Galway. The hermit found by Brendan in the Land of Promise. Saint Brendan himself on these cold seas before me. Saint Brendan himself? . . . Saint Brendan the Voyager.

(*A ship's siren is heard in the distance*)

What is that new noise? I have never heard it before. Hos omnes invoco in auxilium meum.

(*The siren comes nearer*)

Another temptation would it be? Is it from hell this time or merely from the old gods of Ireland? If only I had my sight! How long ago was it the *last* monster came —

(*The siren is now very threatening*)

And he roared no louder than that. And then there was the time that the mermaids sang to me — when I still had my sight and the other thing. Even that temptation did not trap me. But from that day on I reduced my diet — God told me to.

(*Muldoon has now come ashore*)

MULDOON Stay here by the dinghy, the three of you. I will go up myself and talk to him.

(*The Hermit hears him from his higher position*)

HERMIT They're coming again — the demons. The saints preserve me once more! Saint Michael and his angels stand around me —

MULDOON (*from below*) Father! Father, may I —

HERMIT Demon! Don't touch me! In the name of the Blessed Trinity —

MULDOON I am no demon. I'm a man.

HERMIT No men come here. You must prove it to me. I'm blind.

MULDOON Then you must take my word for it. I am a man, I swear it.

HERMIT I need more than your word; they have fooled me before. Come up here and let me feel your body — a demon's body is cold, yet it makes one's fingers tingle. But, *if* you are a man, be careful; there is little room on this ledge.

(*Muldoon clambers up and joins him*)

Are you here? Let me feel you.

(*The Hermit passes his hands over Muldoon's body*)

Yes, you have the pulse of a man. Where do you come from?

MULDOON Ireland.

HERMIT I come from Wales. But that was before you were born. Tell me: what do you see?

MULDOON What do I see?

HERMIT What do I look like to you? Do not lie to me.

MULDOON (*feeling for his words*) You look ... to me ... like the oldest man in the world. Naked ... a cage of bones ... your face lathered with bog cotton.

HERMIT But what do you read in my face?

MULDOON There is so much hair I read nothing.

HERMIT That is just as well. When I lived in the world I never stopped sinning. All the sins that there are except murder.

(*A seal, as it seems, barks in the distance*)

Was that a seal? They come here rarely now. There is not enough for them to eat; the fish are few in these seas — as I knew when I still ate fish. All I live on now is limpets or winkles and seaweed. It is better, to keep down desire.

(*The seal barks again — nearer*)

I think that seal means harm. What was I saying, my son?

MULDOON Father, forgive me, I am pressed for time. For years that I cannot count I have been chasing a murderer. They call him the Lord of the Eskers.

(*There is a pregnant pause*)

Father! What has happened? Where have you gone?

HERMIT Say that again — the name of the man.

MULDOON The Lord of the Eskers.

HERMIT I never heard of him.

(*The seal barks — nearer still*)

The bark of that seal makes me shiver. Oh for a fire — it is forty years since I saw one. But if I had a fire on this rock, I would never let it go out. And as each new night drew on — tell me, my son, is night coming now?

MULDOON No, Father; it's high noon.

HERMIT As night drew on I would rake the fire to preserve it and this is the prayer I would say: 'I rake this fire as the pure Christ rakes all. Mary at its foot and Brigid at its top. The Eight Highest Angels of the City of Grace preserve this house and its people till day!' I mean 'this rock and its hermit till day'.

(*Muldoon drops his dagger on the rock*)

You dropped something. What is it?

MULDOON Only a knife.

HERMIT A knife? Let me feel it. I like the feel of a knife.

(*Muldoon is about to hand it to him but Skerrie once again intervenes*)

SKERRIE (*calling from the distance*) Muldoon! Muldoon! Come at once!

HERMIT There is that seal again.

MULDOON (*calling back*) What is wrong, Skerrie?

SKERRIE Come at once!

MULDOON Forgive me, Father, I must go.

HERMIT One moment, son. The knife!

(*There is a pause while Muldoon scrambles back down to the dinghy*)
He has gone — and the knife with him. Mary, Queen of the Angels, Fountain of the Gardens, Star of the Sea, as the night falls, I rake this fire on the rock. The Eight Highest Angels of — Fire? But it's out! Mother of God, it's gone out!

(*A harp paints a ship becalmed and them on board her bemused*)

URSACH Muldoon, we are becalmed.

MULDOON So is my will-power; the thrust is gone out of me.

SKERRIE And it is time. Will I sing you a lullaby?

(*She croons something that suggests the Hebrides*)

CORMAC Muldoon! Muldoon! Look over the edge.

VOICES Would you believe it!
The saints preserve us!

JESTER The most beautiful town you ever saw. Glossy black cows in the streets, a white horse drawing a chariot —

MULDOON What are you babbling about?

(*From below them they hear drowned bells*)

SKERRIE It is the Country-under-the-Sea.

MULDOON I have often heard of that country. Perhaps we will get there some time.

URSACH You can only see it when it's crystal calm. I have seen it twice but no good came of it.

CORMAC Don't they all wear wonderful colours!

JESTER And don't they all look very busy and brisk!

CORMAC That's because they're going to church.

MULDOON Church?

CORMAC Can't you hear the bells?

MULDOON I wish I was with them.

SKERRIE Don't say that, Muldoon.

JESTER I could look at this moving picture for ever. That yellow-haired girl with the flowers in her pitgails! D'ye know, I think it's a wedding.

CORMAC You're right. Those bells are wedding bells.

MULDOON But why are they beginning to dance as they walk?

JESTER Because they're happy, I suppose.

URSACH That's no dancing, that's a ripple. Between them and us. Just the wisp of a gust.

CORMAC He's right. Now they're walking steadily again.

(*Pause*)

JESTER Another ripple!

URSACH The calm is ending.

MULDOON No, stay! Stay there! Let me join you!

SKERRIE You can't. Your time has not come.

JESTER You can hardly see them now. Just a coloured blur. A blur!

MULDOON Goodbye down there! God be with you!

URSACH Get in the main sheets! The wind's rising.

(*There is a great flapping of sails and creaking of a wooden ship*)

SKERRIE So much for the Country-under-the-Sea. It is too late to escape, Muldoon.

MULDOON Did I say I wanted to escape?

SKERRIE You did not. I saw it in your eyes.

URSACH Steer 155.

VOICE 155, sir.

(*Suddenly, if unobtrusively, they are aboard a steamship*)

JESTER What I always say is: there's nothing like a deckchair.

(*Pause*)

CORMAC I don't know what's wrong with me. Fool, do you know what's wrong with me?

JESTER Nothing, Cormac — except that you're going to die.

(*Pause*)

URSACH This tiller is no longer obeying my hand. This has never happened before.

SKERRIE Everything has got to happen some time.

(*Pause*)

SKERRIE Don't you think so, Muldoon?

MULDOON What?

SKERRIE Everything has got to happen some time. But that time is fixed; you can never jump ahead of it.

MULDOON I can jump ahead of it.

SKERRIE How?

MULDOON Ursach, where are we? How far from land?

URSACH Two and a half leagues.

MULDOON Then lower the gangway.

URSACH I will not. Even if this tiller — but it isn't a tiller, it's a wheel.

MULDOON What are you playing at? Lower the gangway!

SKERRIE You are all at sixes and sevens. Where do you think you are?

MULDOON *When* do you think we are?

CORMAC I'm sorry, Muldoon, but nobody lowers a gangway in mid-ocean.

MULDOON Oh, so nobody does? Then I'm nobody. I, nobody, alias Muldoon, hereby command my crew to lower the gangway and step on it. If Muldoon can't come to the island, then the island must come to Muldoon!

(*And so it does*)

JESTER But we don't want that island. Just look at it!

CORMAC Where did all those people come from on the quay?

JESTER For that matter, where did the bloody quay come from itself?

MULDOON This is an order — Lower the gangway!

(*As the gangway is lowered the crowd on the quay become threatening*)

CORMAC Before you go ashore, Muldoon my foster-brother —

MULDOON Yes, my foster-brother, what?

CORMAC Those people don't look too friendly.

CROWD (*from the quay. Off*) It's he! It's he! It's the very man! It's he!

MULDOON You're right, they're pointing at me.

CORMAC They seem to know you, Muldoon.

MULDOON But I've never seen one of them before!

CORMAC That could be because they have no faces.

SKERRIE Muldoon, you mustn't go ashore.

MULDOON Why not?

SKERRIE I smell death in the air.

MULDOON Then we will all take our weapons.

SKERRIE No, no! Weapons will be fatal.

MULDOON That's what they're for, Skerrie. And I don't want any more losses. We lost two good men not so long ago.

URSACH *We* lost? *You* lost! Liam and Eamonn.

MULDOON Silence, Ursach! Strap on your sword. And listen all of you! This time we all go ashore — except Skerrie. And we all go ashore fully armed.

(*They cheer and go clattering down the gangway*)

CROWD It's he! It's he! It's Muldoon!

MULDOON Yes, it's I, Muldoon, and I'm coming!

(*He leads his crew down the gangway and in among the crowd on the quay. Not all in the crowd are new to us*)

FUNSTER Why, if it's not my old friend! Muldoon, my dear chap, have you heard this one?

MULDOON I thought I left you at an auction.

FUNSTER Yes and I lost my face there. But not — perish the thought — not, never, my sense of humour. A funny thing happened to me on my way to this island on the eve of this battle —

(*The crowd laugh. A familiar voice rings out*)

BRANWEN Olwen! Look here, girl! Muldoon!

OLWEN The young man who ran away from us.

BRANWEN Though he's not such a young man now.

OLWEN But we look the same, don't we?

MULDOON Except for your lack of faces.

OLWEN Oh, don't you think figures more important?

BRANWEN Never mind faces or figures, we've both got new jobs, we're happy.

OLWEN And I've got more than a job. I've got a nice little cottage.

MULDOON With bells on the bed?

OLWEN Bells, Muldoon bach? A whole symphony!

BRANWEN But listen to me; *I* have a bower of birch trees with honey-suckle and hot and cold water —

(*Another familiar voice intrudes*)

MILLER Is it Muldoon? the name's Miller.

MULDOON Ah, the Miller of Hell.

MILLER Certainly not. I am a promoter. How can I promote you?

MULDOON You can help me to find the Lord of the Eskers.

MILLER Still on the old tack? If you take *my* advice —

INVENTOR Muldoon! You missed an experience.

MULDOON Who're you? Oh, of course, the alchemist.

INVENTOR Excuse me: nuclear scientist.

MULDOON I thought you had blown yourself up.

INVENTOR Me? But I'm a dreamer; I only blow up other people. Which reminds me: I'm looking for a passage to the mainland.

MULDOON I'm not going to the mainland.

INVENTOR But that's where he is, you know.

MULDOON He? Who?

INVENTOR The person you're looking for. Though why you've got to use a knife when you could do it by remote control —

QUEEN You! I knew I should find you again!

MULDOON The Queen of the Twilight! I thought you were killed by the sun.

QUEEN I thought so too. I fainted. When I recovered I was out in the open under the blazing blue bowl of the sky and the flowers were all open and the birds all singing and at once I thought of you — because it was you who gave me this.

MULDOON Why are you the only one here with a face? Not but what the face has changed.

QUEEN Of course it has. I am now Queen of the Morning.

(*A seal barks in the distance*)

QUEEN Was that a seal? It sounded like a seal.

INVENTOR It couldn't be a seal. It came from the liner.

(*The seal barks again*)

QUEEN It does come from the liner.

INVENTOR Excuse me, madam, I speak as a scientist. Seals are not found on liners.

(*The seal barks a third time*)

QUEEN Well, in that case, it's not a seal — but, whatever it is, it's my enemy.

SKERRIE (*off*) Muldoon! Come back! Before it's too late! Gather your men and come back on board!

CORMAC Muldoon, Muldoon, I've been looking for you everywhere. I have a singing in my ears. I had it once before — on the eve of a battle.

QUEEN A battle, did you say? I can prevent your battles. Where are my handmaids? Branwen! Olwen!

BRANWEN
OLWEN } Here, lady.

QUEEN Have you the baskets with the doves of peace in them?

BRANWEN I have the white doves.

OLWEN I have the black doves.

QUEEN Good. Now stand back all of you. I will have no fighting on this island. Branwen! Olwen! Let loose the doves of peace!

(*There is a whirring of pigeons rising and then a cooing and whirring mixed*)

MILLER Very well promoted! More grist to my mill!

CORMAC Up the white doves! The whites for ever! Down with the black doves! Down with them!

URSACH Down with your white doves, Cormac! And down with you too, damn you!

(*Muldoon's crew divide into two parties to fight each other to the death*)

CROWD Up the Whites! The Whites!
Up the Blacks! The Blacks!

MULDOON Stop fighting! Cormac! Ursach! Fiosta, Brian, all of you! Stop fighting! Put up your swords!

CORMAC Swords? Give me my sten!

(*There is a burst from a sten gun and then mixed machine-gun fire, grenades, etc.; then silence except for odd groanings*)

QUEEN I didn't mean this to happen.

MULDOON Queen of the Morning? You are still Queen of the Twilight. As for your doves of peace —

URSACH Muldoon! Muldoon! Come and listen before I die.

MULDOON Ursach! . . . Yes, Ursach?

URSACH Listen, I have something to tell you . . . about your mother . . . your mother and the Lord of —

(He gasps and can say no more)

MULDOON Goodbye, Ursach. God have mercy on your soul.

CORMAC Is that Muldoon? Can't see for the blood in my eyes.

MULDOON Cormac! You're still alive!

CORMAC No, I'm just going. We have all killed each other. It is your move now, Muldoon.

MULDOON Goodbye to you too, foster-brother.

INVENTOR Excuse me, Muldoon, why not call it a day? I take it you're returning to the mainland now?

MULDOON *Now* I might as well. I have lost every man of my crew.

JESTER Always excepting me.

MULDOON You! But I saw you fall!

JESTER That was a stage fall.

SKERRIE *(calling)* Come on board! Hurry! Hurry!

INVENTOR Yes, hurry. The world won't wait for us.

(They hurry. The Queen has the last word)

QUEEN Branwen! Olwen! Call in the doves of peace!

(The woodpigeons, still cooing, return to their mistress while Muldoon sails back to the port which he left so long ago. But this time he travels in a speedy modern liner)

INVENTOR My dear fellow, do tell me more. You really mean that Muldoon is engaged in a kind of vendetta?

JESTER He's been on it since — never mind when.

INVENTOR But that sort of thing's so old-fashioned. Apart from being somewhat inhumane.

JESTER What are *you* going to do when we get to the mainland?

INVENTOR But I've told you already.

JESTER You have. You're going straight to the municipal authorities to borrow their pneumatic drills. And then you're going to take up the world.

INVENTOR Oh, not the whole world, I'm only going to drill through the crust. Just to prove that the earth is hollow. The municipal authorities have been very kind and enlightened.

JESTER I always wondered why they called it the Port of the Unwise. How did you persuade them in the first place?

INVENTOR Oh, I didn't have to persuade them. It was all arranged by a man called Miller —

(*The ship's siren sounds: they are approaching port*)

JESTER Well, would you believe it! We're practically there!

(*The siren sounds again. Farther along the deck Skerrie is briefing Muldoon*)

SKERRIE When you go ashore now, Muldoon, just remember what I have been telling you. What you've got to do, do quickly. And above all, when you leave the castle, come straight back here to the quayside —

MULDOON Where you'll be waiting for me.

SKERRIE Where I'll be waiting for you. And what was the one other point?

MULDOON I am not to go near the square. But you did not tell me why.

SKERRIE Our friend over there will be using the square and only a fool and his road-drills will stay with him.

(*The siren sounds a third time and the noise dissolves into the noise of road-drills. This is the port and this is the square in it*)

JESTER I may be only a fool —

INVENTOR Speak up, I can't hear you.

JESTER I may be only a fool but I can't see the object of this.

INVENTOR I've told you a dozen times: to prove that the earth is hollow.

JESTER If it is, what will you do with it?

INVENTOR It will aid my more general thesis that the centre of every-thing is nothing.

JESTER Oh, I see. All nice and tidy.

INVENTOR Your friend, Muldoon, when he gets to the castle, will probably prove something similar. But he's only one door to pass through; his test will be over sooner.

(*Muldoon is already waiting at this door*)

PORTER Now who is it you're wanting to see?

MULDOON The Lord of the Eskers. Is he in?

PORTER Of course he's in. What name will I say?

MULDOON *I'll* say it.

PORTER Muldoon?

MULDOON You never heard of me?

PORTER No, sir. Just wait here a moment, please.

(*Hollow steps receding — distant murmur — steps returning*)
The Lord of the Eskers never heard of you either.
But don't be shy, go on in.

MULDOON I won't be shy. Nor will this knife be shy.

(*Muldoon brushes off the porter and as he enters the castle, his steps ring hollow. When he reaches the central chamber he is met by a little boy*)

I am Muldoon. I have come here at last to —
Where is the Lord of the Eskers?

BOY You asked to see *me*?

MULDOON You?

BOY What do you want with me, old man?

MULDOON I wanted vengeance but — where is the Lord of the Eskers?

BOY I told you already. It's me.

(*Pause*)

MULDOON I see it now. How long have you held the title?

BOY Two or three years. Since my father died.

MULDOON I am too late then. He died.

BOY If you had any request of him —

MULDOON I had one request only — to kill him.

BOY What! To kill him! Why?

MULDOON It was he that killed my father.

BOY I do not believe it.

MULDOON It's true.

BOY But when and where? He never killed anyone.

MULDOON It was with this knife. In a church.

BOY In a church? Oh, that was my grandfather.

MULDOON And he's dead too?

BOY No one knows. He abdicated long before I was born. He put himself to sea in a boat without oars for penance. He would be shockingly old now.

MULDOON To sea . . . for penance? Did he come from Wales?

BOY Of course not, he was the Lord of the Eskers. But he had been brought up in Wales and his wife, my grandmother, was Welsh. They say he was very unfaithful though.

MULDOON I must go back then. To the island before the last. But I think I no longer need this.

BOY Why are you offering me this knife?

MULDOON It belongs to the Lord of the Eskers.

(*In accordance with Skerrie's instructions Muldoon returns with all speed to the quay. But the Inventor is still busy in the square: his drills are about to break through)*

INVENTOR You can leave me, you know, if you're frightened.

JESTER I'm frightened all right but I'll stay with you for the laugh. Mother of God, there's Muldoon coming out of the castle. Well, he got the killing over quickly. Look at him now, he's breaking into a run.

INVENTOR Why should I look at these figures of the past? When I've almost broken through to the future! If you *must* look at something, look at this!

(The drills break through with an enormous noise. This noise continues and grows)

JESTER And on the seventh day . . . he created nothing at all.

INVENTOR Are you looking? The dust is thick but —

JESTER I can see all I want to.

INVENTOR I can't, I'm blinded with the dust. What can you see? Tell me!

JESTER I can see nothing at all. Nothing, pure undiluted nothing. I mean: the whole thing's hollow.

INVENTOR Hollow? Then I was right!

JESTER You were indeed! *Dead* right!

(Things begin to explode)

INVENTOR Eureka! Eureka! It was worth it!

JESTER The laugh is on me. I was dying . . . to get one.

(The explosion reaches a climax just as Muldoon arrives on the quay-side)

SKERRIE Quick now! Into the boat! Before the tidal wave comes.

(He jumps in. It is a motor boat)

Now then. Start up the engine!

(The motor boat starts and they head once again for the open sea)

MULDOON Look back. You can't see where it was.

SKERRIE All the houses have gone down the hole. The Port of the Unwise has vanished.

MULDOON The castle's gone too. The Lord of the Eskers is dead.

SKERRIE Yet you still want to see his grandfather?

MULDOON I don't want to see him but I must.

SKERRIE Why?

MULDOON I don't know.

SKERRIE When you saw him before you still had the knife. But now, Muldoon —

MULDOON Don't go on. This has all happened before. I know what you're going to say next. And I know, though I cannot face it, I know what's about to happen.

SKERRIE That's the double vision of the mind. I know it too, I'm afraid. In a moment we shall see the rock of the hermit, he will be standing there waiting —

MULDOON And beside him a woman, old, very old, but still straight —

SKERRIE And you know who she is?

MULDOON No.

SKERRIE I do.

    (*The engine stalls*)

MULDOON Damn it, the engine's stalled. Wait now till I crank it —

    (*He tries to crank it but fails*)

What's wrong with it, I wonder.

    (*A voice from the past calls out across the water*)

MOTHER Take your head out of that box! Look up! Raise your head, man, look at me!

MULDOON Christ upon the naked tree! This has all happened before. The rock, the old hermit standing there, the woman beside him, waiting —

Woman! Old woman! Who *are* you!

MOTHER I *was* a woman but now — Let the scales drop from your eyes.

    (*They do but he cannot accept it*)

MULDOON No! No! No!

SKERRIE Don't close your eyes, Muldoon. Look at her!

HERMIT She is your mother — and she's dead.

MULDOON And what has she to do with you?

HERMIT Everything, my son, everything.

MULDOON When you say 'my son' . . . do you speak as a man of God?

HERMIT I speak as a man who once was a man of sin.

    (*Pause*)

MULDOON Mother! Is that true?

MOTHER I was his mistress. You are his son.

MULDOON Then the man who was stabbed in the church —

HERMIT It was I who stabbed him.

MOTHER It was I who planned it. That man was my husband but not your father.

MULDOON Then this quest of vengeance . . . ?

HERMIT I had been unfaithful to her.

MOTHER Yes, I wanted him killed. It was only the reason was different. But now we are back together and he is about to die.

HERMIT Yes, Muldoon, my son, I am about to die. And may God have mercy on your soul.

MULDOON On my soul! And yours?

HERMIT Your mother and I will dissolve in foam; we shall have no souls between us.

MOTHER Give me your hand, lost love of my life! Goodbye, Muldoon my son. Hand in hand your parents are now about to leave you.

MULDOON I can't see this! I can't! I won't!

(*There is a double splash as the two bodies hit the sea*)

SKERRIE Open your eyes again. They have gone. They are foam already.

(*Pause*)

MULDOON Did you know, Skerrie?

SKERRIE Who was your true father? I knew that only just now — just before I stalled your engine. And that changed everything else.

MULDOON What else?

SKERRIE I thought I could break the rules but you human beings are too difficult.

MULDOON Let us go, Skerrie; I'll start up the engine again. We'll leave this deserted rock and —

SKERRIE It is not deserted, not yet. Look up, Muldoon, see who's there!

MULDOON Mother of God! Who is that naked man?

SKERRIE He also has been waiting.

(*Yet another voice from the past calls out from the same rock*)

DROWNED MAN I have, Skerrie. For you.

MULDOON What do you mean? Who are you?

DROWNED MAN You met me before. Many years ago. Only you have grown older and I, Muldoon, have not.

SKERRIE Yes, you have met him before. When you first saw him he was still one of you; under your eyes he became one of us.

DROWNED MAN Will you come with me now, Skerrie?

SKERRIE Not till you have answered three questions. When did you first meet the sea?

DROWNED MAN In a singing shell and the music haunted me.

SKERRIE Why did you become a seaman?

DROWNED MAN Because I had heard of the joy of the sea.

SKERRIE Thirdly and lastly: what *is* the sea?

DROWNED MAN The first and the last thing, the cradle and grave of life, the mother and mistress of all of us.

And now — will you come with me?

SKERRIE Yes, now I will come; you are one of my kind.

MULDOON She will not; you will have to fight for her.

SKERRIE Muldoon! Muldoon! Would you strike a drowned man?

MULDOON A drowned man? Now I remember! But *that* man became a seal.

DROWNED MAN And a seal I am. Look, here is my skin.

SKERRIE Put it on, be quick, put it on! Then dive from that rock. I will join you.

MULDOON Skerrie, you can't, you've been with me so long, without you I would be nowhere —

(*The Drowned Man, a seal again, dives from the rock*)

You're right. He's a great grey seal.

SKERRIE Give me your lips, Muldoon. Our first kiss and our last. I thought I could break the rules — I could have perhaps if you'd helped me.

The engine will work when I've gone. Goodbye — and your strange God bless you.

(*She dives overboard and the splash ripples outwards*)

MULDOON (*calling*) Skerrie! Skerrie! ... (*and then to himself*)

Two round heads swimming away.

(*calling again*) Goodbye then, Skerrie.

(*A seal barks*)

MULDOON So here am I at the end alone in a small boat and it has all been for what? I thought that vengeance was mine but the fates took it away from me and what was I avenging anyway? My mother's name and shame — and my father's — are lost for ever in foam, the port from which I sailed is a gaping hole in the globe, my foster-brother and my friends are dead, and Skerrie ... Skerrie has left me. Well, let's try once more. She said it should work now.

(*He makes two vain attempts at cranking; at the third the engine starts and the motorboat carries him away*)

PERSONS FROM PORLOCK

the story of a painter

Persons from Porlock (broadcast 30 August 1963, Third Programme) was Louis MacNeice's last play-production, uncannily predictive of his death four days after the broadcast.[1] It tells the tale of a fictitious painter of the time, Hank, who strives in his art, but who is repeatedly distracted or interrupted in his craft through money problems, war, women, commercialization, drinking, and the like. He takes up a hobby of cave exploration; and finally he meets his end in a Yorkshire cave, Skrimshank's, with a caving pal, while voices real and imaginary sound in his head. The well-known Coleridgean title is referred to in MacNeice's brief introductory article as well as in the play itself. The play is noteworthy for its use of pot-holing sound effects. The text is taken from the script (the only copy left) in the BBC Play Library, Broadcasting House, photocopied from roll film by the BBC Written Archives Centre; there are some passages in the script which MacNeice deleted, and which were all excised when the play was published by the BBC in 1969.

When Coleridge failed to complete his 'dream poem', *Kubla Khan*, he laid the blame on 'a person from Porlock' who had called to see him on business, thus fatally interrupting his writing. Taking the phrase 'person from Porlock' to represent any unforeseen interruption of the creative process — or, going deeper, those forces which are always odds on against an artist — I have dramatized the story of a fictitious painter of our time.

We begin with him as an art student in 1936 at the time of Picasso's Guernica exhibition in London: he is then an enthusiast for what would now be called 'commitment'. When he is beginning to find his vision, he is interrupted by the war, in which he has his experiences in Burma that have a lasting effect on him. Subsequent interruptions and frustrations include those occasioned by the lure of commercial art, by drink, money troubles, and women. Over against all this stands his one recreation: speleology.

As a painter my hero believes — to use a stock distinction — in making images rather than gestures and, after the war at least, tries to go his own way, undeterred by changes in fashion. As a person he often behaves badly but, I hope, emerges as on the whole sympathetic or at least understandable. Fictitious though the whole story is, I have drawn upon my own experiences and upon my observations of artists I have known.

As the story covers more than twenty years, I have had to break it up into a large number of scenes. The dialogue is naturalistic and the main characters are meant to be characters and not mere vehicles of the theme, but there are, to provide latitude and contrast, occasional digressions into scenes of hallucination. I intend the story primarily as a story but it involves some implicit comments on the conditions in which artists have to work in this country today.

CHARACTERS

HANK	DIRECTOR OF GALLERY
SARAH	BAILIFF
PETER	DOCTOR
MERVYN	POLICE OFFICER
MOTHER	PROFESSOR
SERGEANT	WHITE
FOREIGN MAID	MRS BEETON
VOICES	RED LADY
MAGGIE	BARBAROSSA
DONALD	JAP
TONY	THE PERSON
JOCK	

PERSONS FROM PORLOCK

ANNOUNCER When Coleridge failed to complete his dream poem, 'Kubla Khan', he said it was the fault of 'a person from Porlock' who had called to see him on business. To his 'no small surprise and mortification' this interruption destroyed his vision. Many lesser artists than Coleridge meet with interruptions of this sort. What follows is the story of an imaginary painter who had his Persons from Porlock.

HANK So there it is, Sarah. I've told hardly anyone else about this. I suppose it's made me rather anti-women. On the other hand it may be what made me take up painting.

SARAH What I don't understand, darling...

HANK Go on.

SARAH Is your mother dropping you cold like that?

HANK Well, my father insisted, you see.

SARAH No doubt. But seeing how small you were and how much you depended on her —

HANK I couldn't compete with this out-of-the-blue Don Juan. I forgot to tell you the first time he came he gave me a bar of marzipan. Marzipan! That was him.

SARAH Do you ever see your mother now, Hank?

HANK Of course not. I think she's in the South of France but I don't even know what her name is. It wasn't Don Juan she married, you see. Well, that's all; let's get back to the Guernica Exhibition.

SARAH Yes, wasn't it marvellous today!

HANK Funny to think Picasso was once a cubist.

SARAH Well, thank God all that lark's over. Being a woman I just never rose to this abstract thing. Now nobody need even try.

HANK How could they with what's going on in Europe! I sometimes feel guilty not being there, you know.

SARAH Europe?

HANK Spain, silly. And not to paint. To fight. Or do you think that also's to do with my mother?

SARAH Of course not, Hank.

HANK I never know my motives one hundred per cent — do you? Ready for bed, darling?

SARAH It's early. Let's go first to 'The Plough' and have a beer.

HANK Haven't got the price of one.

SARAH I have. Just. Us poor impoverished art students!

HANK I hope Peter's not in 'The Plough'.

SARAH Why?

HANK He enraged me today at the New Burlington. Saying Picasso would cash in on anything.

SARAH You shouldn't pay any attention, Peter's not really serious.

HANK Except about mountaineering. That's what he should be teaching.

SARAH Still, to be fair, we've got worse instructors than Peter.

HANK That's not saying much. Anyhow, I sometimes doubt if art can be taught at all. But, if Peter *is* in 'The Plough' and starts talking again about today's exhibition —

(*Fade up slight pub atmosphere and behind*)

PETER You see, Hank, the point about today's exhibition is it's so jolly and flip. Have another pint?

HANK Yes, thank you.

PETER And you darling?

SARAH A half please.

PETER Two pints and a half please miss. Yes, people say it's all a practical joke. What's wrong with that? Practical's something that works.

SARAH But really, Peter! Furred cups and saucers and —

PETER Sex, my dear, sex. But the high spot was Dali in his diving suit. Trying to control those two borzois. You know what happened of course: the breathing apparatus went wrong. That will teach him to go diving in the New Burlington Galleries.

HANK When I think that only last year in those very same bloody galleries —

SARAH Yes. Picasso. Guernica.

PETER Guernica, my dear? Ancient history.

HANK People are still dying in Spain.

PETER And Picasso's still nobly declining to die. Anyhow, he painted Guernica just to cash in on the fashion.

SARAH Peter, how can you!

HANK Peter, if you're going to talk like that —

PETER Now don't get all starry-eyed and stupid. Only one good artist has been inspired by war and that's Goya.

SARAH I can't see how anyone comparing these two exhibitions —

HANK Surrealism! What does it add up to?

PETER What does Guernica add up to? Wait till we have a war of our own. Which we shall of course. Next year or the year after. And if you two think that's going to help your painting . . . It'll just cut you off from the Continent, you'll be more insular than ever.

HANK Are we any more insular than you?

PETER But of course you are, my dear boy. Partly because of your puritanical mentalities but even more perhaps because you've never painted abroad. Don't you realize that the light in this country —

HANK I don't think light is of primary importance.

PETER Oh, don't you.

SARAH Peter, what are *you* going to do when the war comes?

PETER Me? Camouflage perhaps. Hank will be too young for that.

HANK I don't think I'd want it anyway.

PETER You mean you'd rather fight?

HANK Whatever happens, I'll get through.

SARAH What do you mean, darling? Through it alive?

HANK No, through it as me. And that's not quite the word either.

PETER What an odd obscure fellow you are, Hank. You know, if you two got married, they mightn't call Hank up so quickly.

SARAH That's impertinent of you, Peter.

HANK Yes, Peter, for God's sake! We've only just stopped being students and we haven't any money between us — Anyhow, I'm too fond of Sarah to marry her.

SARAH And that goes for me vice versa.

PETER Sorry, I seem to be obtuse. I'm taking a holiday next week.

HANK Snowdonia again?

PETER No, Yorkshire. And this time not up. Down.

HANK Meaning?

PETER Meaning speleology. Caves and pot-holes and things. In the North they call it 'pot-oiling'.

HANK When I was little my mother used to read aloud to me. And one book she read was by Jules Verne.

PETER *Journey to the Centre of the Earth*?

HANK That's right. It got me completely fascinated.

PETER Hank! You've been up mountains with me. Why don't you come down a cave for a change?

HANK Well, in a way I'd like to but —

SARAH You go, darling. It will give me a chance to clean up the studio.

HANK Just a moment, both of you. There is one small snag.

PETER What is it?

HANK I suffer from claustrophobia.

(*Pause*)

PETER Oh. Well perhaps this might cure it. I knew a chap who had no head for heights and he made a few parachute jumps and —

HANK It cured him?

PETER Completely.

HANK Right. I'll have a go.

PETER That's fine. I'll let Mervyn know.

HANK Mervyn?

PETER He used to be a Welsh Nationalist and this, I suspect, is a substitute. He has some rather quaint habits though. He's got to make jokes and they're always the same jokes. For example when he's leading, groping on ahead, and he calls back over his shoulder just to be sure you're OK, well, how do you think he puts it?

(*Cross-fade pub atmosphere to cave atmosphere and behind*)

MERVYN (*calling*) How now, old mole?

(*Silence*)

Hankey! I said: How now, old mole?

HANK (*calling*) Oh me? I'm OK.

MERVYN (*calling*) How's the other old mole?

HANK (*calling*) Peter, you OK?

PETER (*calling*) I'm OK. How are you?

HANK (*calling*) Fine.

(*To self*) I'm not though. Talk about back to the womb! Difference is the womb was soft.

MERVYN (*calling*) Hallo there! I've reached the pitch. Luncheon will be served immediately. One pork pie per head, bar of chocolate, tube of condensed milk.

HANK (*to self*) Moles. That tiny dead one on its back. Holding up its hands like a suppliant nun. Mummy took it away, threw it in the dustbin.

MERVYN Come on old mole.

HANK Here I am.

MERVYN Sit down. Don't impale yourself on a stalagmite.

HANK I don't see any stalagmites.

MERVYN There aren't any. Don't mind me, I'm just a mad hatter. But if you want stalactites and stalagmites, just wait till you see Skrimshank's.

HANK Skrimshank's?

MERVYN Hush, it's a secret. My Unknown Quantity. I've only so far explored the first chamber but, man, it's a symphony in dripstone. The chamber ends in a chimney, that's what we go down next.

PETER We?

MERVYN I'm talking about Skrimshank's.

PETER I guessed you were.

HANK Why is it called Skrimshank's?

MERVYN Skrimshank's Cave. I called it that. It was I discovered it, you see. But I'm keeping it dark from the fraternity.

PETER Well, do I gather you're inviting both of us?

MERVYN To Skrimshank's? Yes, of course. We'll beat the bastard between us. Eat up your lunch, boys, we've got to descend that pitch.

PETER Mervyn says Skrimshank's is a maze of galleries. With a number of chimneys and chambers and quite a few traps.

MERVYN That's all conjecture, mind you. How do you find this underworld, Hankey?

HANK Hank.

MERVYN Hank.

HANK I find it . . . excitingly timeless.

MERVYN That's right. You leave time outside. With the weather.

PETER The weather outside can affect us inside though.

MERVYN Yes, that's only too true. What else do you notice about it?

HANK Well, er . . .

MERVYN Don't you find it pure? Unsullied?

HANK Unsullied? Yes. I suppose so.

MERVYN I know so. And you like it?

HANK Oh yes.

PETER There, I knew your little trouble would be cured.

MERVYN Action stations! Out with the lifeline, Peter. (*Hums*) Have you seen the lifeline man, the lifeline man, the lifeline man . . .

(*Fade out humming and cave atmosphere*)

SARAH The buses are hopeless, darling. Let's go by Underground.

HANK Damned if I will.

SARAH Why?

HANK It's under ground.

SARAH But seeing now you're a speleologist —

HANK Well that makes me feel sick too. But at least it has its compensations. Henry Moore for instance.

SARAH Henry Moore?

HANK He comes from Yorkshire too, you know. Remember those reclining figures with holes in them? That's the landscape all right. Well, if he can do it, why can't I? I'm set on getting through, I told you.

SARAH Through which, darling? Skrimshank's Cave or your problems as an artist?

HANK Through both of course. But Skrimshank's will have to wait. Mervyn's going off for two years to the Andes. Peter'll let me know when he returns.

(*Knock on door*)
SARAH Come in.
(*Door opens*)
SARAH
HANK } Oh, Peter!
PETER Heard the news?
HANK Mervyn's back?
PETER Russia have signed a pact with Germany.
HANK } What?
SARAH } No!
PETER So I'm going to rub up my camouflage.
SARAH You mean the war's on?
PETER The war's on, so Skrimshank's, I'm afraid, is off. Mervyn's on the reserve, you know.
HANK I didn't know.
PETER What will you do, Hank?
HANK In the war? Wait till they conscript me.
PETER That's right. Don't volunteer.
HANK I won't. I've got things to paint.
SARAH I wonder where they'll send you.
PETER Maybe nowhere.
HANK Maybe. Or maybe worse than nowhere.

MOTHER Burma! But are things bad in Burma then?
SARAH They're cut off — surely you've heard that. So that must be why I've not heard from him.
MOTHER So my poor lamb's in Burma! They told me you were the only one who might know. You see, he hasn't any relatives. Present company excepted and perhaps I don't really count.

(*Pause*)

Or do I, my dear?

(*Pause*)

Well, I can't force you to answer. Did he ever talk to you about me?

SARAH Yes.

MOTHER What did he say?

SARAH You can guess, can't you?

MOTHER Of course you would see it from his angle?

SARAH Mrs Hankey, why did you come back?

MOTHER Well, my dear, I just didn't want to be occupied. I mean Vichy France is not as bad as the other but even so, my dear, things were terribly difficult. And, when this awful war broke out, I was all set to go to Venezuela. Now I'll have to wait till it's over.

SARAH But first you'll wait to see your son?

MOTHER Yes, of course, my dear. What do you think I am?

SARAH May I ask you something?

MOTHER Anything you like, my dear.

SARAH It's not what I like but what I must. Why did you never get in touch with him before?

MOTHER Oh I tried to, my dear. Repeatedly. It was his father, you know.

SARAH His father's been dead some time.

MOTHER Yes, poor old man. Oh, I know I'm terribly to blame but I'm not quite as bad as you think. If you could only imagine how completely cut off I felt —

SARAH As completely as Hank?

MOTHER Year after year, but I can see it in your eyes: you just don't believe me, do you?

SARAH Mrs Hankey, would you like a drink?

MOTHER Oh, how very kind of you to ask me! But isn't it unfair with these war-time shortages —

SARAH Oh, *that's* not unfair. I can offer you beer or gin.

MOTHER I can't drink beer, I'm afraid, but if you could spare me a teeny weeny gin —

SARAH Say when. (*spot*)

MOTHER Just the width of an eyelash more, my dear. Thank you, you're a darling. What very good taste my boy has, taking up with a girl like you. By the way, talking of Venezuela, my friend out there is in oil —

('*All clear*')

What's that?

SARAH The All Clear.

MOTHER The All Cl — ! Do you mean to say, while we've been talking, there's been an air raid on?

SARAH It's been on for hours — not that anything seems to have happened. You must have missed the Alert.

MOTHER Good God! Well, cheers.

SARAH Would you like another?

MOTHER Well, in the circumstances —

SARAH You're welcome. But, while we've been talking, by the way, there's also been a world war on. It moved to France and you left there. It moved to Burma and he went there. Though whether there'll ever be an All Clear for that — he's cut off, can't you understand? Cut off in a pocket, surrounded by screaming Japs. For all you or I know, he's dead or a prisoner. And you sit there, dreaming of Venezuela.

MOTHER Now, I beg you, don't get hysterical; I know exactly how you feel, my dear. I feel all the same things too but I'm older and so I don't say them. All one can do is pray and have faith.

SARAH Pray and — Cheers!

MOTHER Cheers again, my dear.

(*Fade up jungle night bird*)

SERGEANT What was that, Mr Hankey?

HANK Some bloody night bird, Sergeant.

SERGEANT Not a Jap imitating a bird?

HANK Could be a bird imitating a Jap. How far do you think they are now?

SERGEANT Oh, fifty yards, as usual.

HANK Do you think they feel as blind as we do?

SERGEANT Probably don't but they ought to. This is a blind bloody war. What you might call a ghost war. Always working in the dark and the mud and —

HANK How now, old mole? Sergeant, have you ever gone caving?

SERGEANT How do you mean, Mr Hankey?

HANK Exploring caves — what they call speleology.

SERGEANT Well, when I was a kid at the seaside —

HANK No, this is a serious thing like mountaineering. It's a perfectly grown-up thing. But those caves are darker than this even. There are also things called traps.

SERGEANT What do they trap?

HANK The cavers.

SERGEANT Just like us in the Fourteenth Army too. The whole bloody
Arakan's a trap. We're all proper Charlies to be here.

(*Pause: explosion of V2*)

PETER Good God, Sarah. Do you often have this sort of thing?

SARAH That's what we call a V2, Peter.

PETER Well, it shouldn't be allowed. Not the first time I'm home on
leave from Shepheard's Hotel in Cairo.

SARAH Tell me, Peter, are you good at camouflage?

PETER Rather a dab in fact. Between ourselves I had a lot to do with
Alamein. But to return to higher things —

SARAH No, Peter, I'm sorry, but definitely no.

PETER Hank wouldn't mind.

SARAH I'm not sure about that. But even if he wouldn't, I would.

PETER All right, let's drop it. This your latest?

SARAH It's my only painting in six months. I'm kept so busy in the
Min. of Inf.

PETER 'm. It's interesting. A bit Little England, of course.

SARAH Well, what do you expect? As you said yourself, this war would
enhance our insularity. But what, may I ask, have *you* been painting?

PETER I have painted one mural for a pasha. To amuse his women —
which, I am told, it did.

SARAH Peter, will you go back to teaching after the war?

PETER I very much doubt it. I met some charming chaps in Shepheard's
who think they can get me into advertising. That's the coming career,
you know. Now if Hank was interested —

SARAH He wouldn't be. Hank will go straight on painting.

PETER He shouldn't.

SARAH Why the hell not?

PETER Because he uses painting as a therapy. Which is worse than
people like me who use it for fun and games.

SARAH But supposing he does use painting as a therapy —

PETER He'll just be terribly disappointed. It won't be good painting
and it won't be good therapy. Besides, Hank will always need money.

SARAH Yes, that I must admit: his tastes do get more and more
extravagant.

PETER What about this cow of a mother of his? How's she off for the
lolly?

SARAH Peter, seriously, I'm scared about that woman. And I don't even
know if Hank will agree to see her.

PETER But he must, you must fix it, darling. And you'd better have all your plans ready. Any day now this war's going to come to an end.

SARAH The war in Europe, you mean. Hank's may go on for ever. I mean, the Japs won't surrender.

PETER Don't you worry: something will turn up to fix them.

SARAH I pray to God something does.

PETER To go back to Hank's mama, you're keeping in touch with her?

SARAH Oh, I've never seen her again and don't want to. Apart from anything else, she's on the bottle. But I promised to telephone as soon as Hank came home. It's some number in Shropshire.

PETER Safe hotel no doubt.

SARAH Oh, no doubt. But if Hank, as I suspect, won't ring her himself, why, then I'm prepared to do it for him.

(Pause: dialling and cross-fade to ringing of telephone)

FOREIGN MAID 'm? Yes? please. I am sorry. Madame is gone away it is now three weeks. Yes. Gone away. I am sorry. To Venezuela.

(Receiver replaced)

SARAH Hank! *(begins to sob)*

HANK It's what I expected. She's gone to Venezuela. But for God's sake stop crying. My mother means nothing to me now.

SARAH How do you know?

HANK Let her go to bloody Venezuela: you and I are going to the Victoria and Albert. To see what the boys have been up to. They, after all, are the civilization I've been fighting for.

(Fade up picture gallery atmosphere and behind)

VOICE A Makes one feel so terribly insular.

VOICE B Not Matisse.

VOICE A No, not Matisse, of course not.

VOICE B But Picasso, yes.

VOICE A Picasso, definitely yes. It's something we just can't do.

VOICE B Perhaps it's because we weren't occupied.

(Up buzz of voices and behind)

VOICE C Jennifer, have you seen that? What do you think it is?

VOICE D It could be a woman, mum.

VOICE C A woman? With one eye sideways and one eye frontways —

VOICE D It's what they call distortion, mum.

VOICE C I'll say it's what they call distortion! I've a good mind to ask for our money back.

(Up buzz and behind again)

PETER Hank!

HANK Peter!

PETER Well, you old so-and-so! You're looking terribly well, Burma must be healthy.

HANK You should try it some day.

PETER So you've just got back in time for your idol's exhibition.

HANK My idol?

PETER Picasso. Well, I wouldn't mean Matisse, would I?

HANK He *was* my idol; it's funny.

PETER What's funny?

HANK Well, I don't think he is any more, it may be I'm just out of touch but ... you know how I felt at the time of the Guernica exhibition?

PETER Well, you've got older since then.

HANK I've been in battle since then. And now — oh, perhaps I've gone blind but I don't think Picasso's saying anything. It's all too bloody virtuoso.

PETER Well, I'm more than inclined to agree with you. What about your own work, Hank?

HANK Well, you don't think I painted in the jungle, do you? I've lost five years and now I've lost the studio. But the moment I can find four walls and a roof —

SARAH I know of a studio, darling. A huge one, just the place for us. We could cook there, sleep there, everything. The only trouble is it's shockingly expensive.

HANK Oh, don't worry about that, I've got my army gratuity. Just tell me where it is and we'll take it.

PETER That's the spirit; more power to your elbows. But Hank, if you do need money, just let me know because I've got a proposition —

HANK Thank you, Peter, at the moment I just don't fancy propositions. All I need is a canvas and a brush. And four walls and a roof and Sarah. And then I can get through. I know I can.

(*Fade out art gallery background*)

No, I can't! I can't, I can't, I can't!

SARAH If you're going to destroy that canvas too, I'd like you at least to pay me for it.

HANK Don't sound so acid, Sarah.

SARAH Sorry, darling, I saw your point with the last one but this one was coming on well.

HANK Here you are: paint over it. Sarah, I'm sorry; I've had it.

SARAH Had what?

HANK The painting business. I lost most of it in Burma and the little bit left over I lost in Venezuela. And now go on: despise me for my self-pity.

SARAH Hank, come and sit here beside me; I've got things to say to you. I know I've said them before but —

HANK It's no good saying them again, I take that back about Venezuela. But as far as Burma is concerned —

SARAH Darling, I know it was ghastly.

HANK It wasn't, you know, all of it. Some of it was bloody funny and some of it was even inspiring. There was one particular morning when the word inspiration applied. This was after the monsoon, there was sun, one could really see things. There was a river with bamboos reflected in it. I thought to myself: here it comes, this is vision again, I've still got it. And then the thing happened — the worst thing I met in Burma.

   (*Pause*)

SARAH Go on, darling.

HANK The worst thing I met was the worst thing I did. I was looking idly — yes, idly — through my binoculars and there at two hundred yards, bang in the open, was a tiny Jap soldier enjoying a crap. Just having a crap on his own without a care in the world. Well, Lance-Corporal Potter by ill luck was standing beside me with a rifle and it suddenly, just for the hell of it, occurred to me to try my eye. I never really expected to hit him — as you know, I'm not a good shot — and when I did I almost shook hands with myself. Lance-Corporal Potter was properly impressed too. I was so pleased I felt it had made my day. But that only lasted half a minute or so. And then I thought, well I thought what a thing to do. And I suddenly hated not only the war but myself. And as for the vision that had just been with me, that finished it.

SARAH I understand, darling, but that must have happened to so many people. It's all part of it, surely?

HANK All part of what? Of a lost lousy world. Look at what ended that whole war. We were delighted at the time of course. By the way, you remember that letter I got this morning?

SARAH About artists' careers being interrupted by the war?

HANK Interrupted! The understatement of 1946. Have we got a Coleridge in the house?

SARAH Coleridge? I'll look.

HANK When one's interrupted one can't pick it up again. It's happened to me all my life. My mother's lover with the bar of marzipan, and then the war itself and —

SARAH Here you are; service! *Collected Poems of Coleridge.*

HANK Now wait till I find it; this is all about me, darling. Here you are: 'Kubla Khan: or, A Vision in a Dream'. Bamboos reflected in the river and blue mountains beyond. A vision in Burma on a sunny morning. This is what old Coleridge said:

(*Reading*) 'On awaking he appeared to himself to have a distinct recollection of the whole, and taking his pen, ink, and paper, instantly and eagerly wrote down the lines that are here preserved. At this moment' — here it comes, Sarah — 'At this moment he was unfortunately called out by a person on business from Porlock, and detained by him above an hour, and on his return to his room, found, to his no small surprise and mortification, that though he still retained some vague and dim recollection of the general purport of the vision, yet, with the exception of some eight or ten lines and images,' — look at that thing on the easel there — 'all the rest had passed away like the images on the surface of a stream into which a stone had been cast, but, alas! without the after restoration of the latter.' There you are, Sarah, that's me. No small surprise and mortification. It's happened before and it will happen again.

(*Telephone rings: receiver lifted*)

SARAH Yes? ... Oh, Peter? ...

It's Peter for you, he's got one of his famous propositions. But watch it, darling. Don't commit yourself.

HANK Hullo, Peter! ... What? ... Next week-end? Yes, I'm doing nothing. I'm always doing nothing these days ... No, she won't mind. Yes, I'd love to.

(*Receiver replaced*)

(*Fade up cave atmosphere and behind*)

MERVYN (*calling*) How now, old mole?

HANK I'm all right, Mervyn.

MERVYN Not dropping those pitons are you?

HANK I'm not dropping anything, Mervyn.

MERVYN Only the gentle dew from your armpits. Well, join me here and we'll wait for Peter.

(*Scrabbling of rope-soled shoes on rock*)

You see. I told you about the dripstone. Stalactites and stalagmites, gympsum flowers, the lot!

HANK What I like about caves is their names.

MERVYN Oh yes, their names, man, they're marvellous. Alum Pot and Gaping Ghyll, Lost John's Cave and Wookey Hole.

PETER Here I am, Columbus. And here's the missing life-line. So we're all set for the drop. How deep is that damned chimney?

MERVYN I'm in no hurry; sit down and get your breath, man. Hank here and I were just talking about caves.

PETER How did you stumble on that subject?

MERVYN What a pity it is, you know, once the trippers are in. Take the biggest cave in the world, the Carlsbad Cavern in New Mexico. Do you know it has an intake of five hundred persons per hour? They whiz down by elevator eight hundred feet and what do they find when they get there? A quick feed restaurant and a male voice choir on record. Commercialization! You'd think we had enough on the surface.

PETER (*low*) Talking of commercialization, Hank, you won't forget —

HANK No, I won't.

PETER It shouldn't interfere with your own work, you can always do that on the side.

HANK On the side? Oh, yes. Of course.

PETER So that's a date? We'll lunch with Alec next week?

HANK And take a long spoon. Yes, that's a date.

MERVYN Action stations, boys! Shoulder your tackle! Chimney's just thirty yards ahead. Onward Christian cavers!

PETER How deep is it, Mervyn?

MERVYN How would I know? Fifty feet, perhaps sixty. We'll drop a stone and find out, but I hope your lifeline's not rotten.
(*hums*) Have you seen the lifeline man, the lifeline man, the lifeline man,
Have you seen the lifeline man
(*fading*) Who lives in Skrimshank's Cave?

(*Lose cave atmosphere: pause: door opens*)

HANK (*singing on approach*)
Have you see the lifeline man, the lifeline man, the lifeline man,
Have you seen the lifeline man
Who lives in W1?

SARAH Hank! You've obviously had a good lunch.
Where's Peter?

HANK Left him with Alec.

SARAH Alec?

HANK The chap he wanted me to meet.

SARAH So you're on Christian names already?

HANK It's a Christian name world, Alec's.

SARAH And you're proposing to join it?

HANK We need the money, Sarah.

SARAH And how will you get it?

HANK By drawing things.

SARAH Advertisements you mean?

HANK Oh, no. Illustrations to women's magazines. And strip cartoons if I'm lucky. Oh, maybe an ad just once in a while. I've appointed Alec my agent.

SARAH Mervyn rang up when you were out.

HANK Mervyn! Why?

SARAH To send you his apologies. The next expedition's off. He's suddenly been invited to some do in the Pyrenees. Some archaeological do. But about Skrimshank's: he says when he comes back to tell you: all you need now is more rope.

HANK All I need now is more rope?

SARAH You remember the proverb, of course?

HANK Sarah, you're a bitch.

SARAH I'm a what?

HANK A bitch. B–I–T–C–H. I thought you'd be pleased that we're now in the money.

SARAH That *we're* now in the money?

HANK Well, you don't suppose that, when I'm rich, I'm going to leave you out of it!

(Pause: fade up ringing phone: receiver lifted)

MAGGIE Hullo! . . . Yes, of course this is Maggie . . . Oh, Sarah darling! After all this time! Whatever have you been doing with yourself? . . . Yes, I *am* still looking for someone to share the flat . . . You mean *you* would like to? But what about Hank? . . . Out! How do you mean out? . . . But lots of people are commercial artists . . . Yes, I've seen those strips they're very clever. I don't think one should be snob about it . . . On the bottle too? But that's nothing new, darling . . . Worse? How much worse? . . . Oh really? Well, you know you're always welcome *here* . . . Oh, as soon as that? Marvellous, darling, I'll expect you.

(*Receiver replaced: pause: fade up Peter*)

PETER Well, that's my second point. And my third point, Hank —
you're not listening!

HANK I got your first point, Peter: that's all I need. You got me into
all this and now you're running me out of it.

PETER I'm doing no such thing, I'm merely tipping you off. Alec says
they're getting tired of it. You're always being so behind-hand.

HANK Well, when I'm beforehand, what happens? The Art Editor
sends it back to me. Look at this: they even rejected this. Because I
drew the bride's nose straight: they said it should have been tiptilted.
As if brides couldn't wear straight noses! Women's magazines! You
can have them.

PETER But it's not just the women's magazines. Alec says your comics
for teenagers —

HANK You're out of date. I've packed that in already.

PETER Well, now we come to the worst thing. Worst because it's the
most lucrative. That daily strip cartoon of yours in the Daily —

HANK Stop! I know it brings in the money but I just can't keep up the
pace. If I work till four in the morning I can only do two in the day.
I'm going to pack that in too.

PETER But you told me it had been an education.

HANK That was two years ago.

PETER But you'll keep on the women's mags?

HANK Yes, if they'll keep me on.

PETER Well, that brings me to — forgive me mentioning this but
Alec — well, frankly, it's about your drinking. Alec says unless —

HANK Alec says! Alec says! Sarah sent that one up long ago.

PETER I wish you'd listen.

HANK Do you know how long it is since she left?

PETER Sarah? Three years? Four? How long?

HANK *I* can't remember! But she never came back for her paintings.
Those are all hers in the corner.

PETER And that canvas on the easel?

HANK That's mine. That surprised you, Peter, didn't it?
(*Pause*)
Well, come on, what do you think of it?
(*Pause*)

PETER 'm. It looks as if you've joined the British Romantics. No, that's
not a sneer. The British Romantics with a difference.

HANK Can you guess what that was suggested by?

PETER Skrimshank's?

HANK Got it in one. Perhaps you *could* have taught art if you'd gone on.

PETER You think it's a pity?

HANK Maybe. It's a far greater pity that Mervyn's living abroad.

PETER But haven't you heard? He's back.

HANK Back! Since when?

PETER Two months ago, actually. And any day now he's going to have another crack at Skrimshank's.

HANK *I've* not heard anything about it.

PETER Well, er . . . You mean you'd still be interested?

HANK I'll always be interested. Tell Mervyn, will you, I'm interested.

PETER Yes, of course, when I see him. There's nothing definite yet you know.

HANK And tell Alec I'm through.

PETER What?

HANK Tell Alec I'm through with commercials.

PETER Why should I?

HANK That's right. Why should you? He's not your agent, he's mine. You can't sack him but I can. And I *will*; it will be a pleasure.

PETER Hank, you mustn't! You'll ruin your career.

HANK Ruin my what? I'm about to cross the Rubicon. That's the Rubicon there. That little black object with a dial on it. That's my Rubicon, Peter.

PETER Now, Hank —

HANK And I cross it simply by dialling.

(*Dialling and fade out*)

MAGGIE I saw Peter today, Sarah.

SARAH Yes, Maggie?

MAGGIE He told me something that should please you.

SARAH What's that?

MAGGIE Hank has dropped the commercials and is starting to paint again.

(*Pause*)

Well, aren't you interested?

SARAH Not particularly.

MAGGIE Well, of all the strange girls —

SARAH Three years ago I would have been.

MAGGIE Peter's furious, of course. It's made trouble between him and this Alec man.

SARAH Is Hank still hitting it hard?

MAGGIE Oh, I don't know anything about that. Though Peter did say he was high when he made the great renunciation.

SARAH Dutch courage. No. It won't work.

MAGGIE Darling, why don't you go and see him? After taking a step like that he must need someone to talk to.

SARAH Hank can find plenty of sounding-boards.

(*Fade up moderate clapping*)

HANK Thank you, ladies and gentlemen. I very much appreciate the quite undeserved speech of thanks that the gentleman in the Old Etonian tie —

1ST VOICE It's not as a matter of fact.

(*Laughter*)

HANK Old Carthusian tie made in response to my lecture. I've enjoyed coming here more than I expected. And I hope I've said one or two things that may give you to think.

(*Giggles and whispering*)

About Henry Moore, for instance. Did I make my point about Henry Moore?

2ND VOICE You did. Several times.

(*Giggles*)

HANK The point is this, you see; the point is this. The point is — oh yes: in this country for the first time since, for the first time, in this country sculpture has now got ahead of painting. So we painters have got to catch up, we've got to beat the bloody hour-glass.

3RD VOICE Language!

(*Laughter*)

HANK What are you laughing about? Yes, that's right, beat the bloody hour-glass. Action stations and get on with it. But when I say action stations I don't mean action painting. I'll tell you a secret: I don't like action painting. When I want to paint I paint and, when I want action, know what I do? I go down a bloody pot-hole.

3RD VOICE Language!

(*Laughter*)

HANK Who said language? I'll tell you something. You people don't speak *my* language. But let me tell you something. Next week I'm going exploring. Exploring a cave nobody knows about. And the man I'll be with, the man who discovered that cave — he's worth all you lot put together —

4TH VOICE Shame!

HANK He speaks my language all right. Because I'm an artist and he's a speleologist. Yes, old Mervyn speaks my language.

(*Fade up cave background, with stream, and behind*)

MERVYN (*calling*) How now, old mole?

DONALD (*calling*) Wait for me, Mervyn, my light's gone.

MERVYN (*calling*) Hasn't Peter got a light?

DONALD (*calling*) Yes, of course.

MERVYN (*calling*) You wait for him then. I'm busy.

    (*Pause*)

DONALD (*calling*) Hurry up, Peter, my light's gone.

PETER (*calling*) Coming, Donald.

    (*Effect of rope-soles on rock*)

(*To self*) Really, this boy Donald! First he drops the eats in the stream ... next he gets stuck in a squeeze ... and now for good measure his light's gone. Still we had to have three.

Hullo, Donald! Got your spare battery?

DONALD I've got no spare battery.

PETER Then I'll give you mine. Hold this torch.

DONALD Peter, I'm loving every minute of this.

PETER Are you?

DONALD Greatest fun I ever had in my life. I shouldn't say it, I suppose, but I'm glad your friend had 'flu.

PETER Between ourselves, he hadn't.

DONALD Eh?

PETER Mervyn wouldn't take him.

DONALD But why? I thought he was quite an old hand at it.

PETER He's become, well, perhaps a rather shaky hand. And he didn't really like it all that much. He suffers from claustrophobia, you see.

HANK (*shouting*) Let me out! Let me out, let me out, let me out!

MAGGIE But you are out, Hank, you're in the park, you've just been having a nap on the grass.

HANK The park! Who am I with?

MAGGIE Me! But you mustn't shout. People are staring at you, ducky.

HANK Me? Who's me? Who's you?

MAGGIE Maggie. Don't you remember? I called on you this afternoon and then you took me out to dinner.

HANK What did we have for dinner?

MAGGIE Oh really, Hank! Those perfectly lovely scampi and —

HANK He wouldn't take me down his bloody cave.

MAGGIE What cave? Who wouldn't?

HANK You wouldn't know! Who are you, anyway?

MAGGIE I told you. I'm a friend of Sarah's.

HANK Oh Sarah. How is Sarah?

MAGGIE I told you: she's quite all right.

HANK Did Sarah ask you to call on me?

MAGGIE Well, not exactly but —

HANK Kiss me.

MAGGIE No, no, Hank, not in the park.

HANK Yes, that's right, we must wait till Sarah goes.

MAGGIE Sarah's not here.

HANK I thought you just said she was.

MAGGIE Darling, you're a little confused. I'm going to take you home now.

HANK Yes, take me home. And then you know what? You and me'll have a little nightcap.

MAGGIE A little one, yes; not a big one.

HANK Why not a big one?

MAGGIE Because tomorrow you've got to see Tony.

HANK Who's Tony?

MAGGIE Oh God, darling, I told you! The man who can get you in on television.

HANK Oh yes, I remember. Animated cartoons. Damned if I want to do those.

MAGGIE Now don't be naughty. You promised. Come along, get up. Easy now, I'm taking you home and giving you a tiny nightcap and then I'm setting your alarm clock.

HANK No, no clock. No time under ground, you know.

MAGGIE I'll set it for 11.30. That will get you to lunch on time.

HANK Don't want lunch.

MAGGIE It's with Tony.

HANK Tony? Oh yes.

MAGGIE You promised.

HANK Then you stay with me till the alarm goes off.

MAGGIE I'm afraid I can't do that.

HANK Oh yes, Sarah, you can. You always used to, damn it.

MAGGIE Hank! I am not Sarah.

HANK Then there's no obstacle. First taxi home, then tiny nightcap, then set alarm clock, then bed for both.

MAGGIE Not for both. For you.

HANK But I can't sleep alone, Sarah. The dark's full of traps, stream keeps rising, poor old moles get drowned. Little drowned nuns with little hands still praying.

MAGGIE We're going now.

HANK That's right: going. Going to nightcap, then bed, then alarm clock. Alarm and despondency, alarms and excursions . . .

   (*Alarm clock*)
Sarah! Turn that off!
   (*Alarm clock out*)
My God, who are *you*? Have we committed adultery?

MAGGIE That didn't arise, darling.

HANK Then let it arise now.

   (*Pause: fade up restaurant background and behind*)
TONY So you see, Hank — sorry you've eaten nothing — when we saw those strip cartoons it struck us all simultaneously that your style was just like Bill's.

HANK Bill's?

TONY I've been telling you: Bill Trueman. The man I want you to work for.

HANK I don't believe my style is just like his. What would I have to do?

TONY Just what I explained. He does the key drawings, you do the fill-ins.

HANK Why can't I do the key drawings.

TONY Because animation is a very special technique. If you have a real flair for it — and my guess is you probably have — why, then, within a year or six months or even sooner you can branch out on your own and form your own animation company. Just as Bill Trueman did himself. How does that prospect tempt you? Orders coming in from here, there, and everywhere. The tobacco people, the ice-cream people, the detergent people, the lot! That's where you may be in a year or so.

(*Fade out restaurant atmosphere*)

MAGGIE Darling! A man rang up today. He wants you to animate whats-its-name toffee.

HANK Oh hell, Maggie! I've enough on my plate already. If I take on one more contract, I *will* have to get another assistant.

(*Fade up piano — one finger — tune of 'have you seen the mocking bird?'*)

PETER Sarah, look at the screen! This commercial.

SARAH Ugh! What about it?

PETER It's Hank's.

SARAH That beastly little bear with toothache?

PETER Not toothache, darling, that's toffee.

(*Recorded voice of singer:*)

Have you seen the Toffee Bear, the Toffee Bear, the Toffee Bear, Have you seen the Toffee Bear?

Yum! Yum! Yum! Yum! Yum!

(*Recording out*)

SARAH Poor Hank! How ghastly for him!

PETER Sarah?

SARAH Yes?

PETER If I may ask, why do you go on living here?

SARAH Why, you know: I took over the lease two years ago.

PETER Yes, from Maggie: that's what I mean.

SARAH But I'm the sole tenant now.

PETER Well *that*, in fact, is what I mean. I'd have thought the associations — After all, we all know where Maggie's living.

SARAH Peter, you're bloody impertinent.

(*Pause: fade up Hank whistling toffee bear tune*)

JOCK Mr Hankey!

HANK (*stopping whistling*) What, Jock?

JOCK I've got a complaint to make.

HANK Well I've a complaint to make too. You are still unable to get the rhythm. I've just been flipping over the cells and I'm afraid it won't do. Sorry, Jock, but it's bad animation.

JOCK Yes, I agree, it won't do. You're three weeks behind with my wages. Norman and I are fed up.

HANK I've explained to Norman and you: I'm in the same position. No one ever pays me on the dot —

JOCK That's your affair, you're the boss. But speaking as a wage-slave, wages are wages. And how with all your contracts you can get so behind hand . . .

MAGGIE Why with all your contracts you're always in debt is something beyond my understanding.

HANK Like many other things.

MAGGIE A month or two ago you had four figures in the bank; now you're in the red. I just can't think how you manage it.

HANK Can't you? Take a good look round this studio — or rather it used to be a studio, now it's like a call-girl's dream.

MAGGIE Thank you.

HANK You might also look in that pier glass. What you have on your exquisite torso isn't exactly sackcloth.

MAGGIE Well, at least your drink bills are down.

HANK I told you to stop that parrot cry. 'I saved him from a drunkard's grave. I saved him for the commercials.' Twenty-five frames per second which means about sixteen drawings, most of which I have to do myself because my assistants are imbeciles — Maggie, I think I've had it!

MAGGIE Had what?

HANK Commercials.

MAGGIE Oh, and what are you going to do then?

HANK What I was born to do. Paint.

MAGGIE Hadn't you better wait till you're out of the red?

HANK No, Maggie: life's too short.

MAGGIE You've not even paid the rent and the rates.

HANK I'm forty-two and I've never had a show. It's time I did.

MAGGIE But you haven't any pictures.

HANK That can be corrected. It will take me two years.

MAGGIE What am I to do for the next two years then?

HANK Whatever you like. Stay on here if you like.

MAGGIE That's very kind of you.

HANK But I warn you: I'll have to clear the decks. Once I start to paint I can't have all these carpets and armchairs and things. And I'll need all the cupboards available. That one and that one and that one —

MAGGIE That one's my wardrobe.

HANK Not any more it's not.

MAGGIE Hank!

HANK What do you mean 'Hank'?

MAGGIE So you're now even grudging me a wardrobe!

HANK You can hang your clothes in the bathroom.

MAGGIE I can what?

HANK It was you who wanted a bathroom — it cost me — what? — to put it in.

MAGGIE I didn't know you'd paid for it yet.

HANK I haven't but that's not the point. You wanted that bathroom. Now you can hang your clothes in it.

MAGGIE I'm not removing a single thing from my wardrobe.

HANK If you're not, I am.

MAGGIE Hank!

(*Double doors of cupboard thrown violently open — hangers pushed along rail*)

HANK Here! Catch!

(*Dress on hanger clatters on floor*)

And this (*effect*). And this! (*effect*) ... And this and this and this and (*effect*). And this disgusting monstrosity.

MAGGIE Hank! Stop it!

(*Effect*)

HANK And this little piece that's ten years too young for you.

MAGGIE OK. Where are my suitcases?

(*Long pause: fade up Hank whistling 'Onward Christian Soldiers'*)

PETER Hank, I'm astonished.

HANK (*stopping whistling*) What by, Peter?

PETER By all this work. You've done all these in a year, you say?

HANK One year and one month.

PETER Including those jumbo-sized canvases? Hate to think what they cost.

HANK Never mind the quantity. What about the quality?

(*Pause*)

PETER May I be candid?

HANK Of course.

PETER I don't think people will like them.

HANK Look, I don't want to know if they'll be in the top ten. I'm asking if they're good.

PETER To tell you the truth, Hank, I don't really know. You see you used to be a man for line but the line seems to have gone.

HANK I had too much of that in the cartoons. But you're wrong; it's still there — underneath.

PETER Trouble is painting's a visual medium.

HANK If you look long enough, the line will emerge.

PETER At art shows people don't look very long. You want to sell your pictures, don't you?

HANK Of course. I've got debts to pay off.

PETER What are you going to ask for these?

HANK Nothing less than three figures.

PETER Even the tiddly ones?

HANK Even the tiddly ones.

PETER It's your first show, remember.

HANK 'How can I forget?' says balding young artist. If the war hadn't happened, if Alec hadn't happened, if Maggie hadn't happened — Do you ever see Sarah now?

PETER Once or twice a week.

HANK I'd like to have her opinion.

PETER Well, ask her to come and look at them.

HANK How can I! I've only seen her once since the Maggie business.

PETER She doesn't seem to resent that, you know.

HANK No?

PETER Oh, she resents Maggie all right but, as between herself and you, she'd admit it was she who left you. She's a very honest girl, you know, Hank.

HANK Of course I know. That's why I want her to see these pictures. She's the one person I could trust to give me an honest opinion.

SARAH If I'm to give you my honest opinion, I think what you mean is valid — it's something that comes from the depths — but I don't think you're getting it over. There are four to five where you do — take this one for instance —

HANK I like that one myself. Do you know what it is?

SARAH A dead mole.

HANK My God, you're perceptive, Sarah. Most people would think it was an abstract.

SARAH It's a dead mole and it's praying. Of course, I must confess, you told me that story.

HANK What others do you like?

SARAH Well, that — and that — and that.

HANK And this?

SARAH No, definitely not.

HANK What's wrong with it?

SARAH Nearly everything.

(*Pause*)

HANK I know what's wrong with my work. You used to be here to criticize.

SARAH But you didn't get through even then.

HANK I think I might now. Will you come back, darling?

SARAH You are funny!

HANK Funny!

SARAH Egocentric. This is not a bad one either. I like the beam of light playing on that fan-vaulting, bringing out those blues and greens and yellows –

HANK You think it's a church, do you?

SARAH Isn't it?

HANK No, it's a cave. The first chamber in Skrimshank's.

SARAH Oh dear, old Skrimshank's! I'd forgotten Skrimshank's.

HANK Forgotten? I wish I could! Mervyn refused to take me the last time.

SARAH Why?

HANK Why do you think? And Peter tells me they all get stuck at a trap and Mervyn's named it the Stygian Trap – sometimes his humour is a trifle macabre.

SARAH I've forgotten. A trap means . . . ?

HANK It's where there's an underground stream and the rock comes down so low that you can't get through without swimming under water. Mervyn's been abroad ever since then, so nobody's conquered that trap yet. But I hope to be in on it yet. What do you think of this?

SARAH Hank! Can't you really tell the difference? Between these two.

HANK No, I can't. They're all equally me.

(*Pause*)

SARAH In that case I'd better come back. I'm a fool of course but –

HANK Sarah!

SARAH And we'll have to work like mad if you're going to have your show next spring.

(*Fade up art gallery background and behind*)

VOICE A Can't make head or tail of it.

VOICE B Did you ever hear of this man Hankey before?

VOICE A What's the point of painting in black on black?

VOICE X How he's got the nerve to ask three hundred for that!

VOICE Y Rather a come-down after that German group.

VOICE X I notice nothing's been sold so far.

    (Fade out background)

DIRECTOR OF GALLERY Well, Mr Hankey, I know it's disappointing. But I warned you: these things are a gamble. It's a pity you clashed with the Young German Exhibition — and then there's that disciple of Pollock's —

HANK Yes, emperors all of them.

DIRECTOR Emperors?

HANK Emperors' new clothes. Not a bit like my stuff.

DIRECTOR Well, at least we did sell five. Though not, I agree, at the prices in the catalogue. And I think, if I may say so, you were rash to spend so much on the frames. At a guess these must have averaged ten pounds . . . twelve?

HANK More like fifteen. And I haven't paid for them all yet.

DIRECTOR Fifteen? And what about the —

    (Fade up knocking on door: door opens)

BAILIFF Are you Mr Hankey? I expect you can guess who I am. I have to present you with this.

HANK What is it?

BAILIFF Well, sir, I'm afraid it's a Court Order. And it's my duty to quarter myself upon you until such time as this debt is paid. But I'll try not to get in your way, sir; it's fortunate perhaps you have such commodious premises.

    (Pause)

HANK Supposing I write you a cheque?

SARAH Hank, you know you can't!

BAILIFF I'm sorry, sir; I couldn't accept a cheque. I am only allowed to take payment in cash.

SARAH Show me that bit of paper. Good God! Never mind, I'll be back with the cash in an hour or two. Give the gentleman a cup of tea.

HANK But, Sarah, wherever are you going?

SARAH Never mind, darling.

    (Door opens and closes: pause)

HANK Do you really want tea? Or would you prefer Scotch?

BAILIFF Oh no, sir, thank you. Tea is my customary tipple.

HANK You don't mind if I have Scotch?

BAILIFF Naturally not, sir. De gustibus, as they say ... Excuse my asking, sir, but are you a professional artist?

HANK What do you think all these things are?

BAILIFF I can see they are paintings, sir, but I thought it might just be your hobby.

HANK Hobby! It's my bloody cross.

BAILIFF Oh. There's something else I'd like to ask, sir.

HANK Ask away.

BAILIFF This is purely professional curiosity, as the question, it transpires, will not arise, but this very large room we're in, is this your only sitting-room?

HANK This room is a studio but it's also my only sitting-room, *and* my only bedroom.

BAILIFF Hm, in that case there wouldn't be much to distrain on. Please forgive me, sir, I'm talking to myself. We'd have to leave you the bed of course. And most of the rest would appear to be the tools of your trade.

HANK 'Appear to be' is right.

BAILIFF If I may importune you again, sir, why do you have more than one easel?

HANK Because I need more than one.

BAILIFF That one there, sir, surely is an exceptionally large easel.

HANK It is. It cost me a hundred.

BAILIFF Excuse me, sir. A hundred?

HANK Once upon a time it belonged to a very famous artist.

BAILIFF I see. Raises an interesting problem. The question of course will not arise but —

    (*Kettle whistles off*)

HANK Sorry. That's the kettle.

BAILIFF (*to self*) Interesting problem, yes ... Was your easel really necessary? ... A hundred? Remarkable.

HANK (*approach*) How do you like your tea? Strong? Weak? Medium?

BAILIFF Just as it comes, sir, just as it comes. I notice you possess an exceptionally large tea-pot.

    (*Pouring effect*)

HANK Well, see if you can drink your way through it before the lady comes back. And I'll drink my way through this.

BAILIFF Not through all the bottle, I trust, sir!

HANK That depends when she comes back.

    (*Bottle and glass business*)

    Well, cheers.

BAILIFF Cheers, sir.

    I've often wondered how it feels to be an artist.

HANK How does it feel to be a bailiff?

BAILIFF It is rather . . . an ambivalent feeling. On the whole, sir, I am
quite relieved that my little boy's not going to follow in my footsteps.
He is only eight and a half but he knows what he's going to be already.

HANK And what is he going to be?

BAILIFF A racing driver, sir.

HANK Good for him. Well, cheers.

BAILIFF Oh didn't I say cheers? Cheers, sir.

    (*Fade and pause*)

SARAH Hank! How could you! This bottle's empty.

HANK He distrained on it. He drank it. Didn't you?

SARAH Didn't who?

HANK My friend over there.

SARAH Your friend over there's just left. With his pockets full of fivers.
He asked to be remembered to you.

HANK He distrained on your gin as well.

SARAH You mean that on top of all that Scotch you —

HANK No, he did; didn't you, sir?

SARAH Hank, there's no one there.

HANK Yes there is, there always is. 'Who is the third who walks always
beside me?' Tell you what, let's all three go out and celebrate.

SARAH Hank, you'd better go to bed.

HANK No, we must go out and celebrate. I've got the car round the
back and —

SARAH You've got the car round the back?

HANK If you don't believe me, look from the bathroom window.
(*Humming*) Onward Christian painters
Marchin' through the muck —

SARAH (*approach*) Hank! Give me the keys.

HANK What keys?

SARAH The car keys.

HANK Haven't got them.

SARAH Oh blast you! (*Pause*) What's this in your pocket then?

HANK This is the key of the Kingdom.

SARAH Hank! Listen! Go to bed. I'll be back when I've put it in the
garage. But do be good and go to bed: you're nine-tenths out already.

HANK Right. I'll be good. I'll go to bed. See you later, darling. See you later, sir.

SARAH (*moving off*) Ach!

(*Door bangs: pause: telephone rings for some time: receiver lifted*)

HANK Yes? Who is it? . . . Who?! . . . Hospital? What hospital? . . . Who? . . . In my car? Yes? . . . How bad is she? . . . Broken ribs and — I'll come round at once — . . . Oh I see, tomorrow. Tomorrow then. Give her my love. Tell her I'll see her tomorrow.

(*Receiver replaced: pause*)

SARAH The flowers are lovely, darling. How's your hangover?

HANK The worst ever.

SARAH I wish it was the last ever.

HANK I'm sorry, Sarah.

SARAH The ironic thing is it's I who'll be losing my licence.

HANK Oh they'll probably just endorse it.

SARAH I'm afraid not, Hank — driving across the red like that. I'm lucky not to have killed anyone.

HANK But you never drive across the red.

SARAH I was thinking about you, darling.

(*Pause*)

HANK Darling, what was the name of that doctor?

SARAH What doctor?

HANK The one you once asked me to go to. You know: the one who does the Cure.

SARAH Oh, Doctor Butler. Why?

HANK This time I'll go to him. He can slang me all he wants but —

SARAH He won't slang you, darling. But you'll have to tell him all about yourself.

DOCTOR And that, of course, has a great deal to do with it. The last twist of the knife was when your mother went to Venezuela. All along, subconsciously, you felt it was your fault. It's appalling to think how many mothers have made their sons alcoholics. For, not to mince words, Mr Hankey, that's what you are. Your mother started it, your failure in the art world continued it. As an artist you've always felt inadequate: therefore, subconsciously, you set out to destroy yourself. It's just because you're a creative person and because in the creative field —

HANK Doctor Butler, I wish you'd stop using that word.

DOCTOR I can't. For you it's the key word.

    (*Pause*)

HANK What are you going to do to me?

DOCTOR Nothing very frightening. First we'll give you some injections to clear your system of alcohol. Next come some dashes of vitamins. After that it's up to you. We'll supply you with pills but you'll have to promise to take them.

HANK I've heard of those pills. They're the ones that make you feel like death.

DOCTOR Only if you drink — and then you'd feel worse than death. But you will take them, won't you?

HANK Yes, I will, Doctor; thank you.

DOCTOR Good man. And, I assure you, in no time at all you'll feel different. You'll find yourself able to work again, you'll even be fit to take up your caving again, or pot-holing or whatever you call it, if you still want to keep up that hobby.

HANK Oh, it's more than a hobby, Dr Butler. But I don't know if Mervyn will take me again.

    (*Fade up cave*)

MERVYN (*ordinary voice*) How now, old moles?

DONALD Fine, Mervyn, fine.

MERVYN And you, Hank?

HANK Yes.

MERVYN You both had a long enough rest?

DONALD Yes.

HANK Yes, Mervyn.

MERVYN Right. On your feet! Next stop the Stygian Trap.

    (*Cross-fade plink-plonk to running stream*)

HANK So this is the Stygian Trap? I expected something more sinister.

MERVYN Well, the stream's low today; in fact today it isn't a trap at all. See there; headroom for swimming!

DONALD Headroom! I wonder if that's so all the way.

MERVYN As far as I can see with this torch. It's because we've had so little rain lately. Now, boys, the plan is this. I'll swim through with this line: if it's too far to shout I'll communicate by jerking. The usual code. Clear?

DONALD Clear. The usual code.

HANK Clear, Mervyn.

MERVYN When I'm through —

DONALD I follow?

MERVYN No, Hank will follow.

HANK Right, Mervyn.

MERVYN And I warn you: that water's icy.

DONALD Well, good luck, Mervyn.

HANK Good luck.

MERVYN See you later, boys. Right. Wet hand and tilt!

> (*Heavy splash and noise of swimmer receding — then stream running as before — fade out — pause — and fade up again*)

DONALD He's been gone a long time. No tug on the line even yet?

HANK Not the shadow of a tickle. Donald, what ought we to do?

DONALD We'll just have to wait. Try calling again.

HANK (*calling*) Mervyn! . . . Mervyn! . . . Can you hear me?

> (*Pause*)

I think I'll go through myself.

DONALD He'll murder you if you do that. We've got to wait till he tells us.

HANK But supposing he doesn't?

DONALD Don't suppose things like that, Hank.

> (*Pause: sudden increase of stream noise — and build behind*)

Hank! Do you hear what I hear?

HANK My God! It must be raining outside.

DONALD Is the stream higher?

HANK I'm just trying to check. I noticed a funny bit of crystal in there in the wall of the tunnel — No, my God, it's submerged!

DONALD The water can rise very quickly in these places.

HANK (*calling*) Mervyn! . . . Mervyn! . . . Mervyn!

Donald, I'm going through.

DONALD No, let me.

HANK I was to follow, Mervyn said.

DONALD Right then, but watch yourself. If you can't get through —

HANK I'll get through. But obviously, with all this noise, we can't communicate by shouting.

DONALD That's all right, I'll take over the line. Where is it?

HANK The line? . . . Good God, it must have been swept away.

DONALD Then you won't be able to communicate.

HANK Well, that's my fault isn't it? I had it in my hand.

DONALD Hank, you know something? You may get through from here because you'll be swimming down stream. But how once the river's in spate you could possibly swim back against it —

HANK I used to swim for my county.

DONALD Well, even so ... All *I* can do then is wait.

HANK 'They also serve,' like the man said. See you later, Donald.

DONALD Good luck, Hank.

>   (*Violent splash*))

>   (*Calling*) Good luck, Hank!

>   (*Build water noises to peak, then cross-fade to telephone ringing: receiver lifted*)

POLICE OFFICER ... Yes, this is the police station ... What! Two men cut off in a cave? And the entrance is flooding rapidly? What cave is it? ... Skrimshank's? Never heard of it ... Right, we'll pick you up and you'll lead us there.

>   (*Pause: fade up. Hank humming against stream background — gradually lose latter*)

HANK (*humming*) Have you see the lifeline man, the lifeline man, the lifeline man — Eh? It's gone quiet — by comparison. Rain must have stopped outside. Perhaps Mervyn could hear me now. (*calling*) Mervyn! ... Mervyn! ... Can you hear me?

>   (*Pause*)

So you're there! Thank God for that! Are you all right, Mervyn?

>   (*Pause*)

Not broken anything?

>   (*Pause*)

Fine. Then you can climb up to me. I'm up here on a ledge, miles above the water, it's safe, we can both wait here till it subsides.

>   (*Pause*)

You don't know how to find me? I'm sorry. My battery's gone — can't think why — but light after all is not of primary importance! If you just follow my voice — it's an easy climb, but you must hurry. Right, Mervyn. Are you coming?

>   (*Pause*)

Mervyn, are you coming?

>   (*Pause*)

You answered just now — or did you answer just now? (*To self*) No, Hank you fool, he didn't answer just now. That's what's called wishful thinking.

Hallucinations. But not due to alcohol. No, Doctor Butler, truly. I took my pill this morning, I've never lapsed once, Doctor Butler. But

I've just thought of something funny: Doctor Butler, you look like a butler.

DOCTOR (*as butler*) Herr Professor Lidebrock.

HANK Oh, my dear Professor, I've always wanted to meet you, since my mother used to read me your adventures. How you went down the volcano and ran into all those mastodons. But, of course, in your case you got out again.

PROFESSOR That was because I am a character in fiction.

HANK I'd forgotten that! So you are.

PROFESSOR Jules Verne invented me. But who, mein Herr, invented you?

DOCTOR Mr Jim White of Texas.

WHITE That you, Hank? What you doing in that little rat-hole, buddy? Why can't you get you a man-sized cave like I did? It's got two elevators now — cost a hundred and sixty thousand bucks. And a male voice choir on record. State of New Mexico gave me a bookstall down there. Most subterranean bookstall in the world. Sells only one book — mine: all about the Carlsbad and how I discovered it. Way it came about was when the bats flew out.

HANK (*humming*)

Bats in the Carlsbad,

Bats in the belfry,

Bats in —

(*speaking*) Bats in my bloody stomach! When did I last have a meal?

DOCTOR Mrs Beeton.

HANK Ah, Mrs Beeton! 'What feast is toward in thine eternal cell?' Not soya link sausage again, I hope? We had enough of that in Burma.

MRS BEETON Take five dozen eggs and a thirty-pound turkey, an armful of parsley and a pinch of gypsum —

DOCTOR An Officer who has been Attempting to get in Touch with You.

BAILIFF Mr Hankey! How nice to meet you again. The circumstances are not as propitious as last time and I fear they have sent me to distrain on this cave. Unless the little lady with the cash —

HANK She's not here!

BAILIFF In that case I must make an inventory. Perhaps you'd be so kind as to tell me which are the tools of your trade. What about these stalactites and stalagmites? Oh, and this hour-glass?

HANK Don't you dare touch that! That's what I've got to beat.

DOCTOR Pablo Picasso.

HANK And about time, too. I've a bone to pick with you, Pablo. You may be a genius but you've done us wrong. Grievous spiritual harm. You set us all doodling when we should have been painting pictures. And why are you not wearing your diving suit? After all, Salvador Dali did.

BAILIFF Excuse me, Mr Hankey, but, talking of bones, I've just found some. Am I right in assuming that, if they're prehistoric —

DOCTOR The Red Lady of Paviland.

RED LADY Here I come, dancing all in my bones —

HANK Don't wobble like that. It's bad animation.

RED LADY In my old red bones all made up with ruddle. Dr Buckland found me in Goat's Cave down in the Gower Peninsula. I was the only lady there, the others were all riff-raff — bears and hyenas —

HANK Come off it, you're no lady. You're a Cro-Magnon Man.

DOCTOR The Emperor Friedrich Barbarossa.

BARBAROSSA Tief im Schosse des Kyffhäusers
bei der Ampel rotem Schein
sitzt der alte Kaiser Friedrich
an dem Tisch aus Marmelstein.
I am returned from my cave to redeem my people.

HANK You hear this fellow in the cellarage?
We're not your people, Emperor. Go and wear your new clothes somewhere else.

DOCTOR Corporal Hokusai Hirosaki.

JAP Lieutenant Hankey, I presume?

HANK Yes, Corporal.

JAP You should have waited.

HANK Waited for what?

JAP You should have killed me later. Or not at all.

HANK Or not at all. But, truly, I never expected to hit you.

JAP It is a pity. I was an artist too.

DOCTOR Mrs Hankey, mother of the accused.

MOTHER My long-lost boy! It seems an age since I've seen you.

HANK Only some thirty-five years.

MOTHER Still I saw your little girl-friend: pretty in her way. She gave me some lovely gin. Have you got some lovely gin?

HANK Certainly not. I promised Dr Butler. And Sarah.

BAILIFF If there's any gin in this cave, I'm afraid I'll have to distrain on it.

MOTHER Well, never mind: I had a couple before I came. But *I've* brought *you* a present. All the way from Venezuela.

HANK What is it, mother?

MOTHER A bar of marzipan.

HANK (*screams*)

DOCTOR A Person —

>   (*Hank stops screaming*)

A Person . . . from Porlock.

HANK Not another!

PERSON Another — yes. But the last one.

HANK Haven't I seen you before somewhere? Of course I have: I painted you.

PERSON In black on black. And not a bad likeness. How do you like my dark zone?

HANK I like it all right but it's taken Mervyn.

PERSON I've taken Mervyn.

HANK Just like a person from Porlock. Always interrupting things.

PERSON But what have I interrupted? I thought I'd arrived on cue. Mervyn cued me first. Then you.

HANK I don't know what you're talking about.

PERSON No? It's the first time, I must admit, I've had an appointment in Skrimshank's. But in many other caves and pots, none of which now you will ever visit —

HANK Why? I'm not too old.

PERSON People have invited me along and I always make a point of being there. In the Bertorelli Chasm, in Wookey Hole, in the Grotte du Nirzou, in the Trou de la Creuse — excuse my accent, it's because I come from Porlock — in the Gouffre de la Pierre-St-Martin, in the Font-Estramar resurgence. And now, for the first time, in Skrimshank's. Your friend Mervyn was a man after my heart.

HANK Was?

PERSON Was.

HANK And me?

PERSON Till just the other day I had my doubts about you. You made too many excuses. Still, in the end you behaved well to Sarah.

HANK I love Sarah.

PERSON And the day before yesterday you swam through after Mervyn.

HANK The day before yesterday? I swam through today.

PERSON What did Mervyn say? There's no time in these places.

HANK Anyhow, I said I'd get through and I have.

PERSON Yes, you have — in more senses than one. The ironic thing is: this will sell your pictures.

HANK (*yawning*) Why? I don't understand.

PERSON You're sleepy, aren't you?

HANK I'm glad it will sell them — if there's anything in them.

PERSON Of course there's something in them.

HANK Thank you. But tell me — before I drop off — why is this going to sell them?

PERSON Because they will say he met a noble — well, a noble person from Porlock.

APPENDIX 1

Author's Introduction to Christopher Columbus:
Some Comments on Radio Drama (*1944*)

(*i*) *Apologia*

After deciding to publish this radio play I was asked to write an introduction
to it and I suppose that, if one is worth doing, so is the other; the book-
buying public is still very ignorant of radio. Radio plays and 'features' (dramatic documentaries), when laid on the printed page, tend to lose even
more than do plays written for the theatre. But *Christopher Columbus* is
something of a special case in that it is unusually long and is written throughout in a more or less stylized form and with comparatively long sequences
(scenes) which therefore make less demands on a reader's imagination. I am
having it published not only because I hope that it will be readable but
because it may interest some members of the more literary public in a
popular art-form which still is an art-form. In the following pages I shall
talk about radio-dramatic writing. My generalizations, like all generalizations, will be only approximately true and will be coloured by personal bias.

In the following pages I do not attempt to do justice to the more topical
species of radio documentary. This species is large and elastic and, at its
best, can compete with the best journalism (or cinema newsreel) and the
best short stories (or topical story-films). This species has enormous possibilities but these are outside the scope of this introduction. I am limiting
my attention to that kind of radio-dramatic writing – historical or imaginative – which might loosely be called 'creative'.

(*ii*) *Requirements of the Medium*

'Creative' works written for broadcasting, while having a vastly larger public
than stage-plays, novels or poetry, get, in the ordinary sense, very much
less publicity. They are heard once and no one has a chance to go back to
them. Only a few periodicals carry radio critiques and these are sometimes
written by persons who have not fully taken in the aims and limitations of
the medium. If you cannot enjoy the spoken word with your eyes shut,
don't try to criticize radio.

Sound-broadcasting gets its effects through sound and sound alone. This
very obvious fact has two somewhat contradictory implications: (1) A good
radio play or feature presupposes a good radio script; (2) such a script is
not necessarily a piece of 'good writing'.

This second point needs amplifying. The good writer who writes only
for the page concerns himself with words alone; the radio writer has to

think of *words in the mouths of actors*.[1] Consequently those subtleties which
the ordinary writer uses in rhythm or phrasing – or thought – will often be
superfluous and sometimes detrimental to the radio writer. An analogy (apart
from the legitimate stage, where, thanks to visual compensations, a playwright can often get away with literary excrescences) can be found in the
writing of lyrics for music; if you write a lyric to be set it is in most cases
unnecessary, if not indeed injurious, to employ to any extent the more
fancy tricks of prosody; your significant variations of rhythm, your internal
rhymes, your off-rhymes and assonances and technical surprises, will get in
the composer's way; it is *his* job to add the significant variations.

This subordination in radio of words to words-as-they-are-spoken has
for the writer both its regrets and its rewards. He may have to lay aside
some of his technical equipment but, provided his piece is well produced,
he can count on his words regaining those literary virtues which literature
itself has lost since it has been divorced from the voice. He can for example
write the same line five times to achieve five different effects. Or he can
write deliberately flat, understate, with the knowledge that this understatement will be heightened as required by the voice. The voice too will help
him to squeeze from a cliché that expressiveness which many clichés still
retain. These possibilities, I feel, should be peculiarly welcome to many
contemporary writers. With a literature so old as ours and a contemporary
diction so vulgarized, precise and emotive writing comes to depend more
and more upon twists – twists of the obvious statement or the hackneyed
image. To do this on the printed page requires constant ingenuity and often
leads to an appearance of being too clever by half. In radio, without sacrific-
ing simplicity or lucidity, you can often leave the twisting to the voice. But
while being thus indebted to the voice for special effects, you must never
attempt effects which voices cannot procure. Your trade is in words-as-they-
are-spoken – and words-as-they-are-heard.

(iii) Requirements of the Audience

The radio writer is not only limited by his medium; he is also limited by
his audience. This audience, which should be reckoned in millions,[2] is under
no obligation to listen to him. The writer therefore must make his work, if
not intelligible, at least interesting to the millions. This in general precludes
an esoteric content or manner, an obviously highbrow approach, or anything
which puts too great a strain on a simple man sitting by his fireside.

This synthetic figure of the Ordinary Listener tends to become a bugbear
to radio writers and producers; it would be very natural to draw the inference
that to hold the attention of this listener a writer has got to 'write down'.
(By writing down I mean pandering – writing by standards which the writer
considers low.) This inference would be false. Radio writing must, in the
majority of cases, be popular; it need not ever be vulgar. The argument for its
vulgarity rests on a misconception of our old friend, the Man-in-the-Street.

I admit that the man-in-the-street cannot be assumed to have much intellectual apparatus and is not as a rule prepared to make great intellectual efforts. That is why he cannot cope with the higher sciences or philosophy. But radio-drama – like the other forms of drama – is not a higher science; it appeals to the emotions rather than to the reason and requires a sensitive more than an educated audience. In making this distinction I do not forget that aesthetic sensibility can be developed by education but I refuse to believe that men and women in the street are as insensitive or as emotionally atrophied as is sometimes assumed by the intelligentsia. The trouble with 'ordinary people' is not that they have innately bad taste but that they can be easily conditioned to admire what is vulgar and emotionally false. Give them a year of the Wurlitzer organ and they will not stomach a symphony orchestra. Write down to them and they will never look up.

If then the radio writer must not write down, how is he to get on terms with this unseen audience which is so easily bored, so attuned to bad art, so unconscious that it is an audience? I would answer that the first thing he must do is to forget about 'literature' and to concentrate upon sound (see Section *viii*). This is not to deny literature, for this is how literature began – the Homeric or Icelandic bard shouting over the clamour of the banquet, the 'tale told in a chimney corner' while tankards clatter and infants squawl and somebody makes up the fire and old men snore and cough. The radio listener listens in a terribly everyday setting; there is no auditorium to beglamour him and predispose him to accept you; if you want him to accept you, you will have to seduce him by sound and sound alone. But seduction is a necessary part of many human relationships and here, as elsewhere, can be achieved without either lies or crudity.

(iv) Radio-Drama and Poetry

All the arts, to varying degrees, involve some kind of a compromise. This being so, how far need the radio dramatist go to meet the public without losing sight of himself and his own standards of value? He obviously cannot aspire to the freedom of lyric poetry written for the page; he must work to the limitations, already described, imposed both by medium and audience. This audience he must regard, if only because of its size and diversity, as a primitive one; to reach it he must move on a more or less primitive plane. But what is primitive is not *ipso facto* crude or false or childish or even outmoded. This plane precludes the higher mathematics and the more erudite *nuances* of symbolist poetry; it does not preclude the basic human emotions or their broader forms of expression. It does not therefore preclude the broader forms of poetry.

For man, we should always remember, is born poetic. Hence the predominance of nursery rhymes in the nursery and of poetry in all early literatures. Poetry, in this one sense at least, is more primitive than prose; it was easier on the ear and less strain upon the mind. That is why radio drama – not because the medium is new but because of its primitive audience – might reasonably be expected to demand a poet's approach. And poets on the whole do seem more at home on the air than novelists, say, or essayists.

But the modern public, we shall be told, is not at home to poetry. This I do not believe. The man-in-the-street who admires Walt Disney, is not a scientific 'realist'; he is ready to welcome certain forms of design, rhythm, and fantasy. He may dislike *the idea of poetry* but that is because he has been conditioned to think of poetry as something too sissy, infantile, difficult or irrelevant. Thus the mere sight of verse on the page (like a menu printed in French) is enough to frighten him off. Verse, however, when coming out of his radio set, will not strike him – at least not too aggressively – as *verse*; instead of prejudging it as a piece of highbrow trickery he will, like the audience of the primitive bards, listen to the words, or rather to the sounds, as they come and will like them or not according to their emotional impact. Since the defence mechanism of his prejudices is suspended, this impact may often be surprisingly weighty.

When I spoke above of a 'poet's approach' I did not mean this narrowly in the sense of versification (see the next section and Section *vii*) but it is worth stressing the point that it is fairly easy to get away with verse on the air. Write a piece of dialogue or narration in an obviously rhythmical but not too strait-laced verse-form and the radio audience will accept it, thinking of it probably as just a powerful bit of language. The academic listener on the other hand – not that academics often listen – will find himself in an unusually normal position; not having a printed page to ponder and scan, he will be unable to decide by his eye that the poet's words have no rhythm and will have to allow his ear to admit what rhythms emerge.

(v) *Construction in Radio Drama*

If radio drama is poetic, its poetry – like poetry in general – must consist of a great deal more than rhythmical patterns of words; it presupposes a wider and deeper pattern beginning with a careful and intuitive selection of material and culminating in a large architectonic. The first virtue of a radio script is construction. A novel can legitimately be rambling and discursive, a narrative poem can be padded with decoration, a short story can be a chunk of impressions, Belles Lettres can be merely 'belles', but a radio play or feature must have a dramatic unity; in the jargon of the trade, it must have the proper 'builds' and an 'overall' shape.

It is as a builder in this sense that the radio dramatist, however prosaic or colloquial or dry his dialogue, is by his nature nearer to the poet than to the journalist.[3] This is true of 'features' as well as of plays. The radio feature is a dramatized presentation of actuality but its author should be much more than a *rapporteur* or a cameraman; he must select his actuality material with great discrimination and then keep control of it so that it subserves a single dramatic effect.

In achieving a dramatic unity the radio writer must, as a rule, be more economical than the playwright proper. For (1) he normally has a much narrower time-limit, usually from thirty to sixty minutes; (2) his speakers being invisible, he has to take many more pains to 'plant' his situations; (3) his audience having no visual aids to imagination or memory, he must be much more careful not to confuse them with sideshows or bore them with dull patches or strain their memory with references back — if there was just one key line you can never be sure that they caught it. Characters and situations must be clearly established and the line of development be strong and simple.

Yet, when you look at the theatre, you find you have your compensations. Provided you make clear your transitions from scene to scene, you can take many more liberties with time and place; you are free of the dead hand of the Three Act tradition. You can jump from India to the Arctic and from 1066 to 1943. You can make a point with a scene consisting of three lines and no one need fiddle with a curtain or black out the lights. And you can, with less fuss and more credibility than on the stage (and perhaps than on the screen), introduce — if you want to — allegorical speakers or choruses. You can again, with the help of music and recorded effects (but see Section *viii*), present all sorts of scenes — especially scenes of action — that the theatre can rarely attempt. You can finally (though this applies mostly to features) get an effect, if you want to, of up-to-the-minute actuality, a set-piece as vivid as a running commentary. With all this you must remember that you cannot compete in trappings or tricks with either the cinema or the theatre; your medium being sound alone, you must stand or fall by the use you make of words.

(vi) Radio Craftsmanship

If the overall planning of a radio drama needs a certain creative artistry, its detailed working-out needs craftsmanship. Radio is not a good channel for souls in flux, for the kind of inspiration that sings and does not count the cost. A radio writer must write to an exact scale, with every link made firm and no loose ends; he must not only, as I said, woo his audience cunningly; he must work to hold their interest; two or three minutes of even legitimate boredom may bring their hands to the knob that switches him off.

Another reason for craftsmanship is the fact that many radio scripts are, inevitably, commissioned work, and that the persons who commission such work must inevitably judge it by more or less professional standards. This is not to deny that it is the duty of any broadcasting institution to invite *spontaneous* contributions from 'outside writers'. It is merely to recognize the obvious fact that an organization working on such a scale cannot depend entirely on spontaneity and must therefore partly rely upon such writers as are prepared to practise radio-writing as a *craft*. That this fact, though repugnant to some artists, is not incompatible with art, is proved by those many periods in history where the basis of the arts has been an accepted triangle – patron, professional artist, and public. I do not suggest that this triangle is to be found at its best in the world of radio today; there are too many factors – commercial or bureaucratic – that confuse, hamper, and vulgarize. One virtue, however, of radio's contemporary triangle is that it insists on a function of words which salon-writers are perhaps too apt to forget; this function is communication. The distinction of 'communication' from 'self-expression' is misleading. If compelled to communicate with a fair-sized public, a writer may sometimes find himself expressing bits of himself that he had lost.

To prevent misunderstanding, I should add that I do not hold that the writer's[4] chief job is to write for a majority public – let alone pander to it. There are many themes which can only be understood by a minority; there are certain treatments which only a minority will appreciate. To assert, as some do, that all art should have mass-appeal is like asserting that all mathematics should be 'for the million'. On the other hand, there *are* themes and treatments which the masses and the writer can enjoy in common. These are for the most part the same themes and treatments that have been ousted from the literary salon and abandoned to the films and the newspapers. A writer in reclaiming them is at the same time giving himself a tonic (a dose of earth and ozone) and helping to correct the public's taste. Such a reclamation is possible in radio which in spite of its many temptations to vulgarity, is at least more free from those temptations than either the press or the cinema.

(vii) The Importance of 'Story'

What are these themes and treatments? The themes consist, roughly speaking, of anything that in a newspaper sense can be called a 'story' – the Trojan War, the Hound of the Baskervilles, the story of a penny, Elsie's week-end. The treatment, roughly speaking, will be broad, lucid and dramatic – dramatic in the Aristotelian sense that the central event, or theme, will be central and everything else, including characters, subordinate.[5] As compared with most contemporary literature, the objective elements will preponderate over the subjective, statement over allusion, synthesis over analysis. We are at a far remove not only from Proust or Joyce but also from Shaw's conversation plays and the middlebrow 'psychological' novel.

Writers of my generation, brought up on chunks of life and the stream of consciousness, must often have envied the old-fashioned story-teller – or the modern writer of detective fiction – this element of plot, of simple progression from event to event. But stories in themselves – *contes*, *Märchen*, *muthoi*, or what-have-you – being essentially primitive, had become as suspect to many modern writers as the literary element in painting had to many modern painters. This was partly because his background tends to make the modern writer an introvert and partly because at this stage of our literature there already was a glut of books which relied chiefly on story. Now however our background is changing and forcing us again to take an interest in what people *do*. And, if we want to present what they do, we can still avoid the staleness of the printed word by resorting to other media; and one of these is radio. I for one, having always preferred the Icelandic sagas to the modern novel, am only too pleased to discover that a medium exists where a saga treatment is still feasible.

An early and excellent example of a popular story treated broadly, rapidly and vividly with all the resources of radio was *The March of the '45* by D. G. Bridson (first transmitted by the BBC in 1936). This programme followed Prince Charles Edward from his landing in the Hebrides to his final defeat at Culloden, peaking the action with bagpipes and Jacobite songs and covering the transitions with a quick-fire verse commentary skilfully varied in form to match the changes of mood. This achieved a total effect unattainable on the stage and less simply attainable on the screen. (Most film directors have yet to learn not to sow with the whole sack; the talking film still suffers from trying to do too much at once.)

Regular listeners to British radio will have noticed, at least in these recent war-years, a predominance of stories of the hot news variety. This was inevitable and it must be admitted that radio is an adequate medium for topical *rapportage* and realistic impressionism. But my own opinion is that the radio play (if not the radio feature) can only reach its heights when the subject is slightly larger, or at least simpler, than life and the treatment is to some extent stylized – when, we might say, it is competing with the Soviet art-cinema rather than with Hollywood or the standardized news-reel. I found this borne out in practice when I was asked to make a radio adaptation of Eisenstein's film *Alexander Nevsky*. This film, which disappointed some English intellectuals because of its lack of subtlety in characterization, its complete innocence of psychological conflict, its primitive pattern of Black versus White, was for those very reasons easily transposed into a radio form, Prokofiev's incidental music which had been an integral part of the film helping equally in its turn to integrate the theme on the air.

(viii) Radio Production

This mention of music brings me back to my main thesis that, while in radio drama words are of the utmost importance, the radio dramatist must think in terms of sound rather than of words alone. He must therefore be studio-conscious, remembering what results can and cannot be obtained from a limited number of microphones, a control panel and a gramophone turntable. There are some veterans of broadcasting who go so far as to say that no radio script can be more than a very rough notation for the producer, a hunk of raw material which can only take on shape in transmission. This is an overstatement – a really good script should survive a bad production –

but it is undeniable that to write a really good script you have to remember not only the microphone which is going to accept it but the loud-speaker, or rather the million loud-speakers, which are going to deliver it.

A surprising number of persons appear to be completely ignorant of *how* a radio 'show' gets on to the air: it is even sometimes assumed that a radio play or feature goes out without any rehearsal. For this reason I do not think it superfluous to add here a few remarks on production. If we leave aside the more technical but minor points of acoustic perspectives, of balance, fading, etc., there are three ingredients, apart from the words themselves, which are of primary importance — voices, effects, and music.

(ix) *The Voices*

The voices of radio actors come in for a lot of criticism, much of it justifiable but some of it unjust. It must be remembered, in comparison with the theatre, that the radio actor, because he is not seen, is at a double disadvantage; he has to rely solely on his voice both to establish himself as a genuine character and to distinguish himself from the rest of the cast. On the whole, actors on the air probably use a less phoney delivery than actors on the stage, but the grease-paint voice will stick out all the more when there is no real grease-paint to look at and when the listener, instead of being self-consciously seated on plush and transported out of reality by coloured lights, is listening to dramatized speech in the too-too real context of his home. As for the differentiation of characters, you can put twenty-one Oxford undergraduates on the stage, short and long, blond and black, all drawling away in the 'Oxford manner', but you cannot do that on the air without causing hopeless confusion.

In both these respects the writer can make things much easier for his cast. He must 'envisage' what kinds of voices will be heard together on the air and he must apportion the lines in such a way as to help any necessary contrast. Another very important point: remembering that much of the colour of radio is achieved by variations of tempo, he must avoid writing, as it were, by the metronome; taking a bird's-eye view of the needed contours of his programme he must undulate his scenes and the dialogue itself accordingly.

(x) *The 'Effects'*

'Effects', in the sense of naturalistic noises contributing atmosphere or establishing a fact, are of two kinds — records on a gramophone or spot effects in the studio. The trouble is that they often sound what they are — that is, a put-up job. They are, however, sometimes necessary for reasons of vividness and economy. A cow mooing will call up a farmyard more quickly and more vividly than a paragraph of word-painting; all you need is a decent record of a cow. If there is only a bad recording available, it is better to word-paint or else to do a cow on the trombone. In my own opinion musical effects often can — and should — be substituted for naturalistic ones, though this is of course less feasible when a programme purports to be a direct transcript of actuality.

Those effects which one would most welcome are also too often those which least ring true. This is so with all noises that suggest enormous power and express this power by volume; on the air their volume disappears. A writer therefore should not, after building up to a battle, say, or a thunderstorm, rely upon mere effects to point the climax; *if* he must use these effects, he should frame them very carefully with words. And, as regards recorded effects (the notorious example is the BBC seagull), he must remember that, as with some repertory actors, they may become much too familiar to the listening public and therefore defeat their own end and make the whole scene unreal. In general, a radio writer should only ask for effects when they are (*a*) practicable, (*b*) an asset to his story. They must not be over-used nor indulged in for their own sake.

(*xi*) *The Music*

The use of music in radio features and plays has always been, and remains, a subject of controversy. Like naturalistic effects, it has too often been inserted from the mere love of variation or the mere fear of boring the audience with long stretches of speech; there is no evidence, however, that the public is really so allergic to the naked word. What music can very often do is to compensate for the lack of the visual element, to establish an emotional atmosphere or to register a change of mood more vividly, and more quickly, than words alone. In radio it is used in two ways — (1) by itself, before, between or after the spoken passages, (2) as an atmospheric background to speech. In either case it should serve a functional purpose.

Music by itself is chiefly useful either as a link or to make an emotional peak. In a form which tends to involve many short sequences and therefore many transitions in space and time, an appropriate musical link will smooth over the transition and will often, in some cases, convey information less creakingly or cumbrously than words will; the impersonal Narrator who says 'And now we take you to August 1914' is a bore; it is preferable to play *Tipperary* (reinforced, if you like, with marching feet). Information can of course be given in another way by specially written music of the descriptive kind sometimes used on the films — music, that, like onomatopoeic language, achieves a *similitude* in sound to the object described.

Radio's other use of music is as background to speech. This is often very messy. The ear finds it difficult to follow two things at once. In general I would say that background music should not be used for realistic sequences (with the exception of scenes where the music is an important part of the *real* background, e.g. lovers in a dance-hall) but should be reserved for stylized pieces of writing as when a narrator is speaking in verse or a character thinking aloud (like a factory worker soliloquizing to the rhythm of a machine or a traveller to the rhythm of a train).

A small minority of radio-dramatic programmes, of which *Christopher Columbus* is one, were conceived from the start as joint literary and musical works. In such cases the above remarks still apply. The music, though much more conspicuous, must still be strictly functional, subordinated to the dramatic purpose of the whole; the music must not attempt to usurp the primary role and turn the whole thing into a concert.

(*xii*) *Conclusion*

Most of the above generalizations are elementary, although many radio-dramatic works, including my own, often fail to conform to them. I have been expressing what I consider the norms of this kind of writing, but I should now add the warning that here, as in any other medium, it is fatal to let yourself be victimized by 'the rules'. G. K. Chesterton said that, if a thing is worth doing at all, it is worth doing badly. A similar paradox is true of any artistic medium: if its rules are worth keeping, they are also — on occasion — worth breaking. I trust therefore that this Introduction will not be regarded as an *ex cathedra* lecture. In any art-form a practitioner must be an empiricist. Any generalizations which he makes should be proved or refuted in practice. The medium is there for anyone who wants to degeneralize.

I would here make acknowledgement to Mr Dallas Bower who suggested the programme in the first place and later produced it, and to Mr William Walton whose music supplied a third dimension that this printed text must lack.

L.M.

Addendum (to p. 397): I had overlooked a case where radio scores most heavily, i.e. in *soliloquy*. Try any of Shakespeare's self-communings close to the microphone.

APPENDIX 2

Author's General Introduction to The Dark Tower and Other Radio Scripts (*1947*)

The interest shown in such few radio scripts as have been published (the most notable recent example being *The Rescue* by my friend Mr Edward Sackville-West) has encouraged me to publish some more of my own. I do this not only because like all radio writers I feel frustrated each time a script has been broadcast but in the hope that a selection of dissimilar pieces may throw some light on the medium. I have chosen *The Dark Tower* because I think it is the best radio script I have written; the others are included as fairly clear-cut examples — I would certainly not say models — of different types of programme. All of them seem to me worth reading.

Having in my Introduction to *Christopher Columbus* essayed a general exposition of radio-dramatic writing, I will not labour again those main points which I still consider valid, e.g. that 'the first virtue of a radio script is construction'. But I would like in some respects to correct myself. That the radio writer 'must move on a more or less primitive plane' is, I think now, an overstatement or at least misleadingly expressed. What the radio writer must do, if he hopes to win the freedom of the air, is to appeal *on one plane* — whatever he may be doing on the others — to the more primitive listener and to the more primitive elements in anyone; i.e. he must give them (what Shakespeare gave them) entertainment.[1]

In the same Introduction I wrote: 'As compared with most contemporary literature, the objective elements will preponderate over the subjective, statement over allusion, synthesis over analysis.' This again I want to qualify; the comparison with contemporary *literature* may have misled me. The 'psychological' novel, concerned chiefly with 'subjective' experiences, deals largely in *oratio obliqua*; even that kind of *oratio recta* used to represent 'the stream of consciousness' is usually not much more than a shorthand for the page. But when no character can be presented except through spoken words, whether in dialogue or soliloquy, that very *spoken-ness* makes this distinction between subjective and objective futile. A character in a radio play, as in a stage play, may say things that actually he never would or could say — the author may be making him utter what is only known to his unconscious — but once he has said them, there they are! As objective as Ben Jonson's Humours are objective. To take an extreme example, Virginia Woolf's novel *The Waves* is often quoted as subjective writing *par excellence*; the characters, thinking in the first person, say things they never could have formulated, being even as small children endowed with the brilliant introspection and the sad philosophy of their creator. I am confident that this method, though probably not this application of it, would be feasible on the air. Listeners might not accept Virginia Woolf's long-windedness, her preciousness, the sameness of her characters, the lack of a 'story' — but that in no way proves them 'allergic' to subjectivity. Once your characters speak speakable lines — once, to use a horrible piece of jargon, the subjective is objectified — you can get away with anything *so long as you entertain*.

Similarly, the distinctions made in my quotation between statement and allusion and between synthesis and analysis are perhaps equally worthless. It would have been safer to say that in radio dialogue we need a number of things which *sound like* statements — but in spoken dialogue that goes without saying; no two people can keep up a conversation which is one *hundred* per cent surrealist. As for allusion, not only is it difficult in any context to make any statement which is not also an allusion, i.e. suggestive of something beyond its own definitive meaning, but in all *dramatic* writing a word, let alone a phrase, pulls more than its dictionary weight; the pun is only the crudest example of a procedure familiar to, though not of course formulated by, everyone. In characterization equally, Mr X, who may appear to be talking at random and naturalistically, can really be talking succinctly and also symbolically, revealing himself — or whatever else is meant to be revealed — by a process of implicit logic. 'Implicit' is here, as in other creative writing, a keyword. Even in the psychological novel, if it is a good one, the psychology is implicit; for explicit psychology we go to the textbooks. This is all I meant in subordinating analysis to synthesis — but this too could have gone without saying or at least I ought so to have expressed it as not to preclude 'psychological' characterization from the sphere of radio drama.

But criticism comes after the event; it is no good talking about radio until you have experienced it. It may therefore be instructive if, dropping generalities, I make a short confession of my own experiences as listener, script-writer, and producer. Before I joined the BBC I was, like most of the intelligentsia, prejudiced not only against that institution but against broadcasting in general; I rarely listened to anything except concerts and running commentaries on sports events. These latter, which gave me a pleasure distinct from that which lies in *seeing* a game or race, should have provided a hint of radio's possibilities; my prejudice, however, prevented me from exploring the possible pleasures in wireless plays and features. Since then I have listened to many examples of both and must confess that often they give me no pleasure at all — but this proves nothing; we have all met the same disappointment with books, plays, and films. What does prove a point to me is that *some* plays and features have excited, amused, moved me. So the wireless *can* be worth listening to. But next: is it worth writing for?

Many writers are deterred from radio drama by fear of the middlemen and by dislike of actors. They expect their work to be doctored from the start and travestied in the presentation (which has of course sometimes happened — as it has happened both on the stage and page). But while no production will ever seem perfect to the author, the questions are whether one can gamble on a reasonably good production and whether such a production is better than none. Your answers depend on whether you really have an itch for drama; if you have, you must want sooner or later to write dialogue to be spoken somewhere — and it is no more likely to be spoken badly on the air than anywhere else (the wireless lacks the body of the stage — but also some of its impurities). If *you* provide a good script, the odds are that it will gain by being broadcast; in fact, if it loses, while it may be the fault of the production, the more likely inference is that your script was not radiogenic (a handy word, though jargon). The predominance of adapted stage-plays in BBC programmes has probably discouraged a number of writers, for many of these plays do lose on the air (at least as compared with the stage); few of them are radiogenic. Transposition from one medium to another is usually unfair to both. Which is why we must remember that the script-writer is a peculiar species.

The all-important difference between visual and non-visual drama, while discouraging some, may encourage others towards radio, for here and here alone can one listen to calculated speech divorced from all visual supports or interferences — even from a printed page. It would be a great pity if television were ever completely to supersede sound broadcasting as the talkies superseded the silent films. That cinema revolution was inevitable but through it we lost the unique pleasure of watching a story told visually, dispensing with people's voices. But sound alone is for most people more potent, more pregnant, more subtle, than pictures alone and for that reason — regardless of the material pros and cons of television — I hope that sound broadcasting will survive, dispensing with people's faces. As with many other media its narrow limits are also its virtue, while within those limits it can give us something unobtainable from print (though print of course will always retain its proper autonomy). When I first heard a piece, which I had written for broadcasting, broadcast, I was irritated by details of presentation but excited and delighted by the total effect (there was more to my script, I felt, than I myself had realized). The mere fact that one's words issue from other people's mouths, while gratifying no doubt to an author's vanity, is also a welcome release from his involuntary egotism. Most novelists and poets, I think, envy the playwright that specious present and that feeling of *sharedness* which are given to a play by every fresh production, just as they envy the painter as composer-executant the excitement of his manual craftsmanship and the immediate impact of his completed work (which also can be shared by several people at once). When you have written for the page, you do not see your readers reading you; which is just as well as you could never tell if in their heads they were 'hearing' you properly. But in broadcasting you can, given the right speakers, force your listeners at least to hear the words as they should. The point is that here we have a

means by which written lines can emulate the impact of a stage or of a
painting and give the writer that excitement of a sensuous experience simultaneously shared with many which is one of the joys of life. This pleasure in
a thing-being-performed-and-shared, while obtainable in all sports and some
of the arts, is sadly lacking in the world of literature today. It is a pleasure I
have often received, though mixed at times with mortification, when hearing
my own scripts broadcast. It is succeeded, as I said before, by a feeling of frustration – because it is 'over'; but in that it is not of course unusual.

I have stressed this fact of pleasure because some people assume that
writing for the wireless must be hackwork. It often is – for the salaried
script-writer because he must turn his hand to many things, some of them
dull, for the occasional writer (less forgivably) when he deals with an uncon-
genial subject for money or writes badly because he is merely writing for
money. But it often is not. Broadcasting is plastic; while it can ape the Press,
it can also emulate the arts. Yes, people will say, that is theoretically true
but in practice you will never get art – or anything like it – out of a large
public institution, encumbered with administrators, which by its nature must
play for safety and to the gallery. This is not the place to dispute this at
length but I would maintain that in this country such an institution cannot
be really authoritarian; with ingenuity and a little luck a creative person can
persuade (or fool) at least some of the administrators some of the time.[2]
And, thinking of the vexed question of commercial broadcasting, I would
add that many of the more original programmes by my friends and myself
(this book shows examples in *The Dark Tower* and the 'March Hare' scripts)
would have been no more acceptable to sponsored radio than to the biggest
and vulgarest profit-making film company. For its acceptance of such experi-
ments I am very grateful to the BBC.

In this age of irreconcilable idioms I have often heard writers hankering
for some sort of group life, a desire doomed to disappointment; the modern
writer – at any rate the modern poet – is *ipso facto* a spiritual isolationist
who will lose far more than he will gain by trying to pool his mentality with
those of his colleagues. Thus of the several dozen poets whom I know there
are very few with whom I would wish to discuss poetry and only, I think,
one from whom I would often accept criticism. This solitude (which inciden-
tally has nothing to do with the Ivory Tower; there are Group Towers too,
remember) is *in our time* salutary – but here again we cannot but envy
playwrights, actors or musical executants. And here again I for one have
found this missing group experience, in a valid form, in radio. Radio writers
and producers *can* talk shop together because their shop is not, as with poets,
a complex of spiritual intimacies but a matter of craftsmanship. Though the
poet of course is also – or should be – a craftsman, the lyrical poet's technique is – or should be – closely wedded to his unique personality and there
is no more point in defending your own personality than in impugning your
friend's. But radio craftsmanship, like stage craftsmanship, is something

much less private; we are fully entitled to discuss whether dialogue rings true, whether the dramatic climax is dramatic, how well the whole thing works. This is refreshing for a writer.

The popular assumption that all radio professionals resemble civil servants (resting on that other assumption that civil servants are automata) is flatly untrue. The department to which, at the date of writing, I belong in the BBC, would compare very well for intelligence with almost any contemporary salon of literati; my radio colleagues would be found on the whole quicker-witted, more versatile, less egocentric, less conventional, more humane. But, apart from these relishes to discussion, the reason why we can work together enjoyably and effectively is that in every case our work must go through the same mill, i.e. into a microphone and out at the other end through a wireless set. This very simple physical fact is such a bond of union as is rare among creative writers, playwrights again excepted. For we share the excitements and anxieties of *the performance*. This is especially so if we are our own executants, i.e. writer-producers. There are obvious drawbacks to this combination of functions – Mr A as writer may see so clearly what he means that Mr A as producer will fail to notice when the meaning is not coming over – but it does put a writer more closely in touch with his work-in-performance than he can be anywhere else unless he is Mr Noel Coward. We know what happens to a film script when the multitude of 'experts' gets hold of it. On the stage there is no such multitude but there still is considerable interference and few writers have the chance, the time, the knowledge, or the capacity, to become stage-producers. But radio production being comparatively simple, not a few writers can learn to handle it – at any rate well enough to gain more than they lose (this especially applies to 'experimental' scripts where the pioneer, though an amateur, has an advantage over the professional geographer).

The script itself, after all, is only half the battle and the writer who merely sends in a script and does not go near the studios is working largely in the dark; whereas a writer who produces his own scripts will cut his coat according to his cloth. Since I have been producing my own programmes, I find that I both avail myself of facilities which I previously overlooked and avoid awkwardnesses which I previously imposed on my producer. Thus an earlier version of *Sunbeams in his Hat*, entitled *Dr Chekhov*, was so written as to be almost unproduceable in places[3] at least without the use of multiple studios, as I typically had not envisaged the studio set-up. When I came to rewrite it for my own production I eliminated these difficulties and in so doing found I had made the script not only more manageable but more compact, more lucid, more convincing. Similarly, as regards both music and actors, the writer-producer has the advantage of being able to decide at an early stage who is going to do what. Thus, when he has a composer to write special music, he can not only get this music to fit the script but adjust his script on occasion to fit the music. He also has the say in casting, which is especially important in broadcasting both because of the shortness of rehearsals and because of the microphone's transparency to anything ham or unintelligent. In writing my more recent scripts I have always had an eye on the kinds of actor available and so avoided demanding the impossible and, when I could, the improbable; sometimes I have, from its conception, written a part for a particular actor, e.g. the Soldier in *The Nosebag* for Roy Emerton and the March Hare for Esmé Percy.

The preceding paragraph was intended to amplify my point about work-in-performance. While it is obviously not normally feasible for 'outside writers' to produce their own work, it is desirable, if not necessary, that they should be studio-minded; then they can explain to their producer what they want done without being embarrassing or nonsensical. I would like finally, since the chief object of this introduction was to disprove the assumption that broadcasting is 'inhuman', to inform my readers that every transmission of a play or feature, however unimportant the programme, should have — and usually has — the feeling of a First Night; it is something *being made* by a team of people.

For each of the scripts in this book I have written a separate introduction; but they all have this in common that, whatever my sins in either respect, I enjoyed both writing and producing them. The programme on Chekhov was suggested to me by my employers but the others I proposed myself. This gives me the opportunity of expressing my gratitude to the head of my department, Mr Laurence Gilliam, who is as willing to accept such spontaneous suggestions as he is to allow an elastic treatment of those other programmes which 'have to be done'.[4]

Notes

Christopher Columbus

1. Notes in the BBC Radio Archive, London.
2. See notes 3–18 below for author's notes.
3. MacNeice's note: 'Somewhere between radio pageant and pageant proper comes the new form *Son et Lumière* where the history, say, of a group of buildings is presented by recorded sound – voices, music and effects – combined not with dressed up actors but with permutations of lighting effects. This is naturally limited to special places and purposes.'
4. MacNeice's note: 'The radio convention of the Narrator seems to me often abused when used, as it is commonly used, merely to convey information; information can usually be conveyed through the mouths of the characters proper; the chief virtue of a Narrator is that like a Greek chorus, he can shake himself free of realism and speak – if needed, in an unrealistic manner – to heighten an emotion or point a moral or suggest a historical perspective.'
5. MacNeice's note: '*The King of Portugal* at the time was John II. The Portuguese were then the world's champion explorers but Columbus's proposals were apparently too vague for their liking. He wrote many years later that the Lord shut the King's eyes and ears and all his senses to the truth.'
6. MacNeice's note: '*Antonio de Marchena* was not, I believe, present at La Rabida when Columbus arrived there. However, I required his presence.'
7. MacNeice's note: '*That the world is a sphere* was, contrary to popular tradition since, generally admitted at this date by educated persons. Globes were already in use but the Tripartite World was commonly thought of as on *top* of the globe. It was therefore the fear of getting *under* the world that deterred would-be circumnavigators.'
8. MacNeice's note: '*The Marquesa's song* I wrote as a deliberate pastiche of fifteenth-century Spanish Romance poetry.'
9. MacNeice's note: '*The Royal Commission* did exist and did reject Columbus's proposals but there seems to be some doubt as to where it met and how often and under whose presidency. I have ignored these doubts. I have also presented Talavera and the Commission more as Columbus saw them than as they really were.'
10. MacNeice's note: '*Beatriz Enríquez* gave offence to some radio critics who, if they did not assume that I had invented her, tended to complain that this *affaire* was inconsistent with Columbus's character. She was in fact the mother of Columbus's son, Fernando Colón (though I have

post-dated his birth), but little more is known of her. I introduced her not to modify but to emphasize her lover's single-mindedness.'

11. MacNeice's note: '*Luís de Santangel*, apart from making a loan to Isabella, seems largely to have been responsible for her consenting to Columbus's expedition. In a more psychological treatment of this story he should feature quite largely, as should Ferdinand.'

12. MacNeice's note: '*The signing-on of jailbirds* is a stock part of the Columbus legend and may be mainly, or merely, legend. I retained it for its wider truth — that most great projects are achieved through the use of unlikely instruments.'

13. MacNeice's note: '*Martín Pinzón* is another figure whom I have not given his historical due. In any play which concentrates on the First Voyage itself he might well be the deuteragonist.'

14. MacNeice's note: '*The double refrain* of this shanty is taken from a poem by Lorca and means: 'Because I am not (any longer) I and my house is not my house.'

15. MacNeice's note: '*This quotation* from Seneca's *Medea* was translated by Columbus himself in his *Book of Prophecies* (written in AD 1501).'

16. MacNeice's note: '*The sighting of land* is another disputed point. The tradition is that, while Pedro Gutiérrez was the man who established the light, one Rodrigo de Triana (or Juan Rodriguez Bermejo) was the first to see the land itself. In any case Columbus himself pocketed the promised reward.'

17. MacNeice's note: '*The identity of this island* is still uncertain and it is not agreed by all that Columbus named it San Salvador.'

18. MacNeice's note: '*A new world* is a phrase that Columbus would probably not have used. But what else was it?'

He Had a Date

1. Quotations from the title card index, BBC Radio Archive, London.
2. *Radio Times* 102: 1322 (11 Feb. 1949), 7.

The Dark Tower

1. MacNeice's note: '*Roland as a boy* was, in the broadcast, brilliantly doubled by Cyril Cusack.'

2. MacNeice's note: '*The tolling bell*, instead of being done by percussion alone, was reinforced and made ultra-suggestive by strings. Apart from percussion and one trumpet (reserved for the Challenge Call) Benjamin Britten confined himself in this programme to an orchestra of twenty-six strings from which he got the most varied and astonishing effects.'

3. MacNeice's note: '*The Child of Stone* puzzled many listeners. The Mother in bearing so many children only to send them to their death, can be thought of as thereby bearing a series of deaths. So her logical

last child is stone – her own death. This motif has an echo in the stone in the ring.'

4. MacNeice's note: '*The Verbal Transition* ['Go quickly' repeated] from one scene to another is controlled from the panel and need not seem either abrupt or confusing. It only makes a change from the musical transition but has certain positive advantages; e.g. as here, irony.'

5. MacNeice's note: '*The Soak* I should have called Solipsist if that word were known to the public. His alcoholism is an effect rather than a cause. Robert Farquharson wonderfully achieved the right leer in the voice and the dream-like sinister undertones.'

6. MacNeice's notes: ' "*I'm dreaming you*" is a famous stumper for reason. Compare *Alice Through the Looking Glass*, the episode of Tweedledee and the Red King:

> " 'And if he left off dreaming about you, where do you suppose you'd be?'
> 'Where I am now, of course,' said Alice.
> 'Not you!' Tweedledee retorted contemptuously. 'You'd be nowhere. Why, you're only a sort of thing in his dream!' " '

7. MacNeice's note: '*The Stentorian Voice* butting in here changes the scene with the speed of a dream. Radio, like dreams, having no set stage, can disregard spatial conventions.'

8. MacNeice's note: ' "*The sea today*": this covers a number of days. The developing false idyll of Roland and Neaera is intercut with the voices of people playing tombola – always the same again. The idyll also is merely killing time.'

9. MacNeice's note: '*The Mirage Sequence* needed a great deal of rehearsal but the stunt came off.'

10. MacNeice's note (1947): '*The Final Decision* may, I think, be too abrupt for a listener – though in life such a complex psychological conflict can, of course, resolve itself abruptly.' [Editorial note: MacNeice expanded the passages of the Final Decision in his versions of 1950 and 1956.]

11. MacNeice's note: '*The Last Scene* is naturally the nearest to Browning. Compare:

> Not see? because of night perhaps? – why day
>   Came back again for that! before it left,
>   The dying sunset kindled through a cleft:
> The hills, like giants at a hunting, lay,
> Chin upon hand, to see the game at bay, –
>   "Now stab and end the creature – to the heft!"
>
> Not hear? when noise was everywhere! it tolled
>   Increasing like a bell. Names in my ears
>   Of all the lost adventurers my peers . . .'.

Prisoner's Progress

1. *Radio Times* 126: 1626 (7 Jan. 1955), 5.
2. In World War II René Cutforth (1902–84) served with the Sherwood Foresters in Abyssinia and Libya, was captured in the Western Desert and spent 1942–5 in prisoner-of-war camps in Italy and Germany. After working for the BBC news, he was sent as war correspondent to Korea: his reports home made him 'famous' (see his *Korean Reporter*, 1952). Later he went freelance – Obit., *The Times*, No. 61795, 2 April 1984, 14. – The title of his autobiography *Order to View* (1969) was borrowed from MacNeice's poem of that title, March 1940 (*Collected Poems*, 1979, 169–70).

They Met on Good Friday

1. Note on the title index card, BBC Radio Archive, London.
2. *Radio Times* 145: 1882 (4 Dec. 1959), 6.
3. Sir Thomas (D.) Kendrick, *A History of the Vikings* (1930), 297.

The Mad Islands

1. Note, in *Radio Times* 154: 2003 (29 Mar. 1962), 39.

Persons from Porlock

1. Note in *Persons from Porlock and Other Plays for Radio*, introd. W. H. Auden (1969), 108: 'It was Louis MacNeice's last production. When he went into the studio, after an expedition to the Yorkshire moors to record potholing effects, the illness which was to cause his death was already on him, and he died on 3 September [1963].'
2. *Radio Times* 160: 2076 (22 Aug. 1963), 44.

Appendix I

1. MacNeice's note: 'The term "actors" is to be taken to include persons from real life enacting themselves.'
2. MacNeice's note: 'While I am in favour of occasional special programmes for small minority audiences, radio as an institution is, like the cinema, obliged on the whole to envisage a regular public large enough to keep the radio business going.'
3. MacNeice's note: 'The Greek derivation of "poet", though hackneyed, is still worth remembering.'
4. MacNeice's note: 'I am speaking here of the writer in general.'
5. MacNeice's note: 'Compare the remarks of W. B. Yeats on Tragedy.'

Appendix II

1. MacNeice's note: 'The reception of *The Dark Tower* supports this. Many listeners said that they enjoyed it, found it "beautiful", "exciting", etc. — but had "no idea what it was about". In fact they were caught by the "story" but I flatter myself that, in passing, the story "slipped over" some meaning on them.'

2. MacNeice's note: 'I am not suggesting that, as things are, all our administrators need persuading or fooling.'

3. MacNeice's note: 'For which I now apologize to Mr Stephen Potter — who in producing it saved the situation.'

4. MacNeice's note: 'The foregoing Introduction was written before the BBC "Third Programme" came into being. This new programme — for the first time, I believe, in radio history — assumes that its audience is going to *work* at its listening. So there is less question than ever of playing "for safety and to the gallery".'

Select Bibliography

BOWER, DALLAS, 'MacNeice: Sound And Vision', in T. Brown and A. Reid (eds.), *Time Was Away: The World of Louis MacNeice* (Dublin, 1974).

COULTON, BARBARA, *Louis MacNeice in the BBC* (London, 1980).

—— ' "An Air-Borne Bard" ', in *The Honest Ulsterman* 73 (Sept. 1983).

HOLME, CHRISTOPHER, 'The Radio Drama of Louis MacNeice', in J. Drakakis (ed.), *British Radio Drama* (Cambridge, 1981).

LEWIS, PETER, 'Radio drama and English Literature', in P. Lewis (ed.), *Radio Drama* (London, 1981).

MAHON, DEREK, 'MacNeice, The War And The BBC', in J. Genet and W. Hellegouarc'h (eds.), *Studies On Louis MacNeice* (Caen, 1988).

MCDONALD, PETER, *Louis MacNeice: The Poet In His Contexts* (Oxford, 1991), ch. 6, 'Parable'.

PAULIN, TOM, 'In the Salt Mines', in *Ireland and the English Crisis* (Newcastle upon Tyne, 1984).

REID, ALEC, 'MacNeice in the Theatre', in T. Brown and A. Reid (eds.), *Time Was Away: The World of Louis MacNeice* (Dublin, 1974).

RODGER, IAN, *Radio Drama* (London, 1982).

SIDNELL, MICHAEL J., *Dances of Death: The Group Theatre of London in the Thirties* (London, 1984), ch. 10, 'Louis MacNeice and the Group Theatre'.

SMITH, R. D., 'Castle On The Air', in T. Brown and A. Reid (eds.), *Time Was Away: The World of Louis MacNeice* (Dublin, 1974).

THWAITE, ANTHONY, 'Memories of Rothwell House', in *Poetry Review*, 78/2 (Summer 1988).

WHITEHEAD, KATE, *The Third Programme: A Literary History* (Oxford, 1989).